Building
a Philosophy
of Education

HARRY S. BROUDY

Professor of Education
University of Illinois

Building
a Philosophy
of Education

SECOND EDITION

PRENTICE-HALL, INC.
Englewood Cliffs, N.J.

PRENTICE-HALL EDUCATION SERIES

John S. Brubacher, *Editor*

Second printing......March, 1962

Library of Congress
Catalog Card No.: 61–8710

Printed in the United States of America

08629–C

To My Father

Preface

My purpose is to furnish a guide to the philosophical treatment of educational problems. Such a treatment, if it considers the widest range of evidence relevant to educational problems, is synoptic; if it examines the adequacy of this evidence, is critical; and if it tries to relate the solutions to each other in such a way that they are logically connected, is systematic. I have tried to fulfill all three requirements.

The method employed throughout is to begin with an educational problem and to see what makes it controversial or difficult to solve. Sooner or later this search reveals certain presuppositions about the ultimate nature of truth, goodness, and the nature of man. This method differs from that which begins with a standard position in general philosophy, for example, Idealism or Pragmatism, and then traces out its educational consequences. I have indicated the reasons for my choice of method in Chapter 1.

Although facility in dealing with educational problems philosophically rather than acquiring *a* philosophy is the primary goal envisioned for the reader, I have not simply presented him with a variety of solutions from which he may choose. The beginner is not yet capable of making a critical choice, and I do not believe all alternative solutions are equally defensible.

Consequently, a solution is suggested and defended for each problem raised, and to the extent that these solutions are synoptic, critical, and systematic, they do constitute a philosophy of education. Should the reader disagree with the solutions proposed, there should be little trouble in finding where the disagreement lies, and where my arguments cease to be convincing. Indeed, it is by search for such disagreements and through the construction of counterarguments that the critical powers of the reader will receive their most fruitful development.

The view expounded here may be called a form of Classical Realism: Realism, because it accepts as regulative principles the idea of a truth independent of the individual knower, and the idea of structures in the universe, man, and society that are normative for man's striving toward the good life and for the education that will help him to achieve it; Classical, because the fundamental notions about the structure of human personality, its goals, and its destiny owe much to the theories of Plato and Aristotle.

It is my conviction that such a view, freed from distorting historical accretions, is a highly perceptive and intelligible account of human experience—an account that many modern theories of personality and education knowingly or unconsciously presuppose. Events and their educational reverberations since the first publication of this book in 1954 have strengthened this conviction. Cognition, systematic study of subject matter, creativity, and individuality have come to the fore as objects of pedagogical interest, while the current uneasiness about excessive togetherness, other-directedness, and social engineering make self-determination, self-realization, and self-integration more appropriate than ever as the goals and characteristics of the good life.

Analysis of current educational problems leads me to emphasize the role of the school in the cultivation of the intellectual values. This role does not point to a "traditional" school, but rather to a curriculum, organization, and methodology that take account of the contributions of psychology, the science of education, and the more basic contributions of Dewey's Instrumentalism.

The readings suggested at the end of each chapter—works on general philosophy, philosophy of education, and professional education—should be used as supplements to fill the gaps in previous preparation or as resources for more intensive study.

The book is divided into three parts; the first edition had two. Part I treats systematically of such problems as definition, aims, and the good life; Part II analyzes the educational task into the different types of value experience that make up the fabric of the student's life. Part III contains chapters on curriculum, methodology, and organization of the school system. Placing these chapters in a separate part and at the end of the book will, I believe, strengthen the logical structure of the work and allow the value materials to be presented earlier in the course.

Although the whole book has been carefully scrutinized for opportunities to remove obstacles to clarity, by and large the substance and style of argument have not been altered. The most important substantive change comes in the chapters on curriculum. A somewhat different principle of selection of studies has been employed, and this entailed changes in the classification of both the contents of the curriculum and its organization at the secondary level.

The book is intended for a semester's work at either the undergraduate or graduate level. By varying the supplementary readings and the level and detail of the class presentation, the instructor can use the volume over a wide range of learning readiness. Although the book has not been criticized for being too easy, the comments I have received from teachers and my own experience indicate that it is well within the comprehension of college undergraduates. It is, however, neither so simple nor so wise as to render the knowledge and experience of the instructor superfluous.

Comments and criticisms of numerous teachers, students, reviewers, and colleagues have helped shape the new edition. I am indebted especially to Forest L. Shoemaker, B. Paul Komisar, and Lawrence G. Thomas for their detailed analyses of the first edition and their suggestions for revision. They are not, however, responsible for any resultant sins of omission or commission.

I am deeply grateful for the many hours that my wife, Dorothy, contributed to the preparation of the manuscript and to the other chores associated with the making of a book.

HARRY S. BROUDY

Urbana, Illinois

Table of Contents

xi

PART III   THE GOOD LIFE AND THE
           SCHOOL

PART | I

MAN, SOCIETY,

AND THE SCHOOL

CHAPTER | 1

Definition and
Philosophy of Education

Education is something men argue about. Often
it is praised; more often it is blamed for what happens to men and
nations. The words "ought" and "must" pervade educational discussions giving them an imperative and urgent mood. One feels
that something can and should be done—presumably something
different from what is being done.

In such a situation there is always the disturbing possibility that
the words being used in the argument may not denote (point to)
the same activities nor convey the same meanings to the disputants.
The word "education," in its long journey through human history,
has acquired ballast and barnacles in the form of subordinate and
partially allied ideas that now travel along with it as if they were
an original part of the keel itself.

The most familiar meaning of the term "education" identifies
it with the *process* of instruction and training that goes on in an
institution of learning, in a school.

In the last fifty years another meaning has become familiar:
that which refers to the art or science or both of carrying on in-

3

struction and training. There are departments of "education" at
universities and teachers colleges devoted to the study and teaching
of "education" in this sense of the word.

These two meanings are fairly clear. Not quite so precise is the
meaning of education when it refers to the *result* of training and
instruction. We speak of a man having had a good education or
not having had a chance to acquire one. We then mean either that
he has or has not attended a school or has not attended it long
enough. It is not uncommon for us to remark that Peter So-and-So
may have gone to college, but it did not give him much of an education; or we may marvel a little at Gregory This-and-That who
has never seen the registration office of a college yet behaves like
a man of culture and learning.

This little ambiguity, resulting from the fact that the processes
of instruction may or may not leave permanent or desirable results,
leads to an even cloudier meaning of "education," what Funk and
Wagnall's *College Standard Dictionary* calls, "The systematic development, cultivation of the natural powers, by inculcation, example,
etc."

The same dictionary gives "the training of animals" as one of the
definitions of "education," but in the discussion it remarks: "We
speak of the *teaching, training,* or *discipline,* rather than of the
education or *tuition* of a dog or a horse." But why this fastidious-
ness? To teach a horse tricks is certainly to develop his natural
powers systematically.

To add to the complexity of meanings, there is the common asser-
tion that the environment is "educative," as when a person is said
to have received his education in the school of hard knocks or in
prison—an education that is apparently not systematic at all.

All that has been said thus far is intended as a justification for
an attempt to fix the meaning of education a little more precisely—
at least for the writer and the readers of this book.

Education as Control of Learning

Let us then, as a sculptor might, hew away quickly those sections
of the stone that obviously will not figure in the final form of the
statue. No meaning of the term "education" intends to include any
process that cannot be altered by human effort, or one that will take

place without any such effort. No meaning of education, for example, envisions giving a man an extra arm or leg, or changing his nervous system or the method of circulating his blood. Nor does one undertake to educate the hurricane, the fog, or the seasons of the year; rather do we hope to educate men to control these events or to adapt to them. In other words, let us exclude from the proper meaning of education those changes in behavior or structure that are caused by maturation and physical accidents.

This leaves us with a vast number of changes in behavior that are due to *learning*. Such changes differ from those that take place in a chemist's test tube or are exemplified by one rock falling on another. No matter how many times a given amount of base and hydrochloric acid meet in the test tube, if the conditions are kept constant, the same thing happens. Neither the base nor the acid nor the test tube *learns* anything. Similarly, no one has been able to teach one rock to "duck" when another rock is about to fall on it. But throw enough rocks at a cat or a dog and they learn, we say, to avoid the missiles. Learning, then, in its most general meaning, is the kind of change that uses the results of previous experience. The dog swerves at the upraised arm of his tormentor *because* of what he has undergone and done previously. If the acid did suddenly change its attitude toward the base, it would never occur to a respectable chemist to believe that this might be due to the experience of the base with the acid on previous occasions.

Learning goes on wherever living tissue can retain its own history for use in subsequent predicaments. Some learnings are conscious; many are not.[1] To the extent that entities do retain their experiences, and to the extent that what is retained shapes subsequent responses, learning is about as avoidable as breathing.

Clearly, therefore, education has something to do with learning. Is it equivalent to it? Is it a division of learning? Or is learning a subdivision of education?

If learning and education are to be taken as equivalent, then we must be willing to call every chance conditioning—many of which occur without our knowledge or anyone else's—education. If, at the age of three, the sight of a tomato coincided with a violent

---

[1] Psychologists refer, for example, to latent learning and unconscious learning. The public was agitated some years ago by television advertising that utilized subliminal stimuli to persuade the viewer by suggestions he could not consciously perceive.

gastric disturbance so that one subsequently hated tomatoes, the hate certainly was the result of learning, but in what sense can it be called the result of education? Only in the sense that a man's education is the sum total of all his learnings. But if we keep in mind that men are disposed to argue about what education ought to be, it should be evident that only that phase of education which is under the control of man is fit for argument. Since all learning is not under the control of man, some of it has to be excluded from any profitable discussion about education—precisely that part which cannot be controlled.

This leaves us with the term "education" as relevant only to that part of learning which in one sense or another is under the control of men, with the degree of control varying according to circumstances. Therefore, we can speak of various kinds of education:

1. *Milieu education.* There is the kind of learning that takes place almost automatically. We have thus learned apparently without any design on anyone's part to walk on sidewalks; to eat certain foods and to avoid others; to live in houses, etc. These are customary ways of doing things in a particular culture. At one time there may have been a reason for doing them this way rather than that, and there still may be. If economic conditions were appropriate, we would, no doubt, learn to relish rats and grubs.

A society will deliberately try to insure the younger generation's conformity to these folkways and *mores,* but since the process can be trusted to go on more or less automatically as a by-product of ordinary living, the deliberative element is not always apparent. We may call this *milieu education* or education by *social contagion.*

2. *Informal education.* Other learnings are produced with conscious intent, but the producers are interested primarily in activities other than instruction. They may impart knowledge or information (instruction); or they may on occasion exercise the pupil in the formation of a habit (training); but this is not their sole or even their chief business. This is *informal* education. Parents give a great deal of it; employers give some to their apprentices; and the theatre at times to its patrons. When it is said that education does not stop with schooling, and that schooling is often the least important part of education, the intent is to emphasize the importance of informal education.

3. *Formal education.* Finally, there is *formal* education in which the intent to teach or train, or both, is clear and where an institution

is designated to devote itself primarily to this task. Schools from the kindergarten through the university are institutions devoted to *formal* education. Churches, when they establish schools, are engaged in *formal* education; some of their other activities may be designed to promote learning, but they are likely to be informal.

The distinction between formal and informal education is important. In the first place, many agencies in our environment do educate. These may produce learnings that reinforce those of the school, interfere with them, or be wholly unrelated to them. For example, the father who preaches the virtues of economic competition may be interfering with a teacher in school who may be preaching the virtues of economic co-operation.

We thus have the problem of co-ordinating diverse educations that Plato tackled head on in the *Republic*. The state, he decided, would censor all poetry, music, and drama. It would control *all* educative enterprises, formal and informal, so that the future guardians would everywhere encounter the same attitudes toward courage, temperance, wisdom, and justice. To label Plato's solution as autocratic, undemocratic, and totalitarian does not provide a better solution to the problem of the relation between formal and informal education.[2] We are still quite helpless in coping with the influence of the movies, comics, magazines, and television on young children.

Another, less important, reason for making the distinction between formal and informal education is the commonly accepted distinction between schooling and learning on one's own, i.e., *self-education*. The belittling of formal schooling is still a popular pastime in our culture, even though this culture is the best customer the schools ever had. But it takes no great psychoanalyst to trace it to an uneasy reverence for schooling. A man with a degree from a well-known university may be a fool and a failure, but we are likely to be surprised if he is either. On the contrary, the self-educated man bears the burden of proof that what he got from his own efforts is as good as the standard brands. When it turns out to be, it is an occasion of so much amazement that we can safely regard it as a rare occurrence. On the whole, however, the distinction is a healthy one. It keeps formal educators from getting stuffy about their results, and it

---

[2] For a defense of Plato see Robert Jordan's chapter, "The Revolt Against Philosophy: The Spell of Popper," in *The Return to Reason*, edited by John Wild. For more complete bibliographical information on items cited in the footnotes, consult the General Bibliography.

brings home to all of us the possibilities and importance of self-education. Indeed, the differences among schools of educational philosophy can be reduced to their different answers to the question: What sort of formal education is the best guarantee of successful self-education in subsequent years?

In its broadest and most general usage, therefore, *education is the process or product of a deliberate attempt to fashion experience by the direction and control of learning.* Formal education refers to the process as it is carried on in schools.

On this definition it would be inaccurate to speak of an "educative environment" unless one meant that the environment was trying directly or indirectly to teach something to someone. To say that one *learns* from the environment would be true but not enlightening because there is nothing else from which one can learn. It also would make us cautious about such phrases as "learning by or from experience" and for precisely the reason that all learning is from experience and through it.[3]

Some practical considerations

Do definitions of education make any difference in the practice of education? Charles Peirce, the forerunner of modern American Pragmatism, and William James, its most prominent publicist, agreed that definitions which make no difference in practice are for all practical and theoretical purposes the same.

One cannot be sure whether people line up their practice to fit their definitions or *vice versa.* They may fashion their definitions to give what they do a respectable air of theoretical consistency. Yet, granting this possibility, once the definition is framed, it does tend to crystallize and congeal the practice which it justifies, so that further deviation from it is discouraged as not being quite respectable.

In the definition given in this chapter there was an admitted attempt to restrict the use of the term "education" to the *deliberate* direction of learnings, namely the direction chosen by the teacher, whosoever the teacher in any given situation might be. Obviously

[3] Everything depends, of course, on the meaning given to "experience." Thus, for Dewey, sticking a finger into a flame is not experience until we perceive the relation between the flame and the pain. *Democracy and Education,* p. 163. In more customary usage, experience refers to everything of which we are aware, i.e., any and all consciousness.

this point would not have been stressed if some educators or philosophers of education did not fail to make this distinction. The equating of growth, life, learning, and education by John Dewey,[4] although perhaps not to be taken literally, has persuaded many professional schoolmen that the boundaries between the school and the community should be abolished wherever possible. It has persuaded them, and they have helped to persuade parents, that the duties of home, government, church, and school overlap so much that separation of them is perniciously artificial and naive. It has been the cause of the endless admonitions to public school teachers that their responsibility as teachers extends far beyond the classroom. How far it extends is impossible to say because if all life is education, there is no logical reason for setting the boundaries anywhere this side of the grave.

The proposed definition makes a real distinction between teaching and learning, contrary to a rather widespread mode of speaking. Many educators glibly pronounce the dictum: "If there is no learning, there is no teaching." This is only a way of speaking because no educator really believes it to be true, or if he did he would in all honesty refuse to take most of his salary. There is a difference between successful teaching and unsuccessful teaching, just as there is a difference between successful surgery and unsuccessful surgery. Both good and bad operations are performed by people called surgeons, and fees are collected for the successes and failures indiscriminately. To teach is to try deliberately to promote certain learnings. When other factors intrude to prevent such learnings, the teaching fails. Sometimes the factors are in the teacher; sometimes in the pupil; sometimes in the very air both breathe, but as long as the effort is there, there is teaching.[5]

Oddly enough, those philosophers of education who are most sensitive to the multiplicity of factors that go into deciding whether learning will take place or not are least sensitive to the absurdity of making the teacher responsible for factors over which he has no control. Of course, teachers usually refuse to take such responsibility, but the more sensitive they are morally, the more their consciences bother them for every learning failure. *Mea culpa*, they secretly cry; not a few of the very best teachers leave the field altogether be-

[4] *Op. cit.*, p. 62.
[5] For an extended discussion on the linguistic aspects of this point, consult Scheffler, *The Language of Education*, pp. 41 ff.

cause they have taken what at best is a careless *cliché* to be a moral and pedagogical imperative.

Even if it were true that there is no teaching where there is no learning, the converse—there is no learning if there is no teaching —would be false, and if the morally serious teacher is discouraged by the falsity of the first statement, the morally indifferent teacher takes advantage of the falsity of the second, since learnings do accrue regardless of teaching.

Maintaining the distinction allocates to the teacher a definite area of responsibility. There are procedures that one can rightfully expect he will follow, and there are results that he can conscientiously try to achieve. By limiting his responsibility, we can give a definite meaning to the responsibilities we assign. There is no meaning without limitation, or more colloquially, everybody's business is nobody's business.

Teaching and pupilage are genuinely correlative terms as teaching and learning are not. A teacher when teaching is always teaching a pupil, and pupilage is the state of being taught. Education, as here defined, always implies a teacher-pupil situation. Even in self-education the relation is present, although the distinction is within one person rather than among different personalities. Even in milieu education, in which one generation teaches another, it is not wholly absent.

So there is a practical difference. By our definition, education is restricted to the deliberately undertaken direction of learning. For learnings otherwise produced it takes no credit and no blame, although it does take them into account. Operating on this definition, schoolmen would be less eager to promise to remedy the weaknesses of all social institutions by what they do in the classroom. Taken seriously, this definition tends to distinguish sharply among the roles of the teacher, the citizen, mother, father, or soldier. Opposite tendencies are encouraged by the Experimentalist or Deweyan definition. Definitions of education not only can make a difference, but what is even more important, they do. Is there then any basis for preferring one definition of education to another, or is this a matter of mere words or personal taste?

Here we are venturing into deeper philosophical waters. We are asking whether definitions are conventional (agreements on the usage of words) or real (reflecting the structures of reality itself). I believe, of course, that this definition is to some extent a real definition; that it does follow the articulation of society into different agencies, each having a specific role to play or function to perform. Education is one such institution and has its own primary function. This function differentiates it from other agencies and their roles. (See Chapter 4.) This belief is rooted in a metaphysical doctrine that there is a natural order in the universe resembling the division of labor found in all organic life and even in the inorganic realm. Some of these ideas will be elaborated in future chapters, but it is only fair to let the reader know why one definition is preferred to another. Since this is a book on the philosophy of education, it cannot simply register the author's preferences. Such preferences may be interesting and satisfying, but unless they are grounded in some theory about the nature of reality, the nature of truth, and the nature of goodness, they are hardly philosophical.

Defining Philosophy of Education

If education is now defined, then we are ready to inquire into the meaning of the philosophy of education. Far from being a simple matter, this inquiry has engaged the serious efforts of nearly all professional philosophers of education for many years. The results, however, make it clear that no book in the field can safely assume any common understandings as to the scope, method, and literature of the philosophy of education.

Traditionally, technical philosophy has included the following major fields:

Metaphysics. If men were never deceived by their experience, it would never occur to them to ask whether anything is real or only an appearance. If we never asked this question, we would never develop science or philosophy. But because the straight stick seems bent in the water, because the dream's promise is not fulfilled, and because men say one thing and do another, we inquire into what is *real* and what only *seems*. Metaphysics probes into our beliefs about reality: about the reality of trees and skies, death and freedom, the world and the self. Does mind have the same sort of being as physical objects? Does God have the same kind of being as do molecules and electrons? Is there an unchangeable being as well as a changeable one? What characteristics must anything have to exist? To change? Is there a design or purpose behind every change or are all or some changes due to chance? These are some of the topics studied in metaphysics (sometimes also referred to as ontology or the science of being). Some of these questions will be taken up in Chapter 5.

Epistemology. This is the branch of philosophy which studies the structure, methods, and validity of knowledge. Or as Hocking (in *Types of Philosophy*) puts it, epistemology deals with "beliefs about belief." Is genuine knowledge attainable? Our senses err and our reason leads us to contradictory conclusions; can we trust either or both? The sceptic says "No." Other philosophers more optimistically say that we can know some things but not others. Or we may ask for the source of our knowledge. Does it come from sense experience, from reason, or from some combination of both? Do we get different kinds of knowledge from these two sources? How much does the knower and how much does the object contribute to the final knowing experience? What is the criterion of truth that we use or ought to use in estimating the reliability of our knowledge? Some of these questions will be discussed in Chapter 5.

Logic. This is the study of the rules and techniques of reasoning. Formal logic studies the way propositions are related to each other so that we can judge whether our reasoning is valid or not, regardless of *what* the propositions assert. For example: If Boston is south of Miami, and if Miami is south of Havana, then we can conclude formally that Boston is south of Havana, even though the *content* of the propositions is false. Knowing the rules and techniques of reasoning may not make our thinking more profound, but it prevents our making invalid jumps from premises to conclusions.

Ethics. This study, also referred to as moral philosophy, deals with judgments of approval and disapproval, rightness and wrongness, goodness and badness, virtue and vice. In short, it deals with the principles of conduct which help us judge whether a choice or an action is good or right. For further discussion of ethical problems see Chapter 10.

Aesthetics. This discipline raises the question as to what makes us judge an object as beautiful or ugly. Is it merely a matter of individual taste? Or are there principles to which we can appeal to support our judgment? Does a school, for example, have a *right* to shape the pupil's taste in art and music? These problems will be discussed further in Chapter 9.

These are the disciplines one would study as a major in "philosophy" at a college or a university. If we ask what a philosophy of education might be, the most obvious answer is: It is philosophy *applied* to education. This is straightforward enough if only we can be sure about the sense in which "applied" is to be taken. Two such senses suggest themselves:

1. Inasmuch as education aims at something called the good life, it is in ethics, metaphysics, and epistemology that we should find the formula for it. Pick a philosophy and see what sort of education you need to bring that kind of good life about. The model of this type of approach is Plato's *Republic*. There he asks: If justice is what I have found it to be, then what kind of state does it require? And what educational system will produce the individual that will make such a state possible? Using this method we can elaborate every philosophical position into its educational consequences—if any: Idealism, Scholasticism, Dialectical Materialism, Pragmatism, Existentialism, etc.[6] We begin by asking what a given philosophical system has to say about the nature of reality (metaphysics), the nature of knowledge (epistemology), and the nature of goodness (ethics), and then deduce the kind of curriculum, method, and school organization that would seem to follow from it. In other words, this approach leads one to believe that if we know what an educator's philosophy is, we can predict what sort of school he will advocate.

2. Another way of applying philosophy to education is by using the tools of technical philosophy to discuss educational theories critically. For example, in a book on principles of education the author might urge that the schools reflect the will of the majority, but on occasion that it should stand firm for what it knows to be right. On what theory, if any, can he hold to both of these views without falling into self-contradiction?

Or to take another example, the philosopher of education might concentrate on analyzing the language used in educational literature. Needs, interests, the whole child, and learning by doing are a few of the terms encountered in educational discussion. What do they really mean? Do they mean what their authors presuppose? Do they refer to anything we can locate in experience or are they empty phrases? This latter approach may be called "analytical" and is

[6] The National Society for the Study of Education: Forty-first Yearbook, Part I, *Philosophies of Education*, and the Fifty-fourth Yearbook, Part I, *Modern Philosophies and Education*, furnish good examples of this approach.

finding strong support especially among some of the younger workers in the field.[7]

The second approach is always valuable because it is always good to be critical, logically cautious, and willing to examine all data that might have a bearing on the problem at hand. It reduces the non-sense uttered in the name of educational discussion and deflates the slogans to which workers in the field become so readily and passionately attached. This approach ferrets out the causes of misunderstanding and tests out "new" solutions in idea before they have a chance to do much harm in practice. Nevertheless, the second kind of "applying" does remain largely supervisory and disinfecting, just as the first kind of "applying" is likely to remain tightly bound to the demands of a particular kind of "ism."

Both approaches are in use but each leaves something to be desired. The first approach concentrates on labeling views about education with an appropriate "ism" taken from general philosophy. Presumably some people regard this as important. Unfortunately, knowing that a particular educator, e.g., Jacques Maritain, is to be labeled as a Thomist, or that Kilpatrick is an Experimentalist, tells us little about what he will say on problems of the curriculum, educational policy, organization, and methods of teaching. Not all topics in general philosophy are equally instructive about problems in education. Perhaps the chief value of this approach is that it gives us a broad justification of life styles or value patterns. Idealism, Realism, Pragmatism, Thomism, and Existentialism do advocate distinctive life styles and as such they prescribe in a general way the aims for an education that will help people to live according to these life styles.[8]

In this book the philosophy of education is regarded as the systematic discussion of educational problems on a philosophical level, i.e., the probing into an educational question until it is reduced to an issue in metaphysics, epistemology, ethics, logic, or aesthetics, or to a combination of these. Because the whole book will be an exemplification of this approach, no extended discussion of it is needed here.

[7] Cf. O'Connor, *An Introduction to the Philosophy of Education;* Scheffler, *The Language of Education* and *Philosophy and Education;* and a collection of essays by various authors entitled *Language and Concepts in Education,* edited by B. O. Smith and Robert Ennis.

[8] A thorough discussion of this question is to be found in the readings suggested for this chapter.

What is needed is the elucidation of what is meant by "philosophical level."

We can distinguish several levels of discussion in talking about any problem that is not completely trivial. Although they are not mutually exclusive and subdivisions of each type can easily be imagined, they may help to differentiate a "philosophical" discussion of educational problems from other kinds of educational interchanges.

The emotional level of discussion

At the emotional level discussion consists largely of each party expressing how it feels about the matter at issue.

Suppose the issue is whether a new elementary school is to be organized around an activity program or conducted on the more conventional subject matter lines with which the adults in the community are more familiar. On an issue like this there will be persons who, for one reason or another, hated or loved their own elementary school days, teachers, books, and playmates. They can take a position in the controversy with practically no thought whatever.

For example, teachers successful in a conventional school may be alarmed at the proposed innovation of an activity school and rebel against it out of fear; those who would like to see these teachers squirm a bit might favor the proposal precisely because it would produce the squirmings.

Challenged by the opposition, each side can think up good reasons for its own views, but essentially the views themselves remain expressions of emotional commitments that are perhaps as opaque to their possessors as to the observers. Liberals in politics and education who for a long time believed that sensible logical discussion would solve all antagonisms are now more sophisticated, realizing that attitudes are not moldable at the will of the holder and not always open to his conscious inspection.[9]

The factual or informational level

If the emotional level does not produce a decision—and it will not unless one side exercises preponderant power—then cooler heads, i.e.,

[9] It is this disturbing fact that has made Existentialism and group dynamics —very different movements—so relevant to our times.

those whose hearts are not so heatedly committed to either side of the controversy, may suggest "getting the facts." On this level the issue will be reduced to getting information about the relative costs of the two types of program: the costs of the buildings and furniture required, cost of teachers, etc. One can imagine both sides agreeing that one or the other plan will cost more in the short run, but the side getting the worst of this informational affray will argue that "in the long run this will prove a false economy." What facts shall we summon to help us to decide how long a "long run" should be, and what is the difference between true and false economy?

Facts may be marshalled to show the relative effectiveness of the two types of program on achievement examinations in the regular school subjects; or experts may be called in to testify as to the success of the two plans. For example, communities which have used the activity plan may claim that the number of commitments to the psychoneurotic clinics has been considerably reduced and that their jails are practically empty of young offenders.

It is clear that sometimes the ascertainment of fact settles an argument. If both sides are really concerned only with dollar and cents economy as reflected in the next year's tax rate, then it is relatively easy to decide for one plan against the other on the basis of accurate information. If both sides wish to make their decision on the basis of pleasing the greatest number of voters, then the public opinion poll can settle the argument by feeling the public's pulse. It is only common sense to ascertain the facts, especially if both parties can agree as to which facts are relevant. But disputes cannot always be settled by summoning the facts. Even in our own little problem it is extremely doubtful that the impassioned battlers will be converted by the facts as such.

The explanatory or theoretical level

Mere marshalling of facts is fruitless unless guided by some theory that marks out some facts as relevant and some as not. The fact that boys are red-headed may on the surface have nothing to do with the issue in question, but who is rash enough to say that being red-headed is totally divorced from that complex of facts we call success and failure in life? Surely the kind of school we are to have has something to do with success and failure in life.

So we need a theory to make sense out of the facts. A theory is a set of ideas so related to each other that they account for or explain a set of facts. Thus if we are acquainted with the theory of how light travels, we can explain why it is that a stick partly in the water seems to be bent. If we are familiar with Freud's theory of the unconscious, repression, and resistance, we can explain why dreams occur when and as they do.

What sort of theories do we use in discussing problems of education? Clearly they are theories about how human beings behave and learn and theories about how they *ought* to behave and learn. The first kind of theory we draw from psychology and social sciences such as economics, sociology, anthropology, and the like. We may call them empirical or scientific theories. The latter we may call axiological or, more generally, philosophical theories.

Why do controversies such as these persist if there is a body of fact and tested theory that points to their solution? For one thing, in the social sciences that have bearing on our daily life, the facts are so numerous and diverse that no theory has yet succeeded in unifying and explaining them to the experts in the field.

For another, a conflict of attitude is rarely the result of a conflict between ignorance and knowledge, between one theory and another. The opponents of school integration are not persuaded by psychological facts or theories, nor are the more violent partisans of the activity or traditional curriculum. Persisting controversies are invariably the results of conflicts about what we believe is fundamentally valuable.

In our own example, theories about mental health and how adjustment in the community takes place could be cited to justify one type of program as opposed to another. Suppose, for example, one side argues that the activity program makes for co-operative attitudes and that these are needed for both democratic living and for mental health. The other side could point to facts that are explicable by another theory. For example, it could argue that none of the great advances in human knowledge came about in committees, but were rather the products of individuals devoted to some goal not usually shared by the group.

Nevertheless, it is our intellectual duty to exhaust the possibilities of science in the solution of problems before turning elsewhere. It is all well and good to cry that we have to go beyond science for the secret of the good life, but it is well to get *to* science before going *beyond* it.

The philosophical level

If the facts and scientific theories cannot settle the controversy, and if the disputants still wish to continue a rational discussion, they have to pass to another level of argument, namely, the philosophical. Here the disputants defend their value commitment in terms of a theory about what is *really* true, *really* valuable, and *really* real.

Are there any truths about the world, about man, or about goodness that are universal, eternal, and valid for all men in all circumstances? If so, then do not these constitute the basis for a fixed curriculum that should be mastered by every child—with pleasure if possible, but with a little pain, if necessary? Is the good life not an appropriation of the things that the race has found to be satisfying? Is not, therefore, the traditional school with its emphasis on mastery, on intellectual absorption, and on self-discipline the only sensible means for achieving the good life?

But if one is convinced that all this talk of eternal values and truths is moonshine: that truth varies with the climate, the Dow-Jones averages, and the peculiarities of our ancestral superstitions, then does not the newer school with freedom for the individual to develop his own truth and his own destiny seem the logical and sensible alternative? Or are there intermediate positions between these extremes?

Here we have reached the ultimate in the possibilities of discussion. It may be that no agreement is possible; certainly if one cannot get agreement on this level, there is no deeper level on which the disputants can take refuge. Some other device such as "role-playing" or sharing common tasks might be invoked to soften the conflict, but on the purely intellectual level the possibilities are exhausted when we have failed to achieve agreement on issues in metaphysics, epistemology, aesthetics, and ethics. For these are the most general aspects of all human thought and furnish the basis and validation of all human knowledge in any field. Hence we call this level the philosophical level, and this approach, the most fundamental philosophical approach to educational problems.

On this view educational problems that can be settled by seeking out the facts, or which cease to be controversial in the light of a reliable scientific theory are not, strictly speaking, problems in the philosophy of education. For example, which method of hand-writing instruction produces a given degree of legibility in a month is not a philosophical problem, nor is the proper beginning age for reading instruction. But whether teachers in the elementary grades should be required to have any mastery of the liberal arts is, and so is the question as to whether the church or the state or the family shall be responsible for the educational program.

Accordingly, the remainder of this book is organized with a view to exploring a number of educational issues to the depth of their philosophical roots. As we seek the answers, it will become clear that we have to resort to views about reality, about knowledge, about goodness, and about beauty, and what views we have about these may determine our choice in these practical issues.

Summary

In this chapter we undertook two tasks: (1) to define the term "education" in such a way that we could distinguish various kinds of education; (2) to mark out the limits of the discipline we call "philosophy of education," showing its relation to the discipline of general philosophy. It was argued that philosophy of education can have its greatest value if it explores educational problems so that the controversies about them are pushed back to metaphysical, epistemological, aesthetic, and ethical issues. To do this, we have to see how each educational problem shapes up on the emotional, factual, and scientific level of discussion. It is only when these levels yield no clear-cut solution that we have to take up the problem at the philosophical level.

PROBLEMS FOR DISCUSSION AND RESEARCH

1. Trace several controversial issues in education or in some other field through the levels of controversy discussed in this chapter.

2. Read at least a chapter in metaphysics, logic, ethics, epistemology, and aesthetics to get a preliminary notion of what these disciplines are like. See Suggestions for Further Reading below.

3. Read through the table of contents in books on the history of education, principles of education, educational psychology, and the philosophy of education. Can you make any observations as to similarities and differences?

4. Take one controversial educational issue. Pick out the points of agreement and disagreement between the parties involved. On what points do the disputants seem most reluctant to compromise?

5. List the points or arguments or conclusions in this chapter that seem to you to be (a) erroneous, (b) unconvincing, (c) irritating. Can you put your finger on just *why* they are (a), (b), or (c)?

Suggestions for Further Reading

For fuller bibliographical information on the books listed below, consult the General Bibliography.

The suggested readings at the end of each chapter are samples of the kind of materials the student may use to supplement the text. Gaps in the student's background and special interests, or the desire to get points of view other than that of the text, can serve as guides in the selection of items to be read.

With regard to the nature and scope of education, the philosophy of education, and general philosophy, the following unit may be worth the rather close study it requires, especially in advanced classes:

Broudy, H. S., "How Philosophical Can Philosophy of Education Be?"
Price, Kingsley, "Is a Philosophy of Education Necessary?" in *The Journal of Philosophy*, 52:22, October 27, 1955, pp. 612–633.
Symposium on the philosophy of education based on these articles in *Harvard Educational Review*, 26:2, Spring, 1956.
A review of this symposium by the author is to be found in *Harvard Education Review*, 26:3, Summer, 1956, pp. 286–292.
A Symposium: What Can Philosophy Contribute to Educational Theory? with papers by C. J. Ducasse, William K. Frankena, and Kingsley Price, and comments by H. S. Broudy, George E. Barton, and Israel Scheffler in *Harvard Educational Review*, 28:4, Fall, 1958.
McMurray, Foster, "An Autonomous Discipline of Education," *Educational Theory*, 5:3, July, 1955, pp. 129–140.

In the field of general philosophy for purposes of sampling the various fields:

Hocking, *Types of Philosophy*, and books of readings such as
Edwards and Pap, *A Modern Introduction to Philosophy*,
Wheelwright, *The Way of Philosophy*,
Smith and Grene, *From Descartes to Kant*.

With respect to books on philosophy of education, examples that utilize the standard views of general philosophy as a point of departure are:

Butler, *Four Philosophies*.
N.S.S.E., Forty-first Yearbook, Part I, *Philosophies of Education*, written by philosophers of education, and
N.S.S.E., Fifty-fourth Yearbook, Part I, *Modern Philosophies and Education*, written by general philosophers.

The logical problem of definition is discussed in textbooks by McCall, Parker and Veatch, Leonard, and Black. See General Bibliography.

2

The Good Life as
the Aim of Education

If education is not an haphazard enterprise, then the most obvious question one can ask is: What is the goal, purpose, or objective of this enterprise? Educators and citizens never tire of asking this question, and often insinuate that some educators do not know where they are going, or that if they do know, the road they are taking will never get them there. One also hears complaints about the confusion in education, and this confusion is laid at the door of a corresponding "confusion" of aims or objectives.

These accusations may be well-founded, although it is hard to believe that teachers and administrators spend their professional lives in aimless motions. Possibly the confusion is caused by the different meanings that are entertained whenever aims are discussed. A deeper source of confusion, however, is the lack of unanimity as to what constitutes the good life. Both kinds of confusion have to be cleared away before we can get on with the building of a systematic set of beliefs about education.

Granted there are aims in education, whose aims shall we talk about? The teacher's? The pupil's? The parents'? Those of the school committee? The Legislature's? Those of the newspaper editor? The adolescent in coming to school may have as his chief aim nearness to other adolescents. His parents may cherish hopes of having a lawyer in the family. The high school principal dreams of becoming a superintendent, while the newspaper editor believes that the school should teach everyone to be self-reliant and to shun help from the government. All are sure of their own aims, but *only* of their own. Is it any wonder, therefore, that they believe there is "confusion" about what education ought to be doing?[1]

Levels of Educational Aims

Another source of confusion is the fact that one man's end is another man's means. To promote certain learnings, e.g., long division, may be an end for a teacher on a certain day of school, but certainly the learning of long division is not the final goal of the school or even of the teacher. She may be that very rare teacher who regards the collection of her salary as the end of education, but to the community the payment of her salary is a necessary albeit disagreeable means toward something else.

If, therefore, we wish to talk intelligibly about the aims of education, we have to specify on what level of generality the discussion is to take place. It is thus quite possible for a group of school supervisors to discuss aims of education solely in terms of supervision, and for a group of administrators to do so in terms of budgets. These discussions can be profitable provided supervisors and administrators do not secretly differ among themselves as to the purposes that supervision and administration are to serve.

But suppose that one administrator feels that the purpose of the public schools is to provide each pupil with adequate vocational training, whereas another is convinced that the schools should confine themselves to a rather simple program of general education. In that event, what one says about an adequate budget will be incom-

---

[1] For sample lists of educational aims and objectives, see Bobbitt, *Curriculum Construction in Los Angeles;* N.E.A. Commission on the Reorganization of Secondary Education, *The Cardinal Principles of Education;* U.S. Bureau of Education Bulletin, 35:11–15, 1918. Also N.E.A. Educational Policies Commission, *The Purposes of Education in American Democracy,* and American Federation of Teachers Committee on Educational Reconstruction, *Goals of American Education,* Chap. 2. But there is no dearth of current lists; there is scarcely a community without one of its own.

prehensible to the other. If they are to communicate at all, they will have to abandon budgets for a while, at least until they can come to some agreement on a higher level of generality, namely, that of the purpose of the schools.

If, as so often happens, the differences among levels in aims are overlooked, controversy becomes muddled. A teacher complains that the lack of strict discipline in the home interferes with her attempt to get homework done. A mental hygienist replies that strict home discipline develops a feeling of hostility in the child, whereas some industrialist predicts that unless children learn to do an honest day's work the economy will collapse. Each of these remarks might be true, but they pass each other without really meeting.

Or take another common controversy in education. College professors almost without exception wince when they have to read the writing of freshmen. Sloppiness of expression and scrambled thought irritate a specialist anxious to get on to the advanced phases of his specialty. He mentally awards the high school of America a "D" for the quality of its teaching. On the other hand, the mental hygienists, dealing daily with neurotics, are impelled to say that emotional and mental health are far more important to a democracy than English composition, arithmetic, and literature. From them American education also gets a "D." The Classicist, especially if he has lived in Europe, notes the American public's taste in books, music, and painting and likewise gives American education a "D." Clearly, each of these critics of American education has an aim in mind. All have a view of the good life which probably is pretty much the same. But each has concentrated on that particular set of *conditions* prerequisite to the good life in which he is an expert and in which his pupils are rank amateurs and beginners. Each specialist quite properly regards the demands of the others as outrageously one-sided, and the public school educator quite properly regards them all as less than sane.

The discrepancy in aim-levels is most noticeable in the pupil-teacher relationship. The premedical or pre-engineering student is, if unenlightened, impatient with courses in literature and music appreciation. The prospective elementary teacher shrugs her shoulders at statistics and philosophy. The little fellow in the grades, with better excuse, resigns himself to the vagaries of well-meaning but incomprehensible adults. This discrepancy has resulted in one of the most important educational proposals of our times, namely, to begin instruction with the aims or problems of the learner rather than those of adults. However, as we shall have many occasions to observe, it is one thing to take the felt wants of children as a means of disclosing to them their more fundamental wants, and it is quite another to deny that there is any difference between them.

In other words, we can be intelligent about our common search for means when there is no disagreement about the ends they are to serve. If we are agreed that it is good to know long division we can investigate scientifically the best means for securing this knowledge. If someone questions the value of learning division, however, the investigation of the best means, for the time being at least, loses its point.

Is there any stage in the educative enterprise at which we can say that we are all agreed on the end? Or is it sufficient for the enterprise to say that if pupils solve their immediate problems intelligently from day to day there is no need to ask about ultimate goals?[2] The answer to the first question is in one sense affirmative and in another sense negative. It is affirmative in that the good life is the goal of every choice, for no one knowingly chooses evil. It is negative in that it would be difficult for men to agree (except in very general terms) on just what the details of a good life would be.

There is no simple affirmative or negative answer to the second question. Those who are satisfied with short term goals have a strong faith that intelligence consistently employed on any problems whatever will in the long run add up to a good life, i.e., a life of intelligent action. Those who are not satisfied believe that our conceptions of the good life are strategic for the solutions of our day-to-day problems. To solve them intelligently, they would argue, is to solve them so that a step nearer to the good life is taken. Otherwise a solution that is intelligent for a restricted end may very well frustrate a longer range goal.

We have then an awkward situation. All men agree that the ultimate justification for any educative enterprise is that it can promote the good life for its beneficiaries. On the other hand, there seems to be very little agreement as to what makes a life good. This lack of agreement led the Instrumentalists and Experimentalists to argue that whatever the good life may be, it cannot be specified

---

[2] "Educators have to be on their guard against ends that are alleged to be general and ultimate." John Dewey, *Democracy and Education*, New York: 1916, p. 127. Used with permission of The Macmillan Company.

in advance; only intelligent experimentation with experience can disclose what is good. The crux of the problem turns out to be whether we can discern any general features of life which we can say will make life good for any man. If we can, then there is some sense in saying that the aim of education is the good life. If we cannot, the argument must go to the Instrumentalists.

The Concept of the Good Life

The good life has two correlative subdivisions: the good individual and the good society. It is useless to try to settle the issue of priority between the good individual and the good society because one cannot even be defined without reference to the other. The good life reveals itself in both. It arises when the individual behaves in certain ways toward other men and when the group is so structured as to help him to live well.[3]

There is a sense, however, in which the individual is of more direct interest to the teacher than the society. It stems from the fact that teachers work with individuals directly, and the immediate fruits of their work are changes in individual behavior and demeanor and not in the social structure. But this behavior and demeanor are *for* a life in society; hence, the teacher represents the demands of society to the pupil. Yet he represents the individual's demands upon society also. This is a difficult maneuver unless he places himself at the vantage point of the good life from which both are derived.

The task for a philosophy of education is accordingly outlined. It is to transcribe the good life, the good individual, and the good society into learnings that presumably will contribute to their production. This means the establishment of a hierarchy or grading of means and ends so that ideally each educational activity, however minute, finds its justification in the next higher level of aims.

The classroom teacher needs the vision of the good life as a directive that makes sense out of long division, but he is not on that account an educational philosopher or even a school superintendent. The latter needs the vision to make sense out of his busy days and

[3] This does not mean that we cannot distinguish between them. We define eggs in terms of chickens and chickens in terms of eggs, but both have other characteristics as well, and this enables a chicken to eat an egg—an ability it does not share with the egg.

nights, but he is not a specialist in long division. The industrialist and the factory worker both need the vision of the good life, but they are not related to it as is the educator.

The educational philosopher also has his specific position in the journey to the good life. He is responsible for framing the vision itself out of the philosophical work of the past and the present in such language and form that all the *echelons* of educational workers can comprehend it. And, we may add, in such form that all citizens can get a working understanding of it.

In the second place, it is up to him to trace the connections between the good life and the educational conditions that will contribute to its production—and to do it in the light of the best evidence available and with the most rigorous reasoning of which he is capable. If this description gives too much scope to the educational philosopher, it should be remembered that even he is restricted to his specific job. He is not a statesman, theologian, metaphysician, sociologist, or administrator. He is not a master of their specialties as they are not masters of his—to think critically, synoptically, and systematically about the relations of education to the good life.

Subjective estimate of the good life

The history of civilization is also a history of attempts to define the good life. Aristippus thought the secret was pleasure, the most intense and riotous available. Epicurus agreed that pleasure was indeed the greatest good, but he exercised such caution in avoiding pain that he got himself a bad name for nothing. Mill[4] also argued that pleasure was the highest good, but he was fussy about the *kinds* of pleasure and not so fussy as to who would have them; hence, he argued for the greatest happiness of the greatest number. Aristotle decided that happiness was best achieved in a life devoted to the practice of virtue. Christianity counseled love of God and neighbor as the key to the good life. Others have plumped for power, fame, social service, the simple life, the busy life, and even learning.

If we look about us or read the confessions and aspirations of our contemporaries, we have to believe that life can be good in Hollywood, Washington, on a Vermont farm, and the New Mexican desert. Lives of the great and the humble, rich and poor, the handsome and the ugly can all be good. There is an almost endless

---

4 John Stuart Mill, *Utilitarianism*, Chap. 2.

variety of life styles in which men say there is satisfaction, just as there is an endless variety of lives which men judge to be miserable.

Is there any sense in asking whether there are any features that are common to these variations? The answer is, of course, that we do not have much choice in the matter, for whenever we aver that lives so different as those led by St. Francis, Socrates, and Abraham Lincoln were good, we mean something, even though it is not easy to agree on what that meaning might be.

The educator has even less choice because he believes that he is trying to lead his pupils toward the good life. Different though each pupil may be from all the others, it will never be the case that persistent lying, crime, laziness, and ignorance can in his particular instance add up to the good life. Even though one boy can achieve the good life in the army, another in the church, and still another as the local street cleaner, what makes their lives comparable at all is a basic design for the good life that each in his own way exemplifies.

When we ask whether a certain man's life—say that of Benjamin Franklin or of F. D. Roosevelt—is good, we refer to at least two judgments. First, we want to know whether Roosevelt himself thought it was good, and, in the second place, we have to inquire into the judgments of other men. Let us call the first judgment— that which a person makes upon his own life—the subjective judgment or estimate, and let us call the judgment other men make upon it the objective estimate.

Let us first examine the grounds upon which the subjective estimate is made.

1. Certainly a life in which physical pain predominates throughout its span will not be judged good by the sufferer. Disease, grinding poverty, unceasing toil can and have been endured. A man may indeed reap no little satisfaction from such endurance, but he can hardly be expected to be happy about the need for enduring it. If such a man should judge his own life to be good, it would be in spite of the pain and misery, for no man desires pain for its own sake, and, unless the suffering is a means to something less painful, it is about as near to a pure evil as can be imagined.[5]

2. To be judged good, a life must not be predominately terrifying. A little danger winds up the spring of life, but long periods of danger

[5] To what extent man is unconsciously a pain-seeking animal is a profound question, on which see Reik, *Masochism in Modern Man.*

sooner or later make cowards of us all. The most disturbing of these
perils do not necessarily threaten us with bodily harm. The dangers
of losing prestige, security, and love, although not so violent as the
dangers of war, are even more potent in their destruction of confidence. Certainly no chronically anxious man is happy or would
judge himself to be.

Perhaps no man is free from such fear, and no man can fit himself
so snugly into the scheme of things as never to fear that he may
be shaken out of it. But the happy man finds means of allaying
that sense of insecurity. He has, for example, one or more persons in
the world who love him just because he is he and no other person.
Mothers, wives, fathers, and husbands are supposed to furnish this
unswerving, unquestioning love to their spouses and offspring. This
is a love that does not evaluate the worthiness of the beloved. Black
sheep and wayward mates are loved in spite of their demonstrated
unworthiness. Such love bolsters the sense of a person's security
whether he is six months or sixty years old. For even men of modest
intelligence know or at least suspect that they are somewhat short
on merit and therefore crave the earthly grace that an unselfish and an
unquestioning love supplies. So great is this craving that unless it
is satisfied few, if any, men would call themselves happy or their
lives good. This theme has an unfailing attraction for novelists and
dramatists. That the rich, powerful, talented, fortunate, but unloved
man should wistfully eye the man blessed in this respect, if in no
other, is accepted by high and low as quite understandable.

3. Physical well-being and love, however, are not enough. The
person has to feel that he counts for something and that he deserves
to. He needs a sense of power and accomplishment; he needs the
conviction that his presence makes a difference in the world; he
needs to be needed. Here, too, most men are not overly confident
about their own judgment. They seek outward proof of their merit
in the form of recognition, titles, better jobs with bigger desks, and
prizes in competitions of all kinds. To be sure, some are satisfied
with very little merit, and still others deceive the world and often
themselves. But such deviations are relatively rare. Most men are
not happy unless they can respect themselves, whatever their standard for self-respect happens to be. Accordingly, a life of which
they are secretly ashamed will hardly be judged by them as good.

A more fundamental form of this craving for accomplishment
is the desire to exercise one's potentialities. Some men do seem to

be content to leave their talents undeveloped. Unused power does not seem to disturb them overmuch, but one wonders whether upon self-examination they are as happy about it as they seem to be. The contrary is certainly more often the case, and the bitterest accusations against life come from those whom circumstances have rendered far less effective than they are convinced they could have been.

4. Finally, to be judged as good or satisfactory, life has to have a tension toward the future. A simple word for it is "excitement." Another word is "zest." Boredom and happiness exclude each other. But for life to be interesting and absorbing means to have a stake in future events. People who do not own stocks are not interested in the stock market, and those who do not bet rarely go to the races.

This is naturally the most subjective of all the criteria of the good life. It is difficult to name anything in which somebody does not take a keen interest. On the other hand, the crime reporter after seven years or so finds that even crime has its routine, and that it can be very dull indeed. But whatever the individual's capacity for excitement or boredom, he will not judge a life good that, rightly or wrongly, he finds dull, slack, and unsurprising.

Objective estimate of the good life

So much for the subjective estimate of the good life. Such estimates are made by the individual of his own life, and there is no way that we can get inside his experience to make sure that what he reports is what he actually finds. If a man feels miserable or happy or contented, then it has no meaning to tell him that he feels otherwise; he is the final arbiter about what is at any moment in his conscious experience.

And yet all of us are forever judging the goodness or badness, the happiness or misery, of other people's lives, and as often as not our judgments do not agree with the subjective estimates of the lives we so judge. When a Hollywood star heavily endowed with health, wealth, beauty, love, and fame reports in the revelations of her inner life that she is profoundly unhappy, and that her life is not good or not so good as she would wish, most of the readers either refuse to believe her or wonder what is the matter with her. If she is not happy, she certainly ought to be, and if what she has does not add up to a good life, what in this world could make it better?

We are equally incredulous about the reports of obscure people who judge their interminable drudgery and their endless commerce with the commonplace as making up a good life. In other words, the objective and subjective estimates do not always agree. When the educator is speaking of the good life as an aim of education, does he have in mind the subjective estimates of his pupil, the objective estimates of the world, or both? If they do not agree, which is to take priority?

Let us, therefore, see how these criteria are used to measure the goodness of life as others live it.

1. It is pretty well agreed that pain, hardship, and physical deprivation are at best necessary evils. People who desire them for their own sakes are regarded with the greatest suspicion by psychiatrists. Many subjective and objective estimates agree on this. When it comes to *what* is painful and *how* it shall be accepted, the agreement becomes very rough indeed.

A man suffering acute aftereffects of alcohol is by his own testimony ready for death as a desirable alternative to his distress. He finds it difficult to muster sympathy among his fellows, first, because they regard the distress as unnecessary and avoidable, and second, because usually the results are not immediately fatal. Let the cause of the distress be an incurable cancer and the world is unanimous in judging it as irremediably bad.

The objective estimate, therefore, measures physical suffering not only by its intensity and duration, but also by its causes and probable effects. The sufferer also takes these causes and effects into account, but during the suffering they have much less weight for him than for the unaffected observer.

Moreover, this objective observer uses a yardstick that is often quite different from that used by the sufferer when he estimates physical hardship and deprivation. For example, to some the prospect of living in a dingy flat with no hot running water seems an intolerable hardship; to others, inability to change suits every day may be regarded as the depth of misery. Consequently, individual objective estimates are likely to vary as much as subjective ones in this matter. However, when we pool our judgments, a good deal of the unevenness cancels out, and the yardstick we actually use represents an average expectation. If most people in a culture have hot running water, the lack of it is judged as painful; if most people do not change suits every day, the subjective misery of those who would like to do so but cannot will be dismissed as nonsense.

The educator perforce adopts a rough yardstick of this kind as he envisions the life of the pupil. Certainly he will want to help the pupil avoid unnecessary hardship and pain so far as learnings can accomplish this. He knows that knowledge, skill, and ingenuity both in the individual and in social arrangements can mitigate physical ills and hardships. Physical handicaps and diseases due to ignorance, human callousness, and carelessness have no place in the good life, not only because they are experienced as painful by the subject, but also because of their crippling effects on other possibilities of value realization, i.e., because they bring emotional pain along with them and block the possibilities of achievement of which the individual might be capable.

Yet it is elementary wisdom to realize that pain, suffering, and hardship are not always avoidable, however clever we are. Hence, in the judgments about the goodness of life, the objective observer uses another yardstick, namely, the *attitude of the individual toward these evils*.

How to deal with pleasure and pain is the central theme of ethical studies, and the virtues are the dispositions we build up to deal with them successfully.[6] Courage is the right disposition toward the pains induced by dangers; temperance is the right disposition toward bodily pleasures and pains; liberality is the right disposition toward the pleasures and pains of giving and receiving material goods; justice is the right disposition to the apportionment of pleasures and pains among our fellow men. To maintain these right dispositions, whatever right may turn out to mean, is the essence of good character.

Therefore, whenever we judge the lives of others we look not only at the pains and pleasures we presume they are having, but also at their attitudes toward them as revealed by words and actions. The man who suffers what he must with great courage, and the man who does not place too high a value on bodily pleasures for himself or others is judged as having qualified for the good life in this respect, at least.

For those individuals who suffer because they refused to develop the virtues above described, we have some pity and somewhat more contempt. For those who suffer from evils thrust upon them but

---

[6] This topic is taken up again in Chap. 10, but sooner or later the student should dip into Aristotle's *Nicomachean Ethics*, especially Books II–V.

who do not have the virtues to endure them properly there is pity mixed with regret that these virtues were not cultivated.

Hence, the educator makes character development co-ordinate with knowledge an aim for the individual—knowledge to avoid and mitigate evils and character to secure the best possible balance among pleasures and pains over the long pull of a lifetime. These two are not separated because prudence is the virtue of using knowledge to deliberate about what the virtuous action is to be, and the habit of so using knowledge is itself one of the most important of the virtues. But as we shall have occasion to note, the method of teaching knowledge and forming character (the virtues) differ in many respects, and the question will inevitably arise as to what formal education can do in the way of character formation.

We see then how it is possible for Mr. X to feel that his life is good or not good and yet find that his peers do not agree with his estimate. At this point we might simply assert the priority of the group judgment and tell Mr. X to get in tune with his universe no matter how he happens to feel. But on what grounds can we assert it so that it will be convincing to Mr. X? As we shall see, it must be on the grounds that the virtuous life necessarily must be the pleasant life and indeed the happy one—insofar as life is in the control of the individual.

2. With regard to the second criterion, namely, that of emotional security and insecurity, the relations between the subjective and the objective estimates are similar. At the outset we would all agree that a life filled with dread, anxiety, frustration, despair, and loneliness is not good. But whereas physical ills and hardships are often the result of factors over which the individual has little or no control, it is not so clear that emotional suffering is due entirely to external causes. Only in recent decades has the view become prevalent that such suffering is due to environmental forces over which the individual has as little control as he has over slums and war. Because these ills are not always physiological in origin, it is commonly believed that they are more preventable and remediable by some effort on the part of the sufferer. The Stoics, who held that all evil consists in the opinions we have of it, were among the precursors of mental hygiene, and those who practice virtue according to any of the formulae suggested in Western or Eastern civilization have the promise of the inner peace so requisite for the good life.

The situation is immensely complicated, however, by the circumstance that the sufferer of emotional aches and pains can conceal them from others and even from himself. The genius may feel miserable; we wonder why. The banker who seems happy and prosperous may commit suicide. The wife, outwardly a model of domestic bliss, may inexplicably elope with the town ne'er-do-well. The obedient well-behaved child may take to setting fires. Conversely, the subject may so successfully hide his insecurity that he may feel happy enough most of the time, while his outward behavior may invite the scrutiny of the psychiatrist or even that of the perceptive layman. Thus the model of domestic bliss may busy herself so assiduously in perfecting her domesticity that her behavior becomes rigid and compulsive. The floor must be washed every week, then every day, and finally twice a day. Or she may so successfully conceal a desire to run away with the town ne'er-do-well that she reveals it only in her excessive zeal to ban obscene literature.

To the educator, the problem of the good life in this area once more falls into two parts. Clearly, some fear and anxiety can be alleviated by knowledge and skill. But what about emotional maladjustments having their origin in what psychologists call childhood or infant conditionings? What about the child who feels rejected by his parents and feels that he will always be rejected? What about the child whose physical endowments are so poor that he is consistently repulsed by his peers? What about the person in whom compensation for insecurity has gone so far that no one dares to love him freely?

The mental hygienists certainly have a point here, and the educator grants it. But this problem, like that of character formation, has different meanings for different conceptions of education. Is the education of young parents the task of formal education? Is the proper emotional adjustment of infants the problem of the school or of the home? If the home does not do its duty in this matter, does it become the primary task of the school to correct the mistakes of the home?

3. On the third criterion, namely, sense of worth and achievement, there is again no disagreement about its importance, but only on what constitutes it. Here the objective judgment has in mind the demands of society and the way in which the individual meets them. A man's life is not regarded as much good if he cannot sup-

port himself and his family or if he cannot render the services as-
sessed upon him by the community, country, and friends.

The objective judgment goes further. It grades the goodness of
lives by the amount of service so rendered. A peasant maintaining
his subsistence level, paying his modest taxes, and playing his little
role in the army, church, and community is not judged to have lived
so good a life (other things being equal) as the great heroes, leaders,
scientists, statesmen, and artists.

In other words, the concept of differences in capacity enters into
the judgment. It is in every case better that a man fulfill his
possibilities for the good life than that he should fail to do so, and
in this respect heroes and peasants both get "A" for effort. But if he
who might have been a fine scientist is content to fulfill his life as
a simple peasant, our judgment will not be lenient. Undeveloped
potentiality is viewed with regret and often with impatient anger.
Delightful as a hobo's life may be to him, we do not approve the
delight if his talents are great. On the other hand, delusions of
grandeur and levels of aspiration for which there is no adequate
talent impress us as pitiful.

For the educator potentiality for achievement becomes central.
How can we estimate these potentialities? How far should a person
carry his formal education? For what type of life work does he show
the greatest promise? At what levels can he enjoy and create values?
What kind of social order is most conducive to the development of
these potentialities? What sort of schooling will insure such a
development?

4. Does the objective estimate of the good life take into account
the dimension of boredom and interest? Unquestionably it does, but
once more the perspective from which life is judged is somewhat
different from that of the individual. One may feel bored and dull
because of the lack of variety in life. Even steaks and gay celebra-
tions as a steady fare can pall. Or one may find that life is dull
because the future holds nothing that one wants very much or no
surprises in connection with getting it. The inveterate desire to
gamble may very well be a symptom of a life that has lost its
capacity for surprises and tension. Gambling caters to these cravings
as do political campaigns and sporting events.

From the objective point of view a life to be good not only must
have tension, but it must be a certain kind of tension, or rather the
tension must come from a certain kind of activity. The tension to

qualify as good must issue from striving after a goal that somehow contributes to the common good. A man who has led an interesting life by hopping from one job to another, from one country to another, or from one romantic partner to another may excite secret envy, but if we admire him at all, it is because he displays an unconcern for security and convention, a kind of courage and daring we ourselves do not possess. And yet there is resentment mixed with this admiration, for we realize that his freedom and insouciance are bought with our slavery and timidity. He can afford neither to toil nor to spin because we do the toiling and spinning for him.

We therefore demand in our reflective judgments that the interesting quality of life come from commitment to great goals that develop the individual's powers for the common good. Such commitments call for courage and never are so certain as to eliminate the risk and excitement attendant upon difficult tasks. This judgment is a reflection upon the nature of man: that his most important dimension is that of the future and not the present; the important dimension of his life is "what might and what ought to be" rather than what is and what must be.

It is clear from all this that our subjective and objective estimates of what makes life good may not coincide. Our subjective yardstick is marked in degrees of satisfaction, or what broadly might be called degrees of pleasantness. Which experience will prove to be satisfactory or otherwise cannot be predicted even by the individual himself. So much depends on what he contributes to the experience and so relatively little on the nature of the experience as such. The subjective yardstick can be used only by one individual on himself, and he is the final authority on what he finds when he applies it.

The objective estimate, on the other hand, is based on what we conceive would be satisfactory to the group as a whole and in the long run. From the group we learn what qualities of character and of behavior it has decided by centuries of trial and error *do* lead to the group welfare—and we learn to admire them in ourselves and to demand them from ourselves as well as from others. In short, they first become a debt to the group and later a debt to ourselves.

And so it happens that although military service is satisfactory to the group, it may not make the soldier happy, and the Jobs of the world wonder why a good man should suffer so much while the wicked prosper. We can shrug off this situation as a cosmic mystery, or we can be confident with the Stoics that it all does make sense when the final accounts of the universe are cast up, or that malignant fates pursue men to thwart their most decent aspirations. Or we can say that the individual is corrupt by nature and is thus always out of step with society, or conversely, that society is so corrupt that it is forever making its individuals wretched.

Uniting subjective and objective estimates

Any view that separates the subjective and objective estimates too much is in for trouble both theoretically and practically. Theoretically, a universe in which individual goodness or rightness contradicts goodness in society is an inconsistent and clumsy universe.[7] Practically, such a radical separation makes it next to impossible to motivate the individual to correct or modify his own actions when they run counter to his impulses and desires. We may indeed admire and respect the upright but unhappy soul, but we are not eager to exchange places with him.

The solution, it would seem, lies in the promise that if we order our conduct in accordance with certain principles, we shall not only win the approval of our fellow men, but we shall also experience pleasure, and this pleasure will be greater, more lasting, and more satisfactory than the pleasures that accompany action not so ordered.

Such a promise is implicit in the principle set out by Aristotle's doctrine of pleasure. He holds that every activity is completed by its appropriate pleasure. Each of the senses and every act of body or mind has its attendant pleasure.[8] There is pleasure in seeing, hearing, eating, running, and thinking, and each activity is intensified by its proper pleasure and hindered by the pleasures attendant on other activities, ". . . for people who are fond of playing the flute are incapable of attending to arguments if they overhear someone playing the flute."[9] Alien pleasures do pretty much what proper pains do, "since activities are destroyed by their proper pains."[10]

Pleasure, therefore, is a sign that some function is being carried

[7] Immanuel Kant, realizing this, postulated God, Freedom, and Immortality so that the discrepancies between merit and happiness in this world could be corrected in the next, *Critique of Pure Reason*, Transcendental Doctrine of Method, Chap. II, Sec. 2.

[8] From *Nicomachean Ethics*, translated by W. D. Ross, Clarendon Press, Book X, Chap. 4, 1175a, 21–22.

[9] *Ibid.*, 1175b, 3–5.

[10] *Ibid.*, 1175b, 16–17.

out well; pain is a sign of the contrary state. Pleasure as such is not bad but is actually a sign of some degree of goodness. But pleasures vary in quality as do the activities they complete, the higher the activity, the higher the pleasure. What then are the "higher" activities? For Aristotle, man's highest activities are those which distinguish him from other forms of organic life, viz., the activities of thought. Consequently, the activity of choosing our acts in the light of thought (prudence or the use of practical reason) and the use of reason to apprehend the nature of things (its theoretic activity) are the highest activities, and the pleasures accompanying them are the highest pleasures.[11]

The virtuous man becomes the yardstick for the good life, and it is a yardstick that does justice to both the individual subjective estimate and the social objective one. It represents the search for happiness and pleasure, but it is an enlightened reflective search. It stands as a corrective to individual caprice and to social rigidity. The formula for the good life prescribes the development of our human powers so that they function with a minimum of friction and waste. When such is the case, the group becomes the good society, and the individual not only meets its demands but is genuinely happy in doing so.

The Good Life as an Educational Aim

No one would disagree with what has been said about the desirability of framing a vision of the good life as the ultimate aim of education, but there would be some serious objections nevertheless.

1. It would be objected that the "good life" is a very general expression and that aiming at it is like aiming at the sky. An aim, if it is to direct activity, has to exclude much more than it includes; the target is always a minute portion of what we can see.

In a sense, this objection has been met by the analysis of the subjective and objective estimates of the good life and by trying to show that there is a way of uniting the two. How well we shall succeed in overcoming this objection depends on how clearly we can indicate the kinds of behavior that give life the quality of goodness and those which do not. In other words, we shall have to

[11] *Ibid.*, Book X, Chaps. 5–8. It should be noted that happiness is not the equivalent of either pleasure or virtue. Friendship, some worldly goods, and a little luck as well as virtue are needed to achieve happiness.

indicate what we mean by a human capacity or function operating well or badly. When, for example, is the human power to think functioning well? Can it also function less well? If so, what are the signs of such mal-functioning? How does it happen that a human function can operate both well and ill?

How useful the conception of a good life will be for education also depends on how well we can identify and estimate the potentialities of the individual pupil in each of the major human powers. Can we estimate the power to think? Can we diagnose the individual's capacities for realizing economic, social, aesthetic, and religious values? Further, even if an individual's capacities can be estimated, is there anything the school can do to foster such powers in a given direction? Can the school improve the powers of thought, feeling, and imagination?

If these things can be done, then the objection of generality and also of unpredictability will be met at least in part. We cannot predict the particular acts by which the individual pupil will achieve or fail to achieve security, freedom from pain, and a sense of accomplishment, but perhaps we can predict the *form* such activities will have to take if the resulting life is to be judged as good.

In anticipation of the coming chapters, we shall call these forms: *self-determination, self-realization,* and *self-integration.* We shall try to show that any act to qualify as contributing to the goodness of life will have to be measured in these three dimensions.

2. But on what *grounds* do we make such pronouncements? This brings us to the second great objection to the good life as an ultimate aim of education. The issue here is difficult but clear. It is simply whether the term "good" refers to what some person or persons happen to like at any given moment, or whether there is a structure in the human personality, i.e., human nature, that defines what is good whether the individual feels it to be good or not at any given moment.

This issue will come up in every one of the subsequent chapters. On what grounds can we demand of ourselves or of others that one action be chosen over another? Why should men postpone the satisfaction of some of their cravings when to satisfy them would be so pleasant? Why should I sacrifice for the common good when my own good is clear and imperative? Why should our enemies be converted to our system of values?

Of course we can force the recalcitrant pupil, neighbor, citizen, or enemy to do our will if we have the power and are willing to exert it. This is a famous argument, *argumentum ad baculum* (the argument of the club), and it is one of the wonderful mysteries of human life that we do not accept it as valid. Animals never question the social reality and validity of brute force.

But the only alternative to the club (and the club may be psychological and subtle as well as physical and brutal) is persuasion, an appeal to the rational powers of our adversary. Only if we can show that his values run counter to *his* own self-determination, realization, and integration can we persuade him rationally. But, you say, suppose he does not want to determine himself, realize himself, and integrate himself? I will admit that I could not argue with such a creature, but I would also wonder why I was still calling him a man.

Put in another way, the task that confronts any view holding to an objective concept of the good life is to show that human nature has a structure that is everywhere the same, and that this structure demands for its own preservation the form of action characteristic of the "good" life.

Some writers who do not hold to an unchanging form of the good life, who hold rather that good is whatever a culture defines it to be or whatever any person feels it to be, or whatever circumstances dictate it to be, do not face such a task. An opinion poll provides an answer to their problem. On the other hand, they do not really need a *philosophy* of education either. For a philosophy is needed only when one is trying to *argue* that one value system or one form of life is really superior to another, and that one view of human nature is truer than another.

But the serious philosophers who defend the relativity of human experience are also striving to find norms that will clearly differentiate between good and evil, and their attempts to validate such norms without the aid of absolutes is an intellectual enterprise of no mean order. How successful they are is another matter, but their attempts prove that the concepts of the good life and human nature are not meaningless notions.

Summary

Educational controversies often get nowhere because the parties involved have educational aims in view that are not on the same

level of generality. The highest level of such aims is some notion
of the good life. When we try to formulate such a notion we find that
although we agree pretty much on the features of a life judged to
be good, we employ one yardstick in measuring our own lives and
a somewhat different measure for the lives of others. The subjective
estimate is based for the most part on how pleasant or satisfactory
our own lives seem to us. Objective estimates also insist on pleasantness, but they subordinate it to duty to the common welfare, quality
of character, and a rough notion as to what we have a right to
expect from life in an average set of circumstances.

The subjective and objective estimates can be united by the
Aristotelian doctrine that perfect functioning of any human capacity
is accompanied by pleasure. The happy life is therefore the outcome
of the virtuous life, and this, in turn, comes about as we cultivate
our human capacities to the utmost. For education, therefore, the
good life as an aim translates itself into a program of helping each
individual lay the groundwork for such cultivation.

The two main objections to this kind of view are: (1) that the
good life is too general a notion to be valuable in directing education,
and (2) that it cannot be defended on rational grounds. The remain-
ing chapters are devoted in large part to the meeting of these
objections.

PROBLEMS FOR DISCUSSION AND RESEARCH

1. Study pp. 161–195 in Brubacher's *Eclectic Philosophy of Education* on various conceptions of aims in education. How does our own
discussion apply to these views?

2. For advanced students the same sort of analysis should be made
on the material in the Forty-first Yearbook of the N.S.S.E., Part I,
Philosophies of Education, or the Fifty-fourth Yearbook, Part I.

3. Surveying the American scene, can you construct types of lives
that would be regarded as good by considerable portions of the population?

4. Study the memoirs of Winston Churchill, or the life of Albert
Schweitzer, or Thoreau. Are these lives "good"? If so, what makes them
good?

5. A good insight as to what happens in society and education when
agreement on the good life breaks down is furnished by the first six
chapters in W. O. Stanley's *Education and Social Integration*. This topic
lends itself to a panel discussion or round table.

6. Study a list of objectives in a curriculum plan for some school system. See if you can arrange the aims listed there in some hierarchy on the basis of levels of generality.

SUGGESTIONS FOR FURTHER READING

For fuller bibliographical information on the items listed below, consult the General Bibliography.

Brubacher, *Eclectic Philosophy of Education*, Topic 8.
———, *Modern Philosophies of Education*, pp. 105–112.

For the Classical Realist approach:

Aristotle, *Nicomachean Ethics*, Book X.
Plato, *Republic*, 400 C–403 C, 521 C–531 C.
Wild, *An Introduction to Realistic Philosophy*, Chap. 2.

For samplings of the Instrumentalist or Experimentalist views:

Childs, *Education and Morals*, Chaps. 2, 3.
Dewey, *Democracy and Education*, Chaps. 4, 8.
Mason, *Educational Ideals in American Society*.
Wynne, *Philosophies of Education*, Chap. 10.

For some other views:

Bagley, *Educational Values, passim*. (Essentialism.)
Cunningham, *Pivotal Problems of Education*, Chap. 8. (Roman Catholic.)
Finney, *A Sociological Philosophy of Education*, Chap. 4. (Conservative and institution-centered.)
Kneller, *Existentialism and Education*, Chap. 5.
Ulich, *Fundamentals of Democratic Education*, Chaps. 3, 4. (Idealism.)

A critical survey of various sets of educational objectives will be found in:

Smith, *et al.*, *Fundamentals of Curriculum Development*, Chap. 7.

3

The Structure and
Dynamics of Personality

We have outlined the characteristics of the good life as an ultimate aim of education, and we did so after examining what men judge to be good in estimating their own lives and the lives of others. We concluded that although the subjective and objective estimates often and perhaps always differ, there is an underlying unity out of which both estimates emerge. This underlying unity we may call the nature of man or the structure of human personality.

Therefore we must seek those general features that characterize all men regardless of their variations. The educator transacts his business with individuals, but he will understand them and his own task only as he sees in them instances of mankind in general.

The Appetitive Principle

Desire, want, lack, and need initiate and maintain all life. These terms are all names for an unsettled state in the organism that produces tension just as the damming of a river, the coiling of a spring, or the compression of a gas produces a tension that concentrates energy. This energy when released will do work; it constitutes power. Every philosophy recognizes this motive principle as the basic condition of any life whatsoever. What differentiates the numerous grades of life are the *forms* that this appetitive principle takes. A cabbage needs nutriments from the soil, water, and sunlight. A cabbage worm needs a cabbage.

Desires as tissue needs

At the simplest level the appetitive principle reveals itself as a need for what will maintain and reproduce the tissues—what have been called physiological drives or tissue needs. Unless such tissue needs are satisfied, no life is possible. We are justified, therefore, in calling them *necessary* conditions of human life.

History provides two extreme reactions to this basic fact. There is a long and respectable tradition dating at least as far back as Socrates that although tissue needs may be *necessary* conditions for life, they are also necessary evils. Many forms of religion regard these lusts of the body as obstacles to the spiritual life. They are to be minimized, disciplined, and controlled so that they will interfere as little as possible with the higher desires of the soul and the workings of the mind. Yet none of these religions, however much they may welcome release from the body, deliberately counsel suicide.

The other reaction to the tissue needs is that they alone are basic, that all so-called "higher" forms of desire and life originate in these needs, and that they never rise as far above their origins as man would like to believe. From the ancient Greek materialism of Democritus and Epicurus down to modern Marxism, this tradition has regarded it as a part of wisdom to see human life as a brief trip from dust to dust. The trip can be rendered more tolerable by making the satisfaction of tissue needs easier and surer. It is not quite fair to say that the materialist wants a life of bread alone, but until sufficient bread is provided, he is likely to be impatient with schemes for doing without it.

Such differences in point of view about the physiological needs serve notice that in man, at least, desires are not restricted to the level of tissue needs. A cabbage deprived of what it needs dies quietly. We do not pity the cabbage because we assume that the cabbage is unconscious of both its life and its destruction. A cabbage may need sunlight, but it does not yearn for it.

Consequently, awareness or sentience is the first requisite for doing anything about tissue needs except taking them for granted. If the filling of tissue needs did not give pleasure and the denial of them pain, they would be unconscious mechanisms that either occurred or didn't occur; the spiritualists would not deplore them nor the materialists exalt them.

Sentience, or being able to feel needs and their relief, is not enough to account for the strategic role desires play. Imagine a life in which nothing but the immediate present moment is ever experienced. I feel hungry and slightly painful, then more hungry and more uneasy, then I encounter food and there is relief, then there is sleepiness and I sleep. Now I feel cold and then warm, etc. Very possibly some animal forms exist on this plane, but certainly such creatures do not worry about whether their desires ought to be satisfied and how. Indeed, with no future and no past, what could worry mean for them?

We consequently have to notice another fact of life. It is that protoplasm can retain pleasures and pains *beyond* their immediate occurrence. Some of the circumstances under which tissue needs were felt and satisfied in the past can come to serve as signals or signs that satisfaction is in the offing. When this comes to pass, we say that the organism has *learned* something. A rat that has learned to run a maze in the process of getting food no longer lives exclusively in the present moment. It uses its past to anticipate the future. In addition to the organic messages from the stomach there can now be anticipatory feelings of pleasure when the progress in the maze is customary and promising, and there can be feelings of pain when the experimenter is frustrating its efforts.

Thus the simple tissue need for nutriment has expanded to include a desire for certain *experiences in the maze*. There may even be a desire to see the experimenter. These new desires were not created by tissue needs themselves, but rather by the fact that the activities of the past are not entirely erased from the rat's nervous system and continue to operate in each succeeding "present." Psychologists refer to this somewhat simple knitting together of what previously were separate elements as conditioning, as when a dog learns to respond to a bell as if it were food or a signal of impending food [1]

Our simple natural bodily needs proliferate into *acquired* desires —not for food merely but for certain flavors, table settings, and utensils. The desire for sex activity is not merely a response to hormone activity but can be aroused by thoughts about the opposite sex, by seeing parts of the anatomy not ordinarily exposed, by the sound of the voice, or by certain articles of apparel. The number and variety of objects that can become symbols of sex activity is so great that it is impossible to say, *a priori,* what object if any could not under appropriate circumstances become one.

Symbols as objects of desire

Men desire not only what their tissues demand, but they gradually come to love with equal ardor the signs and symbols of such satisfaction. These signs achieve an autonomy[2] and power of their own which is to a large extent independent of their origin and often cannot easily be traced back to them. A husband comes home tired and irritable. His wife serves a soggy meal. If the husband is angered, it is not because his nutrition has suffered, but because the ill-cooked meal symbolizes an incompetent wife or an unloving one or both. But an unloving wife symbolizes in turn an unfortunate or an unworthy husband. We are now a long way from tissue needs, but the anger and unhappiness of the husband are no less genuine for all that.

This expansion of desires through learning, imagination, and symbolization has at least two results. One is that not all desires are "necessary" in the same sense that food is "necessary" to life. If they are to be called "necessary," it is in the sense of the psychological necessity to preserve the personality and a sense of well-being. Certain strivings are as natural to the human personality as are its cravings for food, and like all cravings they can become overlaid with desires that are not so natural. Through imagination and symbolization they can be transformed into perverted and warped desires or into the noblest aspirations and ideals.

The other result is that proliferated, symbolic, or derived desires

---

[1] For a thorough discussion of modern theories of learning by conditioning see Mowrer, *Learning Theory and Behavior.*

[2] What G. W. Allport has dubbed "functional autonomy."

can be satisfied by a wide range of action. The satisfactions are as varied as are the desires themselves, so that although imagination creates a mighty burden for man, it also provides to some extent the means for bearing it.

What has been said about the proliferation of desires should not give us the notion that each one of us independently builds up his own desire system out of sheer imagination. By far the bulk of our desires comes from the culture which has already put its labels of "desirable" and "undesirable" on the objects with which men are engaged in their daily life. For some this simplifies the problem of deciding what "ought" to be desired; for others, the cultural stereotypes complicate matters even further.[3]

Another characteristic of the desiring element in human nature is its blindness, although the blindness is not complete.[4] There is what Cannon[5] has called the "wisdom of the body"—that remarkable system of checks and balances for the maintenance of the bodily economy. But it is a relatively fixed and therefore myopic wisdom. The glandular fireworks that put the body into readiness for emergencies make men football heroes, but may give them ulcers when they become executives. The wisdom of the body is insufficient to recognize poisons by taste or to give advance warning of the imminence of injurious viruses, cancerous growths, or atomic radiations.

To say that a desire is blind is to say no more than that a craving is imperious in its demands for immediate satisfaction. It does not of itself foresee that it may lead to pain, to excess, to satiety, and even to revulsion. It does not see that it may conflict with other needs and desires.

Desire, the power behind all human action, reveals itself as a rational core of necessary tissue and psychic needs enveloped by what we learn to love or hate through education, through our powers of imagination, and through more or less haphazard conditioning. It is clear, therefore, that at the human level, desires of either the body or the personality will not automatically organize themselves into the good life. We cannot trust desire to differentiate between the real needs of the individual and his "felt" needs. We are

---

[3] In *Human Potentialities* Gardner Murphy refers to these cultural shapings as the second human nature.

[4] Aristotle noted that some of our appetites have a tendency to obey the rational principle.

[5] Cannon, *The Wisdom of the Body.*

led accordingly to the next stage of our search, viz., the principles by which the motive power of desire is controlled and organized.

Education and the appetitive principle

The clearest form of such control is found in the training every child receives in what to love and what to hate. Plato, in the *Republic*, recognized this so clearly that he prescribed for the infancy and childhood of his philosopher kings a rigorous period of conditioning that would make them love and hate what their mentors would have them love and hate. He also established a censorship of all literature, drama, and music so that the adult population could not easily contaminate this training.

Plato has been severely criticized for this. To impose adult likes and dislikes on helpless infants smacks of high authoritarianism. Unfortunately no one has discovered a sensible alternative. Every community has a ready-made set of attitudes, likes, and dislikes that it foists upon the younger generation more or less successfully without thinking very much about it. In any culture—democratic or autocratic—the imposition of love-hate patterns is the rule and not the exception.

If we throw out Plato's rigorous and radical solution to this problem, the problem does not disappear; it is merely shifted into the lap of parents and citizens. Parents have to try as best they can to form certain attitudes, and citizens have to control somehow those forces in the community that would subvert their efforts.

Parents realizing the complexity of child training are understandably discouraged, especially when every manual of child care tells them what ought to be done in one paragraph and in the next paragraph warns them that no two individuals are alike and that therefore the rule may or may not be applicable to their child. Parents are urged not to be harsh with their children, yet not to indulge them too much, to socialize them, yet not crush their individuality, and to love them, yet not make them dependent on that love. Aristotle saw long ago that the approximation of the mean between such extremes is not a matter of precise calculation. Only by experience can we recognize the precise moment when a child can stand a little frustration. There is no principle or formula to take the place of such experience. This means that mistakes in child rearing are inevitable,

48 MAN, SOCIETY, AND THE SCHOOL

and that accidents are unavoidable. We may as well recognize these
limitations at the outset for the sake of parents and children alike.
Our knowledge of these matters is still so meager that we cannot
be sure when an error in child rearing turns out to be a mistake or
a blessing.

Protection from unnecessary frustration and pain breeds in the
child a love of parent that makes for emotional security; development of his powers breeds a sense of adequacy. Given these two
assets the child incorporates the attitudes of the parents toward the
values of life, whatever they may be. He will love what they love,
fear what they fear, and hate what they hate. In the absence of these
attitudes learning also takes place and quickly, but what the child
learns is to revenge himself on his parents or his fellow children. He
becomes the neurotic child.

It is not the function of a philosophy of education to expound the
details of child care and training. However, it should be kept in
mind that no amount of scheming on the part of the parents can
wholly eliminate the adventitious factors in the development of a
human personality. Parents can exert only a limited control over the
community and the playmates of their children. Their justification for
arbitrary impositions of attitudes on children must come from their
own power to criticize their own attitudes in the light of knowledge
and reason—which their children as yet cannot do. The rearing of
children is at best a gamble; parents can only make that gamble as
rational as possible.

These simple spontaneous and unreasoned dispositions of feeling
are the raw material which the school and the child's growing intelligence may transform into reasoned and reflective conduct—if
circumstances are propitious. The school has already discovered
that knowledge and exhortation accomplish little in the absence of
this sound raw material. As long as the school ignores this fact, it
will continue to promise what it cannot often deliver—a reformation
of character. The emphasis of modern mental hygiene movements
on emotional health is sound, but the insistence that it is the first
business of the school is more dubious. School is rarely a psychological hazard for children who are emotionally healthy, and it is
rarely a remedy for those who are not. The school's responsibility,
like that of the parents, is not to frustrate the pupil unduly but to
help him bear the impedimenta of life. However, it does not do its
share through the *arbitrary* conditioning that is characteristic of the

early years of home training. Teachers are neither nursemaids nor psychiatric therapists.

Self-Determination

The most general feature of human life is that it is agitated by a set of desires that originate in natural physical and psychic needs, but which end up, thanks to memory and imagination, in a veritable jungle of acquired human wants, needs, and aspirations.

Discovery of the self and the other

Desires are useless without means to satisfy them. The human being has power—the power it transforms from the food it consumes to energize its nerves and muscles. Desires are calls for power. Desires also channel power in one direction rather than another. But to be *aware* of power is also to become aware that one's world is divided into two important parts: the Self and the Other. If every wish of mine were automatically satisfied, I would feel neither effort nor obstacle. There would be no occasion to distinguish myself from my surroundings.

But early in the course of desiring we stumble on the fact that some desires are satisfied and some are not. Sooner or later we encounter objects that we cannot budge by the power at our command —not even by crying loud and long. This marks the discovery of the Other, or that which I cannot control. Selfhood and frustration, if not inseparable, are certainly not far apart. If there were no frustration of any desire—not even the frustration of delay—it is hard to conceive how things or persons could be regarded as other than extensions of one's own body. Through frustration I find that I have desires, satisfactions, and pains; that presumably there exist other I's who behave in a similar way, and that there are Its which behave differently from the I's. In all this confusion only this much seems certain: I have power but not all power is mine.[6]

Because I have memory and imagination, I can remember that satisfying one desire brought pleasure and that satisfying another did not. I can imagine both having my money and the good things

[6] An interesting elaboration of this principle is to be found in Ausubel's treatment of ego devaluation, *Ego Development and the Personality Disorders*, Chap. 7.

it will buy. There comes a time, therefore, when desires are suspected as possible deceivers. Doubt and indecision set in, and I find
myself deliberating on the merits of desires instead of rushing forth-
with to satisfy them. I have at least momentarily separated myself
from the desires in order to scrutinize them, and I keep this tentative distance until I choose one rather than another. I thus find that
I am not merely the sum of my desires.

So we arrive at the notion of a Self, an "I" who *has* desires, who
makes decisions and choices, and who suffers and thinks and acts. In
the history of philosophy this has led to the concept of the Self or
soul as a kind of spiritual substance that remains constant while its
acts and its contents change from moment to moment. It is this Self
which was held to be immortal and immaterial, which could be
saved or damned.

There have been philosophers, like Hume, who could find no such
entity, for whenever they looked for the Self they found only what
it was *doing* and not what it was apart from such doings.[7]

We do not have to settle this metaphysical problem at this point,
but there are certain facts of human experience that have to be ac-
counted for, and some kind of theory about the Self is needed to do
so. For example, there is the fact that human experience has some
continuity despite the gaps enforced on it by sleep and uncon-
sciousness. Amid daily changes and adventures the bulk of my experience seems to cluster about a core, so that it is the same person
who yesterday made a fool of himself, who today is ashamed of having done so, and tomorrow will probably make a fool of himself
again. Not only do I remember what happened to me a week ago,
but I remember it as my experience and not my neighbor's.[8]

William James[9] felt that this continuity could be explained by con-
catenation, or by a kind of overlapping of one experience by its suc-
cessor so that at any given moment any two moments of experience
would have something in common. Bergson,[10] believing that all of

[7] This, however, did not make Hume happy, for he remarks that, "I neither
know how to correct my former opinions, nor how to render them consistent."
A Treatise of Human Nature, Vol. II, p. 317.
[8] For an exposition of self-psychology, see Brightman, *Introduction to Philosophy*, pp. 189 ff. Also G. W. Allport, *Personality: A Psychological Interpretation*, Chap. 13, and Broudy and Freel, *Psychology for General Education*,
Chaps. 2 and 3.
[9] *A Pluralistic Universe*, Chap. 5.
[10] Bergson, *Creative Evolution*, pp. 1–7.

our previous experience is preserved somehow in the present, conceived the Self as something to be caught only in an act of intuition.

We may understand these facts by noting that each human being is a real individual with a style of existence peculiar to Selves. This style we can call its formal structure. This structure remains the same so long as the individual continues to live. Thus he has a certain kind of body with certain kinds of organs that maintain life in certain ways. He also has certain ways of knowing, feeling, remembering, and imagining. These may vary in different men, so that *what* we know, remember, imagine, and feel changes from moment to moment. But the structure does not change so long as the individual remains a man. It is this structure that we can call the substance or the substantial nature of man. The Self is also substantial in this sense. The Self is not a hard bit of something. It is a pattern of activity, and it is with this pattern that we shall be concerned in the remainder of this chapter. It is what we shall mean by human nature. It is this pattern that gives each Self its enduring continuity. At any moment the Self is what it has done and what it is striving to do. And in its waking moments under normal conditions it is aware of this unity of pattern; it is aware of itself. The Self is a pattern for living.

During sleep or deep anaesthesia it is the continuity of the living tissues, each with its own pattern of striving, that keeps the individual's life pattern intact. Only the brain, or rather its highest centers, have interrupted their normal functioning. It is as if, in the language of Aristotle, the nutritive soul—the body pattern—has taken over.[11] Persons in grave stages of illness still live when consciousness is gone, and even physicians speak of a will to live that seems to have nothing to do with the patient's thoughts about the matter.

Self as actuality and possibility

At any moment I, as an actual real individual, am the result of my total history. Everything I have done, thought, sensed, remembered, felt, and imagined is registered in me. Not as they happened originally to be sure but as effects of those happenings. One answer to the question: What am I? is "You are what you have been."

But at every moment throughout that history I was straining toward the next moment, the future, and so was every cell in my

[11] *De Anima*, 412a3–415a13.

body. The whole organism and each part was trying consciously or otherwise to maintain its character, exercise its powers, and spread its effects so as to insure its future. Apart from this straining toward the future, we could hardly distinguish animate objects from inanimate ones; the living from the dead.[12]

Thus at the level of human life where we can not only live toward the future, but also be aware that we are doing so, the Self can be thought of as made up of its envisioned possibilities. What am I really? Perhaps what really expresses me is my hopes and plans—what I would want to be at the next moment of my life. This vision is woven out of my previous experience, but it is a *selection* from that experience on the basis of choice, thought, and imagination.

The Self is what the mind envisions as my possibilities. My real Self is not merely what I have undergone to date. All of that has been rearranged and preserved *symbolically* in the hopes and plans I have for the life I have not yet lived. At each moment I projected my past into a future possibility, and in doing so I was creating my own peculiar individual pattern of being which I could say was "I" and no one else.

Note that I did not create the material for my projection, and that no one else could give this peculiar projection to me. This is probably what Sartre means when he speaks of myself as my project.[13] To be, to exist in that particular way or form we call "human," is to project one's Self out of the actual present into a nonexistent but nevertheless thinkable future. It is the Self as a symbol.

The self as freedom

We now come to another stage in the discovery of the Self and the Other. We have already noted that frustration is the spring of Selfhood. We become aware of Self when we realize that we are not omnipotent, indeed not even so potent as our desires would have us be. And at a stroke our whole being puts a high premium on freedom from frustration.

At first, frustration of desire is felt as bad because it is painful, but later, when we have come to know that some desires are themselves pain-producing, it is not frustration of desire that we rebel against

[12] Wild, "Phenomenology and Metaphysics," *The Return to Reason*, pp. 64–65.

[13] Sartre, *Existentialism*, pp. 19, 37–38.

so much as the frustration of the will or the blocking of our choices. A choice is not merely a desire to do or to have; it is the selection of such-and-such an object following thought, indecision, and deliberation. And whenever we choose, so far as we know we always choose the best under the circumstances. Now if every choice is of the best as the person conceives it to be, then whatever frustrates or impedes the carrying out of the choice seems bad. This is what we mean by freedom of the will: not the ability to do anything we wish or desire, but freedom to carry out our thought-out decisions. Therefore, such freedom is the first good, and whatever impedes it is the first evil.

Once more, what is the Self? The Self is its freedom. It is its duly chosen projects, its choice of a plan of action. So far as you permit me this freedom, you let me *be*. Insofar as you restrict it, you cut down my being. If I choose to be an engineer rather than a doctor and circumstances prevent my carrying out this project, then part of me has been destroyed. To continue as a Self I have to remake myself into a new project.

Thomas Hobbes installed the desire for peace as a means to self-preservation as the first law of nature. But self-preservation properly means the preservation of the Self, and the Self is not only the life we live at any moment, but the projection of it as a possibility in terms of our choice, i.e., our freedom. Hence, the first right of man is freedom, and to surrender this right is tantamount to ceasing to exist as a human being. It is spiritual suicide. Such suicide is not impossible. Routinized habit, drug addiction, or too great a love of conformity are steps in that direction. And there can be such a thing as spiritual murder. It is the destruction of the Self as a creator of possibility. Modern tyrannies have realized that their foes are not destroyed half so effectively by physical as by spiritual murder.

To summarize: as soon as he becomes aware of himself and as soon as he can reflect and choose, the individual man must regard the freedom of his will as a fundamental good and its frustration as an evil. Now we may not agree with him as to *what* he chooses, and we may not grant him the freedom he craves, but this does not alter his claim to that freedom.

All of which leads us to conclude that *freedom or self-determination is one of the natural and essential goals of the human being.* To be good subjectively or objectively a life must give evidence of having been fashioned from within by the person who is living it. *It must not be fashioned by desire solely, but by desires as weighed and chosen by a thinking Self, part of whose very being and essence are the possibilities of becoming what it can envision.*

Freedom of the will

Let a man be the favorite son of fortune. Let circumstances so conspire that without effort on his part there come to him wealth, fame, beauty, and every other good. Certainly he will be envied by everyone to whom these goods come reluctantly or not at all. But does the recipient of such lavish good luck judge his life as good? Enjoyable? Certainly. But never to feel that what happens to him is the result of what *he* does, never to be able to take credit for any accomplishment, that is simply to say that he equals zero. *He* is nothing because *he* does nothing; he is simply a corridor for events which does nothing to affect their flow. Is such a life really human?

On the other hand, there have been lives in which circumstances seemed bent on the destruction of the individual, and yet such lives have been judged good even by the individuals who suffered through them. The life of Epictetus, a slave, may not have been particularly enjoyable; certainly Job's life was not always gladsome, and the life of Spinoza was suffused with suffering. Yet none of these nor their observers would hesitate to judge that in certain respects their lives were good. The clue to the answer here is the same as in the case of fortune's favorite, viz., the existence of a Self that by its exertions gave notice to the world that here was a piece of reality to be reckoned with.

Is freedom possible? What is the Self that we so desire to keep free? Are the current definitions and notions about freedom consistent or compatible?[14]

Let us recall that by freedom of the will we mean nothing more than freedom of choice; freedom to carry out our deliberated decisions. Whatever interferes with this is an impediment to our freedom. There are plenty of such impediments.

We do not, for example, choose our tissue needs: to be hungry or thirsty or sleepy, and regardless of how and what we choose, the ways of things will not on that account alter themselves to suit our

[14] Cf. Edwards and Pap, *A Modern Introduction to Philosophy*, Chap. 5.

wishes. Even our own psychological makeup has a certain fixity and regularity that ignores our wishes. For example, certain inglorious memories persist in returning to our consciousness.

On these grounds some deny to man any freedom whatsoever. They argue that our very choices are determined by forces over which we have no control and that if we feel that we are free and really making our choices, this feeling is due to our ignorance of the causes that make us feel that way. There is, they would argue, a psychological, physiological, and logical determinism that makes up our minds for us.

If there is a thoroughgoing determinism in nature and in man, it is obviously one that permits much variation, and if we ask how these variations occur, we find that the determinism is not so rigid or thoroughgoing as is sometimes believed. If by determinism we mean that everything has a cause, then no rational man would deny it. We could explain nothing if this principle were false. On the other hand, if by determinism is meant that all our experience is the result of physical forces so that our choices are as predetermined as the next solar eclipse, then at least one element of our experience does not bear this out, viz., our power to symbolize.

We noted earlier in this chapter that desires multiply because men can remember and imagine. In brief, an experience leaves something of itself for future reference. A week ago I met a man whom I thoroughly dislike. I have not seen that man since, yet I refuse to attend a party at which I am told he will be present. Clearly, it is not the man's physical presence that is directing my action, but rather some sort of present experience which symbolizes or *stands for* the man and my feelings of a week ago. At this moment I can combine this symbol with the images of my meeting him again and of trying to avoid him for the whole evening, and yet all this takes place while I am in the present. All of this "activity" is taking place in terms of *meaning* and not of events.

Of course there are events going on in my brain, and without such events I could not invent or use symbols. But once a symbol is born it takes on a life of meaning which its neural ancestors did not have. In short, symbols can be manipulated and combined as their referents (what they stand for) cannot. I can think of a golden mountain, the perfect crime, or the most beautiful woman in the world without waiting for these entities to come into being.

Events act on each other, but events do not *mean* each other. They are not *about* anything.

> Thus a tree or a jellyfish or the color yellow or the relation "greater than" are none of them of or about anything else. They are just themselves. For instance, what is it that a jellyfish is about anyway? To be sure, the concept of a jellyfish is of or about it, but it itself is not of or about anything else.[15]

Concepts, ideas, even images do not exist as physical things do. They operate in our acts of knowing and thinking to refer to real things or to each other.

Granted that one has nothing to say about feeling hungry or not hungry—cells and body chemistry see to that—no two men satisfy hunger in the same way, just as they do not sleep in the same way or find their sexual partners in the same way. One can imagine eating dinner out of a can, or at an expensive restaurant, or even omitting it altogether.

One cannot help seeking emotional security—to be loved for oneself, to be reassured that that love will not be lost. But no two men seek it in the same way, which is the despair of the psychiatrist and everyone else who tries to understand human behavior.

One cannot help or prevent the blizzard from its blowing and snowing, but one man freezes to death in it; another enjoys the chance to read without interruption; a third makes a fortune out of snowplows; and a poet writes a description that all schoolboys and girls will have to memorize.

What then is human freedom? It is precisely this possibility of varying our responses to forces that we do *not* control, of creating a world of *possible* responses out of the symbolic representatives of events. The fabric of our memories and of our imagination is woven out of these threads, and they lend themselves to many, many patterns.

Why is it that my idea of the Brooklyn Bridge has no size nor weight of its own? Why can I, in my imagination, take it apart in a trice? Why can I see myself diving from it while half asleep in an armchair? This is the ancient mystery of the nature of mind and meaning on one hand and of physical events on the other. Here is a fundamental duality between two orders of being. We cannot, with

[15] Henry B. Veatch, "For a Realistic Logic," *The Return to Reason*, John Wild, ed., p. 180.

the Materialist, reduce everything to the kind of being physical events have; nor, with the Idealists, can we insist that to be is to be known, and to be known is to have the kind of being an idea or a symbol has. We may conclude with Susanne K. Langer that:

> Symbolization is the essential act of the mind; and mind takes in more than what is commonly called thought. . . . In every mind there is an enormous store of other symbolic material, which is put to different uses or perhaps even to no uses at all—a mere result of spontaneous brain activity, a reserve fund of conceptions, a surplus of mental wealth.[16]

How these two orders of being do come together in knowledge is a technical problem of epistemology which we shall not try to deal with at this point (see Chapter 5). *That* they come together is, however, a fact of crucial importance to the structure of personality.

It is by a manipulation of symbols called "scientific thought" that man has increased the possibilities of feeding himself, of communicating at distances, of traveling at great velocities, and of protecting himself against the ravages of many diseases.

By another sort of symbolic manipulation man has been able to envision himself as more than animal, as divine in origin, or as a source of kindness, love, and beauty. And by the manipulation of symbols he has exfoliated his desires into a multitude of wishes and fancies. He has even envisioned engines of great destruction to increase his unhappiness, and fears and anxieties to becloud his waking and sleeping hours.

Such symbolic possibilities, then, are the raw material for choice and decision; some possibilities are better than others, but the kind of freedom we have been talking about is prior to either. Freedom of speech, freedom of enterprise, freedom of self government, and freedom of religion are rightly prized, not because they always issue in good acts or decisions, but because without freedom there is a limitation of creating and sharing possibilities of any kind. Every man is a potential manufacturer of possibility; to restrict him is to limit possibility; it is to shrink *human* being.[17]

---

[16] Reprinted by permission of the publishers from Susanne K. Langer's *Philosophy in a New Key*, p. 41. Cambridge, Mass.: Harvard University Press. Copyright 1942, 1951 by the President and Fellows of Harvard College.

[17] Perhaps it is to this creative power that Gardner Murphy refers as the third human nature, the first being his biological structure and the second his cultural overlay. (*Human Potentialities*.)

Natural and Reflective Freedom

Because possibilities may be good or bad, the good life depends upon the possibilities we select. Since we have defined freedom as the possibility of possibility, good freedom would, I suppose, be that which selects the "really good" alternatives for thought and action. It is possible, for example, to feed oneself by begging, scavenging garbage cans, or working. If working is the best possibility, it must be so because it feeds one more steadily and reliably than do the other alternatives; because in the long run it is less frustrating than the others. On the same reasoning we would judge artificial irrigation to be a "better" possibility than sacrifice of a lamb to the rain gods.

We can therefore distinguish between *natural freedom,* which is merely the multiplication of possibles (by whatever means—science, fancy, wish, or dream) and *reflective freedom,* which evaluates possibilities in terms of their consequences for the good life as a whole. The former is a precondition of the latter, but the latter is that for the sake of which the former is to be cultivated. Hence we can say that any man has the natural right to think what he pleases and perhaps say what he pleases, but he *ought* to think and say what, after reflection, he believes to be true and valuable. The more we restrict this natural right, the fewer the possibilities from which we can select in our reflective freedom.

We can see now that real freedom consists of reflective choice and evaluation of the possibilities that issue from the symbolic activity of men in their natural freedom. It is knowledge that transforms natural freedom into reflective freedom. The more we know about the ways of matter, life, and men, the more possibilities we can envision and the more reliably we can select from among them.

Possibilities, ephemeral as they are, get their substance from the structure of a world that is not ephemeral. Certain combinations of symbols will work because they are in accord with this structure, and others will not for the opposite reason. Certain behaviors will lead to physical health; others will not. Certain behaviors will make us happy; others will not. Certain organizations of society will produce the good life; others will not. The world is not a chaos. On the contrary, it has a pattern and direction of its own. Every existent thing tends to fulfill itself, to realize its form, and "That toward which an entity is essentially tending, which will realize its nature, is good for it."[18]

The rules of scientific endeavor, the laws of evidence, the laws of logic which prescribe rules for the combinations of symbols, and the laws of symbols themselves are our guides in selecting and rejecting our dreams, wishes, and visions. The greater our obedience to these disciplines, paradoxically enough, the greater our real freedom. But these yokes or guides or channels can never be imposed by one man upon another; one assumes them freely or not at all.

In surveying his aims the educator places freedom or self-determination high on his list. But after analyzing the meaning and nature of freedom, he discerns that two somewhat distinct kinds of education are needed to promote what we have called natural freedom and reflective freedom.

Education for natural freedom

Ability to deal with symbols is essential to natural freedom. The Self increases its freedom in proportion as it can envision alternatives for choice. How can such symbolic facility be promoted through learning?

1. We have to learn what these symbols are. As the infant grows, things and their names become wedded to each other. This naming process accelerates rapidly in childhood. But left to the ordinary demands of everyday life, it may not continue to increase. Only deliberate instruction keeps the growth of vocabulary on the march.

Finer discrimination in the use of language is even less an automatic result of maturation. The terminology of the various sciences, sharp distinctions of meaning, and the use of language to convey small differences in meaning are all *acquired* and rarely without effort and instruction.

What is true of the linguistic symbols is even more evident in the matter of mathematical symbols. Here automatic growth is very small, and intensive instruction is indispensable.

There are also the symbols used in the fine arts. Dance movements are symbols of a sort and so are musical notes, dramatic movements, colors, and lines. The flag, the tombstone, the well-cared-for garden, and the uniforms of the police officer and nurse are all symbols of

[18] John Wild, "Tendency: The Ontological Ground of Ethics," *The Journal of Philosophy*, XLIX:14, July 3, 1952, p. 473.

activities or values current in a society. If education is somewhat less concerned with this latter class of symbols, it is not because they are less useful in life but only because they are learned rather easily without formal instruction. But without intensive and deliberate efforts, the child can well remain relatively illiterate in most of the symbols systems.

2. Yet symbolic facility alone is not enough. We need a disposition to use this skill to produce new combinations. Fortunately, the young child is gifted and eager in this respect largely because he has not yet been cast into rigid molds of behavior by his elders. However, this spontaneity is soon subjected to the pressures of custom and habit, so that by the time he emerges from adolescence, his speech, his clothes, and his preferences are already congealing into relatively fixed patterns. (See Chapter 9.) How to maintain this spontaneity, this natural freedom, in the later years of life is one of our major problems.

To sum up, then, as far as natural freedom is concerned, the educator accelerates the natural growth of symbolic mastery and scope by instruction, and fosters the natural creativity of the child by giving him plenty of opportunity to exercise it.

Unfortunately, natural freedom is, as such, a luxury of childhood. It does not matter too much what the child imagines, dreams, or plans because his action is guided and insured by his elders. The consequences of awkward plans and inconsistent wishes do not fall heavily upon him or upon society.

However, when such protection is withdrawn, as sooner or later it must be, the premium shifts from a wealth of possibilities, as such, to the selections of real possibilities from this wealth. The time has come for the use of the imagination in behalf of constructive activity; for this, mere fluidity of ideas is not enough.

Education for reflective freedom

Assuming that the learner has achieved reasonable mastery of the various symbol systems, education for reflective freedom consists of the various ways in which knowledge can guide practice.

Knowledge is a reasoned selection from the imaginative flights of the human race. Literature and the fine arts represent the more or less successful trials of society in using symbols to express the emotional life of men. They do not close the doors to further experimentation, but they eliminate the need for each generation to repeat the errors of its forbears.

Knowledge, then, is the great liberator if it is used as a guide to further freedom rather than as a substitute for it. Of course, it is better to absorb knowledge than to absorb errors, but simple absorption, although it helps to protect a man from being a fool, does not enlarge his stature as a real person, a real Self. To be real is to be the center of creativity, of possibilities, of projects. Absorption has to be a means to transformation.

Reflective freedom also relies heavily on certain dispositions and habits of thought, such as the disposition to inquire into causes, the disposition to examine propositions in the light of the evidence advanced for them, and openness of mind to alternative hypotheses. These dispositions and habits together make up the liberal or the *freed* mind. Since the disciplines of reliable knowledge were built up by these methods, mastery of a subject means not only an acquaintance with facts, but also the disposition to think about them critically, logically, and systematically.

Perhaps a common school example will help to clarify the relations between natural and reflective freedom. One of the important decision points in school life is the choice of a vocational career. Long before high school the pupil may have imagined himself as a dashing paratrooper, a jet pilot, a space explorer, or governor of his state. This imaginative play of ideas is the exercise of his natural freedom and nothing should curtail it. But reality and knowledge of reality converts some of his imagined possibilities into impossibilities —for him. As he uses knowledge to assay his own talents, the volume of possibilities is further reduced. His choice based on the best knowledge available to him is the product of reflective freedom. The greater his knowledge, the more effective does his reflective freedom become.

Self-Realization

Granted that a life to be judged good should bear the hallmark of self-determination, is it good simply because it is freely chosen? Some philosophers do equate the good with freedom. Sartre, the French Existentialist, says, for example: Once aware that in ". . . his forlornness he imposes value, he can no longer want but one thing, and that is freedom as the basis for all value."[19] Such an extreme view effectively emphasizes the strategic position of freedom, but freedom does not carry within itself the guaranty of its own consequences. Strictly speaking, freedom must be free to make us miserable. *What* is chosen as well as *how* it is chosen has to be reckoned with in the good life.

We are told that on some South Sea Islands life blossoms with ease and happiness in a beneficent climate that makes exertion, competition, and guilt feelings an exception to the rule. What makes the Western man think that the South Sea Island life is not so good as it might be? Even after allowances are made for cultural bias and the strenuous dizziness of American life, there remains a hint of genuine sadness when we contemplate adults behaving like intelligent carefree children. Why would so many of us be unhappy among the lotus eaters?

It is not, I believe, because we have been so conditioned by our culture that we cannot fit into the values of a gentler one. If this were the whole story, we would hardly look on such a culture as a reproach to certain features of our own. It is more likely that our sadness is a symptom of a lost innocence. We are also sad because unused potentialities always make us sad, and the unused power to learn, to know, and to appreciate arouses in us the most profound sadness. The South Sea Islanders themselves would view the failure to cultivate the powers of fishing, dancing, and swimming with disapproval. Cultures differ as to which values are worth achieving, but they agree that not to cultivate the chosen ones is bad.

Capacities and their development

Life then is good insofar as the power to realize value is developed and exercised. The range and diversity of values possible for an individual are limited by: (1) his own innate capacities, (2) the richness of the culture in which he lives, and (3) the education that exploits his capacities.

It is a mark of wisdom not to become embroiled in the heredity-environment debate, especially until we can measure capacity independently of the environmental factors that alone reveal its presence. Yet with monotonous regularity human babies exhibit structural characteristics that are generic to men and not to kangaroos. The

19 *Op. cit.*, p. 54.

large differences of accomplishment amid small differences in environment argue for innate capacities and so do the studies of maturation.[20]

Self-realization gets its particular content from the culture; there is no other source from which it could come. Samoans develop neither their muscles nor their arithmetic on golf courses, and an American, if he is to realize religious values, will probably not do so in a tribal ceremony. How well the innate powers of a Self can be exploited depends on the value potential of one's culture, as the example of the Samoans shows. Exceptional people—especially if they do not mind social discomfort—may rise above the limitations of their culture, but even the most creative thinker can only rearrange objects and ideas already present in it. At the equator even a genius would not be expected to conceive—much less fashion—an igloo. If the ancient Greeks arrived at enough ideas to capitalize all subsequent Western civilization by their free speculation, they did so because the art of playing with ideas, as well as a good stock of ideas to play with, already had permeated their culture.

Particular life conditions can limit the form and degree of self-realization. A scarcity of time for education, or of money, or of opportunity, or a widespread laziness all interfere with self-realization.

Finally, the gap between the potentialities and achievements of the individual may remain wide because the educational arrangements of a culture are inadequate to close it. They can fail either by not assessing a pupil's powers accurately or by not having the techniques or the determination to exploit them.

Criticisms of self-realization

We have been considering the need for self-realization and the obstacles to it. No doubt the term does mean something to users of the English language, but what it means is hard to say. Some philosophers of education have argued that it has no meaning at all, or a meaning so fuzzy as to be useless, or worse still, one that leads to very dubious consequences.

Accordingly, one ought to inquire whether the term does have any meaning, and if so, whether it is clear enough to help us in the

[20] See especially the concluding remarks of C. S. Hall in "The Genetics of Behavior," *Handbook of Experimental Psychology*, 1951, p. 328.

directing of education, in a direction, moreover, that will not involve us in dubious consequences.

In the term "self-realization" are the obvious components self and realization. The Self, as has already been indicated, is a peculiar tension between what we are at any given moment and the possibilities that we envision for ourselves in subsequent moments. The Self is a striving to become a certain kind of person, but it is a striving carried on by a Self that is its own past.

To realize one's self, it would seem, is to fulfill some of these possibilities, especially those determined in our reflective freedom (see page 60). Now in general this makes sense. Ask an adult what his hopes, dreams, and aspirations are and you get a fair notion (if he's telling the truth) of what it is he is trying to realize. If he is yearning to become a member of the country club, drive a fine car, and visit night clubs, and if he is working furiously to make the money such activities demand, there is no mystery about what Self-realization means to him.

But suppose one looks at a lad of nine and asks: What should education help him to become? Is he trying to realize himself? What Self is he trying to realize? Suppose the young chap confesses that his burning ambition at the moment is to operate a space ship. Or that some day he wants to be a deep sea diver. Unquestionably these are envisioned possibilities engendered by the natural freedom of his imagination out of his modest experience. One would have to admit that probably this is his real Self at this stage of the game.

If we are true to the concept of the Self, we shall not as educators dismiss these manifestations of it as simply childish. But we shall not forget either that when reflective freedom begins to sort out these possibilities, the Self will change the direction of its strivings. We do not know what direction they will take, but we have to educate the young man *now*. At this point the concept seems to become fuzzy and useless.

If it is to be cleared up we have to introduce the notion of capacity or potentiality and say that this boy has powers that will in time enable him to do x, y, and z. Our business now is to develop those powers.

Capacities and faculties

However, this gets us into more trouble because modern psychology has been careful to eschew faculties and powers. Educators, when they wish to insult each other, accuse their opponents of adhering to the "old faculty psychology" and "formal discipline."

Modern psychology eschews faculties because a power or a potentiality or a possibility does not exist in the same way as does a table or a chair. To say that man has the faculties of willing, reasoning, imagining, and striving would tempt one to look for them. And when the psychologist does look for them he just doesn't find them, just as he doesn't find a Self. He does find that men perform acts that can be called reasoning acts, willing acts, or imagining acts, but pure reasoning, imagining, and willing he does not find. William James argued that if there were such a thing as a memory faculty apart from this and that act of remembering, it should be possible to improve it in such a way that no matter what material it was called upon to remember it would do so more efficiently. As a matter of fact, education had gone on just such a supposition. That each faculty is to be developed like a muscle is the doctrine of "formal discipline." But when James found in his experiment that learning to memorize one set of material did not help him learn another more quickly, the props were knocked out from under faculties and formal discipline.

Capacities of any kind share the weakness of faculties in that they cannot be directly observed; they are always inferred. Suppose you have driven your automobile at 70 miles an hour on several occasions. If anyone asks you whether your automobile has the capacity to do 70 miles an hour, you will answer that it has. You would not mean that it is now doing 70 miles an hour, nor that it has done 70 miles in the past. What you do mean is that if the car hasn't changed too much since the last time it did 70, it will do it again. Capacity manifests itself in performances and can be detected and measured only by a representative sample of those performances.

In this sense psychology still uses the notion of capacity and potentiality. Indeed it freely uses the terms willing, imagining, thinking, and feeling, and so can you, provided you avoid the term "faculty."[21]

Let us now return to self-realization. What do we mean when we speak of trying to realize potentialities or capacities? We mean

[21] Says Mowrer, ". . . psychology is today again concerned, although under a new terminology, with those 'banished' faculties or 'mental functions,' once known as cognition (knowing), conation (willing), and affection (feeling)." *Learning Theory and Behavior*, p. 20. Reprinted with permission of the publisher.

nothing more mysterious than this: as a result of observing generations of mankind, we have reason to believe that this youngster before us, barring accidents, should be able to think, imagine, feel joy
and sorrow, love and hate, and desire and frustration. Unless he is
wholly different from the rest of mankind, he will want to achieve
something in freedom; he will want to be happy; he will want to be
satisfied with his life as he reflects upon it. The capacities are the
names for the various kinds of value experience that we expect the
individual to have. We do not find these powers existing separately,
and we never find them apart from some specific content. Similarly,
we never "find" the concepts "tree," "energy," or "equation" in the
world around us. "Capacity," like any other concept, is thought and
not found by perception. But the concept points to something real—
a real human power that can take on many different forms. If I
imagine a cow now and a church steeple a little later, do I have
two imaginations? Or is it one imagination operating with two different notions? When we speak of realizing or developing our powers
we do not mean that we can improve our memory, reasoning, or
willing as such. All we can do is use these powers on many different
objects and activities, so that what power is there is as completely
used as possible. But surely the power is there to be used.[22]

Some decry self-realization because it seems to suggest the unfolding of something already present in the beginning, as the oak
unfolds from the acorn. On the one hand, it is objected that such
unfolding makes the process of growth a transitional state lacking
meaning on its own account.[23] On the other hand, it is objected that
we are holding up a goal of perfection for the Self to realize—a goal
that no one has realized and which can be interpreted to mean
whatever anyone chooses to have it mean.

One may answer that self-realization as defined here does not
mean unfolding, but rather the building of a Self through envisioned

[22] There is no uncontrolled power, strictly speaking, but always the power
of a structure, whether the structure be an electric battery, a tissue cell, or an
atom. But the same sort of power can be found in many structures. The experiments on transfer of training do not prove that there are no such powers as
memory, imagination, intelligence, but rather that power developed in one
form (Latin) may not automatically be translated into another form (the writing of English prose). But then neither does the power of an electric dynamo
automatically transform itself into the power exhibited by an electric motor.
[23] E.g., Dewey, *Democracy and Education,* pp. 55–56.

possibilities of value. Only the generic forms of human activity (powers) are given at birth, and not even these in the same magnitude. As for the process having meaning on its own account, let us point out that every time we experience a positive value (satisfaction) or a negative one (pain or frustration) we are being notified that realization has or has not taken place.

Nor does self-realization necessarily mean some impossible goal of perfection, although it does mean self-perfecting. If by perfection is meant the systematic use of our powers to achieve the maximum of value—and that is what we do mean in this chapter—then it is not a mysterious goal at all; it is, on the contrary, what every man is doing when functioning as a man.

Still another criticism is that self-realization is an individualistic ideal and unpardonably overlooks man's duties to society. But in the first place we are not trying to set up an ideal at all. The drive to self-realization is a characteristic of every human personality. Further, no matter how I try, I can realize nobody's capacities but my own. But how can I realize any value or develop any of my capacities without also developing or frustrating the development of the capacities of others? How can I develop myself in a bad culture among undeveloped neighbors? Only a person who has abandoned the development of his intellectual powers could fail to see that the duty of self-realization implies a duty to the realization of all human selves.

The conclusion at which we arrive, therefore, is that self-realization is not a meaningless term, that its meaning can be made clear, and that it does not necessarily lead to any very mystifying consequences —educational or otherwise.[24]

Actually what self-realization means for the educator is rather clear: to measure capacity for value realization and to see to it that the individual pupil exploits these capacities to the full. He looks to the science of educational measurement for help in the former and to the curriculum, method, and organization of the school for the latter. These matters will be discussed in detail in subsequent chapters.

[24] That the notion of self-realization can have scientific meaning is suggested by A. H. Maslow's treatment of self-actualization in *Motivation and Personality* and other writings. Of particular importance is Maslow's attempt to describe empirically the experience of "self-actualizing" persons who are doing more than merely coping with their deficiencies.

Self-Integration

The Self both constructs value possibilities and strives to realize those possibilities, but there is still something missing in our account of the dynamics of the human personality. It is the factor of integration. Without it self-determination and self-realization would go off in all directions. In some people this happens. This club and that cause, this person and that interest, this business or that, in turn siphon off their energies.

Such a life need not be unpleasant. It is hard to chide a man for living this way except on the grounds that he will never amount to much. But if he is amiable and stays out of mischief, is it pertinent to insist that he amount to something? If we nevertheless feel called upon to insist, it is because of our conviction that there is a greater happiness in store for those who organize their energies than for those who do not. Some evidence for this belief is furnished by the fact that flitting from one flower to another is so often accompanied by strong feelings of drift and inner dissatisfaction. We may also ask whether such dispersion of energy will permit self-realization.

Let us call the organizing of one's energies for self-realization self-integration. First of all, why is it needed?

If we could actualize every possibility, we would not need integration. But this is not the case. Some values exclude each other. Values that accrue from social life are incompatible with those of solitude. A life of great deeds is incompatible with one of quiet contemplation. Not all values mix amicably. They force us into choosing among them.

Further, values are not plucked out of the air as the mood moves us. Many of them require campaigns for their conquest. The joys of the intellect, of friends and family, or of achievement in any field all call for preparation and cultivation. These take time and some effort. Once used, time cannot be reused for anything else. Every choice, therefore, is a commitment of the whole Self for a span of time, for better or for worse.

Our desires beat upon us clamoring for action. Which shall we admit, which exclude, which combine? If there is no wholeness to the Self, then there is no way of deciding which desire is more compatible with it than any other. I want to be a clever fellow, a favorite with the ladies, a distinguished scientist, a valiant soldier.

There is something attractive about each of these possibilities, but which of these will more truly express *me?* Anyone who has tried to guide young people cannot have failed to wonder whether Miss X is one person or a half dozen. She seems to have many selves each with a life of its own, a role of its own, and desires of its own. And there is no way of telling which one will turn up at the next interview. Charming as this chameleon-like quality is in the adolescent, to the guidance officer the various selves cry out for integration.

This gives us a clue to the meaning of self-integration. A Self cannot be integrated because a Self is already a principle of unification; it is what unites diverse experience with the flavor of "mineness." When we speak of integration we mean the unifying of many selves within one personality, or the unifying of actions or values so that they blend rather than conflict.

Principle of integration

Underlying both forms of integration is the same principle, that of organic unity. Our bodies are our best examples of such unity. Each separate organ differs in structure from the others, yet in the healthy body all are so co-ordinated that the energies are directed and concentrated as needed. Each depends on the other, yet each works for a common end. Disease is a symptom of partial disintegration. The destruction of a few cells matters little, but when an organ such as the heart, liver, or stomach cannot do its job, the whole organism is endangered.

Experience too seems to need and to have an analogous sort of unity. We are told by the *gestalt* psychologists that patterns of some kind are the ultimate units of perceptual experience. Given a series of dots, tones, or lines, we tend to perceive them in patterns and not as individual dots, lines, etc. The so-called laws of association are also descriptions of the way our experience tends to cluster into units and these units into still larger ones. There seems to be in nature an aversion to loneliness; elements of whatever kind tend to congregate into more or less complex societies and societies of societies. As soon as we acquire a new piece of experience it immediately tends to find a home in some cluster of experience already formed. Some intruders have difficulty in finding a home. They are like foreign bodies that irritate our tissues.

A kindly gentleman, for example, walks down the street. A young boy trails him with hoots of various kinds. Finally, the kindly gentleman slaps the youngster briskly. The youngster flees with a howl. The kindly gentleman does not sleep for a week. The slapping can find no home in his character and probably never will.

Occasionally a new bit of experience nestles into a cluster and transforms it. A boy has many fears, and he has a fear of fears because he has learned that it is wrong to be fearful. Then he discovers that his playmates also have their assortments of fears. He may still retain his own specific fears, but the fear of fears is transformed.

If they become large enough, these experience clusters can crystallize into different selves using the same nervous system to carry on their business but not having too much to do with each other. In extreme instances we refer to such divisions as multiple personalities. Yet even in what passes for normal life we have these clusters. Each one of our interests—sports, vocation, family, church—is a cluster. Each role we play in social life—father, husband, citizen, lodge member—has its own cluster of experience which shifts into focus whenever we play that role.

There are many ways to integrate these selves, some more effective than others. This much we can be sure of: that the personality will try to integrate *somehow*. Even the weirdest abnormalities are peculiar kinds of integration. Therefore, when we regard self-integration as a problem, it is the *type* of integration that is problematical.

Types of integration

1. The social order in which we happen to live always furnishes some pattern of integration. It lets us know what is expected of us, and to do what is expected is one way of keeping the peace with ourselves and the neighbors.

It is a rough scheme, at best, and when a social order itself splits into diverse groups each with its own expectations, then it can no longer serve as an integrative scheme for the individual. Among many social scientists this factor is regarded as an important, if not the most important, factor in the uneasiness of the twentieth century.[25]

25 For a good discussion of this argument, see Stanley, *Education and Social Integration*, pp. 57–60, and Butts and Cremin, *A History of Education in American Culture*, Chaps. 13–14.

Even if our social order knew what it wanted, and even if what it wanted was undeniably good, for an individual to be directed by it in all his choices would be to violate his self-determination. He might end up with an integrated Self, but it would hardly be integration *by* the Self.

2. Another kind of integration comes from adopting a long-range purpose that organizes more or less everything we do as means to that purpose. This project may be to become a great writer, musician, philanthropist, or athlete. Such a design will put order into our choices and furnish us with a powerful incentive to overcome the obstacles and nuisances of ordinary living.

Unfortunately, great purposes are neither inborn nor common. Even when they do capture our enthusiasm and imagination, there still remain the questions as to (1) whether they are worthy of our devotion, and (2) whether our abilities are suitable to that devotion. We can be sadly mistaken on both counts. The prevention and correction of such errors depends, of course, on knowledge and education.

Self-integration requires, first of all, an accurate appraisal of our abilities and strivings. It demands a knowledge of the various steps we are called upon to dance as our social groups pipe their diverse tunes. Next, it demands of us a knowledge about the successes and failures of mankind in its long struggle for integration. From literature, the arts, philosophy, and religion we may get an inkling as to what is worth struggling for and what is not. Finally, we need to know the ways of the physical world in which our lives are acted out, because this world can frustrate the most elaborate schemes for self-integration. Therefore, such knowledge will have to find a secure place in general education, and the habits of acquiring and using and enjoying such knowledge will be the immediate outcomes of formal schooling.

Knowledge, as well as being the great liberator of man and the means for realizing himself—his human nature—is also the great integrator. Knowledge of Self, knowledge of society, and knowledge of nature are the *gymnasia* where we practice the skills and perfect the habits needed for self-determination, self-realization, and self-integration.

These are the dimensions of the good life, and we shall use them repeatedly to test our notions of the curriculum, methodology, and school organization.

The descriptions of the good life in its three major dimensions given in this chapter are necessarily abstract. The number of concrete personality patterns that exemplify the self-determined, self-realizing, self-integrating human being is virtually unlimited. Literature, biography, and history are replete with personality descriptions that can be used both to exemplify the structure of the good life and to test our own knowledge of what each dimension is to mean. For example, Abraham Lincoln's life can be analyzed in terms of whether it was or was not or to what extent it was self-determined, self-realized, and self-integrated, and thus evaluated on the degree of its "goodness."

Summary

Four major principles seem to describe the essential workings of the human personality. These are the appetitive principle that provides the motive power to all of life, and the principles of self-determination, self-realization, and self-integration.

These principles describe the strivings of man as he tries to fulfill his essential nature. The power of symbolization which furnishes the basis for thought, imagination, and memory introduces a new factor into these strivings. They are no longer automatic predetermined struggles, as in the case of inanimate objects and the lower orders of living things. The symbolic power puts us into a realm of the possible, so that our strivings can take on an infinity of forms; they become, in brief, indeterminate, risky, and problematic. We have to search for our essential natures and ends because they are so overlaid by acquired desires and the means of achieving them.

For education each of these principles implies acquisition and use of knowledge. In connection with each principle the role of knowledge was discussed so that in a sense we could prevision what general education would have to include.

PROBLEMS FOR DISCUSSION AND RESEARCH

1. Examine a few texts in psychology of personality and see if there is a common meaning for the term "integration."

2. Evaluate the author's attempt to meet the objections to the notion of "self-realization."

3. What test instruments are available to help the educator estimate the value potentialities of the pupil? To help the pupil evaluate himself?

4. How would a Pragmatic philosopher criticize this chapter?

5. How would a Catholic philosopher criticize this chapter?

6. Analyze and compare two well-known personalities in terms of the three dimensions of the good life discussed in this chapter.

SUGGESTIONS FOR FURTHER READING

For fuller bibliographical information on the books listed below, consult the General Bibliography.

For the more general philosophical treatment of the topics in this chapter:

Aristotle, *De Anima*, Book II, Chaps. 1–4.
*———, *Nicomachean Ethics*, Book X.
*Brumbaugh, R. S., and N. M. Lawrence, "Aristotle's Philosophy of Education," *Educational Theory*, 9:1, 1–16, January 1959.
*Dewey, *Human Nature and Conduct*, pp. 248–264, 303–313.
Hocking, *Human Nature and Its Remaking*, Chaps. 7–11.
Klubertanz, *The Philosophy of Human Nature*, passim.
Mumford, *The Transformations of Man*, passim.
Murphy, *Human Potentialities*, passim.
Niebuhr, *The Nature and Destiny of Man, Vol. I*, Chaps. 1–3.
*Pepper, *The Nature and Source of Value*, passim.
Plato, *Republic*, 434 D–445 B.
*Wild, *Introduction to Realistic Philosophy*, Chaps. 3, 20.

Psychological, anthropological, and sociological approaches:

Allport, *Personality: A Psychological Interpretation*, Chaps. 6, 7, 13.
*Broudy and Freel, *Psychology for General Education*, Chaps. 6, 7.
Frank, *Nature and Human Nature*.
Fromm, *Escape from Freedom*, passim.
Horney, *The Neurotic Personality of Our Time*, passim.
Kardiner, *The Psychological Frontiers of Society*, Chaps. 1–2.
Kluckhohn and Murray, *Personality in Nature, Society, and Culture*, pp. 3–50.
*Maslow, *Motivation and Personality*, passim.
Montagu, *The Direction of Human Development*.

Bearing more directly on the problem of education:

Bagley, *Education, Crime, and Social Progress*, Chap. 7.
*Brubacher, *Eclectic Philosophy of Education*, pp. 67–100.
———, *Modern Philosophies of Education*, Chap. 3.
Cunningham, *Pivotal Problems of Education*, Chaps. 3–4.
Kelley and Rasey, *Education and the Nature of Man*.
Lodge, *Philosophy of Education*, Chaps. 7–9.

* Perhaps more helpful than the other items for the explication of this chapter.

4

Education in
the Social Order

What has been said about the good life can be summed up in the expression, "self-perfection." At birth the tendencies and structure for self-perfection are already present. The forms of self-perfection are self-realization, self-determination, and self-integration. Because of man's symbolic powers, the means to self-perfection vary widely so that the potentialities for both success and failure are enormously multiplied. The success of this enterprise, moreover, depends on forces and factors outside the organism as well as on those within it. Hence we can never know in advance whether an individual life will have a happy, tragic, or an indifferent ending.

Perhaps the most important of these conditions is the social order in which men have to live. When Aristotle said that man was by nature a social animal, he was merely describing a state of affairs. Man is born via a social group into a social group, and for better or worse, through inclination or necessity, heredity or learning, lives his life in a group. Nobody chooses to be born; life is always a social imposition.

The important issue is not so much whether man is by nature a social creature or only becomes one by submitting to cultural pressure; it is rather which social arrangements further or hinder its members' drive to self-perfection.

Social Organization

We shall make the assumption that social institutions develop in response to some need of the group. The family had to come into being if the group was to continue with any degree of stability, and government of some kind was the response to a dislike of chaos or a fear of what Hobbes called perpetual war.

Our second assumption is that the principle of the division of labor applies or could apply to social institutions. Just as each of the committees appointed to plan and execute a dance has a particular and indispensable part of the total work to perform, so each social institution at a given time has a particular task which differentiates it from other institutions. This is its primary function.

Furthermore, each committee member or institution depends on every other. Thus although government has a particular job to do, it depends on the economic agencies of the society for its sustenance. Both, in turn, depend on the schools, and the schools on the government and the economic agencies, etc.

In addition to its primary task—the special job that justifies its existence—each social institution has a subsidiary set of tasks that it regards as necessary to the performance of its primary task. For example, an industrial corporation not only has to produce goods— which is its primary function—but it may conduct research, education, and make contributions to charitable institutions. How much of this secondary work it will do depends on how thorough the division of labor in a society happens to be.

This situation can be viewed from two vantage points. If we are impressed primarily with the division of labor, we will be inclined to favor a clear-cut and fairly fixed "mind your own business" policy for each institution. If, on the other hand, we are impressed with interdependence, we shall find clear-cut distinctions of duties and responsibilities artificial and irritating. We shall encounter this difference of emphasis in controversies about the function of the school, the curriculum, and methodology. Those who favor the activity program and oppose divisions of the curriculum into distinct subject matters are impressed by interdependence. Those on the other side are impressed by the need for a division of labor in any efficient organization.[1]

In arguing that each institution has a special job to do, I shall not try to prove that this is the job it has always done or that it is the only job it could do. But if our goal is the good life, and if social organization is one of the means of achieving it, then one form may be more efficient than another, i.e., more rational than another. This is also what we shall mean when we speak of the "natural" order of society.[2] It is what the order would be if it could be planned rationally to meet the requirements of the good life.

The Role of Government

A rationally organized society has a co-ordinating agent to decide among competing ends and diverse means. It has authority to make and enforce such decisions. From what source does it, or ought it, derive this authority? If what has already been said about the good life of the individual as the final goal of human activity is plausible, then the ultimate source of this authority is what the good life logically requires for its realization by the individuals of the community.

But who is to say what the requirements of the good life are *in any particular situation?* For example, we would all agree that good health is a requirement for the good life; we do not question the authority of the government to make and enforce rules of quarantine, inoculation, and sanitation. But is socialized medicine a logical requirement of the good life in America?

Only particular individual men by exploring the consequences of socialized medicine for the Common Good can decide whether or not it is conducive to it. What we can ask of every man is that consideration of the Common Good always attend his deliberation and his action.

What has been said about self-determination and self-realization

[1] This will be seen more clearly in the discussions of the curriculum in Chapters 12 and 13.

[2] Whether there is a more fundamental meaning to natural order and natural law is an important metaphysical and epistemological question. Cf. William H. Banner, "Natural Law and the Social Order," *The Return to Reason*, pp. 218–234, and Wild, *Plato's Modern Enemies and the Theory of Natural Law*, Chap. 5.

also tells us that the perfecting of human life demands that the individual be consulted about the meaning of the Common Good in particular instances, even if, conceivably, an omniscient governor could make the right decisions without such consultation. A society so governed might be perfect, but it would not be a society of men.

If democracy is to be rationally preferred to other forms of government, it will have to be because it provides the most adequate mechanisms for the consultation of individuals about what is relevant to the Common Good. Insofar as it uses such mechanisms, it is taking seriously the belief that the authority of government derives from the rational assent of the governed. But at the present stage of history this is only a promise that democracy makes; it will be redeemed only when men *are* so consulted, and when men are *able* and *willing* to consult with each other *under their obligation to the Common Good*. This is precisely what Plato in the *Republic*[3] felt they would not do and perhaps could not do. To denounce Plato as an aristocrat does not disprove this judgment. Only a system that actually produced such rational consultation and action could prove him wrong.

There are those who believe that mutual consultation of itself will somehow magically provide the best solutions to social problems, but consultation among thieves produces (at best or at worst) only more efficient thievery. Without the goal of self-perfection of individuals, consultation is futile; without the consultation, the self-perfection is gratuitous.

Dewey makes the goodness of a society depend on the number and variety of interests shared and on the number of members sharing them.[4] Others make the consensus of the group or the widest "community of persuasion" the yardstick for social decisions.[5] Both sharability and consensus, however, assume that somehow these will disclose the Common Good. Neither means, I take it, that what a given group agrees to share or to choose is necessarily good for everyone. It is only when sharability is thought of as *universally* sharable, and consensus as what *all* rational men would agree to, that these become signs of a rational democracy.

Consultation or discussion as such, therefore, is not a guarantee of democracy or even an indubitable symptom of it. It becomes a

---

[3] Book VIII, 555B–562A.
[4] Dewey, *Democracy and Education*, p. 96.
[5] Raup, *et al.*, *The Improvement of Practical Intelligence*, pp. 91–92.

guarantee when it is a means to the discovery or the clarification of
the Common Good in a particular problematic situation. Similarly,
group dynamics make sense when they remove emotional obstacles
to such discovery and clarification; otherwise they could just as easily
bring about agreements among genuine rascals as among misguided
saints. (See Chapter 8.)

Government and education

But whatever the form of government, its essential function of
decision will bring formal education under its jurisdiction for the
simple reason that education is itself a social institution affected by
and affecting all other institutions. For example, education costs
money. This means that part of what is produced shall be consumed
by nonproducers during their educative period. Who is to decide
how much of the nation's wealth can be used in this way? And for
whom and for how long shall education be provided? And which
economic groups should it serve? Since wealth is not unlimited, some
decisions have to be made on these questions.[6]

Furthermore, since the school is a tempting tool to other institutions, there is inevitable competition among groups for the control
of the schools. Who is to adjudicate among these contestants if not
the government?

We have, then, the practical situation in which the government
as an institution can control education just as much as its wishes dictate and power permits. But how does this jibe with the principle of
the division of labor among social institutions? If one institution is
completely under the control of another institution, then it is at best
a subdivision of it. Thus where government completely controls
education, education becomes a part of government. To be an institution in its own right it must have a duty that no other institution
wholly discharges; it must not be completely substitutable. But if so,
then it must have an area of autonomy, however small, that is
complete. There must be some things in which it cannot as *of right*
be overruled by any other institution, an area in which its responsibility and power are never zero.

What this means for federal aid and control of education is hard
to define because so many factors are involved, but as wealth becomes delocalized, e.g., as more wealth is held in the form of

6 Cf. Brubacher, *Modern Philosophies of Education,* Chap. 9.

savings and securities rather than in real or tangible property, more taxes will be collected by the federal government. If the schools are to get what they need in the way of support, and if the schools must be supported at a certain level throughout the nation, federal equalizing of educational facilities seems both indispensable and inevitable.

The role of government in schooling will swell and diminish as schooling affects larger or smaller domains of the public interest and welfare. Constitutional provisions and traditions of local control of schools notwithstanding, schooling will become more homogeneous in character and more centralized in control as institutional arrangements become more and more interdependent.

The most dramatic proof of this is found in the effect of the Russian orbiting of an earth satellite called Sputnik in the fall of 1957. Overnight it became apparent to Americans, as no library of books on sociology and economics could make it apparent, that schooling and national defense were so related that whoever had control of the national defense was also going to have a good deal of control over the schools.[7]

But what government will do and what it ought to do in education may not be identical. If the aim of education is the perfection of human individuals, then government ought not to subvert that aim. If educational science points to certain methods, materials, and organization as good, then government ought not to ignore this judgment. If the first duty of the teacher is to the learner, government ought not to hamper the fulfillment of this duty. On the contrary, the proper role of government is to insist that the school as well as every other social institution discharge its duties and in the best sense of the expression to "mind its own business."

The Role of the Family

The essential function of the family as a social institution is the rearing of children during their immaturity. Children can be produced without a family organization, but the rearing of them for

[7] The huge amounts of money for research and promotion of science education, education for the gifted, and accelerated programs to produce technicians illustrate how social forces will work themselves out somehow and sometimes with unexpected results. For example, the research boom in universities has made it difficult to distinguish—in language, dress, or demeanor —a meeting of educational researchers from a meeting of industrial researchers.

any considerable time would be impossible without some form of such organization. We shall here discuss the family as we know it in our culture, but conceivably some other form could be equally or more effective in the rearing of children and the promotion of the good life in individuals.

As with other institutions, the primary function does not exhaust the activities of the family. The family is an economic unit as a *means* to the rearing of children, but not all economic units are families. The family provides companionship to the marital partners and to the members of the household. At times it is a religious, political, and even a recreational unit. Each of these activities can be carried on outside of a family organization, and indeed, one of the current complaints about our society is that so many of the activities of life are not carried on within the family as they once were.

Family and the school

What, then, is the relation of the family to education as a formal social institution? The rearing of children is perforce one form of education. Parents inevitably will deliberately bend the behavior of their children in one direction or another, and even when they are not deliberately teaching, they willy-nilly produce learnings of one sort or another; indeed, they are often amazed at the learnings they unwittingly do produce.

This much is an old story. Today, however, the educative demand on the family has been so enlarged that many conscientious parents look about for someone to help them with it, the pediatrician, psychiatrist, and, of course, the school.

What has brought this about? Largely, it has been the steady infiltration of Freudian psychology into the thinking of the public. It has brought about the disturbing realization that experiences in early infancy leave ineradicable traces on the record of life. This saddles parents with a frightening sense of responsibility and frustration because their every act is somehow significant, yet there is no sure way of knowing what the significance will be.

Childhood training takes place before the child enters school so that it cannot be shifted directly to the school.[8] When the youngster

---

[8] "It is during the period of intensive socialization, between the years of two and six in European and American societies, that serious conflict first arises . . .

does enter school he brings whatever emotional adjustments or maladjustments he may have with him. Hence the school finds itself confronted with a *fait accompli* of which it has to take account. For it is a simple fact that emotionally upset children learn poorly or learn in a distorted fashion, just as physically ill children find their discomforts more absorbing than their lessons.

So obvious is this fact that the mental hygiene movement has with good logic and commendable zeal argued that emotional health is more important than the cultivation of the intellect, and that the school therefore ought to place it first on its agenda. And the physical hygienists were not slow to intone the same melody in their own key.[9]

If the school accepts the arguments of the hygienists, then it has to take on some aspects of the medical and psychological clinic. For it is only by clinical procedures that remedial work can properly be carried out. The teacher is drawn in as an ancillary to the clinical investigator and therapist. She is required to keep an eye out for emotional and physical maladjustment and, with or without professional advice, try to correct it.

Many intelligent parents would approve this new role for the school. Perhaps the school of the future will assume this role more clearly and explicitly, but two questions inevitably arise:

1. Can the school (that is not yet a clinic), in a relatively short day, counteract influences that have been operating since infancy and which presumably continue to operate during the non-school hours? If the maladjustments of the children are due to poor home or neighborhood conditions or both, just what is to be the role of the school in the correction of them?

2. What about the intellectual skills for which no other agency has the primary responsibility? Will the school have the time or inclination to work on these if its first consideration is to be physical and emotional health?

There is probably no one answer to these questions. The schools, characteristically, have added this program and that procedure, to satisfy parents, schoolmasters, and hygienists. The result is a con-

---

between the child and his would-be socializers." O. Hobart Mowrer, *Learning Theory and Personality Dynamics*, New York: The Ronald Press Company, 1950, p. 519.

[9] It has been noted that education has emphasized the mental hygiene aspects of psychology rather than learning theory. W. D. Spears, "Learning Theory and Objective Psychology," *Educational Theory*, 10:2, pp. 107–119, April, 1960.

glomerate of efforts by which the school can prove that it is trying
to do everything required of it, and at the same time managing to
satisfy nobody.

Role of school and family in training

The role of the school in physical and mental health has two
aspects:

1. Whatever knowledge has to do with these "healths" is properly
within the province of the school. Knowledge about the principles
of physical and emotional health is a proper ingredient of the curriculum.

2. In its operations and procedures the school can exemplify an
atmosphere conducive to both emotional and physical health. Teaching has to be done in some sort of physical and psychic atmosphere,
and psychology and medicine have taught us enough to know what
healthful atmospheres are and how they can be produced. The work
of Lewin,[10] for example, has demonstrated how different social atmospheres affect the personalities of the participants regardless of
what is being taught to them. There is also great promise in the
findings of group dynamics that are relevant to this question. The
school should exemplify in any community what the hygienists could
point to as a model of healthy atmosphere.

Clinical facilities for therapy have to be provided somewhere in
the community, but it does not follow that it must be by the school.
It may of course be convenient for a dental or a psychiatric clinic
to be on the school premises, but this does not mean that they are
part of the school program or curriculum any more than are the
boilers in the heating system.

It is not in the power of the school to establish or perfect the
physical habits that in the long run maintain health. I do not know
whether statistics would prove that the physical education programs
of our schools have actually improved the health of their graduates.
Without being dogmatic, it is not unreasonable to believe that much
of the physical education program is justified by its immediate recreational and social value rather than by its physiological results.
Whether or not habits of sleep, nutrition, and cleanliness are formed

[10] K. Lewin, R. Lippitt, and R. K. White, "Patterns of Aggressive Behavior
in Experimentally Created Social Climates," *Journal of Social Psychology,* 10:
271–299, 1939.

in the school, insofar as knowledge has any effect on such habituation, it is the school's business to provide it.

Much the same argument applies to the emotional habits that constitute good mental health. The social atmosphere of the school will be one vector among the multitude that shapes these habits, but it is difficult to see how the school can make such habits a deliberate objective of its instructional program.

What agencies will take care of those phases of physical and emotional health that the school declines to undertake? Clearly the family—in whose bosom these habits are formed in the first place and nurtured thereafter—and the health agencies of the community whose function is to carry on preventive and remedial work for the Common Good must accomplish this.

The work of these agencies is not to devise schemes whereby the schools can do their jobs for them. It is up to the citizens through their government to provide these public health agencies with the means of carrying on their duties. And these may well include the remedying of housing, sanitation, and even the standard of living so far as they affect the health of the community.

If the school were asked what the ideal home can do as its part in education, it would probably answer as follows:

1. By the time the child enters school, regular hours of sleep, elimination, cleanliness, and diet should have been established.

2. The child should be free from acute anxieties, excessive timidity, shyness, temper tantrums, and belligerence. On the positive side, he should enjoy being with children of his own age, and be able to do most of the things they do.

3. It is the job of the family to establish a set of preferences in favor of the values to be stressed by the school: knowledge, courage, honesty, fair play, and respect for law and constituted authority. These frankly are middle class values. Whether they ought to be *the* values is theoretically another matter. However, in any society there will be a value schema that the adults accept as a basis for moral judgment, and there is unspoken agreement that the young shall adopt it.

It should be clear that such a mechanical training for virtue is hardly virtuous, for it is not the product of the Self. In practice it will exhibit the rigidity so characteristic of moral illiteracy. Those who scornfully call such moral training indoctrination are right. But they are only half right. For we can no more avoid beginning with indoctrination than we can avoid eating the food our culture provides or breathing the air that surrounds us. To be sure, these foods may be meager and the air polluted, just as the values of our culture need not be beyond criticism. Parents have no choice but to condition their children in favor of the values they do hold. Schools, on the other hand, do have a limited choice, but then the doings of the school and home in this matter are not identical.

For, to repeat, the fundamental role of the school is the perfection of cognitive (knowing) skills and habits, and one of these skills is surely the skill of thinking critically about our values as well as about our world, about our health, or about anything else. To *feel* that stealing is wrong can be a product of emotional training; to *know* why it is less desirable to steal than not to steal is not a matter of training; it is a matter of ethical reflection, of knowledge, of judgment, in short, of intellectual activity for which the school has as much responsibility as the parents have for the formation of attitudes. (See Chapter 10.)

This division of labor is crucial. The school can reinforce emotional conditionings and learnings that have already been established. It is rarely in a position to establish them on its own account. If, for example, the little boy arrives in school conditioned to admire skill in street theft, outwitting the authorities, loyalty to the gang against adults, and with a sense of distrust and hostility to school and to teachers as symbols of an already detested social order, then how much can the school do to break up this predelinquent *gestalt?* Indeed, the very efforts of the school to do so may engender greater frustration and hence even greater hostility against the school and what it represents.

School authorities are therefore rash when they agree to assume the responsibility for the conquest of juvenile delinquency. Middle class delinquents, that is, middle class youngsters who deviate from the middle class values, usually feel guilty in doing so. If they play hooky, they know they should not. The delinquent acts may be symbolic revolts against frustration by adults or the symptom of emotional maladjustment, but deep down the middle class delinquent does not *want* to leave his class. Consequently, analysis and guidance often can rehabilitate him. Sometimes a better opportunity to realize the middle class values is sufficient. If a boy is stealing to indulge his desire for a bicycle, it is not too difficult to show him alternative methods of getting a bicycle, but if the boy is stealing because he gets prestige with his fellows in this way, then showing him alternative routes to bicycles is beside the point.[11]

If this sounds unduly pessimistic about the role of knowledge in moral education, then let us remember that given the desirable dispositions to begin with, their elaboration, refinement, and above all their rationalization is neither impossible nor miraculous. Indeed, the whole curriculum is such an enterprise of discovering the rationale of our crude predilections, their inconsistency, their narrowness, and their breadth.

So whether we consider physical health, mental health, or character, the division of labor is essentially the same. The family provides the raw materials by conditioning or training; the school furnishes the cognitive skills and materials by which these are worked up into the possibilities of self-determination, self-realization, and self-integration. If the family can do more than this minimum, it should not restrain itself. But it cannot shift the conditioning to someone else.

At this point it will be argued that under ideal conditions such a division of labor might work. But neither the conditions as they are nor as they seem likely to be are ideal. In the first place, conditioning is not confined to the home, and, further, not all these conditionings are in the same direction. Thus the old "pool-hall" and the church did not have the same influence.

In situations where such conflicts among social agencies do exist, it is the state which in the end has to adjudicate the divergences. The school can also be a corrective agency, but only through the autonomy of knowledge, and we shall see below how difficult it is to establish such a claim in anything far short of a perfect society.

The Role of the Church

Historically, the church[12] has claimed the guardianship of at least some of the values of a culture in the name of their supernatural

[11] Delinquency continues to be a complicated matter: "In the main, studies on delinquency emphasize three or four major causal conditions: (1) Delinquency may be a behavior pattern learned through imitation or instruction, with little or no psychological stress present; (2) it may be the result of frustration and conflict with the delinquent behavior being a meaningful, though socially unapproved, reaction to that frustration; (3) it may grow out of disease or injury, or the causes may be so complex as to defy explanation . . . ," Raymond G. Kuhlen, *The Psychology of Adolescent Development*, New York: Harper & Brothers, 1952, p. 383.

[12] "Church" is used throughout this chapter to refer to religion as a social institution with a specific doctrine, ritual, and an official clergy.

source. Certainly one of the best ways to perpetuate a set of values is to impregnate each generation with a religious allegiance to them, and such impregnation is a kind of education.

The church's claim to superiority over worldly powers is metaphysically sound since the agency that knows the end is superior to those that control or furnish means merely.

But the logical force of this claim rests on an epistemological claim that the church authorities have a special source of knowledge with respect to what is right and wrong. The claim and its foundation stand or fall together.

The claim of the church with regard to education has two aspects:

1. The church claims to be the custodian of certain spiritual truths that have to be transmitted deliberately to each generation. This is usually referred to as "religious education" and comprises the creed, ritual, and literature of a particular faith and usually differs in content for each faith. (See Chapter 11.) Insofar as the American school system has decided to steer clear of such teachings in its public schools, "religious education" is, as the church claims, completely neglected in the public school.

2. There is, however, a broader claim that the church can and has made. It is that since spiritual values are the key values, and since the church is the sole custodian of these, the church has the right and the duty to supervise positively or negatively all educational enterprises affecting its communicants and their spiritual welfare.

Social role of church

The most general statement one can make about the church as an institution is that it is the agency primarily concerned with the group's relation to the Cosmos or Supernature. This is the agency that concerns itself with the demands of the Supernature or God upon the group, the means of meeting these demands, and the proper modes of prayer and communion with God. Whether we agree that there is such a God or not, this much is certain: in every civilization the church has crystallized and sanctified the hopes and value schema of the group. This value schema may have only remote resemblance to the prevailing practices of the group, but it may nevertheless represent its aspirations. The value schema, as so crystallized, acquires a unique quality to which the adjectives "sacred" or "holy" become appropriate.

One of the most effective devices for maintaining a value schema is the emotional conditioning of the young through the vivid story and impressive ritual embodied in group ceremonies. Long before the child is ready to understand the content of the creed, the ritualistic practices have (under the pressure of family, church, and community) become well-established motor and emotional responses —so well established that to refrain from performing them in appropriate situations gives rise to malaise. Long before a Catholic youngster, for example, can understand the "whys" of going to church or of not eating meat on Fridays, and long before an ortho- dox Jewish boy can understand the prohibitions against the eating of pork, both boys will be uneasy if they do not abide by the respective injunctions.

Every religion has not only a theory about God, but also about the world and its relation to God. Ritual and creed are organized around this "knowledge" element as a core. For example, the reading of Torah or Old Testament is part of the sacred service of the Jewish ritual, but many parts of this Testament purport to be an historical account of what happened in the history of the world. Similarly, the Christian religions utilize the description of Jesus' life, death, and deeds as the center of their ritual and ceremony.

There is an intellectual descriptive element in every religion. This intellectual element may be the myths of primitive tribes describing the birth of their gods, or it may be highly developed theology. In either case it provides the frame for the concrete religious activities of prayer, communion, and worship. It is quite possible not to under- stand a word of a religious service and yet to be moved by it to great depths of religious experience.

Leaving aside for the moment the question as to the truth of the intellectual claims of religion, it is apparent that in a rationally ordered society there might very well be an agency that devotes itself exclusively to the cultivation of the religious modes of experi- ence for the direct satisfaction that they afford, and because such emotional conditioning constitutes a group pressure of very effective proportions in behalf of the society's value commitment about lying, stealing, murder, sex relations, honor due parents, etc.

Now it cannot be denied that the intellectuals of the western world have little room in their minds and even less in their hearts

for organized institutional religion.[13] The causes for this are familiar
to the students of history. The rise of natural science cast doubt on
the intellectual elements in religion. Either Darwin or the Old Testament was wrong about origins of species, and either the geologists or
the Old Testament was wrong on the age of the earth, etc.

Nevertheless, a great many intelligent men, including scientists so
great in stature as Newton, did not renounce religious experience
because of these inconsistencies. Such thinkers viewed the intellectual element in religion as an artist views the theme in relation to
a painting, a necessary vehicle for emotional impression and expression. They regarded the first chapter of Genesis as a stimulus
to the religious experience of meditating upon the relation of God
to man rather than as an outline for geology courses.

Some intellectuals have been unable to make or maintain this
distinction and so have decided that if a particular religion contains
statements that are scientifically dubious, then all of it is worthless.
Deeper however than the distrust of the intellectual content of this
or that religious dogma is the more general distrust of any proposition that purports to have its source and validation in a Being
outside of physical or human nature. This general mood is called
Naturalism, and, although there are many varieties of it, all agree
in rejecting the existence of any entity that could be called Supernatural.[14]

For the Naturalist, therefore, the religious experience is a kind
of fiction, and some say that insofar as it can have an effect on the
individual's adjustment, it ought to be used whenever needed. The
status of religion in contemporary psychology is well summarized
by Robert B. MacLeod.

> . . . religion tends to be something secondary to be reduced,
> something peculiar to be explained away, or something of practical
> value to be exploited. In no case have we the invitation to a real
> scientific inquiry into the nature of the psychological phenomena
> of religion.[15]

This refusal to take religious experience seriously on its own
account is perhaps more disturbing to the religious person than

[13] Cf. Lippmann, *A Preface to Morals*, Chaps. 1, 2, and 4.
[14] Cf. *Naturalism and the Human Spirit*, Y. H. Krikorian, ed., and *Philosophy
for the Future*, ed. by Sellars, *et al.* For a critique, see Chap. 3 by Oliver Martin in *The Return to Reason*.
[15] Hoxie N. Fairchild, *et al.*, *Religious Perspectives in College Teaching*,
New York: The Ronald Press Company, 1952, p. 271.

the violent anti-clericalism of Voltaire and Paine. To be told that one is evil is bad; to be told that one is of no account is worse.

In the meantime, while the intellectual was losing interest in formal religion or opposing it, the common man continued to accept the religious teachings of his parents without serious questioning. It is to be doubted that most men think any more deeply or seriously about their religious beliefs than about any other beliefs they happen to entertain. For the average man the sanctions of morality lie in the rewards and punishments promised by his religion, and there is little doubt that he gets genuine emotional support out of these beliefs when his children are born, are married, or when some member of the family dies. These are habitual emotional responses and will recur in appropriate situations all through life—especially if there is some reinforcement through the middle years by church attendance, prayer, and work in religious organizations. There are, of course, all degrees of habituation, and correspondingly there are all degrees of respect for the church and its officers. Some priests, rabbis, and ministers could presumably influence their congregants very effectively in an election, whereas others could not.

What, then, shall be the scope of the religious authority in social or political action?

On the principle of the division of labor it would seem that no other agency is designed to provide the emotional reinforcement of the value schema in precisely the way the church accomplishes it. Hence it would seem that it has a distinctive role in the social structure.

In the second place, it is difficult to see how a church can properly refrain from judging social acts as being either in accord with its principles or not.

In the third place, it is difficult to see how it can properly refrain from stating its moral approval or disapproval whenever it finds itself confronted with a choice.

However, if such rights are granted to the church, can there be any limitation to its social authority? Can it, in other words, be distinguished from government itself? Either government becomes a subdivision of the church, or there must be some limitation on the social authority of the church. Still, if the church is to be distinct from other social institutions, it has to have some area of autonomy where its authority is genuine and final.

Let us turn, therefore, to some of the limitations that might reasonably be placed upon its claims to universal validity and authority.

1. Whenever a church puts forth a dogma or teaching that purports to be a description of some state of affairs that existed at some particular time and place, it subjects itself and the teaching to the tests that science prescribes for such "truth." The description of the exodus of the Israelites is either an historical account of certain events or an allegorical interpretation intended to symbolize and arouse certain religious experiences. If it purports to be the former, the historian has to decide whether the account is probable on all the available evidence. If the latter, then it is no more the historian's business than the chemist's. It is the proper business of the church, and its interpretation is final for those who accept its authority in spiritual matters.

The same reasoning would apply to the life of Christ or Mohammed or the Virgin Birth or the Immaculate Conception. It is only as literal meanings, as descriptions of biological or historical events, that they can be questioned. Conversely, the church cannot disqualify any proposition of science except on scientific grounds, although the spiritual meaning of such propositions is wholly within its province. Evolution as a biological theory is the biologist's business; its meaning for religious experience is the church's business.

2. When a church announces that a specific social or political action is consistent or inconsistent with its own teachings, that decision is binding only on the action of its own communicants who, in accepting membership in that church, have agreed to accept such decisions as final.

3. No religious majority can *of right* promote legislation that forces noncommunicants to act or refrain from acting against their will. The majority, of course, can enact anything it chooses including the abolition of safeguards against the tyranny of the majority. There is nothing to prevent a majority in America from removing the Bill of Rights from the Constitution, but it cannot do so in the name of a reason that commands universal *assent*. Thus a religious sect may be powerful enough politically to ban certain plays and books, but it cannot claim the sanction of the natural law for such an act unless it is already admitted by everyone that it has access to some revealed truth.

These three limitations would hold even if in a given community there were only one church and even if no one ever questioned its edicts. For they flow from the principle of a division of function within a rationally ordered society and not from any particular form of government, church, or their respective fortunes or misfortunes.

Relation to education

The relation of the church to education, accordingly, is as follows: whatever needs to be taught to its communicants in the religious mode of experience—creed, ritual, ceremony, techniques of prayer, and spiritual meanings of all kinds—it is the duty of the church *qua* church to teach.

The peculiar province of the church is faith and spiritual knowledge based on that faith; that of the school is knowledge based on human reason. When a civilization is fortunate, there is no discordance between these two orientations, but civilization is rarely that fortunate, and when this is the case, the church no more than the family or the government can of right insist that the school become a vehicle for its own particular orientation.

The long controversy over religion and education in our own country seems far too complicated to yield to so simple and general an analysis as the division of labor in a rationally organized social order, yet an attempt to apply this principle may not be fruitless.

The arguments advanced by the church for some kind of religious education take many forms. The following list will probably omit some that someone regards as important, but it may serve as a preliminary for analysis of the situation.[16]

1. Some argue that the principle of religious freedom and freedom of conscience is violated when a person is denied the right to learn the religion of his parents. Consequently, each denomination has the right to teach its religious tenets to its communicants. Further, since such a right is empty without means of achieving it, it is concluded that public funds are rightfully used for that purpose.

2. Some hold that parochial schools supported in part or entirely by public funds are the answer. Others hold that the public schools, since they are supported by public funds, should include religious instruction within the curriculum.

---

[16] On the whole question of religious education, consult *Religious Education,* Nov.–Dec. 1953. Cf. also Irwin Widen, "Should Parochial Schools Receive Public Funds," *Educational Theory,* 3:4, October 1953, pp. 293–306.

3. Many aver that the public schools by design or by historical accident are "godless," and that such schools are in fact anti-religious rather than nonreligious.

What can be said about the first argument? It presupposes that a child will not adopt the religious beliefs and practices of his parents unless he is conditioned in its creed and ritual at a relatively early age in life. Further, it supposes that his parents have a right to determine this religious choice for him through such early conditioning. The first part of the argument cannot be denied without flying into the face of too many facts. The latter part has nothing to do with facts at all, but insofar as parents do not question their own religious values, it is a fact that they will inevitably condition their children in a specific religious direction. The question then is not about the very early years but about the years of school age. Do the parents have the right to decide that their children shall have their initial conditionings systematically reinforced by religious education in later years? The legal tradition says "yes" but not in public schools.

I see no way of asserting such a right without also asserting the infallibility of one's own brand of religion, for if there is any chance whatsoever that it may not be infallible, then the rational self-determination of the individual child is violated in so conditioning him that an alternative choice is *a priori* excluded. Yet to deny the individual *any* chance for experience in the religious mode seems no less arbitrary a procedure. It would seem, therefore, that the early conditioning which affords the individual immediate religious experience should be subjected to the same sort of inquiry and criticism that are the fate of any experience in the rational life. But this would mean necessarily the objective study of religion as it has manifested itself in our culture and in other cultures rather than the *profession* or *practice* of any one religion.

Does either the parochial school or the public school afford an opportunity for such objective study of religion? Is it pedagogically possible to do it in the elementary school? Could it perhaps be done in the secondary school? These questions are taken up in Chapter 11.

The question of financial support resolves itself pretty largely into two questions of: (1) equity concerning double taxation for those who send their children to parochial schools while being forced to support public schools of which they make no use, and (2) the practical consequences of public support of parochial schools.

If the community decides that public schools, godless or godful, are in the Common Good, then parochial schools are a luxurious deviation that excuses no one from supporting the public schools, just as doing all our traveling by plane does not excuse us from the host of taxes that automobile operators have imposed on the public as a whole. For it is certain that once sectarian schools begin to vie for public funds on any basis one can think of, the public schools will achieve the status of public cemeteries and public infirmaries. It is not too much to say, therefore, that if the religious interests are politically strong enough to secure tax support for parochial schools, public schools as we know them are doomed to extinction.

There are those who say, of course, that such a fate is to be desired for the public schools because they are godless schools. We have therefore to examine this argument more closely.

The charge that the public schools are godless can mean either that the creed and ritual of any particular religious sect are not taught in them, or that the spiritual values are denied or ignored.

On the first meaning, the charge is certainly warranted, but it is hard to see on what rational grounds this could be regarded as a reproach to the public schools. To do otherwise would be practically impossible and theoretically indefensible. On the second meaning, the charge is unwarranted because the public school personnel, teachers and administrators are just about as spiritual as the population in general from which they are selected. They accept and try to reinforce these values without much question. This may be good or bad, but in any case it does not prove the schools to be godless.

The more serious charge against the public schools is that the religious component of our civilization is nowhere systematically studied in it as a body of knowledge—an omission which is hard to defend on any respectable intellectual grounds if we make any pretense of trying to get our pupils to understand the culture in which they live. Should the public schools undertake this task— and the practical difficulties are legion—much of the controversy on this subject would fall of its own weight, and the way would be cleared for a sharper division of labor between church and school.

Religion, therefore, has an indispensable place in the good life and in the good society. The church as a social institution has a function peculiar to itself and induplicable. It alone can clothe the value schema of the group in the ritual and creed that elicit the religious modes of feeling. It alone can provide for common worship; it alone

can supply to all grades of intellect an orientation to the universe
as a whole; it can and does give an emotional attitude toward life
that could make it more spiritual, more courageous, more honest,
more sacrificial, more devoted, more loving, and more perfect.

The educative role of the church is defined by its function. To
teach the creed, the ritual, and the history of a specific religion is
its responsibility and its charge alone. It may enlist the home and
other agencies to help it, but the final responsibility cannot be
shifted to the family, the movies, the schools, or the newspapers.
When the church steps into any educational activity other than that
for which it is especially responsible, it has to be judged on the same
criteria as any other educative institution, namely, whether it is
forming habits that will eventuate in human beings who can determine their choices in the light of the best knowledge available and
who exemplify in their lives a high order of value attainment and
enjoyment.

Can a variety of churches teaching specific creeds provide the
kind of value commitment needed for social unity in a community,
nation, and world? This is a question that only the churches themselves can answer.

School as Social Critic

So far this chapter has stressed the defensive role of the school
against the encroachments of other institutions on its time and
authority. It is time now to point out that the school can have
something positive to say to other institutions with respect to their
own functions without at the same time performing those functions.

While at no time in a rational social order does the school usurp
the role of government or family or church or science, the school in
its instructional activities perforce has to teach *about* the social
order and its institutions. In doing so, it cannot help judging them.
It cannot teach history without having the pupil read that this state
was bad and that at a certain period in history the church performed
its role well or otherwise.

If the school is committed to the truth in these matters, it has no
choice but to teach the best history, science, and literature. What
is the best? What at any given time the scholars in a given field
agree as being the truth or the best. Put in another way, the school

is the critic of society and of all its institutions because it stands for the good life in general rather than for any local version of it. It stands for the professed ideals of the community rather than the ideals it practices and tolerates. It can therefore demand from the home and the government and the church that they perform their own functions in the social order so as to make education for the good life a reality.

In the thirties and forties educators did undertake to act out the role of social critics and social reconstructionists. Identified with one wing of the movement called Progressive Education, these school-men believed that they ought to persuade their pupils to put into practice the results of their social thinking in the classroom. Some were more vigorous and militant than others. Some joined in the political battles of the time; some were content to make speeches and write exhortations to their fellow educators to become conscious of social evils and the need for social reform. When these educators were able to put their ideas into practice, the classroom was alive with discussions of social problems and activities pertinent thereto.

There is little doubt about the sincerity of these men, and many would fervently agree that they were on the side of the angels in the controversies that engaged them. Yet the public often interpreted their efforts as partisan; alleging that the educators had allied them-selves with one political party rather than another; one economic philosophy rather than another; one economic pressure group rather than another. Educators became in the minds of the public one more pressure group grinding this or that economic or political axe.

These schoolmen did not succeed in selling the American public an image of themselves as interlocutors for the truth or for knowl-edge or for disciplined and informed thinking. Instead they raised in the mind of the public the spectre of a group of political partisans who were using the public schools to gain converts among children for their social and economic preferences.

Why did this happen? For one thing, it happened because some of the issues on which the educators took sides cannot even yet be settled once and for all on the basis of fact or of science. On what scientific grounds can we decide between the desirability of one economic pattern over another? Or of one form of government over another?

For another, the educators were not always experts in the fields of economics, psychology, science, and a half dozen other subjects, the findings of which they purported to use in their arguments.

Further, in their enthusiasm for change and reform they had to attack tradition, fixed principles, and fixed ideals as having no special rights. Having made all principles relative and suspect, it was difficult for them to insist on the superior validity of their own ideals over those espoused by their opponents.

Perhaps the lesson to be learned from this bit of educational history is that the school and schoolmen can serve as critics of the social order only if they can convince the public that they are experts in education, that is, that they know what the dimensions of the good life are; that they are interlocutors for the intellectual disciplines in which the knowledge requisite to the good life is deposited; that they have no private social, economic, or political axes to grind, and, finally, that in some small way their own lives exemplify the good life in their own culture.

Autonomy for Education

What sort of autonomy can be rationally claimed for education? In what sense can it be self-governing?

1. It would be absurd for education to claim authority in any area where it depends on some other agency to do the work. It would be absurd for the educator, for example, to claim autonomy in the raising of funds to support education. Some government might grant it a taxing power and even an army to collect the taxes, but such powers would be granted to it by government and would not inhere in education as a right.

2. Nor can it decide by itself who shall be educated, for how long, in what buildings, and by which facilities, because these all hinge in part on the disposition of economic resources which education does not itself produce.

3. It cannot even claim to determine what the truth or knowledge shall be, for it is itself not *primarily* devoted to research and produces no science except the science of education. It gets knowledge wholesale from the special sciences and retails it to pupils, but it creates neither its sources nor its customers. It depends on physics, chemistry, history, literature, or geography for the ultimate content of its curriculum. It depends on biology, psychology, the social sciences, religion, art, and philosophy for its understanding of the

pupil, society, and values of all kinds. None of these does it bring into being, even though in the last analysis it is their sole support.

In what areas can we sensibly assert the autonomy or self-determination of education? Where can it say that its authority is not to be overridden by any other social agency?

Claims to autonomy

If education has a body of tested knowledge that guides its procedures, and if its practitioners base their art on this body of knowledge, then in certain areas it can claim autonomy.

By "tested" knowledge, I mean not only knowledge as embodied in the natural sciences, but also that which crystallizes out of logic, psychology, sociology, economics, and political science and history—any knowledge obtained by a method that permits confirmation or disconfirmation by all who are willing and able to master the method.

By procedures, I mean not only techniques of teaching, but also curriculum designing, organization, and administration of the school system.

If these "ifs" are satisfied, then education can claim:

1. That it is the final arbiter as to curriculum or what is to be taught. Of course, an individual schoolman may be wrong, but the profession or discipline, as in medicine, will represent the best thinking and the most considered judgment on this matter.

2. That it is the final arbiter in the matter of method or how the pupil and the material are to be taught.

3. That it is the final arbiter as to the organization of the school system into levels of instruction and the conditions for advancing from one level to another.

4. That it is the final arbiter as to who shall be regarded as fit to teach what at any level of instruction. This means that the profession has the right to establish its own qualifications for membership, and that it alone has the right to decide whether any teacher does or does not meet these qualifications.

It should be clear that the claims in these four areas or within any one of them will vary inversely in strength with the amount of controversy among the experts themselves as to what the truth is. Thus we would expect less controversy about what is true in mathematics and the physical sciences than in the social ones, and less in

psychology than in the meanings of democracy. This means practically that where the experts disagree, the decision is made by the
specific educator according to his own interpretation of the evidence.

For example, if medical men were divided on the value of a
vaccine to prevent colds, you would probably act on the faith you
happened to have in *your* doctor. However, if you had strong convictions against vaccines, you might refuse to take one even though
your doctor advised it. You might change doctors to bolster your
inclinations with a medical opinion.

Similarly, when educators do not agree on the merits of a certain
kind of curriculum, a community can either accept the convictions
of their school leaders or get leaders with different convictions. But
when the experts do agree, the community has no such alternatives
because replacing the leaders will not give it anything different in
the way of judgment and conviction. The only recourse then is for
the community to subvert the leaders to its own inclinations, but it
is to resist just this kind of pressure that education must make its
claim and defend it to the utmost.

A special problem arises when the community objects to the
teaching of controversial social, political, or economic questions in
the public school.[17] But as we shall see in Chapters 12 and 13, if
we are to learn about our culture, we also have to learn what its
controversies are and *why* they are controversial. The basic issues in
a controversy are amenable to objective study. To that extent the
school's right to teach them is final. However, in schools where
knowledge and the habits of acquiring and using knowledge take
second place to grinding social, political, and economic axes, the
the teachers are hardly in a position to deal dispassionately with
controversial issues. Therefore, they should not be surprised that
those who do not share their views mistrust their motives and their
methods.

Furthermore, it must be noted very pointedly that we are here
talking about *claims* to autonomy for educators. Such claims may
or may not be honored by the community. No group with political
power will abrogate its activities simply because educators announce
a claim to authority. No society has reached the rational stage and
perhaps none ever will, but if we believe that that is the ideal for

---

[17] Usually it is not the community as a whole that objects, but only the
group whose side of the issue is not being supported.

society, then our efforts to achieve it become obligatory regardless of the actual state of affairs in any particular period of history or in any particular community. Not all patients take the advice of their physicians, but this does not absolve the physician from prescribing according to the best medical knowledge available and from pointing to what the community ought to do for its health.

Conditions for strengthening claims

The claims to autonomy will become more compelling under the following conditions:

1. As the body of educational science crystallizes more and more scientifically warranted views about how learning takes place, how capacities are measured, etc.

2. As the social sciences become more precise in analyzing our social ailments and remedies.

3. As educational philosophies come to agree more and more on the basic values and characteristics of the good life. As this comes about it will become more and more difficult for a community to find a superintendent of schools, principals, and teachers who differ *materially* in these three areas.

4. But there is still another condition. We may call it professional ethics or simply courage. I refer to the claim of the educational profession to have a large voice in determining the legal requirements for the *practice* of the profession and the sole voice in setting the intellectual, pedagogical, and character requirements for *membership* in the profession.

It is only when public schools, colleges, and universities realize that a member of the profession will not take a post that requires him to cut and trim the truth of his discipline to fit local peculiarities of prejudice that the public will come to respect the claim itself. Further, until the profession can define malpractice so that it is able to eject malpractitioners from its membership, it cannot expect respect from the public. Doctors are not disqualified by their patients, lawyers are not disbarred by their clients, nor clergy unfrocked by their parishioners. Educators likewise should not leave it to laymen to pass on the qualifications of their colleagues. But in taking a lofty position educators will have to make professional integrity financially possible. They cannot rely on martyrs who are willing to lose their posts for a principle. There are, for example,

100 MAN, SOCIETY, AND THE SCHOOL

the martyr's career and family to think about. At such a price autonomy may be morally too dear.

The autonomy of education is not made easier to achieve by those educators who proclaim that the schools belong to the community and that, therefore, all segments of the community have a right to shape their policies, design their curricula, select their textbooks, and vote on their methods.

The schools do belong to the citizens. What does not belong to the community is the body of knowledge on which the art of education is practiced, just as the science of medicine does not belong to the citizens. When we call in representatives of labor, religion, and industry to build a curriculum, we are saying: "We want you all to be satisfied; what your children ought to learn is what you can agree upon." This situation is a measure of how far the discipline we call education still has to grow before it is worthy of even the name. The argument that only by such co-operation can we get support for the schools is an even more bitter pill to swallow, for we are buying our support and peace at the price of truth itself. But if there is no truth in these matters, polling the customers is the only sensible way to find out what ought to be taught and how, while the administration of schools is nothing more than a problem in public relations.

It is one thing to acquaint the public with the best knowledge about educational theory and practice; it is quite another to interrogate the public as to what this best practice shall be. Perhaps a deeper cause of this attitude is the failure to see education as an institution with a special primary function rather than as a propaganda agency for all the other institutions. If we keep clearly in mind that no other agency is made responsible for the habits of acquiring, using, and enjoying knowledge in the pursuit of the good life, then it will also be clear in what sense the school is not a servant of the community as much as of truth itself—and that this is precisely what the community *wants the school to be* despite deceptive appearances to the contrary.

Summary and Rejoinders

By outlining the functions of government, the family, and the church in a rational social order, the specific role of the school may become clearer.

1. The school is not a legislative agency that makes laws, nor is it an executive agency that carries them out, nor a judicial agency that passes on their legal merits.

2. The school is not a family. It does not come into being to bring children into existence. Conceivably it could undertake their total rearing from the moment of birth on, as Plato suggested it do for the children of the Guardians. But so long as we do have families in our culture, the school is not responsible for the entire rearing. Especially not for the attitudes formed by relations with parents and other children in the early years of life.

3. The school is not a church. It has no Divine authorization, authority, or special revelation.

4. The school is not Science; it is not the agency that is established primarily for the discovery and development of truth. We shall discuss the role of research in the university in Chapter 15.

5. The school is not an industry or business. It does not produce, transform, transport, or distribute material goods, however much it may be instrumental thereto.

6. The school is established by the group when intellectual habits need to be deliberately formed in all or some of the citizens. We have already hinted at the nature of these habits, and in a later chapter we shall discuss them in detail. That it reinforces some of the emotional teachings of the home and frustrates others; that it tries to promote physical and emotional good health goes without saying, but these latter cannot be the primary goals of the school without disrupting the division of labor within our social order.

When the school performs its primary job well, then anything else it manages to do is "gravy." Anything else it does *without* doing its primary job makes its title to being a school highly dubious.

It will be objected that this account of the various social agencies is too narrow; especially will it be pointed out that it seems as if *only* the church, the school, and the family do any educating. Is not then the theatre educative? Are not industry and our daily work educative? Isn't membership in a lodge or a labor union educative? Do not books, magazines, movies, television, and radio educate?

The answer to this objection is the one that has already been given. These agencies provide learning opportunities, but *incidentally* to other functions that are primary for them. They educate *informally*. When the theatre goes in for deliberate instruction, we call it didactic and stop going. The primary task of newspapers is not to instruct, but rather to report. Only in its editorial columns does a newspaper take an educative role. The same may be said about the educational activities of industries, labor unions, and other organizations.

One of the clearest criteria of educational genuineness is the motivation behind the activity. If it is not the perfection of the individual through the control of learning, it may be any one of many wonderful things, but it is not education. For this reason we can say that when a teacher or educator has as his or her ultimate motive any consideration other than the realization of the pupil's potentialities, he or she is no longer an educator. That educators earn their bread by teaching is important but still incidental. Nuns, priests, and parents who do not earn their living in this way nevertheless can still be teachers in the true sense of the word. When society does not pay its teachers adequately it is the fault of society, and the remedy lies not in education but in statesmanship. All of which means that teachers do at times have to be politicians, but this is never to be confused with their teaching function.

The general objection to this chapter may well be that it sets up essential functions for the various institutions as if they were somehow fixed forever. It will be held that institutions do change their functions as social conditions vary. Why, then, should not the functions of the school also change?

The answer is to be found in the interdependence of these agencies in the social order. In any organization there is the working assumption that each element will contribute its share to the whole enterprise. A failure in any part, if it persists for any length of time, disturbs the whole activity.

When any institution makes one of its incidental or secondary functions dominant, it ceases to do its principal job. To that extent the social order is maimed and begins to disintegrate. Consequently, when an institution changes its function, it makes changes necessary in all other institutions—a total rearrangement of the relations among men, and this rarely occurs without great "times of trouble," to use a phrase of Arnold Toynbee. The progress we need can be achieved by changing the *way* in which a social institution performs its function rather than by *shifting* the function. Children should perhaps be reared differently today than they were 50 years ago, but if the rearing of children is made subordinate to the economic or affectional function of the family, there will be trouble. We have changed our methods of industry, but it will be a sorry day for us all when it makes advertising instead of production its chief concern. The schools have changed their methods and can change them much more without trying to play the role of the family, the church, or the government.

PROBLEMS FOR DISCUSSION AND RESEARCH

1. Evaluate the author's analysis of the "primary" functions of the government, family, church, and school.

2. Can you find instances in our culture where some secondary functions of an institution have become primary?

3. Test the theory of the autonomy of education by applying it to some controversy between school authorities or teachers and some other group within the community.

4. Test the theory of the autonomy of education in a controversy about whether there ought to be sex education in the public schools.

5. Go through a half dozen back issues of *School and Society* and identify those articles that deal with the issues raised in this chapter.

6. Arrange a panel to argue the pros and cons of the position taken in this chapter on the relation between school and family, church, and state.

SUGGESTIONS FOR FURTHER READING

For fuller bibliographical information on the items listed below, consult the General Bibliography.

It might be advisable to begin with statements from the founders of political science:

Aristotle, *Politics*, Book I, Chap. 2; Book III, Chaps. 9, 11.
Plato, *Republic*, Book II.
Wild, *Introduction to Realistic Philosophy*, Chaps. 9–12.

This can be followed by:

Brubacher, *Eclectic Philosophy of Education*, pp. 239–273, 281–298, 325–352.
———, *Modern Philosophies of Education*, relevant parts of Chaps. 8, 9, 13.

The literature pertaining to the relations of the school to the social order is voluminous and in continual production. The items listed below are suggested as points of initial exploration.

On the family:

Burgess and Locke, *The Family: From Institution to Companionship.*
Kirkpatrick, *The Family As Process and Institution.*
Waller and Hill, *The Family: A Dynamic Interpretation.*

School and church relations occupy a central position in American educational literature. What is suggested below must, therefore, be considered as a very small sample of what has been and is being written on the many phases of the subject. The files of *Religious Education* constitute a standard source. An example of direct controversy is furnished by the following interchange:

Bode, Boyd H., "Religion and the Public Schools," *School and Society,* 67:225–229, March, 1948, and the reply by:
Raymond, S., "The Principles of Pragmatism and the Teaching of Religion in the Public Schools," *Catholic Education Review,* 47: 365–379, June, 1949.

Other references to this topic will be found at the end of Chapter 11, but the student might consult at this time:

Brickman, W. W., "Education for Eternal Existence, The Philosophy of Jewish Education," *School and Society,* 57: 554–560, May, 1943.
Butts, *The American Tradition in Religion and Education.*
Henle, R. J., "American Principles and Religious Schools," *Saint Louis Law Journal,* 3:3, 237–250, Spring, 1955.
Johnson and Yost, *Separation of Church and State in the United States.*
N.E.A. Educational Policies Commission, *Moral and Spiritual Values.*
Nottingham, *Religion and Society.*
O'Neill, *Religion and Education Under the Constitution.*

For the relation of school to the state and other institutions:

Bantock, *Freedom and Authority in Education.*
Benne, *A Conception of Authority.*
Bryson, *et al., Freedom and Authority in Our Time.*
Cunningham, *Pivotal Problems of Education,* Chap. 16.
Gentile, *The Reform of Education,* Chap. 1.
Harris, *The Social Philosophy of Giovanni Gentile.*
Hullfish, ed., *Educational Freedom in an Age of Anxiety.*
Kneller, *The Educational Philosophy of National Socialism.*
Lieberman, *Education as a Profession* and *The Future of Public Education.*
Lilge, *The Abuse of Learning* and *Anton Semyonovitch Makarenko.*
Mead, *The School in American Culture.*
Slesinger, *Education and the Class Struggle.*
Stanley, *Education and Social Integration.*
Ulich, *Fundamentals of Democratic Education,* Chap. 7.
U.S. Office of Education, *Education in the U.S.S.R.*

CHAPTER | 5

Reality and Knowledge

In the first four chapters many things were asserted about human nature, the social order, the good life, and the value of knowledge in achieving the good life. Now and then it was hinted that all educational philosophers might not agree on these matters, and that some might be reluctant to grant that we can discover the "nature" of the good life, human life, or of the social order.

We thus come to one of those crucial issues in education that drive us into defining more explicitly what is *really* real and how we can know that it is. In other words, we are forced to make a foray (albeit a necessarily brief one) into metaphysics and epistemology. If the reader is disposed to regard this chapter as a somewhat abstract digression from education, he may be reconciled to it by the assurance that the problems of the curriculum, learning theory, and school organization have their theoretical roots in it.

Being and Knowledge

Knowledge is *about* something—about an object. That object may
be a cow, a set of insurance statistics, the state of the stock market,
or a problem in algebra. And the aim of knowledge is to bring into
awareness the object as it *really* is.[1] Sometimes, of course, it is more
comforting not to know the truth, but ignorance is bliss only when
ignorance is complete. The moment we suspect that the doctor may
have deceived us about our health or the instructor about our
grades, the bliss is gone. Our concern to know objects as they really
are shows that there is a possibility that we can be deceived and
that some of our judgments may be false. A false judgment will not
make us aware of the object as it really is, but as it *appears* to be.
Consequently, if we can indicate the conditions under which our
judgments are true (epistemology), we are at the same time setting
up the standards by which we can distinguish appearance from
reality (metaphysics).

We have no choice but to begin with our experience and the
standards of correct thinking. We have no choice but to judge A
and B as different if we can find nothing important common to both
of them, and to say they are somewhat alike if we do. We have no
choice but to accept one of two contradictory statements and to reject the other. In short, if we rely on our human powers, experience
plus the laws of evidence are all we have to go on in the search for
what is really real and what is really true.

Using these two resources, we find that the world divides itself into
a multitude of different objects interacting in countless ways. If we
now ask for the most fundamental distinction we can make among
all the objects of experience, it would seem to be the difference
between the concrete objects that occupy space, come into being, and
pass away, on one hand, and the images and ideas by which we are
aware of them, on the other.

Awareness is a peculiar transaction. When A is aware of X, X is
present to A, but it is a strange presence, for X is not physically
inside A. I am aware of the keys of my typewriter flicking up to the
paper, yet neither the paper nor the typewriter is inside of me. Nor

---

[1] The Instrumentalist would hold that the aim of inquiry is to clear up a
problematic situation by constructing an "object as known" in the complete
process of inquiry. E.g., Dewey, *The Quest for Certainty*, pp. 189 ff.

does my being aware of the typewriter do anything to the machine. In the world of things such transactions are not to be found. If your automobile and mine collide, we both shall probably have repair bills. When two elements unite to form a compound, the result is different from each of them, and neither comes out of the ordeal unscathed. To be sure, my nervous system discharges some energy whenever I am aware of anything, but it is very doubtful that it discharges twice as much energy when it is aware of two men than when it is cognizing one. The image of the Grand Canyon bulges my skull no more than the image of a flea.

Just as remarkable is another feature of awareness. If we take the color out of a piece of cloth, another color appears beneath it. We cannot take the size out of a suit of clothes without destroying the suit itself. We cannot take the hardness out of iron without performing drastic operations upon its shape and other properties. Yet the mind performs all of these feats of extraction without disturbing the object in the least. For awareness is always a process of abstraction, of concentrating on some aspects of things and ignoring others.

We have already discussed still another characteristic of the mind. It is its ability to combine its images, perceptions, and concepts into patterns with extraordinary freedom. None of us thinks it a very remarkable feat to invoke into our presence the picture of a grandmother who is no longer alive and the notion of tomorrow's breakfast which is not yet cooked. All physical things are chained to the present; yesterday and today have no meaning for an automobile or a bag of beans.

Putting these features together, we have to conclude that in awareness the human mind operates in a way and with elements that to some extent, at least, are non-material. The kind of being ideas have is not the same as the kind of being trees, stones, and birds have. Meanings, ideas, concepts have their being simply in pointing to or disclosing the natures of things, but they are not things themselves. Plato believed that meanings or concepts exist in a world of their own—the world of forms. Aristotle and others held that they are abstracted by the mind from our sense experience, that is, from the interaction of our sense organs with the external world. We shall call this type of being (of ideas) noetic or cognitive being.[2]

Although all noetic being is abstract, not all of its elements are equally so. My image of the fire hydrant outside the window is ab-

[2] Wild, *An Introduction to Realistic Philosophy*, pp. 395 ff.

stract, yet it is the resemblance of a particular object. When we remember and imagine, it is still with images of particular things. On
the other hand, when we decide to *define* a fire hydrant, the resulting *concept* leaves out its redness, its somewhat dignified stance,
and its particular location outside my window. The notion of fire-
fighting instruments leaves out still more of my hydrant, but makes
up for it by referring to the multitude of hydrants wherever they
may be.

For some of our mental constituents we depend on physical objects and physical processes that furnish us with images retained
by memory and aroused in imagination. And some of its objects the
mind invents, e.g., the square root of minus one, quadratic equations,
diverse hopes and aspirations, the perfect circle, and the perfect
marriage. Nevertheless, the ultimate origin of all our knowledge lies
in our awareness of the external world, and it is the nature of this
kind of knowledge that sets up the most persistent problems in
epistemology.

Science and Metaphysics

This external world is a world of space. Things in it have a location and happen at a certain time. When and where are always pertinent questions to ask about anything that is said "to exist." All
real individual things exist and in this sense forms or concepts do not
exist even though it is by their means that we become aware of
"what" does exist.

All real individuals in the world of our experience are changing.
Things are in continuous transformation, changing their size, location, and qualities. Our world is the domain of existence, that is, of
changing Being. To understand changing Being is the function of
both science and metaphysics. The difference lies in the nature of
the questions each asks.

Science wants to know what variables are involved in a specific
kind of change, for example, what variables are involved in the
growth of plants and animals; what variables are involved in juvenile
delinquency or in keeping a satellite in orbit? Science also wants
to answer the question as to how variables vary with respect to each
other. For example, is an increase in national income accompanied
by a decrease in crime? Does the earning power of American males

vary with the amount of schooling they have received? Does the speed of aircraft vary with the temperature of the atmosphere?

As science develops it wants to know whether there is any law or general formula that describes how one variable changes with respect to others. Pressure of a gas, to be sure, changes with volume and temperature, but in what ratio? How much of a change in one will be accompanied by how much of a change in the others? Is there a law, one might ask, that tells how crime or the birth rate or trips to Europe vary with changes in *per capita* income of Americans?

Science, therefore, is interested in finding formulas or the most general forms wherewith to describe specific changes in the world. Each science is concerned with its own domain of changes: chemistry, physics, biology, economics, psychology have their own domain of events which they try to describe and understand.

The test of truth for science is called *empirical verification*. This means that when a scientist can by his formula predict how a change in one variable will be accompanied by a change in other variables, he is on the way to being satisfied that his formula is reliable. But this satisfaction is increased as he or other workers test the predictions and find them to be as predicted. The spectacular predictions of astronomers about eclipses; the success of chemists in making new compounds so that they will have the properties we want them to have, for example, were dramatic verifications of the *formulae* these scientists were testing.

It will be noticed that the inner nature of a thing or an event need not be understood or even talked about so long as the formula "works." If wearing blue neckties were to reduce delinquency in cities, we might proceed to furnish all adolescent boys with blue neckties without knowing why they were so effective in reducing crime. It would not be long, however, before scientific curiosity would impel investigators to search for factors within the blue ties and the crime in order to account for the efficacy of the neckwear. They would be taking a step toward discovering the "nature" of blue ties and crime. How far into the "real nature" of things will science go? This much we can predict: science will go as far as it must to verify the formulas it has constructed and as far as it can to discover new formulas that predict better than the old ones.

Metaphysics, on the other hand, asks a somewhat different set of questions about changing Being. To understand change metaphysically is to find a formula that describes features which are essential to any change whatsoever, that is, which make the very idea of change understandable.

Thus in one of the most famous metaphysical analyses of change Aristotle argued that to "think" change we have to think of something that changes, that is, something that persists through the change as the house persists when we change its color, or the horse persists as it grows from colt to yearling. Aristotle called what makes this persistence possible "matter."[3]

Matter is not made up of little hard particles, but is to be thought of as a principle or kind of being that can be spread out in space and that can take on new forms. It never exists apart from some form, but it is not irrevocably wedded to any particular form. Therefore, matter is a relative term. The bar of steel can be matter for a pair of scissors or a girder for a building, and the girder may be matter for the builder. If, however, we reduce the steel to molecules, and these to atoms, and these to electrons and protons, we are gradually getting to the notion of what the ancients called a "prime" matter, or matter with a minimum of form.[4]

By the forms that give each individual thing its character or "whatness" we can mean:

1. Such qualities as shape, position, size, weight, motion—commonly called the primary qualities.

2. Such qualities as color, odor, taste, hardness, softness, hotness, pitch—commonly called the secondary qualities.

3. Such qualities as beautiful and ugly, propitious or threatening, attractive or repulsive—sometimes called the tertiary qualities.

4. Certain structures that give the object power to affect other objects in particular ways, e.g., that of an acid or of a man.

5. A definition that isolates what is indispensable to its being the sort of thing it is, and certain accompanying characteristics that it always has (necessary accidents) or sometimes has (contingent accidents).

There are many kinds of change, ranging from the drifting of a grain of sand on the beach to nuclear fission. Some changes merely substitute one surface quality for another, e.g., as when a lady changes the color of her lips, cheeks, or hair. Other changes, such as we call growth, follow a fairly regular pattern. Birth and death

[3] *Metaphysics*, Book XII, 2.
[4] Cf. Wild, *op. cit.*, pp. 286–291.

are more radical changes; wholly new forms come into being and pass away. But without the notion of a matter that is hospitable to many forms, we could have only creation and annihilation—not change.[5]

To understand change is to be able to indicate:

(1) the state or form of matter out of which the present thing came,
(2) the agency that brought about the transition,
(3) the form or structure that it now has, and
(4) the direction toward which the thing is trending.[6]

Metaphysics does not seek to control things but rather to discover and describe the most general features of Being. It does not ask: "How does X vary with Y?" Nor, "How does X affect Y?" These are scientific questions. It does ask: "What does it mean to say that anything exists?" "How does one describe change as such?" Cause, agency, substance, attribute, matter, form, actuality, potentiality and purpose—these are some of the categories or notions Aristotle felt were needed to describe what it means for anything to exist.

Some of these terms are not needed in the special sciences but when we include "human being" or the kind of existence human beings lead along with the way stones and stars exist, it is difficult to talk about Being meaningfully without the ideas of actuality and potentiality; matter-form; cognitive being and changeable Being. In Aristotle's system all things were given some of the characteristics of "human being." For example, Aristotle thought of each thing as a composite of matter and form, that is, of the potential becoming actual according to some built-in design. For Aristotle the universe and everything in it was trying to achieve a goal or end natural to it. Such a teleological mode of Being modern science denies to physical objects, although "purpose" is hard to dispense with in discussing human behavior.

There are many systems of metaphysics in addition to those of Aristotle. Idealism is a system of metaphysics which holds that all Being has a structure analogous to that of a human mind or a person. Reality is such stuff as dreams and thoughts are made of. All Being is for the Idealist a kind of cognitive or noetic Being, and changing physical objects are in some sense ideas in the minds of

[5] *Ibid.*, p. 327. Change is central to Instrumentalism, yet the structure of change itself is usually bypassed. Cf. Dewey, *Experience and Nature*, pp. 71–74.

[6] Cf. Aristotle, *Metaphysics*, 1013a24–1014a25, on the four causes.

men, God, or the Absolute. Pragmatism, on the other hand, is reluctant to enunciate a system of metaphysics but there are views
on the nature of reality implicit in it. That change and process are
fundamental; that "real" Being has continuity; that change is evolutionary and purposive are all metaphysical doctrines.

Alfred N. Whitehead is an example of a modern metaphysician
for whom "events" and "process" were the basic categories. He tried
to restate all modes of change and Being in terms that would do
justice to everything from an atom to God.

Sensation and Perception

If we now go back a bit to what was said about awareness, we can
say that in awareness the mind abstracts the forms from individual
things. The forms, unlike their matter, are definite and fixed. Each
shade of color has its own character, so have pitch and each degree
of hardness or hotness. Definitions catch and fix the very structure
of things. When the thing changes, there is a new structure or form
to be apprehended.

How do we apprehend the various types of forms listed above?
We do not, for example, apprehend the workings of a steam tur-
bine by looking at it, nor do we apprehend its color by taking it
apart and studying thermodynamics. We do not know the character
of our friends in the same way as we know the sound of their voices.

We begin our knowledge by apprehending what we have called
the secondary qualities, or those forms that make up the surface of
the object. And these qualities are superficial in another sense also.
For the understanding of steam turbines, thermodynamics is more
important than color-awareness. The chemical properties of water
are more important to our understanding of nature than its appearance. For when we know that water is composed of hydrogen and
oxygen we are in a position to connect water with all other substances
containing these elements. And the more we understand nature, the
better is our control over it.

Nevertheless, we have to begin our knowledge with an awareness
of the surface characters. Our sense organs are the gateways to the
external world; there are no others. These sense organs, however, can
only handle such qualities as sound, taste, touch, odor, and color,
and each can do business with only one of these.

The core of all our knowing, then, is sensation, a process that depends on energy emanating from the external object. Out of the changes effected in the sense organ and the nervous system by light waves, sound waves, pressures, heat and cold, chemical solutions, and vapors, the mind abstracts infallibly a particular color, sound, touch sensation, taste, or odor. It separates the particular sense quality from the complex physical process going on in the sense organ and the nervous system.

The more complete this separation is, the more objective it is, and the more accurately it represents the quality which the object sent out. Thus sight and hearing do their jobs of separation more efficiently than do touch, smell, and taste, with the result that we see the blueness *in* the sky, but we taste the fishiness partly in the mouth and partly in the fish.

Are these secondary qualities really in the object to which we assign them and to which our awareness seems to point, or are they our own creations? Since our retinas and brains are not themselves yellow, green, blue, and all the other hundreds of hues that we do sense from time to time, we must assume that these characteristics are (1) brought in from the outside by the different energy patterns that activate our sense organs (Classical Realism), or (2) that the brain being stimulated causes the mind to *create* blueness, hardness, or hotness as a response (a certain form of Idealism), or (3) that blueness and the other secondary qualities are neutral entities that in one set of relations are light waves, sound waves, but in another set of relations are the qualities we sense (certain forms of Neo-realism).

On the second alternative, all our experience of the secondary qualities as being in the object is an illusion, but a remarkably systematic one. On the third alternative, we have to wonder how one and the same entity can play such different roles simply by interacting with a conglomeration of brain cells.

Unfortunately, the awareness of sense qualities can be stimulated from within our own bodies. Anything that stimulates the auditory nerve will give rise to sound, and various drugs and diseases occasion such internal stimulation. We thus mistake noises originating inside our heads for noises occurring outside our bodies. Some dreams are so vivid that it is difficult indeed to distinguish them from waking experience. All of these circumstances conspire to give us the classic problem of the truthfulness of our senses and whether we can prove that there is an external world that is responsible for our awareness of it.

That we are experiencing a blue color or a high tone or a fragrant odor is indubitable. *What* it is that is causing this sensation is, however, not immediately certain. How then do we arrive at a reliable judgment that we are really sensing the blue from the sky or the red from the fire hydrant and not merely dreaming it?

This brings us to the way in which we apprehend the primary qualities of the object, namely, its size, distance, position, shape, motion, and weight. Because there is no special sense organ to grasp these characteristics, we cannot immediately apprehend them as we do the secondary qualities. Presumably each sense more or less roughly brings with it some clue as to the size, shape, etc., of the object. Colors always have some shape and some spread. We feel objects as large or small to the touch; some odors seem to permeate large areas. The rate at which we apprehend two patches of color or two sounds also gives us a clue to motion, and the clearness of visual impressions allows us to make a judgment about distance.

As a result our judgments of the primary qualities (size, weight, shape) are highly inexact and dubious if we rely simply on the impressions of our senses. Yet this circumstance provides us with a means of correcting them that is the basis of all natural science. For if we doubt what touch tells us about the shape of an object, we can look at it. If we doubt the weight of an object, we can transform the pressure it exerts on our muscles to a pressure on a platform and this into a visual impression of a pointer on the face of the scale. If the stick partly in the water looks bent, we touch it and reassure ourselves of its straightness. In other words, since more than one sense gives us cues to the primary qualities, we can use one to correct the other.

Furthermore, if we doubt whether we are dreaming or not, we set up a situation in which it would be very unlikely that all observers would be dreaming in the same way at the same time. It would thus be very improbable that 10 observers would dream about a red fire hydrant, or that all of them would have certain eye or brain defects at the same time.

Yet we must not forget that although the primary qualities can with appropriate corrections be more surely ascertained than the secondary ones, they too are borne by the secondary ones. If we had no eyes, ears, touch, taste, or smell, we could not measure, investi-

gate, and compare. Accordingly we must grant that unless the qualities we apprehend by our senses are at least on some occasions as
we perceive them to be, we can have no reliable knowledge of the
external world.

If some sense reports are true, then their report that the redness
is in the hydrant need not always be false. The red *as known* is in
the surface of the fire hydrant and, under standard conditions of
the medium, sense organs and brain, is abstracted from the energy
patterns that bring it to the brain. Where the redness as a physiological and physical "thing" is to be located is another matter. This
is not "redness as known" but rather redness as correlated with
non-red light vibrations and nerve impulses.[7]

Any acceptable theory of sensation and perception has to explain
how truth is possible, and also why error is almost inevitable but
correctible. Our errors occur not so much in sensation as in perception. Actually, we rarely sense blueness, hotness, or hardness as
such. Instead, we perceive trees, stoves, sounds from an orchestra,
or a blown-out tire. The tiny core of sense that is set up by the
energy process from the objects is immediately enveloped in layers
of memory, imagination, interest, desires, and thought. And as these
vary with the individual, time, place, and circumstance, so do the
perceptions even of the same object. Thus I see the fire hydrant as
a protection against loss from fire, the insurance man sees it as a
determinant in the rates for insurance, and the salesman of hydrants
from another view. Perhaps the artist, of all people, comes closest
to perceiving the hydrant in purely sensual terms, i.e., in terms of
its appearance. Yet he too sees it not merely as a colored shape, but
as a significant form (see Chapter 9), e.g., as firm, watchful, dignified,
observant, or even as lonely.

Thought also has a part in perception. We recognize the hydrant as
belonging to a certain class of objects, and possibly our knowledge
of hydraulics seeps in also. The causes of the hydrant, its uses, the
way it works—none of these do we sense, yet as our experience grows,

---

[7] If these qualities were merely created by the individual's brain, reliable
knowledge would indeed be an inexplicable miracle, for it would be based on an
illusion; and if the process of sensing were wholly a physical one, we would have
another miracle, for it would be the one instance in which one physical object
was *aware of* another. If a Cosmic Mind projected its thoughts so that they
constituted the objects of the natural world (Objective Idealism), knowledge
would be possible, but it would lead us to wonder why we could not read
this Cosmic Mind directly and with more reliability.

the act of perception so quickly mobilizes these resources that it is hard to tell where sense ends and interpretation begins.

It is clear from this account of the matter that there is no education for pure sensation. We either have the physical equipment or we do not. We either attend to the object or we do not. What we have to educate is our perception so that we come to note the object as it is apart from the variations peculiar to our own condition at a particular time. By training the sense organs we can learn to perceive finer and finer differences between shades of color, differences of sound, touch, taste, and smell. Yet we could not do even this unless a form could be preserved in our memory and reinstated into consciousness by imagination so that we could compare one sensation with another.

Nevertheless, the improvement of perception is not merely a matter of staring harder or listening more intently. It is also *knowing* what to look and listen *for*. A layman listening through a stethoscope hears much but perceives nothing; looking through a microscope he sees much but also perceives practically nothing. To perceive in an object that which is relevant to some purpose means to know how it is connected with other things and how these connections reveal themselves to sense. In other words, the visible structure of a thing means little unless we have its invisible structure as a guide to our perception. And this brings us to the way in which we apprehend these invisible structures that make knowledge possible.

Thought and Concepts

Sense, memory, imagination, and the combination of these in perception provide us with more or less complex images of particular individual things: this fire hydrant, John Jones, the maple tree beside the fire hydrant. But when we use words to talk about the maple tree, we leave out the particular image of the particular tree. The term "maple tree" is a universal; it refers to a concept or meaning that applies to all maple trees.

In other words, all communication by means of symbols is to some extent abstract and general. Communication demands that the communicants entertain identical meanings.[8] The symbols for fire and

8 Wild, *op. cit.*, p. 443.

water may be quite different in different languages and as different
as sounds are from written marks, but the meanings to which they
refer must be the same, or the communicants will be thinking about
different things. The fact that we do on occasion communicate successfully means, therefore, that there is a common meaning which
can be abstracted from sense experience by different minds.

We shall call such a meaning a concept. How is it formed? First
of all, it is rooted in perception. We see an object that is pipelike
and has a certain color and are told that it is called a fire hydrant.
We may on another occasion see the object connected to a hose
from which water is pouring. On another occasion this water may
be directed to a blaze. If on one of these occasions we grasp the
connections among the object, water, and the extinguishing of fires,
we have formed a fairly adequate concept of the object's use. If we
now examine the hydrant in terms of its use, we realize why it has
to have a pipelike shape, why it has connections with a water main,
and why it has valves. We abstract from the particular color, size,
and position of this hydrant and form a notion that embodies its
structure as a *fire-fighting instrument*.

Let us notice what the mind had to contribute to the formation
of the concept: (1) the knowledge that water extinguishes fire; (2)
if water is issuing from one end of the hose, it must have a source
outside of itself; (3) the source must be the hydrant; (4) the hydrant
also must have a source; and (5) there must be pressure behind the
flow of water. These examples are sufficient to make two points:
first, that these are all generalizations about the nature of things
and their connections, and second, that these connections of cause
and effect are not perceived directly by the senses. They are the results of logical thinking which illuminates the connections among
things so that their operation becomes understandable. By perception we note one state of affairs following upon another. There is
the fire hydrant, then a hose is attached, then a valve is turned, and
then water issues from the hose, but that one event is the cause
of the next we cannot observe. The mind infers this connection and
then proceeds to argue that, given the structure of the events, it
could not reasonably be otherwise.

To put it in another way: we perceive the changes that an object
undergoes and then ask about the kind of structure it must have that
will permit us to tie these changes together in terms of cause and

effect.[9] But in order to answer such a question the mind must be able at every step to abstract from the perceptual images those qualities and characteristics that are relevant to the object's doings. This means close study of changes in position, size, chemical composition, and energy distribution.

Thus, by reflecting upon the various forms that an object assumes in our experiences, we approach its essence or its fundamental nature. At this point one might argue that the object itself has no absolute nature, but rather that we give it a nature depending on the use to which we put it. For a grocery man the differences between cabbages and brussels sprouts is important, whereas to a nutritionist the difference is not so important as the difference between cabbage and meat. To some a man's vocation is the essential thing about him; to others it is the way he treats his wife and children.

It is true that we form different concepts of objects depending on our interest in them. But even here, what we select from the structure of the object wherewith to frame our concept is still abstracted from the object and not invented at will. If there were no real differences between cabbages and kings, could we distinguish them at all? In man-made things the structure is designed to achieve some goal, and the essence of such things is found in the adaptation of the structure to the purpose. Church, state, and family were defined in this way in Chapter 4.

In natural objects, however, the fundamental nature of the individual thing is not the use to which we happen to put it, for it would still be a tree, for example, whether we used it for shade, the making of fraternity paddles, or for nothing at all. We determine its nature by its particular place in the whole system of human knowledge. Thus we look in the tree for those characteristics that connect it with the whole realm of things we call plants and living things. We do not define water as that which extinguishes fires, but rather in terms of hydrogen and oxygen, so that we can relate it to the whole array of physical objects.

The nature or essence of a thing is that aspect of its structure which is repeatable in other individual things of the same class. The structure of a fire hydrant or a tree or a drop of water or a human being is repeated in countless objects. Now where is this fire-hy-

[9] In other words, we are asked to frame an hypothesis.

drantness, treeness, waterness, or humanity which lends itself to such a multitude of examples?

This is, of course, the famous problem of the status of universals and is as genuine a problem today as it was in the days of Plato and Aristotle. For whenever we speak of classes of things, men, trees, or books, we do so by virtue of the fact that all the members of a class have something in common. And if we could not speak of classes of things, we not only could not have science, but, as we have already seen, we could not communicate at all.

Those who hold that nothing exists save material physical processes must regard this common nature or meaning as one of these physical processes. But how a physical process which is always particular can refer to another or to a whole class is impossible to understand. If I have only individual images of this tree and that tree, and I use that image to name all trees, then I have abstracted something which is not a particular image. If I say that I have merely associated similar images of various trees so that the name "tree" makes me think of other trees (Nominalism), then it can be asked how I recognized the similarity among these various trees if not by the fact that each had a quality or structure that was repeated at least once.

On the other hand, there are those who argue that universals are created by the human mind and do not exist in the objects themselves (Conceptualism). Now it is true that the mind can form concepts in itself, for there is no limit to what we can imagine and invent. Yet we do speak of one concept being more useful or truer than another, and what is the standard for such a judgment except that one way of conceiving an object discloses its meaning more adequately than another?

Plato was so impressed by the need for making concepts objective that he thought of them as subsisting in themselves as fixed principles apart from the individual objects. Actual trees "participated" in the universal "treeness." Unfortunately, we can enter this heaven of eternal ideas only through our perception of actual individual things, and there is no other way of getting into the eternal realm to check whether the pure idea of treeness is like the quality we note in the birch on the roadside.[10]

The moderately Realistic view that has been urged here is that

[10] Aristotle, *Metaphysics*, 990b1–993a10. Cf. Dewey, *The Quest For Certainty*, pp. 161–163, for a different version.

universals or repeatable natures are in the individual object and constitute its essence or form. The mind frames a concept that abstracts this form from the concrete thing itself. In doing so the mind by means of a concept makes the form of the individual, real, concrete, table, chair, or horse noetically present to the mind. Accordingly, to "know" a chair is not merely to have images of it. It is to recognize it as a *kind* of object (its chairness) having some characteristics that it shares with other chairs but no other objects (a structure designed for sitting); some that it shares with many different sorts of objects (being made of wood or steel), and some that it may not share with any other object (the curve of the back or legs).

Summary

Cognition or knowing, therefore, involves a real interaction of the mind and the world outside of the mind. This interaction is between a brain and sense organs and energy from the object. Awareness of this interaction arises when the mind abstracts the particular qualities of the stimuli. But the object is understood only when the mind by a further act of abstraction identifies itself with the universal or essence or the essential *form* (not the matter) of the object.

This brief account of the structure of knowing was undertaken because we had to give reasons for believing that there is such a thing as human nature which has a structure and dynamics that we can study and understand. In perfecting our concept of man we are forever trying to distinguish what is substantial or essential to his being from what can vary without changing his substantial form (accidents). In the previous chapters we were trying to detect the goal, the purpose, the very end toward which human existence seems to be striving. In this end we find our clue to what is good for man and thereby the goal for education.

In the chapters to come it will be evident that this theory of knowledge lies at the basis of the contention that the discovery of the nature of the world, the social order, and of ourselves is the material with which the pupil is to perfect the habits or tendencies of acquiring, using, and enjoying truth. It will also make clear why we shall think of all learning as a means for purifying the aesthetic, ethical, political, and social experience of the pupil by subjecting it to intellectual discipline. We shall also see that all methodology is a systematic means of preparing the pupil for the noetic insight that is the indispensable ingredient of perception, conception, and reasoning.

The view here sketched regards real things and processes as formed matter. Although form and matter are existentially required by each other, we understand or know by apprehending the form only. We digest food by devouring its formed matter; we understand food by abstracting the form from the matter. Thinking is not digestion. However much our culture has "constructed" our world; however much it has invented its values, these constructions and inventions intend to be regarded as true. Certainly if we teach them, we believe them to be true and, if so, then we mean by this that our constructs are more like reality than false constructs.

The view differs sharply from Instrumentalism on several points, especially on the *meaning* of truth and in the account of the knowing act. On the Instrumentalist view, truth *means* a matching of what one predicts will be the case and what turns out to be the case; it adopts the scientific meaning of truth. The differences between meaning and process, mind and brain, form and matter, are not crucial for the Instrumentalist, just as they are not crucial for the scientist.

But as we have seen and shall continue to see, human experience is a process that is aware of itself, and by being aware of it can go beyond it. Philosophically, this confronts us with a puzzle: practically, it makes education both possible and necessary; unfortunately, it also makes it difficult because it raises the problem of truth and error in both fact and value.

The theory disagrees with Instrumentalism in refusing to identify the act of knowing with the process of finding solutions to practical problems. Problematic situations are stimulants to reflective thinking, but each step of reflective thinking—defining the problem, framing hypotheses, evaluating and verifying them—would be meaningless and impossible unless we could apprehend certain qualities and relations directly and immediately, as the Realist insists.

PROBLEMS FOR DISCUSSION AND RESEARCH

1. List the points at which the theory of knowledge described in this chapter resembles or differs from that of John Dewey. (See Suggested Readings.)

2. In going through the suggested readings, keep track of the arguments that are advanced in behalf of and against various theories of perception and conception.

3. Do you find the account given in this chapter plausible? If not, at what point or points does it cease to be so? Why?

4. To what extent do the educational controversies with which you are familiar resolve themselves into epistemological and metaphysical issues?

5. It has been said that science is not interested in the nature of things, but rather in the observed uniformities of their behavior. What is the relation between the nature of things and such uniformity of behavior?

SUGGESTIONS FOR FURTHER READING

For fuller bibliographical information on the items listed below, consult the General Bibliography.

Epistemology and metaphysics are studies in themselves, and an adequate bibliography for them would have to include most of the major works in philosophy ever written. The items suggested are, therefore, only for purposes of tasting, so to speak.

The view presented in this chapter is a brief adaptation of the material presented in:

Aristotle, *De Anima*, Book II, Chaps. 6, 7, 12; Book III, Chaps. 2–6.
Brumbaugh and Lawrence, "Aristotle's Philosophy of Education," *Educational Theory*, 9:1, 1–16, January 1959.
Wild, *An Introduction to Realistic Philosophy*, Chaps. 13, 18, 19.

The understanding of modern epistemology means the study of at least:

Berkeley, *Three Dialogues between Hylas and Philonous* and parts of *Principles of Human Knowledge*.
Descartes, *Meditations* and *Discourse on Method*.
Hume, *A Treatise of Human Nature*, Book I.
Kant, *Critique of Pure Reason*, passim.
Locke, *Essay Concerning Human Understanding*, especially Books II, III.

From Kant on, theories of knowledge and theories of reality branched out into diverse variations of Idealism, Realism, and Pragmatism. An introduction to this material can be gained from:

Baker, *Foundations of John Dewey's Educational Theory*, passim.
Butler, *Four Philosophies*, Chaps. 2, 7, 12, 18.
Ferm, *A History of Philosophical Systems*.
Hocking, *Types of Philosophy*, passim.

PART | II

VALUES IN THE

EDUCATIONAL ENTERPRISE

6

Education and Values

In Part I were presented some of the problems that confront the educator in fashioning a system of formal schooling in a culture such our ours. There was the problem of so defining education as to set it off clearly from learning in general and from the numerous agencies in our culture that foster learning but not as a primary function. Then there was the problem of determining an aim for the educative enterprise. This, in turn, led to the consideration of the good life. We found that one of the conditions of achieving the good life was a good society. Consequently, we had to examine the roles that various social institutions would play in such a social order. In doing so we arrived at the special role of the school and its relations to other institutions.

We have spoken repeatedly about self-determination, self-realization, and self-integration as hallmarks or dimensions of the good life. If we look more closely at the meaning of these three activities, we find that they refer to the *form* that we give to our choices in weaving the fabric of life. To determine oneself is to choose on rational grounds; to realize oneself is to choose rationally among our potentialities; to integrate oneself is to remove rationally so far as possible the conflicts among our choices.

Whenever we *choose* to perform an act, we do so because (1) we have decided that it is the *right* thing to do; it is what we *ought* to do; it is a claim which we acknowledge; or (2) we choose it because of all available alternatives it is the *best* thing to do; it will lead to more satisfying consequences. The relation between (1) and (2) is the heart of ethics (see Chapter 10), but for the moment it will be helpful to keep "right" and "good" distinct because the term "value" is a more general name for "worthiness to be chosen," and there are situations where we have a problem of what is better, but not much of a problem as to what is *right*.

For example, at Christmastime when I pass Salvation Army charity pots, I feel I ought to contribute more than I sometimes want to contribute. Without figuring out the consequences, I try to meet the demands of the "ought." On the other hand, when I am in doubt as to which of two suits has the better quality for the money, I feel no particular "ought." What I would like to know is which has the greater quality. Similarly, when I wonder whether one piece of music is "better" than another, it rarely enters my mind to ask which one I *ought* to like better.

Questions of "right" and "ought" are distinctly moral questions and have to do with moral values. Questions of better and worse are not always moral questions, but may be raised about any type of value: aesthetic, economic, recreational, or social. Of course, we might argue that we always *ought* to choose the greatest value in any field; that we have a moral duty to realize the maximum of value. Nevertheless, we can inquire into the structure of the separate kinds of value without raising the moral issue at every step of the inquiry.

One can describe the good life as the ultimate aim of education in this way: the good life is the one that realizes the maximum of value, and we shall argue that when the person chooses in accordance with the principles of self-determination, self-realization, and self-integration, he has the best chances of realizing the maximum of value.

Very well then, the *ultimate* aim of education is to establish tendencies to choose. But choice always implies alternatives: better and worse, right and wrong. If the school is aiming at the good life, then it has to make decisions about value, about better and worse, right and wrong. This brings us to a problem that we have met many times before, the problem of standards or norms.

The School and Value Norms

Where does the school get its norms? Where should it get them? Does it make any difference where it gets them? Has it any choice in the matter? What makes the choice of norms so difficult for the school?

1. Custom bluntly defines the right and the wrong, the better and the worse. "This is the way we always have done it" is the first line of justification in any society. People with some pretensions to intellect are critical of custom because so many customs seem senseless. To social reformers "custom" is a fighting word because it is the mortal foe of change. Custom deserves many of the harsh things said about it; nevertheless, most of our preferences in most areas of our lives most of the time are determined by the habits of our ancestors.

Indeed it is only when custom balks some strong desire that it ever occurs to us to question it—even the most intellectual and progressive of us. We would expect, therefore, that the school would get a good share of its norms from custom, tradition, and the *mores* of the group.

It was the custom in my own school days for boys and girls to use separate entrances to the school buildings. We studied certain subjects and read certain books, largely because they were customary. We tormented our teachers with customary pranks and received the customary punishments.

2. What society cannot safely entrust to custom it enacts into law. The law of the land proclaims a set of norms, standards, and evaluations stipulating what the citizens shall and shall not do and often specifying what will happen to them if they disobey.

Many states have laws prescribing that certain subjects, e.g., American history, physical education, or this or that language, be taught. Presumably the legislators felt that such subjects were not sufficiently cemented into the curriculum by custom to be taken for granted. Nor were they too sure that the school authorities, left to themselves, would regard such subjects with proper earnestness.

3. There is a type of standard that is more obligatory than custom and less formal than law. It is a custom that has been affected or infected by the notion of public welfare.[1] Putting a fish on each hill of corn may have originated in the observed improvement it made in corn growing. It could have become an habitual practice without any distinctively moral overtones. However, if the notion got into enough heads that the gods would be offended if the fish were omitted from the planting ceremony, the feeling of "ought" would be born, and the practice would join the tribe's *mores*. Tribal feelings, vague in shape but strong in tone, accompany the *mores*. Our horror at incest, cannibalism, infanticide, matricide, fratricide, and patricide has little to do with moral reflection. It is difficult to say how many of our norms in school and out derive from such *mores*, but in general they are the most powerful of our standards.

4. The beliefs of a group about its relation to the Divine generate almost simultaneously a set of demands of the Divine upon men which can be as strong as *mores*. They define the right and wrong, the better and worse, and often describe the rewards and punishments for obedience and disobedience. It would be surprising indeed if a school did not in some way reflect these standards.

Some difficulties

We may call all of these standards mentioned, "cultural demands." They are relatively fixed at any given time, however much they may change in the course of time. We now raise the question: how do these demands ever come to be doubted, questioned, or defied?

1. When a sufficient number of the group are miserable, or when the group seems to lose its power in relation to other groups, there may arise a dissatisfaction with the standards by which they have been living. We say "may" rather than "must" because in every civilization certain standards that make the group members miserable nevertheless persist. In our own culture, for example, the custom of giving expensive Christmas gifts persists even though it imposes a burden on many people. There is already a small but recurrent rumbling against the commercializing of Christmas which may in time lead to a change in the form of this cultural demand.

2. The more obviously a standard is man-made, the more vulnerable it is. Laws are questioned more readily than *mores*, and civil laws more than religious ones. The injunctions against incest would

[1] Sumner, *Folkways*, p. 30.

not be questioned in our culture even if there were no laws against it. Laws about income taxes are almost always questioned.

3. When one set of cultural demands is juxtaposed to a different one no less powerful, the question inevitably arises as to whether one is more rooted in the nature of things than the other, or whether either of them is.

In modern societies all three conditions have been fulfilled sufficiently so that two typical but inconsistent reactions can be distinguished. One is that all standards are regarded as relative to the history of a particular cultural group. The other is that there is a true set of standards and "our" group has it. The first reaction is found in many theories about values; the second is manifested in the actions of men. Let us look at these two reactions more closely.

Relativity and objectivity of values

Whatever may be our private opinion of people who enjoy foods we abhor, clothes we would not wear, and books we cannot abide, we do not, as a rule, do anything drastic about it. We shrug a shoulder and remark that there is no accounting for tastes. Only when differences in value preferences threaten to turn into serious conflicts between groups or individuals are we seriously disturbed. Only then do we realize that unless there is some yardstick by which preferences can be evaluated in terms of better and worse, and unless such a yardstick is universally accepted, our only alternatives are universal tolerance or perpetual war. Since men cannot achieve the first nor sustain the second, they vacillate between the two; they tolerate what they cannot cure, and destroy what they cannot endure.

That customs and manners should be relative to different cultures is to be expected. Different climates and different modes of agriculture and craftsmanship naturally engender diversity in the ways of life. It is not difficult to see why Eskimos wear furs and South Sea Islanders do not.

It has been stated, for example, that even within our own society, which prides itself on the absence of sharply defined classes, the "lower lower" class differs from the middle class on such matters as standards of right and wrong with respect to sex behavior and aggression.[2] A middle-class citizen finds it incredible that a lower-

[2] Cf. Allison Davis, "Socialization and Adolescent Personality," in *The Forty-Third Yearbook*, Part I of the National Society for the Study of Education, 1944, pp. 208–211.

class juvenile delinquent not only steals automobiles, but also regards the stealing of them as "right" and the not-stealing of them as stupid, if not downright evil. What the good middle-class burgher would prefer to believe is that the juvenile delinquent "deep down" really wants to be honest and craves the approval of middle-class society. Hence he is willing to spend large amounts of money to reform the delinquent and to restore him to his original path of virtue. That a boy should not *want* to reform he can explain only by invoking the principle of depravity, but he is denied even this small comfort because sociological doctrine at the moment does not believe in depravity. Instead, it argues that the delinquent learned his delinquency from other delinquents, and these in turn from others, until presumably we get back to Cain, the first of the juvenile delinquents. To put it somewhat differently, in a delinquent culture group, the delinquent would be a good citizen. Only in a social order in which middle-class citizens make the laws is he a criminal and socially maladjusted.

The noncriminal classes share a firm conviction that to disobey the law is bad, but there is no such agreement about which laws are good. By and large, the "laws of God" are recognized as having the greatest unanimity behind them; the broad principles of right and justice come next, and specific statutes enacted by legislatures and city councils last because they aim to inhibit actions that some people have performed in the past and would like to perform in the future.

For Sumner[3] ethical codes are rationalizations of culturally formed *mores;* for Ogburn[4] the value systems of a culture either conform to the changes in the material culture or create a cultural lag; for Marx[5] moral and even intellectual values are fortifications that classes erect to protect their position in the economic struggle. And even when similar codes and institutions flourish in many regions and times, it is possible to explain the sameness by the uniformity of the life conditions out of which they arose, rather than as symptoms of uniformity in human nature or of any natural law of societies.

In the light of all this evidence for the relativity of values, how do men behave?

They behave as if the relativity theory were true in unimportant

[3] *Op. cit.,* p. 36.
[4] *Social Change,* Part IV, Chaps. 1 and 5.
[5] *Capital and Other Writings,* Max Eastman, ed., pp. 332 and 341–342.

matters, and as if it were false in matters that count. That the Russian Communists should prefer vodka to corn whiskey is understandable and tolerable to most Americans. That freedom of speech is not preferable to a controlled press is much harder for Americans to understand and therefore to tolerate. The more deeply we cherish a value, the more it permeates our character, the harder it is to think of it as relative to our own taste, culture, or upbringing.

The plausibility of the theory that all values are relative, colliding with the fact that men in important matters do not act on this theory, is the constant spur to the search for an objective basis for value. For, at best, a doctrine that holds all values to be relative is a protective theory. It justifies our resistance to aggressive people who insist on their own value scheme as final. But it does not enable us to rally men to wage war on injustice, cruelty, or any other state of affairs not affecting them at the moment.

The school's situation

Men do behave as if, in some cases at least, there were objective standards, i.e., norms or yardsticks, that can and ought to be used to judge conduct. In some fields there is more agreement as to what these standards are than in others. For example, few people quarrel about the rules of mathematics, and, at least among educated people, there is little disagreement as to what constitutes good evidence in scientific statements. When we ask what makes an action in business or daily life "right" or "wrong," there is less agreement. When it comes to deciding what makes one piece of music better than another, or one picture more beautiful than another, then the degree of agreement is low—even among experts in the field.

The school finds itself in a similar situation with respect to values and standards. There is no argument about some of the material it undertakes to teach because the community generally accepts one standard, as in mathematics, and to a large extent, in science. But in matters of politics, art, and economics standards within the community diverge.

As Myrdal has pointed out,[6] not even the American Creed which unites all groups is interpreted uniformly by those groups. Does "economic democracy" mean big business, little business, or no private business at all? Does religious freedom mean freedom from

[6] *An American Dilemma,* p. 24.

interference by other sects, freedom to convert other sects, freedom to have one's children attend parochial schools, or the right to have such schools supported by public funds?

As was noted in Chapter 1, when disagreement and controversy reach this level, they are no longer resolvable by matters of fact or scientific theory. One has to turn to metaphysics, epistemology, and ethics to find a common evaluational scheme that is more than a cultural accident.

The school has only a limited number of alternatives: (1) It can follow the elections and promote the norms of the group that wins; (2) it can try to represent in its teachings the norms of all important segments of the community, at one time or at different times; (3) it can try to avoid materials and studies about which there are serious disagreements in the community; or (4) it can try to set up and adhere to a standpoint that cuts across group preferences by taking its norms from some conception of the nature and destiny of man himself.

None of these alternatives is free from almost insuperable practical difficulties. This being the case, we may as well be guided by the logic of the situation. What is the logic of the situation?

If all that we have said about knowledge has any truth at all, and if what we have said about the school as an agency devoted to the transformation of life through knowledge is not complete nonsense, then it follows that the norms and standards of the school should be as universal as knowledge can help to make them.

General Value Theory

How can knowledge in any of its forms give us a way of judging what we *ought* to choose? In other words, can knowledge give the school objective norms for which it can stand in a heterogeneous culture? These questions in philosophy are studied as general value theory. Especially important in general value theory is how value judgments are substantiated.

The experimentalist theory of value

Experimentalists and Instrumentalists, following John Dewey, believe that one can prove a value judgment to be sound in the same way that one proves a statement of fact to be true. Just as a statement *becomes* true to the degree that it helps to make a precarious, problematic situation less precarious and muddled, so an object *acquires* value when it is chosen to achieve a purpose or to remove a difficulty or to further an interest.

Geiger, for example, says, ". . . values are outcomes of human choices among competing human interests . . . the taste for, say, x becomes a value after it has been chosen over taste y."[7]

If we now ask whether preferring x to y was a *good* choice, the answer would seem to be that that depends on *why* x was chosen. If it was chosen capriciously, then there is nothing further to be said. If it was chosen because we judged that it would promote some activity, purpose, or interest, then circumstances will tell us in time whether our judgment was true or false. X may turn out to be as valuable, more valuable, or less valuable than we anticipated.

Suppose a freshman in college is confronted with a choice between joining a fraternity or spending his money to build a personal library. Suppose he would like to do both but has money only for one. Taking success in college and life as his goal, he weighs the two alternatives and chooses the fraternity. Let us assume that he went through the whole reflective process of studying the connection between books and success and between fraternity life and success. Once he has chosen, the fraternity acquires a value and, according to Geiger, not until then. But whether it is as valuable as our student thought it to be must wait until life confirms or disproves his prior judgment.

Let us note a few points about this account of value experience. First, the fraternity had no value for our student unless he had some interest in it. Second, it did not achieve value until he chose it, and, finally, how much value it had was determined by its effectiveness in solving his problem or reaching his goal. For another student in different circumstances the fraternity might have had a different value. The important point is that the value was not *in* the books or *in* the fraternity. The fact that he had an interest in both only made each a candidate for a class of values.[8] Thus values are relative first to the interests or likings we happen to have, and, second, they are relative to their instrumentality or power to fit into or forward our enterprises.

[7] George Geiger, "Values and Social Science," *The Journal of Social Issues*, 6:4, 1950, p. 9. Published by the Society for the Psychological Study of Social Issues.

[8] "The taste x by itself is a candidate for the class of values; it is not automatically a member of the class." Geiger, *loc. cit.*

What does such a theory mean for value education? The Instrumentalist argues that every problem situation involves a choice—even if no more than between one hypothesis and another. So as pupils try to solve their problems intelligently, they not only gain reliable knowledge about their environment, but they also come to know which choices are more effective in achieving control over this environment. Just as their statements about matters of fact become truer as they are verified in experience, so their judgments about values become truer and their choices correspondingly better.[9]

Further, through our social sciences we can come to know more and more how preferences arise, what conditions govern the choices men do make, and how well they work out in achieving their goals. Human life, therefore, gets better and better as human beings know more and more.

The student may wonder why anyone should quarrel with so sensible and optimistic an account of the matter, and it is not our intent to deny or belittle the truth and value of this account. Nevertheless, it does not seem to be an adequate description of our value experience.

1. Suppose we say that a value does not arise until after a choice is made between competing likings or interests. Now if I choose x over y, I do so either for no reason or for some reason. If it is for no reason, then the choice of x simply announces the fact that my desire for x or my interest in x is stronger or more intense than for y. Thus either x has no value even after it is chosen (since interests as such are only candidates for value), or what value it has comes from the strength of the interest. This leads us to suspect that a choice does not *create* value but only estimates the value in the object which its interests and likings have selected.

On the other hand, if there is a reason for choosing x over y, the value comes not from my choosing x, but from the reason (goal, purpose, etc.) to which it is judged a necessary means. In other words, it is the relation to success that makes the fraternity or books valuable and not my choosing one or the other. I choose them because they are already judged to be valuable, or because something is judged to be valuable in itself, e.g., success.

2. We are trying to show that the Experimentalist account of value judgment will not make sense unless some object or some experience

[9] Problem solving as a method of organizing the curriculum is discussed in Chaps. 12 and 13.

is valuable on its own account and from its own nature. If this is true, then not all values are relative in all respects. If there are instrumental values, there must be intrinsic ones, and without pressing the matter for the moment, we shall conclude that the source of value is to be sought not only in the results objects can have as instruments, but also in their own structure which somehow has the power to make them good instruments.

3. Does the Experimentalist view *really* have some intrinsic values—values that are valuable because of what they are rather than because of what they enable us to do? Geiger says, for example:

> Basic in such a set [of assumptions] would be the possibly primitive notion that the resolution of conflict, the solving of problems, is "good." Perhaps equally primitive would be the assumption that a social group or individual organism be judged by its ability to grow as well as to survive . . . that scientific method is not "merely" a means to some extramural end, but that it contains within itself a dynamic and self-correcting purpose for which no ethical apologies need be made.[10]

This quotation, incomplete as it is, gives us a definitely affirmative answer to our question. At the same time, it makes us wonder whether the Experimentalist view of value is as relative as it makes itself out to be. It also gives us a clue as to the Experimentalist's position on school standards.

4. It would regard the scientific method of inquiry into all problems of choice as its ultimate yardstick. It would treat the value demands of the various elements in the community much as the Bureau of Standards treats any sample of a product submitted to it for testing. It would have to reserve the right for school and pupils to arrive at conclusions adverse to some value claims of the community and even of the nation.[11]

It would encourage, if not demand, that each pupil re-examine such value commitments as he may have already formed in the home, the church, and the community. This would be not only a logical position to take, but a very courageous one. Is it a possible one?

The scientific method is at best a *form* of arriving at a choice. Al-

---

[10] *Op. cit.*, p. 13.
[11] For a good exposition of this view, cf. Lawrence G. Thomas, "The Meaning of Progress in Progressive Education," *Educational Administration and Supervision*, 32:385–399, October 1946.

though loyalty to the scientific method develops persistence, integrity, and open-mindedness, it has no content of its own to tell us for what purpose it shall be used. Here the view needs something like "growth in the ability to control the environment," the removal of conflict, adjustment, etc., to anchor the method in a sort of "temporary" ultimate.

Some Experimentalists, therefore, add democracy to the scientific method as an ultimate yardstick, arguing that all choices be judged by whether or not they are truly democratic.[12] However, this criterion is a cultural one, and it suffers from one great weakness, namely, that what is *truly* democratic is precisely what the fight within a democracy is likely to be all about. Is government ownership of hydro-electric plants really democratic or not? Is collective action more democratic than individual action?

If, then, the school is to take democracy or Americanism as its final yardstick, which version of these ideas or ideals will it take? What is the point of controlling the environment more and more? Why remove conflict? What kind of adjustment is the good one?

We have argued repeatedly that without some metaphysical theory about the nature of the good life and the good society, such questions cannot even be raised, much less receive a definite answer. So long as it shies away from metaphysics and from all absolutes, the Experimentalist school, although it claims the right to examine and criticize the culture, has no adequately grounded theoretical basis for doing so.[13]

Emotive theories of value

Emotive theories of value argue that value statements of the form, "This is good," "This is beautiful," and "This is right," do not really tell us anything about any object or any act. Rather, they indicate what our attitude or feeling is toward this act or this object. Or

---

[12] "As *norm*, the democratic value becomes the nearest approximation to any ultimate ideal that the pragmatist-progressivist is willing to accept." Theodore Brameld, *Patterns of Educational Philosophy*, Yonkers-on-Hudson: World Book Company, 1950, p. 127.

[13] On the other hand, the Experimentalist would reply: "This problem ceases to exist when one declines to require absolute certainty for a presumed value on merely logical grounds. The need for such certainty is eliminated when one's process of making evaluations includes an independent and objective way of testing and improving one's value judgments continuously." Lawrence G. Thomas, *op. cit.*, p. 395.

they may hold that value norms are set up by the prevailing culture. Norms express what most people approve or disapprove or
how the majority feels about certain kinds of acts.

On this view, science can help us decide what to do if we wish to
achieve some goal, but it cannot tell us ultimately which goal is better
than another. As Feigl puts it, "Scientific knowledge, even if it concerns the conditions and consequences of valuations, is in a perfectly
clear sense value-free or value-neutral.[14]

Emotive theories do not say that knowledge cannot modify our
choices or that it cannot change our attitudes. But they do deny that
scientific knowledge can justify rationally any ultimate standard
such as justice, benevolence, or truth-telling. They also deny that we
can find out what man "ought" to value from any description of his
structure, his needs, or his interests. Since this is contrary to the
view taken in this book, a word or two of comment are in order.

If man were like the sun or moon or oxygen or hydrogen, then
no matter how carefully we described his actions or his constitution,
we should never arrive at the notion that he "ought" to behave otherwise than he is behaving. For what would it mean to say that the
moon "ought" to behave differently?

The moon is already behaving according to its nature; it is not
free to do otherwise. If we can meaningfully say that man ought to
do so-and-so, then he must have a natural end to issue the command and a free will to obey or disobey it.[15]

We have tried, especially in Chapter 3, to describe such an end,
and we can only repeat here briefly that the symbolic powers of man
make it possible for him to envision a life in which self-determination, self-realization, and self-integration are possible. Once he
glimpses this possibility, his fundamental goals and obligations are
revealed to him also. Whether he succeeds or not, or in whatever
degree, his obligation is unmistakable. He is obliged to choose the
better in the light of knowledge; he is obliged to criticize his culture
in the light of knowledge—for what is knowledge but a reliable guide
to possibilities of a different and perhaps better mode of life? He is
obliged to examine his wants, needs, and interests to redirect them in
the light of knowledge. In other words, to realize that one can

[14] Herbert Feigl, "The Difference Between Knowledge and Valuation," *The Journal of Social Issues*, 6:4, 1950, p. 41.
[15] Cf. John Wild, "Tendency: The Ontological Ground of Ethics," *The Journal of Philosophy*, 49:14, July 3, 1952, pp. 461–475.

be rational is one and the same thing as feeling obliged to be rational.[16]

What sort of value education would be possible on the emotive or attitude theories of value?

Briefly, it would put the school in the role of attitude changer. Attitudes can be changed by altering the beliefs of pupils, by psychotherapy, by persuasion, and perhaps even by force. The school, however, could not on any rational ground decide what attitudes it should favor or oppose. It would face again the problem of adopting a norm in a culture that has many norms. On this theory the school could not even take the stand that the scientific attitude ought to be cultivated—unless the community itself favored that attitude.

Values as objective

A paragraph or so back we spoke of guiding the value quest by knowledge, but such talk presupposes that knowledge can grasp the value-nature of things, and this in turn presupposes that things do have such a value-nature to be grasped. If there is any sense in which goodness, rightness, and beauty are in things and acts, then the more we know of our world the more we know about its value possibilities.

Any theory that asserts that the value of an act lies in the object or in the relation among objects in such a way that it can be known and judged is an objective theory of value.[17]

One such objective theory holds that the value predicates like good and beautiful are qualities that are immediately known. Like yellow or softness, goodness is a quality of an act or of an object and is immediately felt as such. To say that "goodness" is the ability to satisfy desire or interest or to produce certain consequences is to commit what G. E. Moore has called the "naturalistic fallacy,"[18] because one can still ask whether a desire or an interest is good. The experience of yellow is *caused* by light waves and a nervous system, but this is not to say that the experience of yellow *is* the experience of a nervous system and light waves. Very few people have ever seen a nervous system, and those who have do not report it to be yellow.

16 Cf. C. I. Lewis, "Imperative of Rationality," *An Analysis of Knowledge and Valuation*, pp. 480 ff.
17 Cf. C. D. Broad, "Some of the Main Problems of Ethics," in *Readings in Philosophical Analysis*.
18 Cf. G. E. Moore, *Principia Ethica*, Chap. 4, and *Ethics*, Chap. 4.

Whatever the theoretical difficulties with such a view,[19] it does call our attention to a fact about experience. We cannot talk about yellow unless our conversational partner has directly experienced yellowness. And we cannot talk about goodness, rightness, and beauty unless he has had experiences corresponding to these terms.

Every object and every act to which we attend announces itself as being of a certain quality; yellow, red, beautiful, threatening, good, right, repulsive, etc. We shall refer to this phase of the object or our experience of it as the intrinsic phase. The proposition: "This appears beautiful," can never be false if the speaker is not deliberately lying. But statements like: "This will appear beautiful to me tomorrow," or "to all people with normal eyes," or "to all lunatics," cannot be known directly; whether they are true or not has to wait upon events which verify or disprove them.

Suppose, however, only acts of a certain kind appear moral to qualified observers under certain conditions. This would allow us to say that objects and acts, if they have certain kinds of structure, give rise to certain kinds of feeling in a subject or person who can apprehend the pattern of that structure. If I am tone deaf, if I am a tyro in music, if my intelligence is feeble in moral matters, I shall not apprehend the structure that is there, even though I may perceive some kind of pattern. This is the theory of value that we shall try to elaborate in the subsequent chapters. Here it will be sufficient to indicate some of the reasons for favoring it as a base for value education.[20]

In the first place, it locates the source of values in the relation between the structures of things and the structure of human nature. In this sense values are objective. An automobile is not valuable because I want it; rather I want it because its structure holds out possibilities of experience that I hold to be satisfying.

Secondly, it makes value education not merely a matter of changing people's attitudes by conditioning and other nonrational devices, but, rather, a matter of increasing their ability to apprehend structures in the world that do give rise to value experiences.

Thirdly, we can use the valuable part of the Experimentalist view without confining ourselves to it. It takes experimentation and in-

[19] For example, why do we argue so much about what is good if we can apprehend it directly and presumably apprehend the same thing?
[20] For a psychological treatment of this type of theory, see A. H. Maslow, ed., *New Knowledge in Human Values*, pp. 119 ff.

quiry to discover the structure that underlies value potentialities, but the apprehension of that structure is an insight into the nature of things. It is not merely a notion thought up by the inquirer for the purpose of solving a particular problem.

If there can be a rational basis for promoting the attainment of intrinsic values and discovering the efficiency of instrumental ones, then the educator is, theoretically at least, not in an impossible situation. Further, if self-determination, self-realization, and self-integration are truly the forms of the good life, and if we can say what each of these means for an individual pupil, then we can specify which values promise to promote or hinder the prospect of a good life for him. This program is not impossible, but neither is it easy, witness the kinds of questions that immediately present themselves.

1. The child upon entry into the first grade is already well-stocked with preferences, predispositions, and tastes. Home, friends, movies, television, and the comics have had their innings.

2. Each pupil is the bearer of a unique pattern of abilities, achievements, and possibilities. His potentiality for the aesthetic values may be low; for the intellectual ones, high; for health values, average. Should we try to smooth out these irregularities? Should we encourage a specialization that may bring him distinction in one area and mediocrity or even a deficiency in others?

3. Can we estimate the value potential of the pupil? What instruments are available to the school for such measurement?

The value areas

Because the enjoyment of a fine landscape is not the same as that of a symphony, and because both are different from the satisfaction we get when the components of a puzzle click into place, it is convenient to distinguish different areas of value experience.[21]

Economic values. An object has economic value if it commands a money price. It is a commonplace that we do not value money or material things for their own sake, but rather for the enjoyments they make possible. Economic value is instrumental rather than intrinsic, although the miser may get a genuine and perhaps unique satisfaction from the mere handling of his money.

Health, bodily, and recreational values. Under this heading we

21 For similar lists or tables of values, cf. Everett, *Moral Values*, p. 182, and E. S. Brightman, *A Philosophy of Religion*, pp. 94 ff.

shall include the values of health or physical well-being, play, and all the satisfactions that come from the gratification of bodily needs, such as hunger, thirst, rest, and sex.

Social values. The satisfactions we get from friendship, love, family, and membership in groups are to be included in the social values.

Moral values. These are the satisfactions and dissatisfactions that accrue to the individual in the course of his attempts to make right choices.

Aesthetic values. Perceived objects to which the adjectives beautiful and ugly are relevant give rise in the observer to the kind of experience we call aesthetic.

Intellectual values. We prize or get satisfaction from attaining truth in any of its forms. We say that an object or action has intellectual value if it in some way helps or hinders the finding of truth.

Religious values. If an object by virtue of its relation to the Divine can be called holy or sacred, it is said to have a religious value, and the experience of such objects as sacred or divine is called a religious experience.

Each value area has a subjective and an objective aspect. Sometimes we speak of the value as meaning the individual's experience of satisfaction and sometimes value refers to some property or quality of the object or of an act. This is so because value is a relation between an organism and an object, although we cannot ever be sure just how much each contributes to the transaction.

Intrinsic and instrumental aspects

A distinction is commonly made between valuing and evaluating. Valuing refers to the fact that we are actually prizing something; evaluation is a judgment which asserts that what we prized *really* was or was not worth prizing. Valuing is the intrinsic phase of value experience.

To put the matter more concretely, when we see a dear friend we experience an emotional lift that is not quite like any other feeling. We do not at this moment ask whether we ought to feel this way about seeing the friend, nor do we ask whether he is worth our devotion. He seems intrinsically worthy of such devotion.

On the other hand, any value may have an *instrumental* phase; it may lead to other value experience. Few are the values that do not depend on other values for their own full development. Sunsets and the music of birds, to be sure, are free, but education costs money, so do art objects and admission tickets to plays and concerts. Even religious values, if they are to be realized in a congregation, require clergymen who need some material goods and a church building that is rarely constructed out of piety alone.

The reader can spell out these relations for himself by taking one value area at a time and noting what it contributes to every other value. The point to be stressed is that just as the intrinsic phase of value experience is certain, so is the instrumental phase problematic. For in the moment of valuing something, its ramifications and relations are not apparent. While we are enjoying the solution of a mathematical problem, the uses to which it may be put are not evident and may never become evident without investigation. The taste of wine does not foretell its effects, nor the good deed its blessings.

One type of value can be instrumental to others, but it can also be in conflict with them. The businessman may be too busy for the aesthetic or social values if he devotes himself too wholeheartedly to realizing economic values; whereas the artist may have to live in a garret if he ignores the conditions under which pictures are exchanged for money. We cannot cultivate all values with the same intensity at the same time; every choice is trailed by some sacrifice. Practical wisdom reduces this sacrifice, but the reduction is never complete.

Positive and negative values

It seems odd to speak of a negative value, but aversion, dissatisfaction, and displeasure are as real as their opposites. Negative values are experiences we would prefer not to have and perhaps would give something to avoid.

By combining the intrinsic-instrumental dimension with the positive-negative one we get the following combinations:

1. Intrinsically positive-instrumentally positive, e.g., the eating of a flavorful nutritious food, the reading of a book that is both interesting and instructive.

2. Intrinsically positive-instrumentally negative, e.g., the delights of the drug addict, the alcoholic, betting on horse races (at least for those who lose consistently), and overindulgence of the appetites.

3. Intrinsically negative-instrumentally positive, e.g., a pain warn-

ing that medical attention is needed; the bitter pill or painful sur gery that improves health; the failure that inspires greater effort.

4. Intrinsically negative-instrumentally negative, e.g., all instances of unnecessary and preventable suffering, painful incurable illnesses, cruelty, malice, envy.

In general, men yearn for the first class of values, often succumb to the second, endure the third, and hate the fourth.

Higher and lower values

In common usage the religious, intellectual, aesthetic, moral, and some of the social values are often referred to as the "higher" values, whereas the material and bodily ones are called the "lower" values. The quotation marks indicate that higher and lower are not self-evident in their meanings. Why are the intellectual values, for example, higher than the values of enjoying a beefsteak? If we examine the kinds of books men *do* buy, the kinds of pictures they seem to enjoy, and the number of times they prefer beefsteak to study, we can only conclude that often they prefer the lower to the higher, or that if they prefer the higher, they nevertheless choose the lower.

Underpinning the common judgment of lower and higher is a metaphysical belief that those activities which exercise the faculties peculiar to man or are most developed in man are more real than the activities which we share with the brutes. There also lurks the assumption that what is less common is more precious, so that excellence in the aesthetic, religious, and intellectual fields is more to be esteemed than bodily vigor and physical pleasures.

Such convictions may be sound, but it is difficult to see how one could prove them to a sceptic's satisfaction if that sceptic chose to argue that what we share with the animals is, on the whole, more necessary and more pleasureful than what we enjoy as human beings. He might argue that the rare is the monstrous deviation from the type and endangers it, and is, therefore, less valuable than the common, the average, and the plentiful.

Another way of justifying the common use of higher and lower values is to argue as follows:

1. The aesthetic, religious, moral, and intellectual values are more self-sufficient than the others; they are, on that account, higher. Although truth, beauty, holiness, and good character do depend on money, health, and friends, they can, if necessary, be cultivated and

enjoyed with a minimum of such dependence. Granted one gets a more systematic education if he has the means to pay college tuition and book bills than if he cannot do so, an amazing amount can be learned with very little money. One may not be able to buy masterpieces of painting or season tickets to symphony concerts, yet are the opportunities for aesthetic satisfaction seriously limited by lack of money?

2. These values wear well over the long pull. Physical vigor and bodily delights wane with age; friends and family die; money is a mercurial commodity. Literature is replete with commentaries on the ephemeral nature of worldly goods and pleasures. By contrast the pleasures of intellectual, moral, aesthetic, and religious activity increase with age if for no other reason than that the older we get the less distracting the attractions of the bodily values become. Youth will never take the word of the aged in this matter and it consequently will not undertake in the green years to establish resources for the sere ones. Educators who try to convince their charges that something ought to be learned for possible use in old age are wasting their time.

3. One can argue that the higher values—the values of the mind or of the spirit—pervade life more completely than do the lower ones. Every activity undergoes a change in quality when subjected to inquiry, when explored for its aesthetic possibilities, or for its character or religious value. Houses and food can be made beautiful as well as useful, and the spirit of godliness can pervade family life and conceivably even our economic life. The businessman of high character is a better businessman, and a beautiful dance is as hygienic as an awkward one.

In the long run both lines of justification have to be employed. That a life which is self-determined, realizes potentialities, and is self-integrated, is good, rests on the belief that man's perfection lies in the direction of the higher values. This belief becomes empirically grounded to the extent that we actually find the cultivation of these higher values to be more satisfying than a life which does not cultivate them to the full.[22]

Every man realizes some sort of value in every value area. Every man has to have some material goods, some health and bodily

[22] Compare with the characteristics of self-actualization found by A. H. Maslow as typical of the "peak" experiences of life. See *New Knowledge in Human Values*, pp. 119 ff.

pleasure, and some human associates. His knowledge is never zero; he enjoys some sort of beauty, has some code of conduct, and there are some objects he regards as worthy of his worship.

Men differ in the *kind* of values they make dominant in their lives, e.g., the intellectual or economic, and the *level* at which each of the values is realized. Within each value area we can distinguish higher and lower levels. What differentiates them?

This question might be answered in a number of ways, but we shall argue that it is knowledge which makes the difference. The more we know about a value area, the more discriminating we become. We notice smaller differences; we are aware of more alternatives and, therefore, of more possibilities of value realization. In other words, the more we know about a field, the more "high-brow" we tend to become, and the higher the brow, the greater the ultimate satisfaction. How do we know this? Perhaps from the fact that connoisseurs are rarely content to return to the innocence of ignorance.

For education this is of first importance because knowledge, or rather habits of knowing, are the stock in trade of the school. Insofar as knowledge can do anything for value formation or modification, the school can have a genuine share in the enterprise.

Components of Value Education

It is important to distinguish two kinds of outcomes of schooling. One might be called a test outcome. It refers to a behavior sample that tells us whether the instruction just completed by the school has been successful. For example, if we have been teaching history, a test outcome might be the recall of information contained in the text or it might be the interpreting of a set of statements in the text.

But another type of outcome may be called a life outcome. Here we mean a style of behavior or behavior syndrome in which a person acts out his daily round of duties in a distinctive way. For example, he reads newspapers, brings up his children, invests his money, and goes fishing on week-ends.

The important point about this difference is that we cannot observe the life outcomes in school, only test outcomes. The good life is an ultimate aim of education but it is not a *test* outcome of schooling. As has already been pointed out many times, schooling is only one factor in producing the good life. We try to show that the test outcomes are the necessary conditions for the good life; what we cannot prove is that they are sufficient conditions of it.

Value education involves *perspective* and *deliberation*. *Perspective* is the value-scheme: the list of priorities that a man acts out in his life from day to day. Sometimes it is called a value-hierarchy. Within *each* value area there can be a set of priorities and there can be a set of priorities among the value areas. Thus a man may place religious value at the top of his list, and within the realm of the religious value he may place prayer first.

Deliberation is the process of selecting among value alternatives. It uses knowledge already acquired, knowledge of both fact and value, and although it may prompt us to seek knowledge that is needed but not yet acquired, that is not its primary purpose.

Value education accordingly combines the arts of deliberating, judging, weighing, and criticizing with knowledge about ways and means. The knowledge portion presents no special problem because it can be a test outcome. Using it, however, is largely a life outcome. The problem is then for the school to include within the scope of its instruction deliberative tasks that can be test outcomes and yet be similar enough to life outcomes to give us assurance that success in school will promote success in life.

The source material for perspective is science, history, literature, philosophy, and religion, for these disciplines are different but converging ways of describing and appraising life styles or value schemas. Even the social sciences—economics, social psychology, sociology—while they promise "facts" about human living, never manage to omit judgments as to what the "facts" mean for the good life. They are in a word not "value-free." They subtly argue for what "ought" to be under the guise of telling us what "is."

The material for deliberation is harder to find in books and courses. Later in Chapter 13 an argument for a molar problems course will be presented in detail. Here it is only necessary to note that problems of society and of self are the appropriate materials for developing efficient habits of deliberation.

Summary

This chapter is a bridge between Parts I and II of the book. If we regard the first part as the skeleton of the good life and the education it seems to require, we can regard the chapters to come as the flesh that covers the skeleton. In other words, we shall be concerned with the various value areas of the good life and what they seem to require of a school system.

We have taken in this chapter as our key question: On what grounds can the school justify a preference for one kind of conduct over another? This led us into the examination of general value theory with a brief examination of the Experimentalist theory, the emotive theory, and a theory that tries to establish an objective rational ground for value standards.

The last section of the chapter gives an outline of some of the terminology, areas, and dimensions of value experience that will be utilized in the subsequent chapters.

PROBLEMS FOR DISCUSSION AND RESEARCH

1. From the bibliography suggested below, do enough outside reading to get a more complete awareness of the problems and positions in general value theory.

2. Examine your own school and trace the source of some of its norms for right and wrong, good and bad.

3. Do you find any basic agreements and disagreements as to what practices in the community are really democratic?

4. Examine your own value system. Which values are you willing to regard as relative? Are there any that you would regard as absolute?

5. Try to identify a sample of each of the value areas enumerated in your own experience. Try to distinguish their intrinsic and instrumental phases.

SUGGESTIONS FOR FURTHER READING

For fuller bibliographical information on the items listed below, consult the General Bibliography.

On the philosophical side there is no really easy, simple introductory treatment because the subject is neither easy nor simple. The material dealing with values from an educational point of view is perhaps the best introduction for the student of education.

Brubacher, *Eclectic Philosophy of Education*, pp. 142–160.
———, *Modern Philosophies of Education*, Chap. 5.
The Journal of Social Issues, 6:4, 1950, entire issue.
Maslow, ed., *New Knowledge in Human Values*.

Myrdal, *An American Dilemma,* Chap. 1.
Stanley, *Education and Social Integration,* Chaps. 6–7.

For advanced study in the field of value theory as such:

Dewey, "Theory of Valuation," *International Encyclopedia of Unified Science,* Vol. II, No. 4.
Lepley, *Value: A Cooperative Inquiry.*
Lewis, *An Analysis of Knowledge and Evaluation,* Chaps. 12–13.
Moore, *Principia Ethica.*
Pepper, C. S., "A Brief History of General Theory of Value," in Ferm's *A History of Philosophical Systems,* pp. 493–503.
Perry, *General Theory of Value* and *Realms of Value.*
Stevenson, *Ethics and Language.* (Sets forth the much discussed emotive theory of ethics.)

7

The Economic, Health,
and Recreational Values

This chapter will consider three classes of values that are commonly placed at the lower rungs of the value ladder. But high or low, they involve activities in which all men willy-nilly have to participate and of which, therefore, the school has to take account. We shall be concerned with how the school can take account of them, and what account the individual should take of them in the good life.

The Economic Values

The economic values are the values of commodities in exchange and arise out of the production and use of material goods. They are the fundamental instrumentalities not only of the good life, but of any life whatsoever.

We Americans believe that the production of goods and performance of services are the duties of *every* citizen. Idle playboys are more envied than admired. In a highly complex industrial order no man can hope to supply even a small fraction of his material needs. He therefore depends on every other man to do his share in the economic enterprise. A longshoremen's strike in San Francisco or a rail stoppage in Chicago disrupts the whole nation's production and flow of goods in a relatively short time. Such strikes are moral and political as well as economic problems. It is inevitable, therefore, that in our culture the economic role of man should be strategic, so strategic that our concern is how to prevent it from becoming exclusive.

Understanding the economic structure

One of the outcomes of general education should be an understanding of the system by which material goods necessary for the maintenance of the group are produced, exchanged, and distributed. Such knowledge is systematically developed in the study of economics, although there is scarcely a discipline that does not have some bearing on it.

The goal of the school as we shall see in Chapter 12 is to perfect the *habits* of acquiring and using knowledge about the economic system rather than to accumulate a store of information, on one hand, or direct participation, on the other. It is to direct the "how" of this investigation (on whatever level it is undertaken) and to disclose relationships that the young may not of their own accord discern that we need the teacher. It is also for the teacher to determine how much and what kind of symbolic material in terms of reading and calculating would be useful in furthering insights into the system of economic relationships.

It is important that the study should not limit the pupil to the economic doings of his own immediate environment. For our besetting problem is the national and even international interdependence of production and distribution. To the industrial worker a high tariff on manufactured goods makes sense, but one on meat does not. I am not sure that understanding the situation will change it very much, but it may leave us less prone to regard all economic groups but our own as evil conspirators out to exploit us.

If we ask what are the minimum ingredients for intelligent thinking about economic problems, it would seem reasonable to list the following:

1. The principles of large scale machine industry with its highly developed division of labor and equally well-developed means of co-ordinating the divisions.

2. The relation of large scale industry (including large scale agriculture) to capital formation, consolidation, and movement. How are the enormous sums of money required for large scale industry accumulated and concentrated?

3. The role of labor in such industry; how the level of wages is fixed; the relation of labor to management and capital.

4. How do prices find their level in such a mode of production?

5. The major economic groups or blocs and their interaction in the economy.

6. The role of government in the economy.

7. The role and mechanics of credit and money.

8. Balancing and upsetting factors in the economy.

9. Historical roots of our system to explain some of its present features.

10. Other economic systems and possibly a critical evaluation of them.[1]

Until these basic understandings are effected, questions as to whether we can have a planned economy or not, whether we can have economic democracy, and similar issues are tempting but dubious subjects for high school panel discussions. The student cannot rush out of the panel into the library and rush back with the "information" needed. Principles and understandings are not picked up in reference books; they result, when they do, from systematic study and reflection.[2]

There is much to be said for educators who see in the school an opportunity to produce a generation that will be impelled to make our economic system more rational, more humane, and more in accord with their interpretation of democracy. At least there is much to be said for their goodness of heart. However, if a sound understanding of economic systems—even on the modest scale envisioned in our curriculum—does not accompany discussion and exhortation,

---

[1] For a check list of key topics in economic education see *Key Understandings in Economics*, Council for Advancement of Secondary Education. Cf. also H. S. Broudy, "Educational Theory and the Teaching of Economics," *Teacher Education Quarterly*, 17:2, 59–69, Winter, 1960.

[2] Whether economics should be studied as a separate subject in the secondary school is discussed in Chapter 13.

then the school is being used for propaganda, not education.[3] There is no need to fear controversy in this area if it is based on available knowledge, and much more than any of us can easily master is available.

Role of the individual in the economic order

The understandings accruing from general education should be translated by the individual into relevant conclusions for his own role in the economic life of the community. As far as the school is concerned, this has three phases:

1. *Guidance.* We can legitimately demand that before the completion of the secondary school, pupils know a good deal about their vocational abilities, interests, and possibilities.

Techniques of testing have been developed sufficiently to yield reliable objective data on which appraisals can be made not only by the guidance worker, but also by the pupil and the parents. Furthermore, because the number of possible gainful occupations runs well into the thousands, and because they vary enormously in the kinds of competence they require, it is not unrealistic to envision an ideal of matching vocation and individual capacity for every pupil.

This process of self-understanding and appraisal is worth a great deal of time and money. A man's vocation is too important to be decided by whims of parents or pupils or by drifting with the tides of demand and supply of the labor market. A man's vocation is not merely a means of earning a livelihood; the work he does day after day fashions all his other values, for the type of aspiration he will have, the kind of character he will develop, and the kind of prestige he will feel compelled to gain.

There need not be, as Dewey has so ably argued,[4] an abyss between labor and leisure, between culture and occupation. The very multiplicity of gainful occupations in our country makes the choice

---

[3] "If the schools attempt to teach children how to solve the problems of the day, they are bound always to be in arrears. The most they can conceivably attempt is the teaching of a pattern of thought and feeling which will enable the citizen to approach a new problem in some useful fashion. But that pattern cannot be invented by the pedagogue. It is the political theorist's business to trace out that pattern." Walter Lippmann, *The Phantom Public,* 1925, p. 27. Quoted with the permission of the Macmillan Company. What Lippmann says about the political theorist is also true about the economic theorist.

[4] *Democracy and Education,* Chap. 19.

between such alternatives unnecessary. For if we can find a life's work for every man that stretches his intellect to its capacity, work can be educative, and to the extent that it is educative it can never become drudgery.

To be sure, the choice is far from free. The demand for workers in different fields varies from time to time, but the labor market for various occupations might be neither so glutted nor so impoverished if the matching of individual to job were to become as precise as it can become.

Because vocational interests are not so stable as abilities, the latter are the more reliable clue to vocational choice. When a strong interest in a vocation is not accompanied by a corresponding ability, the interest can often be satisfied by finding a type of work in that field that does match the ability of the pupil.

For example: a boy has an intense ambition to become a doctor. Unfortunately, the boy in seven or eight years of schooling and by performance on aptitude tests has demonstrated to the satisfaction of the guidance officer that, barring a miracle, he will not be able to do the kind of scholastic work required in a medical school. But what is a guidance officer to say to an eager boy and to parents who are ready to sacrifice a good deal to have their son become a doctor?

Suppose that both boy and parents are sensible and agree that the judgment of the advisor is sound. Does the boy have to abandon his interest in medicine? Not necessarily. If he shows some mechanical ability, he may become one of the many types of technicians connected with the medical field. If he has the personality that salesmanship requires, there is open to him the whole field of selling medical equipment and supplies. If he has business and executive ability, he may succeed in hospital management. One can play with the possible combinations for a long time without exhausting them. And what is true of the medical field is no less true of many others.

In a genuine sense, these are not really philosophical problems at all, for their solution is well within the limits of guidance techniques already developed; to provide such guidance services is a problem for the administrator.

2. *Vocational training.* Similarly, the question of specialized training needed by the pupil to fulfill his vocational choices is also outside of the domain of a philosophy of education. What sort of training is needed is up to the practitioners of the vocation to determine. The

educator may contribute the methodology by which such training is achieved efficiently, but it is to the educational psychologist that that one looks for hints in this matter rather than to the educational philosopher.

The role of general education as a preparation for a livelihood will be discussed in Chapter 13, but it may be observed here that the level at which general education has been mastered by the pupil points to the rung on the ladder of occupations to which he can realistically aspire. For one thing, many vocations require formal preparation to which admission is based on achievements in general education, e.g., graduate schools of medicine, engineering, law, etc. In other areas, licenses to practice are contingent upon having a high school diploma or so many years of college. In the second place, well-developed habits of acquiring and using knowledge are no mean vocational weapons in themselves, and employers prize them even above specific skills for beginners on the job. Both of these considerations should militate against too hurried abandonment of general education in favor of the more specifically vocational, although admittedly it takes diplomacy of a high order to persuade an adolescent with an itch for money and independence to remain in general education.[5]

Another area of vocational training falls somewhere in between specialized techniques and general education. It consists of work habits and character traits, e.g., promptness, neatness, orderliness, perseverance, reliability, and responsibility. These are useful in any calling, and certainly no school fails to impress the pupil with their desirability. In one sense, the more the habits of acquiring, using, and enjoying truth are perfected, the more these traits are strengthened, because success in any task (intellectual or otherwise) demands them. Yet the pupil who hands in neatly written assignments promptly, who can be relied upon to do his best at all times, and who persists in his task still may have indifferent intellectual ability. Work habits and IQ do not walk hand in hand. Of the two, work habits may well be the more important. And yet one hesitates to say that the school either develops these traits to a marked degree, or that it should take the responsibility for doing so.

[5] From what can be guessed about the results of automation in industry, a larger proportion of the labor force will be engaged in occupations at the technician level, and this may be interpreted to mean a higher level of theoretical preparation for more people at the high school level.

The reason for the hesitation is that traits of this sort are life out-comes formed by many factors and many agencies. The boy who is obedient in school may be a terror at home. About all the school can do is to throw its influence on the side of the angels and re-ward neatness, promptness, and perseverance while sharply disap-proving their opposites. It can also certify to the employer that a given pupil has manifested these traits to such and such a degree *in school* and leave it up to the employer to infer that he will continue to manifest them in the same degree on the job.

When neatness, orderliness, and perhaps promptness are recog-nized as essential to industrial safety and efficiency, and if the worker desires safety and efficiency, these habits will develop steadily. They can be developed even without this understanding through enforced drill and repetition. Some people would have the school do just that. However, the school cannot duplicate industrial or business situations, and there is no guarantee that mechanical drill, however thorough, will bring about a trait that will transfer to out-of-school situations.

3. *Consumer wisdom.* Because all of us are consumers of goods, and because the variety of goods is so great, wisdom in buying is obviously useful. Hence, many educators have been urging con-sumer education as a desideratum of high priority.

One kind of consumer wisdom is not to consume all of one's in-come. This can be accomplished by thrift, good management, knowledge of goods and materials, and preferably by a combination of all of these. Clearly, thrift can be encouraged and practiced in the school. Good management is hard to teach when the pupil has very little to manage. Knowledge of goods and materials in relation to price can be taught, but the question is where, for how long, and in what detail.

If it is true that women do the bulk of the buying in our country, this phase of home economics seems to cry out for a place in the general education of women, and it would certainly do men no harm. It is difficult, however, to include it in general education without also including the use of household and automobile tools, elements of household plumbing, wiring, bricklaying, gardening, and care of children and their pets. These are all valuable skills for everyone to have, but if we include them all in the curriculum, there would be neither time nor room for anything else.

Consumer wisdom is made difficult to achieve in our country by the fact that we buy largely on the basis of advertised information about brand name products. It would take the ordinary person most of his lifetime to learn the signs of good refrigerators, automobiles, cigarettes, permanent waves, types of food, clothing, intoxicants, insecticides, hair removers, hair restorers, shaving supplies, fertilizers, medicaments, and the thousand and one articles that he has to buy in a lifetime. Having learned about wool, cotton, and silk, for example, he suddenly finds a dozen or more new synthetic fabrics on the market about which he knows nothing.

It is even difficult for the schools to appraise the raucous institution of advertising. To discuss a specific product by name either favorably or adversely means trouble. To urge children to beware of advertising helps little because there are so few products that are not advertised. Above all, it would be an act of national ingratitude to cast aspersions on an industry that brings to our homes the bulk of our entertainment and current information. For if it were not for advertising, we are warned, there would be no radio, television, or newspapers.

On the positive side, some advertising is truthful, and, what is even more important, without advertising there would be no huge markets, and without these no mass production, and without this no cheap consumer goods.[6]

Perhaps the most important aspect of consumer education is the perspective from which the individual views material possessions. Granted that money is a necessary condition for the achievement of nearly all values, how much money does a person need? To what extent should other values be postponed or even sacrificed for it? Should we deny ourselves books, theatre, travel, and sociality because we feel we ought to save for the rainy days of old age? Is a job that jeopardizes health or compromises our character worth having? Is a job that takes us from our families and friends worth the sacrifice?

These questions lead us to examine more closely the relation of material goods to the good life as a whole.

[6] Today buying and selling involve more than caution and shrewdness. They are tied up with credit financing. The consumer can also look forward to greater involvement with problems of taxation, insurance, and investment. All of which argues for economic education but not necessarily for introducing courses in home ownership into the high school curriculum.

Economic values and self-determination

Money is freedom. Poverty or the fear of it binds us to our jobs. To the extent that such bonds and such fears possess us, we are not free. An economic order that would reduce these fears and loosen these bonds would certainly improve the individual life, but whether we could maintain a highly complex industrial system without such "slavery" is not easy to say. Social security plans, old age and unemployment insurance diminish such fears, and because we have been able to maintain a high order of productivity within such arrangements, it is not unrealistic to hope for continued lessening of insecurity and an increase of freedom for the individual worker.

Each person has to decide for himself just how to deal with this fear. Savings through self-denial will make us more independent of our jobs. Yet fifty years of self-denial for five or ten years of independence is a high price. Can the powers of enjoyment survive a half century of postponement? And so often the future never does come, thus making the sacrifice ironic or tragic, depending on the philosophy of the observer. Finally, is it better to be a slave to thrift than to a job?

So it may turn out that money is not freedom after all, or that it does not guarantee the freedom we seek. Certainly it is not a substitute for the confidence that power, skill, health, and competence can give. Even these, without the co-operation of moderately good fortune and other men, will not insure us against untoward events, but what else can the individual man do but develop power, skill, health, and competence?

Perhaps there is one more thing he can do, and that is to learn to enjoy the values that do not depend so much on money. To be sure, this is a negative kind of freedom, but it is not unreal, for it is possible to get positive pleasure from books, nonalcoholic conversation, nature, and friends without large expenditures of money. But, as we shall have occasion to show in the later chapters, such possibilities of enjoyment depend on the individual's education.

To the extent, therefore, that our education provides for self-cultivation, it automatically adjusts our perspective on the place of money in the total pattern of life. Hence, it is often easier to detect a really well-educated man when he is in modest circumstances rather than in affluent ones. For the rich man can buy the appurtenances of culture and so deceive us, whereas the poor man who nevertheless lives well must do so out of his inner resources.

Economic values and self-realization

Self-realization or the development of one's potentialities for value experience is, we have seen (Chapter 3), another indispensable feature of the good life. To what extent does economic activity help or hinder self-realization?

Another word for self-realization is achievement. To achieve something is to exert power in behalf of some goal which the Self has adopted as worthy of its effort. To realize one's Self is to make the Self effective in one's own life or in the life of others. It is to become real, to make a difference in the world.

In our culture wealth is one proof of achievement. Barring such rare occurrences as the inheritance of fortunes or the winning of lotteries, great wealth is the by-product of skill, shrewdness, daring, and creativity. Wealth comes to those who have something people want enough to sacrifice their money to possess. This holds true whether it is the talent of a movie star, a baseball player, or an industrial tycoon. Even when large amounts of money are amassed through fraud and violence, it has been accompanied by an impressive display of power and ability, whatever we may think of the direction these have taken.

Although all earned wealth is a result of achievement, not all achievement is accompanied by wealth. This little truth is perhaps obscured in our culture, but it takes only a little reflection to disclose it. The services most men have to sell are not very scarce. There may be a restricted demand for them, or the public may not value them so highly as it values other things. The financial return for some services, therefore, will remain modest, but the achievement of the person is not to be measured by these returns. Physicians, lawyers, teachers, and clergymen exercise their talents for the benefit of their clients, and although they expect to be paid for them, it is difficult to equate these services with a money value. The art of payment, Plato remarked in the *Republic*,[7] is separate from the art of the physician. When a society fails to pay adequately for these services, it betrays a perverted sense of values, but it does not mean that these services are less valuable in a stupid than in an intelligent

[7] *Republic*, I, 346.

society. The continual struggle among labor, management, capital, and other groups for a greater slice of the economic pie is witness to the discrepancy that men believe exists between the value of their services and the rewards they command.

Some achievements have no money value. The quiet, cheerful man is valuable in any group, but he commands no money price. The good friend, the good citizen, the good character carries no price tag. The dedicated men of science, religion, social service, and art are men of power and creativeness. They make a great difference in the world, but it would be silly to measure their achievement in economic units.

When men of great wealth are asked about their achievements, they rarely point to their bank accounts. Rockefeller, Carnegie, and Ford did not cease their activities when they had more money than they or their children could ever spend. It just happens that in industrial enterprises success means control over commodities, means of production, or distribution, and such power is expressed in terms of money in our culture. Ford could not make a cheap automobile except under conditions of mass production, and mass production involved large concentrations of capital and when successful resulted in a large volume of profit.

Achievement, therefore, has to be defined in other than money terms, and it may perhaps be defined more generally as the production of excellence in any value area. The better mousetrap, the better store, the better friend, and the better book are all achievements because they mark the emergence of a new value or a new level of value. If the school by the devices at its command can lead the pupil to some insight into the relation of achievement to monetary success, it will forestall an unrealistic disdain of money, on one hand, and its worship, on the other.

Economic values and self-integration

Self-integration has been characterized as the ordering of values into a hierarchy so that a person's life has a dominant theme of which all his activities are variations. Negatively stated, integration merely means the absence of conflicts among values within the person.

Economic life can be integrative or disintegrative. Given a vocation that utilizes intellect, strength of character, and social impulses, a man's whole life could radiate from his occupation. He would find his friends among his vocational associates; his reading might be selected for its relevance to his vocation; his house and clothes might be chosen for their appropriateness to his calling. He might develop his courage, honesty, truthfulness, and perseverance all in terms of what his work demands. Whatever aesthetic values he enjoys he may also find in his work; conceivably, to a lawyer the handling of a case may seem beautiful. Some men regard their work as the working out of God's will on earth.

Complete integration of personality around a vocational core is fortunately rare, for whatever else its victim might be, he would certainly be the world's prize bore. But at the other end of the scale is the man whose occupation is so split off from the rest of his life that it becomes like a brace that supports his tissues yet irritates them unceasingly.

This is the potential tragedy of a highly industrialized society in which so many men have to earn their living by routine jobs in which they cannot realize any save the economic values and possibly the comradeship of their fellow workers. These jobs call for no ingenuity, little knowledge, no initiative, no heroism save that of perseverance, no sentiment, no beauty, and no holiness. What Karl Marx said about the degrading effects of mass production on the worker[8] had enough truth in it so that even though the rate of pay for such work in our country is higher than anywhere else in the world, the problem still remains. It cannot be bought off. If men cannot be fully men at their work, they will have to play the man elsewhere, and the wages they will demand will be based not simply on the economic value of their work, but on what it takes to play the man off the job.

And yet money alone cannot do this for the worker. It must be money used for self-cultivation in all the value areas that will restore his self-integrity. Money used for distracting entertainment, aimless racing about the countryside, gambling, alcohol, gadgets, and even for more important matters such as better clothes, houses, and doctors will not do what the worker wants done. Not that he does not have a *right* to these things, but what he needs desperately is a life in which he can be a creator of value, in which he can realize himself, in which some goal broad enough and significant enough to pervade

8 *Capital and Other Writings*, pp. 125 ff.

his whole life overcomes the disintegrating effect of a monotonous occupation.

We may conclude this section on economic values by asking ourselves how the school can help the pupil into a proper perspective from which to view the economic life.

Literature is full of vivid experiments in value. Philosophy on a more abstract level never tires of the theme, but perhaps the most instructive material is biography. Biography has the ring of truth and a comforting concreteness that ought to appeal to adolescents. Every biography is an adventure with values and an individual answer to the riddle of perspective.

The Health Values

Much of what has been said about the economic values will apply to the values of health. Health values have an instrumental structure that every normal person readily discerns. Unlike the economic values, they also have a high intrinsic value, because they give rise to experiences that are immediately felt as desirable for their own sake.

I suppose there are those who are glad they feel well because it enables them to do their work, or serve their friends, or benefit mankind in general, but only the most confirmed hypochondriac fails to appreciate the positive experience of well-being that people in good health have and people in poor health lack. There is a limit to the joy we can squeeze from simply feeling well, and therefore we turn to more interesting activities until pain reminds us that we can never take good health for granted.

Knowledge and habits

Fortunately for us, there is something to be known and to be done about the maintenance of health. We can know a great deal about disease, its causes, and its prevention. What is hygienic both for the individual and for the community is not a matter of guess work. Reliable techniques and knowledge in this area merely await a little more rationality on the part of civilized men for their more effective employment.

The problem of the school, therefore, is simple. The knowledge of physiology and hygiene is part of the physical and biological sciences. These are part of general education, and there is no excuse for anyone who has completed the secondary school being ignorant of these matters.

But as was the case with economic values, so here we have another element in the situation which is not so easy for the school to teach. Knowing that teeth ought to be brushed is not the same as brushing them. To know that we need adequate sleep does not automatically get us into bed at a decent hour. By virtue of the mass media Americans know that overweight is hygienically unsound, but their dietary habits do not therefore change overnight.

Nursery schools do try to form such habits. However, as we ascend the grade ladder, it becomes more and more unusual for children to practice their eating, sleeping, and elimination habits in school under the supervision of teachers. School medical examinations and school clinics can play a notable role in the early detection and remedy of physical defects, but that is not quite the same as the practicing of health habits.

Unless we are willing to embark on some system of state youth organizations that will compel young people to live a number of years under the supervision of health authorities, there seems to be no alternative to saddling the home with the complete responsibility for the formation of these habits.

Perspective in health values

The value of health is so little debatable that the problem of what perspective the pupil should take toward it is academic. Certainly the pupil ought to view health as of the highest importance, to be jeopardized only when the entire value system of the person is at stake.

And with equal certainty, the proper perspective demands that the individual weigh all of his activities with an eye to their possible consequences on health—especially those activities that give bodily pleasure. In our culture there are respectable "vices" that do health no good and may do it some harm. The ingestion of alcohol and the use of tobacco if never begun would never be missed. Because legal prohibition of such commodities has proved ineffective, and laws forbidding their sale to minors equally so, and since the most respectable elements in our community indulge in them, the problem seems to be beyond immediate solution.

There is a deeper problem of perspective with regard to health, namely, that our individual health only partially depends on the care we take of it. How, for example, is one to prevent catching cold? Despite our knowledge of communicable diseases, public morality in exposing others to our afflictions is low. We have not yet convinced ourselves that it is a breach of good citizenship and good character to take our colds into theatres, schools, and places of employment. As far as knowledge is concerned, the school has the unlimited responsibility for teaching the nature of disease communication and prevention. For the habits entailed, it is hard to place the responsibility.

Even when we utilize all we know about disease and hygiene, there still remain diseases of which we know little and others for which no cure is available. Nor do we know to what new afflictions the future will make us vulnerable. Hereditary organic weaknesses and clouds of resourceful viruses and bacteria continue to make the health of man a precarious and wonderful thing.

The right perspective on health, therefore, seems to require that after due precautions have been taken and the best available knowledge employed to avoid or remedy the onslaughts of disease, no further thought be given to it. This resigned serenity only the recognition of impotence can engender. It is about as close as we can get to the golden mean between hypochondria, on one hand, and the blithe disregard of all precautions, on the other.

Just how or by what materials the schools can hope to provide such a perspective I do not know. Writers like Montaigne discoursed extensively on the proper attitude toward health, but even if such selections could be brought together, it is doubtful that they would have much effect on children and adolescents. The health of adolescents is for the most part too good and their sources of energy are too great to make health problems real to them.

We shall not inquire specifically into the relations of the health values to self-determination, self-realization, and self-integration largely because, using the pattern of analysis provided for the economic values, the student can work out a similar analysis for the health values. It will be sufficient here to note that health is a limiting factor to all three and therefore to the possibilities of the good life as a whole. Poor health limits the potentialities we can realize, and it is hard to maintain an integrated personality when ravaged by disease. Yet although it is always good to be healthy, and although no one would choose poor health for any reason, once poor health does afflict us, it may furnish an opportunity for the cultivation of values that otherwise might have been ignored.

It is a tribute to the human spirit that beauty, truth, and character can be developed to a high level despite physical disability. In no other area are the religious values more helpful than in facing with constructive fortitude what cannot in any event be eluded. And if the materials for the teaching of resigned serenity in the face of the inevitable are not too effective for the young, there is no scarcity of literature to inspire the young with the heroism that illness and physical handicaps have occasioned in the humble and the great.

It is to be hoped that the school will not set up a special course on how to be brave though ill. General education itself includes the knowledge of how to live with oneself in the face of this particular kind of affliction.

A peculiar sort of blindness in our culture makes of the Humanities a luxury that the common man can do without. And it is hard to know what to say about such blindness when it attacks the professional educator who perspires so freely and easily in his efforts for a practical education for the "common" man. For if anything should be common knowledge, it is that no amount of skill, knowledge, and good will can bring all the factors that shape our lives under our individual or collective control. For every man, perspective is a requirement that he cannot avoid, and perspective is found in the Humanities—in literature, art, religion, and philosophy. Teaching the means for securing the economic values or the health values, or indeed any other, is incomplete until the perspective from which they are to be viewed is also taught.

The Recreational Values

The word "recreation" calls to mind both its intrinsic and instrumental aspects. The play-mood is probably what we commonly mean by the intrinsic aspect of such activity, and the notion that play somehow helps to restore energy expended in work is the instrumental aspect of recreation.

Like beauty, play is hard to define although easy to recognize. Play is not work even though we expend lots of energy upon it. Play is not serious, yet children's play is to them a serious matter.

There is quite a literature on play,[9] but for our purposes, perhaps it will be sufficient to characterize it as a carefree activity performed for its own sake. On this definition, much of what adults call children's play is not play at all because it is not carefree, e.g., when children play house or school. It is more in the romping, laughing, exuberant expenditure of energy that we get a pure form of children's play. The word "fun," so common in children's vocabularies, refers to pleasurable excitement rather than to humor. They feel no inconsistency in referring to horror laden films as "fun."

In adult life the play attitude is a unique mode of experience. The obstacles in our games are artificial, and the consequences of losing are neither fatal nor far-reaching. There is excitement without too much danger. There is a feeling of freedom from care and anxiety. Such a play attitude is missing in the ardent sports fan and in most of the participants in organized sports, professional or amateur. When the outcome of the game becomes very important and has far-reaching consequences for the individual (losing or winning a large wager, getting a fat scholarship to some university, or getting a raise in pay), then the matter in hand is serious business and not play. The sports enthusiast resents nothing so much as to have anyone—participant or spectator—take a playful attitude toward his favorite "play" activity. The point of all this is that truly recreational activities are not always found in games or sports or even in standard amusements.

The instrumental values of play for children are that it is educative and healthful. Play is a source of experience and provides the opportunity for the development of muscles, skill, and sociality in all its forms.[10] For adults the instrumental value of play is much more complex.

1. Recreational activities are liberating because they are carefree. The individual in such activity has a chance for more self-determination than in work. It allows a flexibility that other phases of life do not.

2. Recreational activities often can be used to develop certain potentialities. This is the hobby phase of recreation. Instances are

[9] E.g., Huizinga, *Homo Ludens: A Study of the Play-Element in Culture;* Groos, *The Play of Animals;* Lehman and Witty, *Psychology of Play Activities;* and Mitchell and Mason, *The Theory of Play,* among many others.

[10] For Froebel play adumbrated the adult activities of man in his transactions with the Absolute. Needless to say, the Froebelian play is not especially playful.

plentiful of men who have thus developed artistic, literary, musical, and manual skills to a rather impressive degree of excellence. In a culture where the economic mode of experience so often restricts the potentialities of the worker, recreative activities may be his salvation.

3. Finally, recreation contributes to self-integration through the reduction of tension occasioned by the stresses of daily life. It is doubtful whether deep-seated conflicts within a personality will be cured by play alone, but we are now thinking of the ordinary man and the ordinary stresses of an ordinary life. In such circumstances play may well be the safety valve that forestalls the explosion.

Recreational values and the school

We have been hearing much in the last two decades about education for leisure time, and the term "constructive use of leisure time" has a firm place in the lexicon of educational slogans.

The argument advanced for such education is that our adult population, by virtue of the shrinking length of the working day and increased automation is bound to have increasing leisure. Unless men can use this leisure constructively, they may use it destructively, *ergo,* let the school get busy to circumvent such a possibility.

Now it is somewhat of a paradox that modern educators have assailed the traditional or classical education as being suitable only for a leisure class, yet when we achieve a social order in which every man can have large chunks of leisure, they have to furrow their brows about what sort of education is suitable for leisure time.

Our first point, therefore, is that general education is itself education for leisure; not for work or for citizenship merely.

That so many adults do not avail themselves of literature, music, and theatre, or even high grade conversation for the filling of their leisure time is probably due to the fact that their general education did not perfect in them the habits of acquiring, using, and enjoying knowledge to the level where these resources could be utilized. For as we shall see in the chapter on aesthetic values, literature, music, theatre, the dance, poetry, and the visual arts above the obviously popular level are closed to people who have not cultivated the skills of using the symbol systems in which they are encased.

Another class of activities have a high recreational value and also provide the physical exercise so badly needed by sedentary workers.

These are the sports and games. It is true here also that unless skill in them is acquired during the adolescent period, the chances of acquiring it in later life are small. It may be argued, therefore, that the school should teach such skills and afford opportunity for their practice during the secondary school period.

One would think that such skills could be acquired in the extensive sports program now so characteristic of the secondary school and college, but the complaint is that adolescents will not engage in such sports actively unless they are required to do so. They are quite content to watch their heroes perform on the diamond, gridiron, and basketball court. Hence, there is the argument that such sports education should not be extracurricular, but rather a regular subject for which time in the regular school schedule should be provided.

Some hardy souls draw a further conclusion: that interscholastic sports should be replaced by intramural sports. This is good logic but poor educational politics because the people will not cheerfully be deprived of their spectacles.

If the school is to take the business of educating for leisure time seriously, it should be really serious about it and require for graduation along with passing grades in English, history, and mathematics, something like the following proficiencies:

1. In at least one team game that can be played in adult life, such as bowling, golf, or softball.

2. In at least two individual sports, such as swimming, hiking, and riding.

3. In ballroom dancing.

4. In at least one manual art or craft, such as silver work, woodwork, weaving, or painting.

5. In at least one card game.

6. In at least one creative art such as poetry, acting, music, painting, interior decorating, etc.

The degree of proficiency could be such as an amateur would need to pursue the activity in adult life.

These activities should not become part of the curriculum. Opportunities, materials, equipment, and instructors should be provided so that each student can fill the graduation requirement. These activities remain extracurricular but nevertheless required.

When the school, through general education and its insistence on a minimum set of recreational skills, has provided a kind of recreational competence, its task is pretty much completed. The only ground on which it can hope that in postschool years people will prefer such activities to attendance at cocktail lounges and watching sports events on television is that we do tend to want to do what we can do pretty well.

The school will be unduly optimistic if it believes that such competence is inevitably followed by use in adult life.[11] For the amusements men adopt as recreation are determined in great part by the company they keep. If our friends or co-workers like to frequent cocktail lounges and play cards, we shall either do likewise or lose our friends. If they are a strenuous crowd athletically inclined, we had better keep in shape for the week-ends we plan to spend with them. With recreational preferences, as with all other preferences, "milieu" education (Chapter 1) is far more potent than schooling, for its lessons are taught incessantly and with the most powerful reinforcement: the approval and disapproval of the people whose good opinion is indispensable to us.

Nevertheless, it is also true that where there is no competence there will certainly be no carry-over into adult life. Hence, the school's responsibility is to *require* such competences, regardless of their subsequent use or non-use. That graduates of our schools do not use what they have learned does not prove that they have not learned it, nor that it ought not to be taught. All it proves is that the milieu into which these graduates were propelled was such as to discourage the use of these learnings, but such a state of affairs is a judgment upon the milieu rather than upon the school.

Perspective in the recreational values

Recreational values can incorporate almost all of the other sorts of value. They do not as a rule give rise to economic values unless one happens to win wagers at cards or at the races. Since the recreational activity is undertaken not for gain but for enjoyment, such economic gains arise incidentally or for the person who professionally provides the means of recreation.

Some kinds of recreation give rise to health values; some destroy or jeopardize them. As to social values, there is less doubt. Recreation is seldom a solitary affair and is one of the best ways of break-

[11] Cf. *Massachusetts Youth Study*, pp. 200 ff.

ing the social ice among strangers. Babies, dogs, and games make formal introductions unnecessary.

A strong school of thought believes that recreation is a great character builder. The playing fields of Eton have been credited with the building of the British Empire. In our own country, team sports are supposed to result in a strong sense of fair play, courage, loyalty, and perseverance. No doubt this is true, although in the nature of the case it would be difficult to prove or disprove such a claim. What the commercialization of high school and college sports does for character has not yet been ascertained.

The high position that commercialized and organized sport enjoys in American culture is perhaps a symptom of our ambivalent attitude toward play. On one hand, a Puritanical strain condemns play as sinful, or at least, as frivolous. On the other hand, the tempo of life is so rapid, competition so keen, that we need large doses of the trivial to relieve it. To regard sport as a serious business—a big industry and its stars national heroes—effects a neat compromise between our play impulses and our play inhibitions, for if play is serious business, it can be neither sinful nor frivolous.

To regard recreation as an opportunity for self-improvement or for the improvement of mankind is to convert play into a duty, and one can hardly be playful about one's duty. On the other hand, the eternal playboy does not carry his share of the load in the social order. Some separation between work and play is needed to preserve the character of each.

Recreation can contribute to the enrichment of aesthetic values and in turn utilize them on its own behalf. Artistic activity can be recreational and vice versa. A similar relation obtains between recreation and the intellectual values, but one is hard put to it to team up recreation and the religious values. When religious institutions carry on a recreational program, it is rarely in the place of worship but in some room separated from it. The gods of the Greeks were playful, but few others in the history of civilization laughed very much.

Yet the intrinsic character of recreation, its playfulness, should not be lost in the good life. For it is a little push of freedom whereby we can hold off actuality and thus be relieved for a moment of its relentless pressure. We need not worry too much about preserving the gravity and seriousness of life; it reminds us soon enough that we can be playful about it only for a short time. Great ideas, like great men, can tolerate the playful touch without losing their greatness. Humor and play wreak havoc only on the absurd, and for this, if for no other reason, they deserve to be the indispensable seasoning to the good life.

The educated man differs from the uncultivated man not so much in the amount of recreation as in the form that it takes. The educated man's recreation is more likely to involve a wider range of values and to reflect his potentialities for enjoyments and for discriminating among them. Above all, he is less likely to confuse the playful with the serious, enjoyment with self-abandonment, and on the whole is less dependent for his recreation on the efforts and resources of others.

Summary

This chapter has examined three classes of values: economic, health, and recreation. With respect to each type of value, we inquired as to its intrinsic and instrumental phase, its relations to other value areas, and the problems it posed for the school.

With respect to each area there is a knowledge or skill element which can be taught, and we found that general education provides for the knowledge and understandings required. On the other hand, the formal school has great difficulty in providing the opportunities for forming and perfecting certain other habits that are required for the achievement of these values.

Finally, with respect to each type of value, we attempted to outline or indicate a perspective from which its relations to other values and to the good life could be viewed.

PROBLEMS FOR DISCUSSION AND RESEARCH

1. Secure copies of a Sunday issue of *The New York Times* or some other large metropolitan newspaper, or copies of weekly magazines such as *Time* or *Newsweek*. Turn to the business and financial sections. How much of them can you understand? How often do you read this sort of material?

2. What do you think of the argument presented on consumer wisdom? Can you make out a case for consumer education as a special course? What form would it take?

3. Organize a debate or panel on some current economic issue. Analyze carefully what educative results accrue from it. If none accrue, why not?

4. Analyze your own perspective on economic, health, and recreational values.

5. Take a biography of some noted American and see if you can extract the value scheme of the man.

6. The treatment given to team sports in this chapter will not satisfy many persons. Construct an argument that would make out a good case for interscholastic athletics.

SUGGESTIONS FOR FURTHER READING

For fuller bibliographical data on the items listed below, consult the General Bibliography.

Brubacher, *Eclectic Philosophy of Education,* Topic 27.
——, *Modern Philosophies of Education,* Chap. 9.
Dewey, *Democracy and Education,* Chaps. 15, 19, 23.
Everett, *Moral Values,* pp. 188–199.
Groos, *The Play of Men.*
Huizinga, *Homo Ludens: A Study of the Play-Element in Culture.*
John Dewey Society: Fifth Yearbook, *Workers Education in the United States,* Chap. 12 and *passim.*
Lehman and Witty, *Psychology of Play Activities, passim.*
Patrick, *The Psychology of Relaxation,* Chap. 2.
Russell, *Education and the Modern World,* Chaps. 10, 11, 13.
Veblen, *Theory of the Leisure Class,* Chap. 14.

8

The Associational Values

Between the birth cry and the death rattle men spend their lives in making demands on and meeting the demands of their fellows. Out of this commerce arise both the positive and negative values of human association. These are so numerous and varied that not even the most minute biography can do justice to all of them in the life of even a single individual. For convenience in discussion, we shall differentiate three types of association.

1. *Affectional associations.* We enter some human relationships for the purposes of getting and giving affection. In these associations we seek what the psychologists call "emotional security," or the assurance that we are loved for ourselves as persons and not merely for what we contribute to others. It is the sort of affection we demand in our infancy and which we dread to lose in later life. (See Chapter 3.) Friendship, parental love, romantic love, and marital love are species of this general type of association.

2. *Status associations.* We join or sometimes find ourselves in groupings that provide prestige for their members. Membership not only in exclusive social clubs, but also in certain social classes, races,

neighborhoods, and societies afford varying degrees of status and prestige.

3. *Functional associations.* Some associations are formed to achieve certain goals. Into some of these associations we are simply born, e.g., the family and the clan. Others we join deliberately: labor unions, consumer co-operatives, political parties, and professional organizations.

Each type of association can serve more than one end. Most of them do. One can love the boss's daughter in all genuineness and improve one's status and economic prospects by marrying her.[1] Nevertheless, it pays to distinguish among them because an association may produce one sort of value and not necessarily produce the others. Marriage may further our economic schemes, or it may not; joining the country club may give us prestige, but it may also interfere with boyhood friendships and economic associations that are incompatible with country clubs.

Further, each type of association makes somewhat different demands upon us and upon education. What it takes to be a good father, a good husband, or a good friend may not be precisely what it takes to be a good lodge member, a good party member, or a member of the 400. It may turn out that the task of education differs with the kind of role and the kind of association we have in mind.

Another reason for making these distinctions is that at least some of our difficulties are explained by the theory that the roles we have to play in various associations conflict. The gentleness of the lover is almost worthless in a political debate; the strong leader of men may be the most inept of fathers. When we use friendship to secure status, we usually destroy the friendship, and when we let friendship influence our roles in business, we may lose the business.

It is a mark of the educated man that he does not confuse the multiple roles he has to play in human associations, and it is the mark of an artistic life that these roles are harmonized. But harmony is not a hash. It is an ordering of elements into a pattern of value. It is a matter of perspective. If, however, the elements are not distinguished, there is nothing to order; we have a hash rather than a pattern.

Values realized in human associations differ also as to the *level* on which we realize them. Friendship is the name for a continuum of

[1] Robert S. Hartman, "Group Membership and Class Membership," *Philosophy and Phenomenological Research,* 13:3, March 1953, pp. 353–369.

feelings that range from casual speaking acquaintance to the almost superhuman passion that Montaigne had in mind.[2] A functional association may range from a simple arrangement to buy coal by the carload to a cartel of cartels. Prestige associations vary from boyhood secret societies to the most exalted ranks of nobility.

These variations give an individual life its unique quality. We all belong to all three types of association; what distinguishes each of us is the precise form this membership assumes and the precise shades of feeling that accompany it.

Affectional Relationships

We do not feel in the presence of our parents as we do in the presence of our child, and neither experience is what we feel in the company of an old and dear friend. As for romantic love, the standard theory is that no other experience is quite like it, and furthermore that no two instances of it are comparable.

Intrinsic and instrumental aspects

Perhaps the immediate quality of these experiences is unique and perhaps not. For one thing, since I can never have your experience, there is no way for directly comparing what you and I experience. In the second place, a feeling cannot be taken out of a person for inspection. Consequently, we cannot assign a name to it that will have a precise meaning. If we could be as precise about our emotional life as we are about the physical world, poets, fiction writers, and artists would be put out of business.

Yet these experiences cannot be completely different because when I say that I am angry, indignant, or pleased, I can be understood, even though the peculiar quality of my anger or indignation may be shared by no one else. This means that whenever we talk about the values arising out of human associations we shall be understood, but the understanding will be confined to the rough identification by the speaker and listener of a class of feelings, e.g., love, hate, anger, and devotion.

In their intrinsic phase the positive affectional values are experienced as valuable on their own account. Our love for an infant is

[2] *The Essays of Montaigne,* translated by E. J. Trechman, pp. 182–195.

what it is. The reflection that such love may spoil him, or that it is a symptom of parental selfishness is another matter and may produce a different feeling. On the other hand, the hatred of our fellows, their cruelty to each other, is immediately felt as evil; the relation of the legal executioner to his victim gives pleasure to nobody, however justified and even beneficial such a relation may be for society.

Can education enlarge the pupil's range of such immediate qualitative experience? In ordinary life the quality of experience is also likely to strike an average until circumstances tumble us into emotional depths we never counted on exploring. Thus most mothers love their children. Yet let a child be kidnapped or lost for several days, and the quality of mother love is so transformed that it can no longer be compared to ordinary mother love.

In other words, human relations are infinitely variable in subtlety and complexity, and the quality of feeling is modified with each variation. Few of us would want to live through some of these variations, yet life becomes superficial unless we can envision and experience levels of friendship, of love, and of family affection that go beyond the routine and the ordinary. How to enable the pupil to extend the range of immediate value possibilities vicariously is, therefore, one problem of education in the social values.

That the affectional values help us to realize other values would seem to need no demonstration, and none will be given. Nevertheless, it may be noted that in affectional relationships we tend to disavow the instrumental aspect. Friends, for example, are useful as well as satisfying, and a good friend offers himself generously for use. Yet let us suspect it was offered to secure some benefit, and the friendship, however beautiful, dies. Men and women often marry for mutual economic benefits, but either would resent a protestation of love as a means of securing such benefits.

The instrumental values of affectional relationships must, therefore, always be kept subordinate to their intrinsic quality or they will not long survive. On the other hand, affectional relations, if they endanger other values, may themselves perish. Thus romantic love, if it causes poverty or loss of status and friends, may fly out the window.

All this being granted, the mighty instrumentality of affectional relations is witnessed by the simple fact that without friends, without love, and without family feeling all the other values are devaluated. What men will do for love they will not do for anything else.

Friendship cannot be completely shut out from money matters, careers, and even affairs of state. A standard objective of college attendance is to acquire useful friendships. It is a rare man who, other things being equal, will not hire a friend rather than a stranger, and it is an even rarer man who can leave friendship out when deciding whether other things really are equal.

Affectional relationships and the school

Why is it that so many adults cannot realize the values of friendship, love, and family? It is hard to be sure whether such inability is really increasing or whether the means of detecting it are improving. But the search for love undoubtedly is the grand quest of our times.

We may classify the factors that stand in the way of satisfying affectional relationships into three sorts:

1. Emotional maladjustment with origins in early childhood or unusual traumatic experiences, that is, people with marked neurotic tendencies.

2. Lack of knowledge or skill, e.g., a boy or girl who does not know how to dress or speak as other adolescents do. Or persons so ignorant about the psychology of human relations that they lose friends and alienate people. Here we may also include lack of self-understanding.

3. Factors that we may call "situational," e.g., very low economic status, unusual demands on one's time or money, such as indigent in-laws and severe and prolonged illness.

If one asks what the role of the school is in satisfactory personal relations, the answer is not simple. This becomes clear when the factors that impede such relations are examined.

1. Take the factors due to emotional maladjustment.[3] It is difficult to see what a school can do in the way of therapy for deep-seated neurotic tendencies except to diagnose the need for it. But it should at least do that.

2. Where affectional relations are impeded by want of self-confidence due to lack of knowledge, skill, and success, the situation is quite different, both theoretically and practically.[4]

[3] For an appreciation of how involved these can get, cf., for example, Mowrer, Learning Theory and Personality Dynamics, Chap. 21.

[4] Thus Mowrer observes: "The acquisition or having of fear depends, it would seem, upon one learning principle, viz., that of conditioning; and the

If we recall that the most general features of the good life are self-determination, self-realization, and self-integration, then it becomes clearer how the school can make its contribution to that power of identification so essential for successful friendship, love, and family life.

To the extent that the habits of acquiring and using knowledge are perfected, the pupil's field of freedom widens, and as it widens, his confidence, sense of power, and sense of adequacy also grow. He feels that he has achieved in proportion to his powers, and that he *merits* the love and esteem of his fellow men as well as his own. He can identify with the Other because he has something of himself to give, and he knows that what he gives of himself is needed by the Other. Without self-determination and self-realization we cannot give ourselves to others because we do not have ourselves to give. He who is not his own master is a poor friend, a distracted lover, and an inadequate parent. But freedom and self-realization together mean self-mastery, the rational self-mastery of the good man. If we cannot give ourselves when we are neither free nor unrealized, neither can we give of ourselves when the Self is torn and divided by conflicting desires and allegiances, that is, when we are not integrated.

General education, therefore, has a great deal to offer to the values of personal relationships, but more through the effects of the total curriculum on self-determination, self-realization, and self-integration rather than through any specific course or courses.

3. Some affectional maladjustments are due to the sheer stress under which individuals find themselves. A student who has to work long and hard to stay in school is cut off from normal avenues to friendships. Poverty can be embittering. Home conditions can be bad enough to becloud every personal relation.

But situational maladjustments are so varied that only individual guidance is of much help. For this reason guidance is indispensable to the school program. Knowledge is always of the general. Situations are particular. Often the connection between them is not obvious—at least not to the pupil. Even group discussions will not always disclose what alternatives are open to me in *my* predicament. Just as knowledge is not always acquired by working out our par-

---

diminution of fear sets the stage for the second form of learning, namely that form which results in the strengthening of overt, problem-solving behavior." *Op. cit.*, p. 587 footnote. Quoted by permission of The Ronald Press Company.

ticular problems, so is knowledge as such not an automatic prescription of what to do in a specific situation.

The virtue of a good guidance program lies in its being concerned with the individual pupil without being personally involved in the student's problem. Such a combination is hard to find. Friends and relatives are *too* interested; outsiders are not interested enough, and neither may have the knowledge or experience of the guidance counselor. (See Chapter 13.)

Pupils as persons

It may well be that the school can contribute most to the success of the pupil in affectional associations by (1) treating each pupil as a valid personality and (2) adjusting the demands of the learning task to what the pupil can reasonably be expected to accomplish.

It is relatively easy for a pupil to become just a name on the records in a large school. If his accomplishments are noteworthy for good or ill, he will be noted, but although this may nurture the feeling of true or false adequacy, it does not nourish the need for being valued for one's self regardless of accomplishment, and that is what emotional security implies.[5]

Although the school cannot substitute for the love of parents, it need not destroy the security that this love has engendered, and it may even counteract to some degree the parents' failure in this respect. But having said this much, it still remains a problem as to how a teacher or a school can manifest a genuine concern for large numbers of individual pupils.

Every ingenious scheme for insuring such concern is undercut by the fact that it is recognized for what it is—a scheme. Nor is it possible in picking a school staff to be sure that every member will really care about individuals, especially the mediocre and troublesome ones.

On the elementary level this factor, commonly referred to as the "love of children," is recognized as indispensable for the teacher. Indeed some think this factor to be so important that they are willing to sacrifice intellectual competence in its favor. Needless to say, it would be fine for the elementary teacher to have both, but if one

---

[5] Following the distinction between security and adequacy made by J. S. Plant in *Personality and the Culture Pattern.*

had to settle for one or the other, it would be hard not to plump for the "love of children."

At the secondary level concern for individual pupils is more dif ficult to guarantee. In the first place, adolescents are harder to love than little tykes whose nuisance powers can more easily be forgiven. Second, high school teachers have to be concerned more directly with subject matter, and finally, the affectional needs of adolescents are much more complex than those of elementary school children. The conviction that his problems are of concern to the school can be conveyed to every pupil by the simple fact of *being* so concerned. There are two respects in which the school can do this:

1. With respect to situational maladjustments, the guidance counselor is the school's instrument for showing its concern.

2. The school is committed to helping each individual realize *his* potentialities—not those of the class. This means that *ipso facto* it *has* to be concerned with Selves or individuals. However, the concern is not a love relation between teacher and pupil. On the contrary, the school *demands* from the pupil that he live up to *his* potentialities and will take no less. Isn't this the highest tribute we can pay to anyone? Is there any more genuine way to acknowledge a pupil's personality, his validity, his worth?

The school can be frustrating to many of its pupils. It can become the place where one will fail, be ridiculed, punished, or humiliated. The school is then perceived as hostile, threatening, and even malignant, and when so perceived, the pupil is better off somewhere else —a state of affairs that he tries to bring about as quickly as possible.

This is not, however, an endorsement of the principle that no pupil must fail in schoolwork, or that he must never be in competition with others. No one, and certainly not the pupil, is really fooled by the subterfuges of schools that try to follow this principle.[6]

Security through confidence

Real emotional security is built up when the pupil realizes that the task assigned to him is not beyond his powers. If teachers take the trouble to discover the learning potential of the pupil and to translate the learning demand to a level not beyond his capacity, then failure is not inevitable, and success is genuine. It does not take

[6] Cf. Woodruff, *The Psychology of Teaching*, Chap. 27.

too many instances of success following effort and persistence to convince the pupil that effort and persistence will bring success in the future, and this is also a form of emotional security.

Nor need the successes so induced be wholly relative to the individual and spurious when compared to those of the other members of the class. Fortunately, the distribution of talents within individuals is uneven enough so that in most cases good diagnosis of such talents discloses a possibility for genuine success in some area of school work. But it is important that when such a possibility is discovered, e.g., in history or dramatics, the individual be pushed to the point where his achievement really approaches excellence.

It will be objected that this method of insuring emotional security is really a method of achieving adequacy. This is true. Adequacy is not the same as security. To be loved for what one has accomplished is not to be loved for oneself. At best adequacy prevents unnecessary insecurity, but such prevention is a legitimate and not an impossible goal for the school, whereas the promise of positive affectional security for each pupil by educational theorists borders on the irresponsible.

No device and no methodology can prevent all children from disliking school, but no child should dislike school because he fears its demands upon him, and no child should ever be bored by school because it does not stretch his intellectual powers to the limit. These are educational sins for which there is little chance of redemption.

Status Associations

High status with our fellows is a most seductive social value. Where status is a reward for achievement, it is proof to the individual that he can properly justify the esteem in which he holds himself. This is eminently satisfying—so much so that we can almost call the desire for such esteem a universal motive.

Achievement and nonachievement status

Medals for heroism, prizes for achievement in any field, and election to honorary societies are symbols of high status. Important positions in the life of the community are also proofs of status by achievement. It is hard to find fault with these status satisfactions and symbols except that they may reflect a yearning for something beyond the achievement itself.

But achievement or not, status men must have.[7] They must convince themselves and others that they have some superiority that raises them above the herd, or at least above some part of it. One method is to select a distinctive characteristic and to make this a sign of superiority. If one is born with a white skin, or yellow skin, or a purple one for that matter, one can invent a theory to connect skin color with high virtue and noble character. If the distinctive characteristic is inherited wealth or distinguished forbears, it is rather easy to become convinced that these are marks of achievement or worth because these fortunate accidents do confer prestige.

If none of these is available for high status, it may be possible to join exclusive clubs, secret societies, and cults of various sorts. Automatically one becomes superior to the excluded ones. A rigid code of belief and behavior will differentiate the members of the group from the nonmembers. A peculiar set of manners, clothing, and insignia will also help to mark them off from the excluded ones. The efforts of the members must be directed to the maintenance of this code rather than to any achievement since their status does not depend on achievement.

One difficulty with such groups is that they form tight enclaves within a larger society. Depending on their size and power, such groups can become parasites on the body politic, irritants, or even dangers.

The problem of status association not based on any demonstrable achievement touches the school in two ways. Directly, schools face the problem of exclusive cliques and clubs on their premises or operating under their auspices. Clearly an institution devoted to the achievement of individuals has no room for associations not based on achievement. But there is an even more fundamental objection to such groups, in that they offer a temptation to substitute status for achievement.

It is argued that people with the same interests ought to associate, and that democracy does not imply that we must invite the total electorate to dinner. The answer to this is that people of like interests ought to associate and no doubt will. Interest associations, however, are not established merely to raise status. They do not need artificial barriers to exclude the non-interested. People not interested

[7] Cf. Murray, *Explorations in Personality*, p. 150.

in photography will not press for membership in camera clubs. One does not have to write into the charters of philosophy, literature, or art clubs that the members must be interested in these subjects. One would merely laugh at a college fraternity restricted to choice souls who are addicted to daily cold showers, but a fraternity that maintains its prestige by exclusion of people on account of race, color, creed, nationality, or income should at least be clear about what it is doing and honest enough not to invent pious and noble reasons for this exclusion.

There is a broader and more general way in which this problem touches the school. General education ought to teach about the nature of such status associations and their role in the development of personality. However, the pyschological needs that drive men into such associations have their origin and reinforcement in circumstances that are rarely within the control of the school. The more the school can contribute to the competence of men, the more will it make the psychological crutches of artificial status associations unnecessary.

Functional Associations

Let us call "functional" those groups formed for the purpose of accomplishing some objective collectively. A baseball team, an association of manufacturers, a political party, a labor union, a league to fight vivisection, and a league of nations are all examples of functional associations. We shall confine our discussion to groups formed to achieve *economic* and *political* objectives because, as we have already noted, without the transformation of material goods and their utilization, no life is possible, and without political activity, no social order would be possible.

There is another reason why in our time these types of groupings are strategic. It stems from the fact that within the last century production of goods has taken on the form of large scale machine industry. This transformation has had a powerful impact on every facet of our lives—from child care to politics. It has created new problems for living and education that grow more acute with each decade.

Consider some of the features of large-scale machine industry that have given rise to these difficulties.

The web of economic interdependence

To operate a modern steel or automobile industry requires, first of all, huge concentrations of money. It takes a great deal of money to construct the buildings, build the machinery, and hire the help before even one unit is turned out for sale. Because large numbers of automobiles are to be constructed simultaneously, the parts needed for all the units under construction must be ready and waiting for the assembler. Given parts must be almost exactly alike because they have to be interchangeable. This means high precision machines and tools. Once the unit is put on the assembly line, every part and every workman must be ready at the right time and at the right place. This requires the planning of every motion and every turn of a screw. A strike in a little plant supplying any part of the automobile stops the whole assembly line. The process demands complete co-ordination of workers, machines, materials, subcontractors, suppliers of raw materials, etc. Karl Marx characterized this complex adjustment of large scale machine industry as the "socialization of production."[8] Not only must workers co-operate, but there must be managers to co-ordinate workers, materials, and machines.

In addition to co-operation and co-ordination within the factory itself, there must be co-operation from and co-ordination with allied industries. For automobiles, such industries as steel, rubber, glass, textile, radio, and many others have to be entangled in the web of interdependence.

There is no point in turning out 10 million automobiles a year unless people will buy them. By turning out 10 million cars, the industry can lower the price, so that 10 million people can afford to purchase them. But if too many people lose their jobs, or if food, clothing, and shelter cost too much, they may not buy the automobiles, albeit for the American public the automobile plays the role of a household god. So the automobile industry demands co-operation from the economy of the whole nation: that the farmers sell their crops, the workers get their wages, investors put up their money, and that other industries lower their prices.

But we have not finished with the business. To run a high speed, mass production, industrial system requires materials from other countries, and it may require foreign markets to soak up the items

---

[8] Cf. *Capital and Other Writings*, Chap. 9.

that cannot be sold profitably at home. If other countries are also becoming industrialized and are also out after raw materials and markets, there will be competition among nations and such competition may turn into war. All of which means that large scale industrialization demands for its very existence co-operation and co-ordination not only within the smallest unit, but among all producers and consumers. The world is the smallest unit of large scale machine industry.

Impact upon the social order and the individual

This demand for global co-operation and co-ordination is unprecedented in world history. When production was carried on by the individual farmer and craftsman, it was a virtue for each man to mind his own business. Even when we entered the manufacturing stage, each little factory was a more or less independent unit with co-operation within the unit, but with only loose connection to other units. In such modes of production, the doctrine of free enterprises competing in a free market was more or less a true picture of affairs. The "laws" of supply and demand regulated prices, wages, and all other variables relevant to the enterprise. Each businessman and each worker was theoretically a free agent—free to buy what he wished from whom he chose, to sell his services on whatever terms he could make.[9]

What we have not yet fully understood is that large scale machine industry is not simply factories grown bigger. It is a change in the very quality of the way goods are made and distributed. What is new is the amount and extent of interdependence that it makes *indispensable* to the operation of the whole system. For it is just that—a vast logical and technological system that can exist only by growing and can grow only by absorbing within itself every phase of life. Sooner or later it affects churches, families, books, pictures, love, and crime.

Old laws crack under the requirements of the system. What does negligence mean when a corporation is alleged to have committed it? What do the anti-trust laws mean when the system demands larger and larger units of production and distribution? What does ownership mean when a million people own shares of a corporation?

[9] Actually power has rarely been distributed so evenly that enterprise was, strictly speaking, really free or the rules of competition really fair.

What kind of family shall we have if the system demands that wives work at gainful occupations? What are the masculine and feminine roles in American life today? Is it masculine to wash dishes and diapers? Is it feminine to drive taxicabs and to operate lathes? What is chastity to mean in an age when women can be economically independent of marriage and technologically free of pregnancy? These are just a few examples of the way in which the economic mode of production makes its impact felt even on the most established *mores* and institutions.

The social order is troubled because the concepts and values on which it was founded no longer fit the conditions in which they have to operate. They carry on but with a grinding sound that signifies dislocation and conflict. The times cry out for a reconstruction of these concepts; it is a call for new meanings.

There is also another kind of impact. As we watch the social scene we note that clusters of men are uniting in labor unions, manufacturing associations, farmers' groups, small business groups, advertising groups, and professional groups. Each group is concerned with furthering its own economic welfare or protecting what welfare it has managed to secure. We see these groups making their appeals to government for laws that will change or preserve certain economic arrangements. Sometimes they are organized into political groups or blocs.

But the system demands co-ordination. Various schemes for total co-ordination make their bid for power.[10] The corporate state is one.[11] Various types of socialism and government control also make their bids. The dictatorship of the proletariat is still another bid. Civil war breaks out when a bid for power encounters sufficient opposition within the nation, but because so few interests are merely national, the chances of confining war within national boundaries are small.

Impact on the individual

The persons within the society are like passengers on a huge liner. They seem to be moving in all directions on the ship, but obviously the ship itself is carrying them in only one direction.

1. The individual finds he is no longer a self-sufficient independent

[10] Cf Mannheim, *Man and Society in an Age of Reconstruction*, pp. 155 ff.
[11] Cf. "The Political Doctrine of Fascism," Alfredo Rocco in Wagner's *Social Reformers*, pp. 643–666.

economic unit. He has to unite with others into groups or blocs working for the welfare of a certain segment of the economic system. The individual realizes that he can have economic and political power only through groups. These groups may not be the "classes" of Marx, but groups they are nevertheless.

2. The individual finds inside himself a replica of the value conflicts in the social order. His family life is different from that of his parents. Certain values he was taught to cherish as a child are no longer cherished by his children. The old books, the old moralities, the old ideals assume an air of unreality in the new system. Thrift, honesty, honor, duty—what do they mean today? The job of integrating his life becomes harder. The sand in the gears of institutions trickles down into his own life, so that although each part of his life makes sense, his whole life does not.

3. Finally, the individual feels his individuality slipping away from him. What he does in the whole system *does* make a difference, but it is hard for him to see *what* difference it makes. What he does can be done equally well by almost anyone else, unless he is one of the small minority who by virtue of great technological skill or managerial ability attains to a more strategic position in the system. He is free only in trivial matters; the important ones seem to be decided by the system.

But status he must have, and some prestige he must have, and security he must have. So he lends an ear to promises of status and security. National exclusiveness, social exclusiveness, blood exclusiveness, religious exclusiveness, imagined superiorities of all sorts, and status associations of all sorts become appealing. He turns to all kinds of devices to guarantee love. Alcohol, crime, violence, promiscuity, distractions—all promise relief from personal insignificance.[12]

This then is a schematic picture of our times. It has an air of desperateness, of crisis, and of lostness. Yet over all is also an air of frustrated bitterness that comes with the realization that somehow this giant of machine industry could be harnessed for a better life if—if only the right kind of functional association could be found to manage it.[13]

[12] A literary generation since World War II has tried to give expression to this mood and Existentialism makes this situation its starting point.
[13] Cf. Gerald Piel, "Human Want is Obsolete," *The Saturday Review*, June 27, 1953, p. 9.

The Democratic Dream

Is there any form of human association that could give some hope of a life of self-determination, self-realization, and self-integration in a complex machine civilization? Can there be the required co-ordination without tyranny? Can there be the required co-operation without coercion? Can there be both co-operation and co-ordination without the destruction of individuality?

We have elsewhere (Chapter 4) touched upon democracy and the social order. Here we have to examine the question more closely.

Historical democracy

On one meaning, democracy is the name of one form of political organization. It is characterized by the supposition that the ultimate sovereignty resides in the mass of the people. Unlike an aristocracy, in which decisions are made by an elite, or a tyranny, in which they are made by an individual, democracy is an arrangement whereby decisions are made by the people. What the Common Good is to be and how it is to be carried out depends on the will of the people.

It is assumed that each individual knows his own interests and will naturally look after them. When the people speak, therefore, their voice represents the greatest interest of the greatest number. There is no logical restraint upon the will of the people. It can decide to restrain itself by law, or it can decide not to be restrained by the laws it has made. It can be represented by kings or parliaments, one legislative body, two, or a half dozen.

Democracy has been, therefore, a protest against tyranny and against aristocracy. When it asserted liberty, equality, and fraternity as its triad of fundamental values, these terms had a definite meaning. Liberty meant freedom from the tyrant's intrusions on personal action and especially from slavery. It also meant freedom from foreign domination. The meaning of liberty depends on which tyrant is to be deposed and for whose benefit. People have spilled their blood for personal liberties only to discover that they were fighting for the liberty of domestic tyrants from the domination of foreign ones.

Equality meant that all votes should count equally, that the law should make no distinction among persons, and that no arbitrary obstacles to opportunity should be imposed by the tyrant or by the aristocracy. Fraternity meant a natural sympathy for the other man— a sympathy such as the tyrant or the elite could not or would not feel for the common man. It meant the taking into consideration of the human qualities of each man when decisions were made. These meanings still reverberate in our own thinking about democracy, and our founding fathers certainly had something of this sort in mind. The foe was tyranny; the defense was democracy or some variant of it.

So long as the industrial system had not established its sway over the civilized world, these meanings were clear and roughly cor- responded to social reality. They helped to develop the technology and conditions for the birth of the industrial system itself. The kind of freedom, equality, and fraternity we had in mind was precisely what a young expanding world needed. As a defense against despot- ism, as a defense against the dominance of an elite of any sort, it was and is an unexcelled formula.

The new democracy

Can these meanings of democracy defend us against the tyranny of a system that has a logic and dynamism of its own?

The amount of co-operation and co-ordination needed to maintain the economies of the 18th and 19th centuries was relatively small. A tolerably free market, and as Mannheim has pointed out, trial and error kept the economy more or less in balance.[14] This situation no longer exists.

1. The Common Good can no longer be ascertained by the people assembling in the market place, or in town meeting, or even in legislative bodies. The truth is that no one probably knows enough to say at any moment what would make the system work best. Certainly the ordinary layman cannot.

2. Nor is it possible to be sure that each man knows what his *own* interest really is. Is it to my interest to have the stock market rigidly controlled or not? Is it to my interest as a government em- ployee to have taxes raised or the government payroll cut? Is it to my interest to have corporations make large profits or not? Is it to my interest to have the testing of atomic weapons stopped? I do not

[14] Mannheim, *loc. cit.*

know. I might gladly vote for my selfish interests—if I knew what they were.

3. Simple sympathy for the sufferings of my fellow man is not enough either. My sympathy for beggars leads me to give them charity. Would it be better if I did not, and rather worked to rehabilitate them? My sympathy for the farmer leads me to favor planting controls so that the market will not be glutted, but is there any logic in an economy of scarcity? Furthermore, every man is now my fellow man—not merely a few in my own home town; not even the millions in my own country.

4. Finally, we cannot afford to let the competing economic groups just fight it out at the elections and hope that somehow everything will balance itself out. The system's logic will not permit it; without co-operation and co-ordination it collapses.

We come to the conclusion that just as the system is a qualitatively new mode of production, so must democracy be a new kind of democracy to deal with it. It cannot be merely a defense against tyranny or elites. It has to be a positive control of the system itself, but the control must be in the hands of the people. Let us see what this would mean.

1. It calls for an electorate that can search for the Common Good through knowledge. Otherwise, it is at the mercy of experts, bureaucracies, and powerful groups who can control the mass media of communication.

2. It calls for an electorate that is thoroughly and almost unanimously committed to a set of values that will furnish criteria for controlling the decisions it makes about the system. Self-determination, self-realization, and self-integration might very well be the new triad. Freedom now means not only freedom from arbitrary restraints on personal initiative, but in addition it is the freedom to know and to determine one's decisions by knowledge. When any decision confronting the group demands as its price the cutting off of any individual from rational self-determination, that decision had better not be made. For the system itself is rational and our control of it must also be rational.

3. What shall equality mean in the new democracy? One man, one vote, of course. That is its minimum meaning. Does it mean equality of opportunity to get ahead in the world without arbitrary restrictions of race, creed, and color? That is still within the minimum limits. We need more than that. It is not enough to remove arbitrary

obstacles to education and the employment of talent. We have to take positive steps to see to it that talents everywhere are maximally developed. Self-realization is a duty, not a privilege.

4. What shall fraternity mean? Sympathy for our fellow man, but a sympathy that is based on an understanding of the common manhood of all mankind, of their common nature, their common problems, and their common destiny in the new world. It is the respect for the universal claim of all men for self-determination, self-realization, and self-integration. It is such fraternity that becomes self-integration, which heals the wounds of lostness, of slipping individuality, of nonentity.

The new meanings of democracy, it turns out, hinge on the positive claims of the individual to the good life by which all functional associations are ultimately to be judged. On what philosophical grounds can such claims be asserted?

Arguments for individuality

First, we may argue that progress demands variation. Individuals may be likened to the small differences that the microphone impresses on the massive uniformity of a carrier wave in radio broadcasting. Without the strength of the carrier wave, the minute variations of the microphone would be immediately dissipated; without the variations, the carrier wave would only emit a uniform hum.

Second, even in a collectivized social order leaders are needed, and unless leadership is simply to reflect the existing state of affairs, it will have to risk some deviation from group norms. That this is risky is witnessed by the fate of leaders in totalitarian states where the hero of today may be the traitor of tomorrow.

Finally, there is the argument that the shrinking of individuality makes one wonder what the purpose of life is anyway. In Chapter 3 we tried to show that the good life is to be measured by self-determination, self-realization, and self-integration, but without individuality what meaning can we give to selfness?

Logically, it is not hard to make out a case for individuality. The facts, however, do not always consult logic, and the facts are—as was indicated earlier in this chapter—not favorable to individuality. On the other hand, if single individuals are shrinking in significance, economic groupings and political groupings are not. They are becoming the real units of interaction on the social scene, and if the individual is in real danger of becoming obliterated by the mass, so is the Common Good in danger of being forgotten by the tight pressure groups that seem to have concentrated all individuality within themselves.

The truth is that once we have granted that the Common Good is prior to the individual good and takes precedence over it, there is no logical point at which we can reverse the course. There is no logical point at which the individual can claim a priority over the welfare of the group, or what it happens to think is its welfare. Larger groups can coerce the smaller ones, and there may be one that can coerce all the others.

If the educator expects to justify the claims of any individual in such conflict, he either has to invoke a natural or supernatural law that is superior to all groupings, or he has to make the individual human personality his ultimate unit of reality and value and endow it with inalienable rights and claims that no body politic can legislate away. It was a set of such rights—the Bill of Rights—that our forefathers with commendable haste tacked onto our Constitution, lest the state which they had created swallow up the individuals for whom they had created it.

How can we assert this ultimate worth of the individual? We could do so on a religious base. If we hold that man is in relation to a Divine being, and that this relation is a personal one—a transaction between God and individual man—then man's worth is immediately vouched for by God's relation to him.

Or we could assert it on the grounds of man's rationality, as Kant did. Since man by virtue of his rational powers can become a moral legislator for the universe (Act only on that maxim of which thou canst will at the same time that it should become a universal law[15]), he alone can have a good will which is good without qualification.

Or we can argue that the nature of all reality is "person-like" or is to some extent an example or a product of mind. Such an Idealistic thesis makes the individual man a living embodiment of the fundamental structure of the universe itself.[16]

There are educators who sincerely and honestly assert the importance of the human personality without having recourse to any

[15] Immanuel Kant, *Fundamental Principles of the Metaphysics of Ethics,* translated by Thomas K. Abbott, New York: Longmans, Green and Company, 1947, p. 46.
[16] Cf. Hocking, *Types of Philosophy,* Chap. 23.

of these arguments. They deny all absolutes and ultimates; they shudder at the word "metaphysics." How they do validate their belief in the worth of the individual is, accordingly, somewhat difficult to say.

Similarly, if one insists that the individual is a product of his culture with every shred of him from toenail to aspirations simply a reflection of the group mind, then it is hard to make out a case for his freedom, his rationality, his creativity, and his ultimate importance. In hastening to throw out the bathwater of laissez-faire individualism, the individual himself can be tossed out too.

Freedom, rationality, and creativity are meaningless words when applied to physical entities. Only individuals with the power of dealing with symbols and ideas can be free, rational, or creative. Only individuals can interact with objects so that value experience comes into being. Every human individual is thus a creator of value experience and is not substitutable. If I enjoy a sunset which you do not see, a value possibility is forever destroyed. To say that value experience is important is merely to repeat what the word "value" means. If everything men do is for the sake of value experience, then the human individual is the ultimate value. There comes a time when it is irrelevant to ask what a man is "good for." Value experience is its own excuse for being. The fact that persons exist imposes on every person this "categorical imperative":

"So act as to treat humanity, whether in thine own person or in any other, in every case as an end withal, never as means only."[17]

This is a metaphysical principle. It can never be derived from science, natural or social. A philosophy that asserts the importance of personality and at the same time denies metaphysical principles is either naive or unconscious of what it is doing. Without such a principle there is no defense against group decision. It alone limits what may be done in the name of the Common Good.

The School and Democracy

The qualifications for the citizen in the new democracy are exacting. Many social theorists including Plato, Pareto, and Sumner have felt that it was an impossible order, and that a society would be lucky if a small elite could acquire these virtues. Plato counseled

[17] Kant, *op. cit.*, p. 5€.

the taking away of private families and private property from the guardians as well as a fantastically rigid education to insure even a handful of men who could be philosopher kings. What chance is there, then, of turning vast populations into philosopher kings? At this point eyes turn naturally to the educator, for in large part the answer lies with him.

The educator will think of this assignment in terms of curriculum, organization, and methodology within a school system. If we analyze the assignment, it breaks up fairly naturally into two major kinds of school outcomes. We shall call these cognitive and attitudinal.

If the new democracy means the common search for the Common Good, then it calls for (1) the ability to carry on the search itself, and (2) the disposition to undertake and sustain it in all relevant situations. The techniques of the search we may call cognitive, the dispositions attitudinal.

The cognitive phase

Take any of the recurring social controversies. Shall we have a system of socialized medicine? Shall the public lands be turned over to private interests for development? Shall we make our peace with Communism or fight it out? Shall the United States trim her sovereignty by joining world or regional organizations? Shall the rights and powers of labor unions be augmented or reduced? Shall legislative bodies have the right to probe into the political affiliations of college professors?

In these controversies there are differences of belief about what *is* the case and what *ought* to be the case. When the controversy seems to be getting nowhere even after long discussion, we can suspect that there exists a difference in such fundamental matters as epistemology and metaphysics. (See Chapter 1.)

1. The first phase of any social problem is to check the beliefs of the disputants about what the facts of the situation are. In school the pupils themselves are the disputants who may mirror the conflicting views found in the press, books, and magazines.

With respect to socialized medicine, for example, the costs of medical care, the number of doctors available in various regions, incomes of doctors, fees charged, hospital charges, loss of wages due to illness, and standards of medical practice are all matters on which, theoretically at least, there is or could be factual information.

Unless there are unresolvable disagreements about the facts in the case, the first phase of the inquiry ends with the establishment of what seems to be the true beliefs about the controversial situation. Some problems will probably get no further, some may not even get that far, but this is the necessary first phase.

2. Simply correcting beliefs about the facts may shift some combatants from one side to the other. A boy who opposed socialized medicine because he believed that anyone could get all the medical care he needed might feel differently if the facts were shown to prove otherwise. The shift would be quite probable if he were concerned chiefly about adequate medical care for the public. Suppose, however, an uncle whom he greatly admires is opposed to socialized medicine; facts may not change his mind or his heart so readily.

In any controversial issue there are usually three groups involved. At each extreme is a small group with strong views. In the middle is a large group that is interested but not violently so. The extreme groups have more than an interest—they have a vested interest. The outcome will directly affect their income, their status, or their value schema. The middle group is most amenable to argument based on facts and information, and because it often decides matters at election time, it is never time wasted to educate this group on any social issue. Since the voter can only vote on one side or the other, there arises the illusion that the whole population is divided into two warring camps. On the contrary, the hope of democratic process lies precisely in the probability that a very large segment of the population is not *vitally* interested in any given issue. It is hard to make converts among vitally interested partisans. Where there is a genuine political interest (and not merely an emotional one), there reason and argument have their most hopeful prospects.

The second phase of the investigation is to determine what values the extremists are defending in the controversy and the beliefs on which they are based. Since the first phase of inquiry discloses some approximation to the real state of affairs, this phase is an opportunity to detect fallacies and rationalizations as well as the motives that are operating on both sides. Only a set of concepts and relationships mastered in the various areas of knowledge prevents this phase from becoming an incoherent verbal melée.

3. Phases one and two should clarify the controversy, but they may also sharpen it. For example, some may feel that socialized medicine will destroy the practice of medicine as a profession. Others will argue that the health of the nation is more important than the status of any profession. I doubt that a high school or college class will resolve this value impasse. It can, however, reflect on what each view will mean for self-determination, self-realization, and self-integration. Philosophy, psychology, literature, and art can contribute something here by way of content, so that even this abstract phase of the investigation need not take place in a conceptual vacuum.

4. In some problems there can be a fourth phase, namely, the projection of possible solutions. This phase will not get very far in complex problems. Nevertheless, projections of solutions are important practice in creative thinking and should not be curtailed merely because they lack utility. After all, it is somebody's creative imagination that may save us all some day.

Thus far we have been discussing the intellectual aspects of dealing with social issues in the school. The view here espoused believes that the study of subject matter, however generalized, will not automatically make itself relevant to any concrete social problem. All knowledge can do is to enable us to structure problems correctly and to deal with them systematically and cogently. The specific studies of actual current social problems cannot be dispensed with, but they are neither "palaver" sessions nor action groups. (See Chapter 13.)

The attitudinal aspect

The democratic man automatically *feels* that in any social matter all concerned with the outcome *ought* to be consulted. It is a sign of democratic growth when the individual feels this way without thinking about it, just as it is a mark of growth in etiquette when one no longer has to figure out which utensil to use for peas.

The democratic man feels that he *ought* to contribute something to group deliberation and decision. Our people are not always too mature in this phase of democracy. In every gathering there are the "passives" who tolerate and even enjoy the exertions of the "articulates." Clearly, this is not compatible with the democratic process. The individual should feel the compulsion to make his contribution and feel guilty if he does not.

The democratic man expects as a matter of course that the group will modify his own wishes and is not emotionally shattered when this happens. There is a sense in which prosperous democratic procedures demand that participants desensitize their egos. It is extraordinarily difficult to persuade people that failure to sway a group or to win an election is not a deliberate attack on their egos. Of course, sometimes it is just that, but not nearly so often as is imagined.

The attention that students of group dynamics are paying to this aspect of group participation is of the greatest practical importance for both school and society. For until participants form this attitude or take this psychical stance, group discussion is as likely to be an arena for the battle of egos as a search for the Common Good. Perhaps there is something to be said for problems courses in which the students are not vitally interested in the matters at issue, for then egos suffer less damage from criticism, difference in opinion, and parliamentary defeats.

Finally, the democratic man, as a matter of habit, is loyal to the rules of the group game. It never occurs to him to ask for a change in the rules in the middle of the game.

These characteristics of the democratic man are attitudes and not matters of truth or argument, even though one can argue that these are good attitudes. A problems course properly conducted over four to six years of the pupil's life should reinforce these attitudes. (See Chapter 13.) They should become a tradition of the school to be absorbed almost unconsciously by faculty and students. They should become part of the *mores* of the school, with no particular surprise manifested when they are present and general disapproval when they are not.

Naturally, if a school does not exemplify these attitudes at every turn in its own conduct and management, they will not become traditional; they will not be contagious, and nobody will catch them. The ticklish point here, of course, is whether a school can be democratic without allowing pupils to make all of the decisions that in any way affect them.

This is an old problem. However, there is a principle that can help us to decide when democratic procedures are in order and when they are not. It is the principle of responsibility. Democratic procedure makes no sense if the participants in a decision have no responsibility for its consequences—especially when the consequences fail to turn out happily.

If a class can take financial responsibility for its dances, it should have a voice—perhaps the whole voice—in deciding how expensive an orchestra it will hire, what the favors shall be, etc. But if it cannot meet an unexpected deficit, the responsible parties cannot abdicate the decision to the class.

Suppose we leave the matter of curriculum to the pupils. Either we really let them decide or we only make believe we do. If the former, who is responsible for wrong choices, choices that are later regretted by the choosers themselves? Can they repair any damage that may result from their decisions? If we only pretend they are choosing while making the decision ourselves, we have to justify a bogus democratic procedure.

Whenever students and faculty are in a position to take genuine responsibility, there is no limitation on the democratic procedure; indeed, there is no logical or ethical escape from it. Power without responsibility is dangerous; responsibility without power is even worse; it is administrative sadism. If we really feel that a group can decide a given matter, then let us not overrule it whatever the consequences may be. If we are apprehensive about the possible consequences, then let us make the decisions ourselves. Honesty in these matters pays.

In each of the preceding examples, responsibility is given the meaning of "making good" the damage caused by one's actions. In current literature the usual meaning of responsibility is a subjective feeling of obligation to carry out a task or to feel repentant if one fails to do so. But social responsibility needs a more objective meaning if we are to talk meaningfully about it in education. Regret and good intentions are necessary conditions for responsible action, but not sufficient conditions. A man is financially responsible if he can command enough money to pay his debts, not merely if he means to and tries hard to do so.

On the meaning suggested, a person cannot be responsible for actions over which he has insufficient control. A child without money cannot take the responsibility for property damage; one with a childish mind cannot take responsibility for his own safety or that of others. Education for responsibility, therefore, means little until the power of the child to carry out his commitments is adequate to these commitments.

Finally, ritual and ceremony underscore the high points of social life. They formalize behaviors that symbolize what the group regards as significant. Birth, marriage, death, and victory are almost always ceremonialized. If we regard democratic behaviors as important, they should become ceremonialized. This has not happened.

We have no colorful ceremonies such as the coronations and royal funerals of England. Even our presidential inaugurations are ceremonially not very impressive. And although we make so much of voting, millions of our young citizens reach voting age each year without the community taking much notice of it.

There is no more emphatic "taking for granted" than is exemplified in ceremony and ritual, for what is so ritualized is unquestioned and almost unquestionable. The content of the democratic procedure is not a matter of ritual or tradition; it is deliberative and rational. The democratic attitudes, on the other hand, although modifiable by thought and knowledge, are relatively constant and are properly produced and reinforced by conditioning, ceremony, and ritual.

Education of this sort will slowly, almost imperceptibly, permeate the mass media as, for example, the concepts of mental health and physical health have done. Here and there a set of parents will bring up a child differently because of it. Here and there a group will think differently about an economic problem because of it. Here and there a picture will be bought, a book read, a piece of music listened to because of it. The net results for each generation will be reduced by the fact that the older generations will dilute them and even distort them. But there will be a net gain—and this gain will be measured entirely by the psychological climate of the home, the press, the radio, theatre, television, and the community at large. It is this climate that will change the conditioning pattern of the coming generation—not very much to be sure, but a change, nevertheless.

It will take generations before a gain large enough to impress the historian will be perceptible. It may be, of course, that catastrophe will break off this slow process, but neither the slowness of the process nor the prospect of catastrophe should interfere with the school's performance of its function.

Education for democracy is enormously complicated by the conflicting demands of our culture. On one hand, maintenance of our interdependent industrial complex society demands an elite of intellectuals—small in number but great in power. Perhaps our survival demands it too. Since the rise of Sputnik, we have been acutely nervous lest our scientific elite fall behind that of Russia. The cry has resounded that American schools had better forget equality of educational opportunity and get busy exploiting the talents of the gifted.

On the other hand, the new democracy demands an unusually high order of general education for all our citizens or the elites may give us a world not worth living in, because scientific and technical elites are not necessarily moral elites or even human elites. We depend on the few, but we also depend on the many.

If we take these two demands seriously, then the new democracy is not the glorification of the lowest common denominator. Rather, education for democracy is a call to abolish the mediocre in favor of high grade individuals.[18] The new age will, therefore, not be the age of the Common Man, but the age of the Common Good sought by uncommonly enlightened men.

Summary

We have distinguished three major types of association—affectional, status, functional—for the purpose of seeing how the school can contribute to realizing each type of associational value.

In affectional associations the problem of the school is to remove insecurity by building up adequacy, and it was suggested that one way of respecting the personality of each pupil was to demand that he achieve what we are quite sure he can achieve.

In status associations the school faces the general problem of nonachievement status groups, and it was concluded that although the school cannot tolerate such groups, its major contribution is the promotion of real achievement so that artificial status becomes unnecessary.

With respect to functional associations, what large scale machine industry has done to the historical meanings of democracy was examined. We then tried to redefine these meanings for the new democracy. Finally, we tried to indicate how the cognitive and attitudinal aspects of citizenship education for such a democracy could be carried on in the school.

[18] "To be a democracy . . . implies a continuous redistribution of power and privilege in the direction of a greater participation by the masses of the people. It also implies that the people, enjoying a greater power and privilege, shall cease to be masses." Ralph B. Perry, "The Meaning of Morale," *The Educational Record*, 22: p. 460, July, 1941.

PROBLEMS FOR DISCUSSION AND RESEARCH

1. Analyze your community to see whether you can find associations to correspond to the types listed in this chapter. Are there any pure examples of each type?

2. Analyze some of the associations to which you belong and the values secured from each.

3. Does your school have the three types of association discussed in this chapter?

4. Is this chapter too pessimistic about individuality in a complex industrial civilization? Does such a civilization create more possibilities of choice than it destroys? Develop a panel on these lines.

5. Can a rationally-planned economy be compatible with democracy? Is democracy possible in our time without such planning?

6. On Topic 5 read in particular the section by Alfredo Rocco in *Social Reformers* by Alfred Wagner, pp. 643–663, and some of Mannheim's *Man and Society in an Age of Reconstruction.*

7. Analyze the extent to which ritual and ceremony are used in your school. What values do they tend to emphasize? How effectively?

SUGGESTIONS FOR FURTHER READING

For fuller bibliographical data on the items listed below, consult the General Bibliography.

There is no end of general literature on the problems of democracy in a technologically complex civilization and of individual adjustment in such a civilization. Just a few samples:

Dewey, *Individualism Old and New.*
Eastman, *Capital and Other Writings by Karl Marx,* pp. 321–334.
Freud, *Civilization and Its Discontents.*
Hayek, *The Road to Serfdom.* (Against social and economic planning.)
Horney, *The Neurotic Personality of Our Time.*
Mannheim, *Man and Society in an Age of Reconstruction.* (Very influential book which sees planning as the alternative to totalitarianism.)
Mosier, *The American Temper: Patterns of Our Cultural Heritage.* (Philosophical approach to the backgrounds of American thought.)
Mowrer, *Learning Theory and Personality,* Chap. 21.
Packard, *The Status Seekers.*
Riesman, *The Lonely Crowd.*
Rocco, "The Political Doctrine of Fascism," in Wagner's *Social Reformers.* (An excellent, concise account of the matter.)

Ware and Means, *The Modern Economy in Action.* (A good general account of economic changes.)

Whyte, *The Organization Man.*

For materials more directly related to education:

Brameld, *Patterns of Educational Philosophy*, especially Chap. 17. (A good exposition of the view that the school is a "social vanguard" to reconstruct the social order.)

Brubacher, *Eclectic Philosophy of Education*, Topics 18, 19.

——, *Modern Philosophies of Education*, Chap. 10.

John Dewey Society: Fifth Yearbook, *Freedom in an Age of Anxiety.*

Raup, *et al.*, *The Improvement of Practical Intelligence.*

Stanley, *Education and Social Integration*, Chaps. 4, 5.

Welsh, *The Social Philosophy of Christian Education*, pp. 66–71.

Woodruff, *The Psychology of Teaching*, Chaps. 23, 24.

9

The Aesthetic Values

We realize aesthetic value whenever we perceive an object as a unified expression of meaningful feeling. Let this serve as a first approximation to a definition of the aesthetic experience.[1]

The Aesthetic Experience

The aesthetic experience is a *special* kind of experience. When I perceive a tree, I apprehend the sensuous quality of its color, its rustling, and its fragrance. I also apprehend them as a *unified* impression; the sense impressions are sorted out in such a way that those representing the tree are in one cluster. But I need not apprehend the tree as a unified expression of meaningful *feeling*. A lumberman may perceive the tree as so many board feet of pine. A tree warden may see it as a tree that needs spraying. Both perceive it as instru-

[1] For an appreciation of the difficulties involved in such a definition, see Vivas and Krieger, *The Problems of Aesthetics*, Sec. 5.

mental to some purpose or goal outside of itself. However, if I see a tree with a "nest of robins in her hair," then my perception is of an object that seems to express by its very *appearance* a unity of meaning and feeling that neither the tree warden nor the lumberman perhaps apprehends. First of all then, the aesthetic experience is a *special* way of perceiving objects, events, or situations.

The aesthetic subject

The aesthetic experience is an interaction of an object and a subject. The subject or the appreciator contributes sense organs, a nervous system, a past experience, and a set or readiness. The lumberman and the tree warden have by past experience so structured their lives that they are more or less *set* to perceive whatever will forward the interests of lumbermen or tree wardens.

1. The aesthetic *set* is often called the aesthetic attitude. It means that we are ready to be stimulated by the appearance or the "look" of an object and to concentrate on that appearance for its own sake. In this set, we are interested in what this tree looks like (lonely, majestic, brave), and not in the price of lumber, the ruthless exploitation of forests, or the health of trees. The aesthetic attitude, therefore, is different from the moral, scientific, or the practical attitudes.

2. The appreciator also imports some of his past experience into the situation. I have watched the sea many times. Infrequently, I have sailed on it. My swimming ability is such that I am a little afraid of the sea. A friend of mine has always lived on the seashore and is thoroughly at home on the sea and in it. We both look at a seascape of breakers crashing on reefs, dark gray sky, and a deep sea swell. What he brings to the picture is not what I bring. We thus get our second main principle: that the content of an aesthetic experience is dependent on what we bring to it as well as on what it brings to us.

3. There is another element in what we bring to the experience. It has to do with aesthetic know-how. Here is a man who has tried to paint the sea. He knows how to give the impression of jaggedness to a rock with a few brush strokes. He has mastered the trick of giving surf a fiercely foaming quality. Beside him is a man who has done none of these things. Will they both see the same things in a seascape?

Let us take a more critical example. Two men are listening to a piece of very modern music. One has studied it for a long time; the other has not. The latter experiences little more than irritation because he misses a continuous melody and a regularly pulsating rhythm. The first man, on the contrary, is absorbed in it. He does hear rhythms; he does apprehend some design in the strange sounds, and the sounds are not particularly strange to him. He anticipates the next phrase because he does know the design of the whole composition. In other words, not all aesthetic objects give up their secrets with equal ease.

The subject, therefore, contributes to the aesthetic experience a set or attitude, his past experience, and some degree of expertness with aesthetic objects.

The aesthetic object

The aesthetic object is what we perceive when we assume the aesthetic attitude. It is constructed out of our inner experience plus the stimuli that come from the physical object. A picture is an arrangement of pigments and shapes. This arrangement was put there by the artist. I can see this pattern, or I can see another that the artist may not have intended. Subjects can even impose patterns where there are none. For example, we arrange a series of uniform hoof beats or clicks of train wheels into rhythms to suit ourselves. But obviously, if I contribute too much to the aesthetic object, the physical object becomes superfluous. We would no longer need pictures or symphonies to give us aesthetic experiences. We could gaze at blank sheets of paper or listen to a metronome and fill in the rest by imagination.

The aesthetic object has ingredients that we contribute and ingredients that we do not contribute. How much each contributes is still an unsolved problem.

1. In the aesthetic object, whether it be a natural one like the sea, a sunset, or a tree; or a man-made work of art, there is first of all a medium, e.g., color, sound, marble.

2. In the aesthetic object the materials of the medium are arranged into some kind of pattern, order, and design. This is its composition. Harmony, balance, etc., are characteristics of design.[2]

2 Cf. Thomas Munro, "The Analysis of Form," Fortieth Yearbook, National Society for the Study of Education, 1941, pp. 358–359; and Gotshalk, *Art and the Social Order*, pp. 108–126.

3. The aesthetic object, if it is man-made, usually has something to express: a message, a meaning, a feeling, some quality of experience.

4. The aesthetic object has a vehicle by which the content is conveyed. It may be the sea, a human figure, a group of such figures, a building, a frieze, a plot, characters, and incidents. The vehicle literally carries the message, the content of what is to be expressed.

The aesthetic act

During the interaction between the physical object and the observer in an aesthetic attitude there emerges an experience that has several distinctive features:

1. The aesthetic object seems to have characteristics that ordinarily we would not attribute to it. We speak of the angry sea, the meandering road, the lonesome pine, the uplifting music. Literally this is nonsense because seas have no emotions; neither do pine trees nor the vibrations of the air we call music. These are figures of speech. But in an aesthetic experience we do not say to ourselves: "I am using a metaphor when I speak of the angry sea." Rather, we mean: the sea *looks* angry; or the music *sounds* uplifting; the texture of the velvet *feels* luxurious. Those who cannot "see" the anger in the sea or hear "upliftingness" in the music (or like qualities) are called literal minded and the aesthetic experience eludes them. That aesthetic objects seem to embody qualities that literally do not belong to them has been explained by some theorists in terms of empathy— an interpretation of the aesthetic experience as a kind of identification in which the observer projected his feelings of action into the object.[3]

2. Bullough, on the other hand, by his concept of psychical distance has emphasized the detachment from the object[4] that is necessary in order that we may view it aesthetically. Some persons cannot go to the movies without crying and some spectators cannot watch a football game without playing every position on the team.

[3] Among them Aristotle, *Rhetoric* III, 2; Robert Vischer, *Das optische Formgefühl;* Theodor Lipps, *Zur Einfühlung,* and Vernon Lee, *The Beautiful.*
[4] Edward Bullough, " 'Psychical Distance' as a Factor in Art and as Esthetic Principle," *British Journal of Psychology,* 5:1913, pp. 87–118.

This kind of identification destroys the aesthetic attitude although it may give us an emotional thrill.

As with empathy, so with detachment; only a certain degree of it is natural to all of us. Almost anyone can view a decorative piece of linoleum without undue identification, but it is more difficult not to identify with a realistic movie, picture, or novel. For example, art magazines very often contain pictures of nudes, and novels may have descriptions of sex love that arouse the ire of morally sensitive citizens. The defense of the publisher is that these pictures and descriptions are not sex but art. What he means is that such pictures and descriptions are to be apprehended aesthetically, with a detachment that prevents identifying the nude with certain sexual impulses. However, the citizen may not be altogether wrong. These pictures and descriptions may not be aesthetically apprehended, in which case he is right in suspecting that, art or no art, they are stimuli to sexual excitement. Empathy and detachment in some situations have to be acquired.

3. In every aesthetic experience the subject is asked to apprehend a complex of elements in a unity, and it is required of the object that it have such patterns. A melody is not simply a collection of notes, but rather a pattern that fits them together so well that in hearing it we are not even aware of the separate notes. Right now I am seeing a seascape on the wall opposite me. If I make an effort, I can distinguish at least 25 different color hues, four or five kinds of rocks, and a half dozen shapes of waves and clouds. Yet the unified impression is one of the sea in a restless mood under a sunny sky.

Now there are all sorts and grades of unity. A simple leaf pattern repeated many times in a fabric has a unity of design; increasingly bright shades of red arranged in a picture from left to right would produce another sort of unity. There is the unity of balance and the unity furnished by clusters of contrasting elements. There is a unity of content and of theme, and finally, the most complete unity of all, the unity of idea and feeling that every successful artistic object engenders in the qualified observer. Some unities are easy to apprehend (the unity of a melodramatic plot), some are not so easy to detect (the unities of modern music), and sometimes, of course, there are no unities to detect.[5]

---

[5] I am indebted for part of this analysis to a syllabus for a course in aesthetics prepared by Professor Richard M. Millard of Boston University.

Education and Aesthetic Experience

By breaking up the aesthetic experience into its more prominent components and activities, the role and task of education in promoting the aesthetic values may become clearer.

First of all, the basis for this kind of experience is an inherent part of human nature. Regardless of culture and environment, men in every station of life are impelled to objectify their insights and feelings in artistic objects.

All of us are fascinated by the sheer appearance of the world around us. Perhaps as Susanne K. Langer suggests, this is the first form of human knowledge, in which objects are seen as symbols of feeling: a kind of animism in which all objects are seen—not inferred—to be the habitat of spirits friendly or hostile, productive or destructive.[6] Among most peoples there is a spontaneous effort to celebrate the highlights of life by pictures, song, drama, and the dance which capture and fix the stirring moments of the hunt and the battle into a form that can be enacted over and over again.

Nor do we have to learn that certain sensuous elements are pleasing in themselves. The color of crimson or gold, certain other color combinations, the textures of velvet, leather, silk, or cashmere have their own qualities. Some are pleasant; some are not.[7]

As for unity, there would be no experience at all without it. Our experience makes whatever sense it does make because it is bundled into clusters and patterns. The first task of the infant is to sort out the stimuli that assail him into some kind of order.

Every element in aesthetics—rhythm, plot, character, balance, symmetry, composition, and beauty—is already familiar to the child when he comes to school. Why, then, do we need aesthetic education?

The layman and the connoisseur

We could argue that if we were educated aesthetically, we would frequent concert halls and art museums and do less aimless auto-

[6] Cf. *Philosophy in a New Key*, pp. 146 ff.
[7] It has been suggested that not all qualities can be admired or apprehended aesthetically, e.g., the quality of being equilateral or serrated. Others like smoothness, high gloss, simplicity can be so admired. Frank Sibley, "Aesthetics and the Look of Things," *The Journal of Philosophy*, 56:23, 905–915, November 5, 1959.

mobile riding. This alone might save many lives and would justify even a very expensive form of art education. Some say aesthetic education makes life richer, whatever "richer" may mean; others regard the aesthetic values as spiritual and on that account more refined and more obligatory upon us than others. In the long run, however, there is no way of convincing anyone that one form of life is better than any other unless he actually finds it to be so.

Let us step from the aesthetic field to the athletic field. Boys play football or baseball because they enjoy doing so. Later, when they watch their high school teams, they realize that their own playing does not compare in quality with that of the trained team. Seeing a college team forces them to judge their high school team as inferior; professional teams reveal a still higher degree of excellence. It is the same game on all levels; the difference lies in the speed, precision, and power with which the actions are carried out. And once this is perceived, the boy or man is never thereafter quite satisfied with inferior performances, even though school spirit and rivalry may make a particular high school game more exciting than a professional one.

If the boy develops his interest in baseball, he comes to make finer and finer discriminations; he tolerates fewer and fewer mistakes; he appreciates little tricks of strategy that the casual spectator never notices. He becomes, in short, a connoisseur to whom little differences make a big difference. Food, clothing, sports, drama, literature, poetry, music, painting, and indeed every human activity has its connoisseurs. We call them "highbrows" especially if they are connoisseurs in areas where we are only "lowbrows." In his own field every man is a "highbrow," but few are "highbrows" in many fields.

Being a connoisseur makes one dissatisfied with anything less than the best, and being a connoisseur means having standards that tell one what the best is. That connoisseurs differ in their standards is beside the point. Two chefs may attack each other with knives over the precise amount of oil to put into a dressing; the layman would not detect any difference in flavor if the amount of oil were doubled or halved. The connoisseur cannot argue the "lowbrow" into enjoying what he judges to be the best; he can only appeal to him to try it and then point out to him what causes the differences. The connoisseur not only has a taste of his own, but he has reasons for that taste.

Because some men are connoisseurs in the arts we can believe that there are realms of experience that would be satisfying if we too could achieve connoisseurship in them. This is the justification for aesthetic education. If we as educators do not really share the belief that we can *improve* taste, our aesthetic education will be insincere; if we ourselves have not taken a few steps down the road to connoisseurship, it will not be very effective. There will be aesthetic activity whether we foster it in school or not, but, uncultivated, it will rarely become the act of the connoisseur.

Aesthetic expression and production

Aesthetic education, like aesthetic experience, has two phases: the production of objects that express a distinctive meaning in some artistic medium, and the contemplation of such objects to apprehend this meaning. The artist specializes in production and expression, the layman in appreciation.

However, there is a larger meaning to aesthetic experience. It is that every man in his everyday activity and in the gradual weaving of his life style is *producing* objects that can give aesthetic pleasure or pain to the beholder.

Physical appearance and physical surroundings. Unless we are hermits, we present our bodies to a fairly large number of viewers every day. We cover these bodies with clothing. The object we thus exhibit can be aesthetically pleasing or otherwise, expressive or otherwise. Indeed our first noting of the stranger is an aesthetic one. His clothing, facial expression, posture, and demeanor all merge in a unified impression of quality. We say he looks intelligent, serene, agitated, energetic, lethargic, crooked.

Appearances are deceptive but for the moment let us confine ourselves to these appearances. An attractive appearance is an intrinsic value needing no other justification. Men, as well as women, prefer to be attractive, although often reluctant to put forth the necessary effort. We have a moral duty to present to the world as attractive a physical presence as we can. If this seems to stringent, then we ought at least to exhibit as little ugliness as possible. To sacrifice all beauty for utility and comfort is a kind of selfishness— a genuine disregard for the sensibilities of those who have to look at us even for short periods of time.

We cannot control physiological changes nor can we do too much with the features bestowed upon us. Our fellows have the duty to put up with them as patiently as we ourselves do. But posture, grooming, and attire are within our control, and one way of beautifying the landscape is to improve the appearance of the people in it. Much the same can be said about the aesthetic quality of our homes, neighborhoods, public buildings, and the other objects that we put out for public inspection.

So much for aesthetic charity to our fellow men. But there is another side to the story. Our bodies, clothes, homes, and communities can express ourselves. One could tell a great deal about people from the appearance of their lawns, hedges, and houses, if they did not express the stereotype of fashion rather than their owners. We shall know that aesthetic education in the schools is really effective when short chunky men refuse to wear clothes designed for tall athletes, and householders refuse to clip miles of hedges when they yearn for rugged rock gardens.

Part of the drudgery of housework, dressing, and chores is that they express so little of what we think it valuable to express. It is difficult to see, for example, what doing the week's wash can express aesthetically. However, the foods we eat, the rooms in which we live, our clothing, and our community need not be wholly meaningless aesthetically.

Speech. Some educators recall with derision the grim efforts of teachers to give elegance to school children's speech. Our ancestors took for granted what psychology has subsequently disclosed: speech has an aesthetic quality that leads to judgments about personality.[8] Even those out-and-out utilitarians—the practical businessmen—are flocking to public speaking courses because they too realize that the aesthetic quality of speech may help sell everything from ideas to vacuum cleaners.

Aside from these practical considerations, the quality of speech is either pleasant or unpleasant, distinctive or humdrum, stimulating or soporific. If others must listen to us, they have the right to expect a modicum of precision in our speech, and they will be grateful for a smidge of elegance and style. American slang, especially of the adolescent variety, is a symptom of weariness with stereotyped modes of speech. But by middle life most of the citizens give up even this attempt at linguistic distinction.

[8] G. W. Allport and H. A. Cantril, "Judging Personality from Voice," *The Journal of Social Psychology,* 5:37–55, 1944.

Dress, houses, and even speech have limits of expressiveness. The Self, if it has any depth, needs other "languages," and these are the media of the fine arts: poetry, music, drama, sculpture, the dance, and all the crafts. These media have high potentiality for expressing our Selves and the way the world and life appears to us—provided we know how to use them.

The school's problem and solution

The school faces two strategic problems in aesthetic education. One is the *freeing* of the aesthetic impulse; the other is the development of techniques wherewith to *express* that impulse.

We know that little children have the aesthetic impulse and do not hesitate to express it in scribblings, fingerpainting, clay modeling, dramatic play, poetizing, and in music-making. The elementary school can take credit for exploiting these natural tendencies, but spontaneous aesthetic activity seems to peter out as the pupil reaches adolescence. Why?

There are reasons for this. For one thing, the practical demands of life become more urgent. In comparison to picking a vocation, acquiring a car, keeping one's parents pacified, and staying out of the juvenile courts, aesthetic activity seems trivial and postponable. This is the judgment of the adult community, and it is echoed by the adolescent. Yet at no time in life does the pupil need means of articulating his jittery perspective of life so much. He cannot express himself very effectively in the economic and social life of the adult community, and although his yearning for independence is strong, his dependence is real and humiliating.

Another reason is the betrayal of the adolescent's aesthetic impulse by inadequate technique. He knows enough about reality to be dissatisfied with childish scribblings and make-believe. Pranks, slang, braggadocio, and defiance express his needs much better. There seems to be a critical point in our lives when command of technique decides whether or not we shall continue to use an artistic medium. If this time is in early adolescence, it would follow that aesthetic education reaches its critical stage in secondary education.[9]

To preserve the aesthetic impulse in the face of the pressure of the milieu is an almost insuperable problem. The school has no

[9] Cf. H. S. Broudy, "Some Duties of a Theory of Educational Aesthetics," *Educational Theory*, 1:3, November 1951, pp. 190–198.

choice save to run counter to the stream of the milieu. Aesthetic considerations have high priority in the life of the school regardless of what is going on outside of it. The school building should be aesthetically pleasing even if it means sacrificing a little utility, although the two need not be incompatible. Teachers in appearance, speech, and general mode of life are called upon to live imaginatively as well as sanely and hygienically. The school's ceremonies and rituals should be marked by high aesthetic quality.[10]

It also means stressing the aesthetic quality in students' appearance, speech, posture, and demeanor. Whether or not life can be beautiful anywhere else, it ought to be so in the school. If form is important on the football field and the tennis court, why is it not important in other areas of school life?

All these efforts may be subverted by the non-school environment, but educators are inclined to sell the permanent strivings of human beings a trifle short. Our communities may seem to be indifferent to the beautiful; they may have to be, or think they have to be, but beauty is irresistible, and they will not thank the school for being as lazy and incompetent about it as they themselves may have become.

So much for the informal mode of fostering the aesthetic attitude in the pupil. The other solution is formal; the perfection of the habits and skills of using the artistic media. Part of this is the teaching of artistic techniques such as drawing, painting, singing, and playing of instruments, acting, etc. Another and perhaps more basic part is the development of sensitivity to aesthetic form in the major media of the arts.

Of all the ingredients in the aesthetic experience, form or design is perhaps the most distinctively aesthetic. We cannot notice the form of anything without the aesthetic attitude. Real objects in the world are always unities of form and content. In ordinary experience we are so concerned with real objects and their relevance for action that it is difficult for us to think of their form apart from some specific content. When we see a chair in a painting, we are more likely to see the chair as an article of furniture rather than as a vehicle for a form interesting to the painter.

[10] Not earthshaking, it is nevertheless somewhat incongruous to impress upon the graduate student the lofty importance of the doctorate and then to hold his doctoral examination in a dusty office or cluttered committee room.

Our ways of apprehending forms thus become congealed into habitual ways of seeing and thinking. They become stereotypes. For creative work such stereotypes hold little promise. Whether we are seeking a solution to the problem of raising a loan, an hypothesis to explain a stubborn disease, or a way of expressing our feelings about a lonely day, we are in search of a new pattern, a new form.[11]

It seems to follow that aesthetic education should begin with an effort to promote sensitivity to form in the pupil. One of the methods for doing so is practice in abstracting form from its content to get the feeling of its partial autonomy. A number of circles, for example, may be arranged according to size, color, position, and in any combination of these. Add a few triangles to the circles, and the number of possible patterns increases enormously.

Music exemplifies repeatedly the multitude of patterns into which a few notes may be arranged by varying pitch, tempo, and rhythm. The same is true of spatial volumes in sculpture and architecture, and no less is true of words. But it requires conscious experimentation with variations in form to sensitize the student to the possibilities of formal combinations.[12]

Experimentation with form leads to confidence in manipulating it, and this is the first step in the creative production of aesthetic objects. Given some command over form and something to express, the matter of technique presents no unique educational problem. Technique by itself may not preserve the aesthetic impulse nor even by itself give us command over it, but pupils do not resist technique when they have something aesthetic to create.

Some facility with forms in many artistic media and enough technique for this purpose is the least that we can ask for in general education. This is a long stride from professional competence, but it is the minimum for aesthetic literacy. To be able to write a poem, to act in a play, to paint or sculpt, to perform on a musical instrument, should be standard equipment for every educated man. That this conclusion has a weird sound shows how neglected aesthetic education is in our times.

---

[11] This calls for creativity which, in turn, calls for what has been dubbed "divergent thinking" and "flexibility of response." Cf. J. P. Guilford, "The Three Faces of Intellect," *The American Psychologist,* 14:8, August 1959, pp. 469–479.

[12] On this topic of form and some practical devices for developing sensitivity to it, see Pearson, *The New Art Education,* Chap. 4.

Levels of aesthetic appreciation

Besides creative expression, the school is naturally concerned with appreciation. By appreciation is sometimes meant:

1. Evaluation in the sense of criticism, e.g., one appreciates a poem when he can weigh its merits on some standard.

2. General approval, as when one "appreciates" geometry, fair play, and democracy.

3. Getting a strong sense of pleasure or excitement in the presence of some artistic object or performance, e.g., as when one *really* appreciates a symphony, concert, or play.

The first meaning has a place in aesthetic education because one would hope that if there is a real difference between good and bad art, the pupil would eventually be able to detect it. The second meaning is too vague to be of much use in aesthetic or any other kind of education. The third meaning is relevant to the aesthetic experience, but emotional intensity is often a function of factors other than the aesthetic object: the fame of the performer or artist, the social quality of the audience, one's costume, one's companion, or even the price of admission.

If we review the features and elements of the aesthetic experience in the earlier part of this chapter, we shall hardly expect all observers to receive the same impression from a piece of music, painting, poetry, or drama. This is so because a very important part of the experience is what the aesthetic subject brings to the experience. The various responses to the object can be made on one or more of several levels.

Perception of aesthetic sensory quality. Look at a good color print of Georgia O'Keefe's *White Barn.*[13] It is a long low barn with a white wall, black roof, a narrow strip of blue sky above it and an equally narrow strip of green in front of it. There are two bluish openings in the wall of the barn, a smaller bluish door, and an even smaller bluish window. In front of the two big doors are a few yellowish steps.

The sky, the green grass, and the roof are in solid flat colors with practically no shading. Taken separately, the colors are pleasing: clear, dazzling white; soft, rich blues; bright green; bright yellow. Even a child of five could not pass this picture without being im-

13 Boswell, *Modern American Painting*, p. 124.

pressed by the sheer appearance—the aesthetic quality—of the colors.

There are also shapes in this picture—very simple ones formed by straight lines, yet having an over-all graceful quality. Now take a look at *Daughters of the American Revolution* by Grant Wood.[14] Every bit of the color looks faded and drab. The framed picture of Washington crossing the Delaware is depicted in dull grays. The skin color of the three women is faded and tawney; their dresses are in equally faded colors. The aesthetic quality of these colors is almost the opposite of those in the O'Keefe picture.

The shapes are equally dull. In other words, the sensory qualities are not particularly pleasant taken either in detail or as a whole. On the other hand, the same painter's *Woman with Plants*[15] has a wealth of coloring, all of it pleasant, none of it glaring.

It is more difficult to speak in words of the sensory qualities of music, but we do describe it as sweet, harsh, fluent, pleasant, stirring, quiet, rich, thin, etc.

The point of these illustrations is that the perception of sensory quality is the simplest and most fundamental type of aesthetic appreciation. Color texture, and shapes are perceived pretty much *as they are* by all observers with normal sense organs and brains. It requires the least amount of learning.

There is a difference, however, between noting that a taxi meter is clicking at every quarter of a mile and noting that it is clicking inexorably. There is a difference between saying that the sky is blue and that it is dazzlingly blue. The aesthetic quality of the clicking is the "inexorability"; of the blue it is the "dazzlingly." It has been suggested that colors, sound, and shapes acquire an aesthetic quality when they have characteristics that remind us of what is important for life itself. Rough, smooth; soft, hard; regular, irregular; clean, dirty; balance, unbalanced—all of these are characteristic of our successful or unsuccessful transactions with nature, and we "naturally" apprehend them with interest.[16]

No small amount of enjoyment accrues from simply noting these aesthetic qualities—when they are pleasant. Some music is simply a succession of pleasant sounds and is enjoyed as that and nothing else. There is not much to be done here, educationally, save to expose the pupil to aesthetic objects in wide variety and to encourage

14 *Ibid.*, p. 66.
15 *Ibid.*, p. 67.
16 See footnote 8 on page 210.

him to note shapes, colors, and sounds that never would have occurred if some artist had not created them. Naturally, the more the pupil creates himself, the more likely he is to develop a psychological readiness to note the variety and richness of aesthetic qualities.

Perception of aesthetic form. Every art object has some design or structure that binds together the aesthetic qualities of its elements. In the *White Barn* the strip of sky is countered by the strip of green grass. The four lightning rods are spaced symmetrically. The black roof gives a sharp contrast to the whiteness of the wall. The two big doors balance, but the little door and window at the left prevent it from being a flat geometrical balance. The white of the wall is repeated in each of the four lightning rods.

The design of *Daughters of the American Revolution* is about as interesting as its color. Although the picture is a horizontal rectangle, most of the lines and masses emphasize the vertical. There is a balance between the two figures on the left and one figure plus most of the picture of the Delaware crossing on the right. There is a sort of rhythm of the three faces with about the same expression and the same skin color.

In the picture, *Woman with Plants,* the central figure is, of course, the woman. The contrast between the coloring of various parts of her clothing is carried further by the softer blurred coloring of the background. The reds show gradual variation from the hands through flower pot, the cameo, to the face. The greenish blue of the sky is repeated in the collar of the dress and in the plants. The elliptical top of the flower pot is repeated in the longer ellipse of the hands encircling it.

In music too there is the structure of the melodic line, the rhythm pattern, the repetition of themes and variations and contrasts of pitch, loudness, and timbre.

We do not, as a rule, deliberately analyze the design of an object in this way, but neither do we perceive it as simply and naively as we do the sensory quality of the separate elements. In the examples we have used, the structure of each picture as a whole is apprehended rather easily because their vehicles are familiar. Barns and women as real objects have a unity of their own. Other designs not embodied in familiar objects are often unnoticed by the viewer unless he explicitly pays attention to them.

There is a sense in which the viewer should not have to pay such attention because, if the picture gives a unified impression, it does so by virtue of its composition. The question is whether the viewer gets an aesthetic unity rather than some other kind. For example, the *Woman with Plants* is not simply a woman against a rural background. That is the vehicle by which the artist is trying to convey an aesthetic impression, but he could have taken a snapshot of his mother and accomplished the same thing if all he intended to show was a woman against a rural background.

In paintings with easily-recognizable objects like flowers, nudes, and seascapes there is danger that the recognition of the object plus a noting of its sensory qualities is all that will accrue. On the other hand, in many modern works of art the design is so complicated that the viewer gets no meaning whatever. The hoots that greet some modern works are occasioned by the frustration of the viewer looking for a familiar object as a clue to the structure of the picture. Similarly, a picture that greatly distorts familiar objects like chairs and human figures leads the viewer to concentrate on the distortion rather than on what the artist had in mind. Scolded by the artist, the untrained viewer feels as if he were being addressed in a foreign language and then called a dolt because he could make neither head nor tail of it.

We thus arrive at a phase of appreciation that does require instruction. If the pupil has had experience in making designs of many kinds, he will more readily apprehend designs that are really creative. For those who lack this training there is no substitute for guided looking and listening. Just looking at pictures or listening to a piece of music is not the panacea for all aesthetic ignorance. Equally doubtful are the contentions of those who fear that to analyze a work of art is to destroy the feeling one should get from it. The feelings the uninitiated do get can stand a good deal of destruction with profit. Anyone who has attended the rehearsal of a symphony orchestra knows that the subsequent hearings are enormously different from the first one.

No composer believes that there are short cuts to the better appreciation of music. The only thing that one can do for the listener is to point out what actually exists in the music itself and reasonably explain the wherefore and the why of the matter. The listener must do the rest.[17]

Once beyond the simple, obvious, and familiar—whether it be in

[17] Aaron Copland, *What to Listen for in Music*, New York: McGraw-Hill Book Company, Inc., 1939, p. 13.

poetry, literature, music, painting, architecture—the aesthetic object demands study. Not that the viewer will not get some kind of impression without it, but it may be a very impoverished impression as compared to what he might get.

This is not a plea for the grammatical analysis of Shakespeare or Keats; grammatical analysis is not a search for design. But whoever has tried to create anything—from a henhouse to a tragedy—knows that the hardest part of all is design. The design is what makes sense in a work of art; without it, an aesthetic object is nonsense, and instruction that does not look for design also approaches nonsense.

How do we foster sensitivity to the formal structure of art objects? By isolating the form from the content. And this is true both in the expressive and the impressive phase of aesthetic experience. Just as in logic we become sensitive to the form of propositions by substituting symbols for words so that meanings of the words do not get in our way, so in an art we have to abstract from the nonformal elements to discern the form.

The pupil's intelligence and previous experience will determine how complicated and subtle a form he can apprehend. There is no warrant for demanding more from the pupil than he can possibly deliver, and no excuse for demanding less. The important matter is to prevent a stereotyping of perception that makes it almost impossible for the pupil to see or hear anything save the standard familiar patterns and groupings.

Modern and more abstract art can be used with profit in the study of aesthetic form because the formal element is so prominent in them. When the story of a poem is too prominent, as in *Evangeline*, it is difficult to pay attention to any save the most intrusive elements of form, e.g., the rhyme and rhythm. In some of the modern poetry the "story" is so well hidden that form emerges as the most interesting thing about it.

Perceiving significance.[18] In the analysis of the aesthetic experience it was noted that the experience was incomplete until the various elements were perceived as a unity of feeling, meaning, and imagery. It is the form that gives the art work its structural unity, but if the artist is successful, this form will be perceived as a unity of

---

[18] Cf. John Hospers, "Meaning in Music," in Rader's *A Modern Book of Esthetics*, second edition, pp. 258–282, from *Meaning and Truth in the Arts*, Chapel Hill, 1946.

feeling and meaning as well. The whole picture, poem, or play feels like something—the feeling seems to be in the work of art itself.

We are now in a realm where it is easier to disagree than to agree. What, for example, is the meaningful feeling of the *White Barn?* If I said that it felt "brilliantly serene," could I get any agreement from other observers? From critics? From painters? Perhaps not much. Yet once this meaning has been suggested, others no doubt might find it in the picture.

It is important to notice that when we speak about the meaning of the picture, we do not mean "whatever this picture makes you think about." It is not a mere association of ideas set off by the object. As a matter of fact, if an art object does set us to thinking, we think ourselves out of the aesthetic attitude; we have abandoned the object and set off on our own private journey. If a farmer seeing the *White Barn* gets to wondering how much it would cost to build one like it, and from that proceeds to calculate how much it will cost to paint his own barn, and from there decides that whoever built the barn in the first place was not much of a carpenter, he can thank the picture for an interesting train of thought, but not for an aesthetic experience.[19]

Yet, by and large, the meaning element in the *White Barn* is not prominent and perhaps not very important. It is an attention-compelling and interesting formal structure giving a unified sensuous impression. On the other hand, *Daughters of the American Revolution* is loaded with meaning and not very pleasant meaning at that. If we take away the satire from the picture, is there very much left to interest us in the way of form and aesthetic quality? This is not a beautiful picture, yet it does convey a meaningful feeling—a unified feeling that has been expressed in a formal arrangement of sensuous material. In *Woman with Plants* the feeling I get is one of simple strength, straightforward faith, gentleness, and unspectacular courage.

[19] Vernon Lee found in *Music and Its Lovers* that about half of those answering questionnaires on listening to music reported that they did have images and ideas that the music suggested. The other half denied having these nonmusical associations and these were the more "musical" listeners. Their minds wandered frequently from the music, but they knew when they had wandered. How much wandering is permissible before the experience ceases to be aesthetic? So long as any meaning or message is seen or heard as *in* the picture or *in* the music, the experience is aesthetic; the moment the focus of our consciousness is shifted from the work of art to what it suggests, we are out of the aesthetic experience.

This element of meaning is the hardest of all to capture for educational procedures. Sensory quality we can point to and experiment with. Form we can discern, point out to others, and create for ourselves. But significance is nothing we can point to and have any assurance that it will be discerned. And if I tell you what you *should* perceive here, is not the point of aesthetic education lost?

Pupils who try to express some significance of feeling in artistic form will be more likely to see it in the works of others. Probably the best education for aesthetic impression is aesthetic expression. What we ourselves have tried to do we appreciate when achieved by others.[20]

What significance we shall apprehend is probably a function of many factors. First is the object itself. It may make the meaning so obvious, clear, or powerful that no one can miss it, e.g., the *Daughters of the American Revolution.* It can play down meaning, put forward an ambiguous meaning, or a very subtle one.

Another factor is the viewer's level of experience. How complicated and subtle is it? How deep is it emotionally? How badly does it crave expression? This has to be kept in mind in aesthetic education for the young. It may well be that some art is not for the young in spirit, experience, and age. Yet there ought to be a progression in the art-needs of the pupil. His feelings at 15 should need a different mode of expression from those he had at 10. The school can only hope that, having mastered the "language" of the various arts, he will discern what he needs in great works of art which men and women with deep, thoughtful, and cultivated experience have found significant.

Can the school cultivate and improve the aesthetic expression of the pupil? Our analysis of the components of the aesthetic experience is not intended as a manual for art and music teachers. It should, however, show what components of the aesthetic experience are amenable to instruction and the sort of instruction that gives some promise of success.

Standards and aesthetic education

The analysis of aesthetic education stressed aesthetic expression as a key to aesthetic impression. The latter is perhaps more im-

---

[20] Said Aristotle: "It is difficult, if not impossible, for those who do not perform to be good judges of the performance of others." *Politics*, 1340b 23.

portant for general education because aside from the professionals not many people will devote themselves seriously to artistry in any form. For most of us the higher aesthetic values will have to be realized through the creation of others. But at what level shall we realize them?

Popular art. It is frequently observed that our level of aesthetic appreciation is fairly low.[21] We are peculiarly vulnerable to this charge because in our culture aesthetic products are likely to be produced for large-scale consumption. This results in a body of commercial art we call popular. This fact has two immediate consequences. First, the popular work must be within the comprehension and suit the taste of the multitudes; the lowest common denominator is the mark at which the artist must shoot. In the second place, works that are not popular in this sense have a difficult time coming to life at all. Serious artists do not have an easy time unless they catch on with the intelligentsia. The intelligentsia themselves cannot remunerate the artist, but fortunately there are those who can and will do so if his "reputation" can be established.

There is nothing wrong with popular art in itself, just as there is nothing wrong with candy in itself. However, if candy so sates the appetite that the child does not get a nutritious diet, there is something wrong with his eating of candy. Popular art becomes suspect if it stereotypes taste and perception and makes it very difficult for the individual to enjoy what he needs and what he might really enjoy.

Aesthetically and artistically, popular art is too flimsy to stand much wear. A song is on the hit parade for a few weeks and everyone is sick of it. Certain types of movies have a vogue and then pass away. Books are best sellers this year and forgotten the next. Now and then an old tune is revived for a new generation; it has another fling at popularity and then subsides once more.

It is not surprising that this should be so. Take any popular song. The melody is catchy but simple. Hear it twice and you can sing it yourself. The rhythm is clear-cut and contagious. The form of the song is standardized in any given period. The sentiment or mood is easily identifiable: joyous love, jealous love, yearning love, despairing love, humorous love, and love betrayed. The lyrics are simple, forthright, and usually predictable. There are exceptions;

[21] For a more or less typical statement of this complaint, cf. Joseph Wood Krutch, "Is Our Common Man Too Common?" *The Saturday Review*, 36: January 10, 1953, pp. 8 ff.

in every period there are those who can win the popular market with more solid fare. In general, however, popular art demands so little of the appreciator that it makes very little change in his experience, and this is a rough but not inadequate definition of the trivial.

One can be sure that if the American public heard nothing but symphonic or operatic music for, let us say, five years, certain portions of it would become "popular," whereas other parts would be left to the "highbrows." The parts that would become popular would be those with good melody, easy rhythms, and clearly expressive of what most people feel. We have such classic favorites now.

For the school the choice between popular and serious art is influenced by the fact that popular art needs no formal instruction for its appreciation whereas serious art does. Consequently, a program of aesthetic education that does not introduce the pupil to serious literature, music, painting, and drama is an indefensible drain on the pupil's time and the taxpayer's money.

Good and bad art. Can we then speak sensibly of "good" and "bad" art? Can we insist that our pupils "ought" to prefer one art object to another?

These questions may be easier to handle if we distinguish three kinds of art standards.

1. *Technical standards,* by which we mean standards of skill in execution of art work; in using paints, musical sounds, or body movements. These standards are fairly objective as far as the experts in the field are concerned.

2. *Formal standards,* by which we mean the degree of success achieved in composition or design. Many of the rules of art have to do with these formal requirements of design (harmony, balance, contrast, unity in variety). Here too there can be a good deal of agreement by the experts, even though the innovators are forever challenging some of these rules and thus breaking ground for new trends in design.

3. *Expressive standards,* by which we mean the degree to which the art object gives to the observer in aesthetic terms a message about life and reality. Here objectivity is much harder to define or to find.

When we say that the pupil "ought" to like Beethoven better than popular ballads, or even that he ought to like one ballad better than another, what are we saying in terms of these three kinds of standards?

Usually, the competent art teacher or art critic means that Beethoven's works have a complexity of design and technical finish that put them in a class well above the ordinary popular ballad. *Hamlet* has a much more complicated design and technical finish than a Western movie. In general, complex art works are more important than simple ones, although there are musical compositions and pictures that are very intricate and skillfully done that seems to be no more than exercises in complexity and skill. It is when complexity is dictated by the theme itself or by the complexity of the experience that the artist is trying to express that it becomes a measure of the worth of an art object.

If the pupil spontaneously or with a little coaxing comes to prefer the kind of art the teacher regards as good, there is, of course, no educational problem. This is rarely the case. As far as the untutored subject is concerned, there is little agreement between excellence on formal or technical standards and excellence on the expressive standard. The agreement grows as connoisseurship increases. If this principle is false, the problem of standards in art education disappears. The educational task, therefore, is to help the pupil learn to enjoy art that expresses the more complex and the more important aspects of experience, especially the kind of imaginative experience he is not likely to encounter in the round of ordinary living outside of school.

There are two approaches to this task. One is the direct approach that tries to disclose to the pupil the structure of increasingly complex and subtle art objects as a means of enjoying them. To do this we can:

1. Begin early and continue late to encourage creative expression in as many media as possible, so that these remain natural "languages" to the pupil.

2. Encourage experimentation with form to make the aesthetic attitude easy to assume and to make the pupil sensitive to form in aesthetic objects.

3. Utilize a wide variety of aesthetic activities and objects to keep in the forefront of the pupil's consciousness the endless possibilities of aesthetic creativity.

4. Introduce him gradually to more complex and subtle art products to see what aesthetic impressions he can receive.

5. Demand and insist that the pupil try aesthetic experience that

requires as much intelligence, observation, and discrimination as his previous achievements indicate he is capable of.

The second approach is indirect. One very simple reason for not being able to respond to *Hamlet*, for example, is that we do not have the level of experience that *Hamlet* represents. The themes of love and conflict in *Hamlet* we find in almost every art work. But what adolescent has lived through the kind of love and conflict that Shakespeare is here trying to express? Is not the "boy-meets-girl" idyll of current movies, or short stories, or popular ballads much more expressive of what the normal adolescent feels than *Hamlet* or *Tristan and Isolde?* Does not movie drama adequately express the trials, tribulations, and triumphs of the average housewife? *Functionally*, therefore, aren't these art objects "better" than operas, symphonies, plays, and pictures that leave them bewildered or cold?[22]

One function of aesthetic education, and perhaps of general education, is so to extend and subtilize the experience of the pupil *vicariously* that he *needs* more complex and subtle art works to express that experience. In other words, *Hamlet* may not elicit the proper aesthetic response from a senior in high school, but it may, if a genuine effort at understanding is made, extend his experience so that love, conflict, and duty achieve a far more complex meaning than they have had in his own direct experience. Whatever contributes to the enriching of experience in the school is laying the groundwork for more mature aesthetic standards.

Therefore, it is no conclusive argument against a work of art that it is not immediately appreciated by the pupil. Nor does it follow that it should not be in the curriculum of that pupil, for it may be serving a broader function in the whole economy of life than immediate enjoyment.

If these principles are followed faithfully by teachers who themselves have tried to realize their own aesthetic possibilities, there is little need to worry about standards because:

1. The standards will be *genuine*, which means that they will not be imposed by the teacher or by the box office, or even by the critics, but rather by the developing needs of the pupil himself.

2. The pupil will not only like what he likes, but he will also know

[22] We have here a vicious circle. The young who are to be educated to like "good" art don't "need" it, and because they don't need it, are likely to resist the education.

why he likes it, and this is the first step toward connoisseurship, which is nothing more than intelligent taste.

3. We need not worry about lack of enthusiasm for the Classics in any field. If the pupil's experience is mature enough to need that form of expression, he will appreciate it.

We have stressed the more intellectual aspects of aesthetic education rather than the emotional and attitudinal ones, and the reasons for this should by now be thoroughly familiar to the student. The emotional and attitudinal aspects of aesthetic experience depend heavily on cultural pressures that are largely beyond the control of the school.

This means that the efforts of the school for 12 or even 14 years cannot guarantee that habits formed in the school can withstand social pressure. Vocation, family, friends, and the community as a whole may counteract a good deal of what the school has accomplished. Yet if the school is true to its function, it must proceed on the faith that the habits of intelligence will seek an opportunity to exercise themselves and in the long run under favorable circumstances will modify the culture so that it is less hostile to the values the school espouses.

The Aesthetic Values as Instrumental

Thus far we have tried to justify the aesthetic values on their power to give a special kind of intrinsic enjoyment. However, we can expect to be told that fine as enjoyment of music, painting, drama, and poetry is, it bakes no bread, fires no locomotives, wins no wars, and raises no corn. On the other hand, such enjoyments cost money. The time it takes to create and enjoy works of art has to be paid for by the whole economic system. Aesthetic education is no less expensive than other kinds of education. Is it not, perhaps, a frill, a delightful adornment of life which, in a pinch, can be dispensed with?

I would not know how to argue that aesthetic enjoyment is as biologically, economically, or politically important as corn or cannons. Nevertheless, the aesthetic values do have an instrumentality that is sometimes overlooked by the practical man.

Aesthetic qualities are consistently used by a culture to guide the choices of its members. The mechanism for doing so is to give an object an appearance which renders it more or less attractive than other objects within the field of choice and action. Let us see how this works in some of the value areas.

1. American industry and business have learned that, of two articles with the same utility, the more aesthetically pleasing will command a higher price. Functional art makes a virtue out of seeing to it that the very form of a house or a car contributes to its usefulness while also providing aesthetic satisfaction. Advertising not only has to be aesthetically pleasing itself, but it also has to utilize the aesthetic qualities of the product it advertises. This is one of its most potent "angles." The prosperity of commercial art is proof enough that aesthetic values pay economic dividends.

2. Darwin concluded that the brightly colored feathers of male birds were no mere accidents. They were means of attracting the females and thus factors in biological selection. Appearance certainly is a factor in human mating. Men should prefer a lovely character in their prospective wives to a lovely face and form, and the wise man, if he must choose between them, will choose as he should. Unfortunately, many a lovely character lacks an exterior sufficiently attractive to encourage males to find out how lovely the character really is. Not only do aesthetic values influence selection in mating, but the effort to become aesthetically attractive has made beauty big business.

3. Aesthetic attractiveness enhances all social intercourse. Other factors being equal, we prefer occasions and associates that afford us aesthetic satisfaction to those that do not.

4. Even in the clear thin air of the intellect, many an hypothesis has captured the belief of men by its aesthetic qualities. A theory that is neat and symmetrical is a tempter. Plato was frankly fearful of the seductiveness of the arts when they intruded into intellectual matters.

5. Adherence to duty in extraordinarily trying circumstances becomes sublime, and there is an aesthetic charm in spontaneous generosity, kindliness, and good will. Dante could not describe the Godhead in terms of goodness and wisdom alone. It had to be supremely beautiful. Religions with aesthetically satisfying ceremony, ritual, and liturgy attract adherents. Says Whitehead:

> The ultimate motive power, alike in science, in morality, and in religion, is the sense of value, the sense of importance . . . This sense of value imposes on life incredible labours, and apart from

it life sinks back into the passivity of its lower types. The most penetrating exhibition of this force is the sense of beauty, the aesthetic sense of realized perfection.[23]

It is manifestly false, therefore, to deny to the aesthetic values a powerful instrumentality. We do not, it is true, always guide our conduct by aesthetic signs because only in a perfect world would the true, the good, and the beautiful coincide perfectly. If perfection has any meaning, it connotes an object or an act that is perfectly adapted to its purpose, exemplifies the truth, and is delightful to contemplate. There are few such objects.

Because aesthetic values do have instrumentality, in totalitarian states the control of the arts is regarded as of no less importance than the control of industry and the military. For the arts clothe ideas, objects, and persons with attractiveness and thus touch the emotions of men. And whoever controls the emotions of men also controls their actions at their very source. That is why in a democracy we must be wary at the first sign of suppression or intimidation of the artist by the state or any group within the social order. It is a sign that the strain of democracy is becoming too great for some segment of that order.

Negatively, value education suffers if the values of a culture cannot be transformed by artistic imagination into seductive, highly dramatic ideals. It is difficult to teach values without aesthetically exciting value models.[24]

Perspective in the Aesthetic Values

It is easy to go overboard about the aesthetic values. In no other value area is the prospect of achieving self-determination, self-realization, and self-integration so promising.

Nevertheless, to cultivate the aesthetic at the expense of the other values betokens either a lack of moral sensitivity or intellectual care-

---

[23] Alfred N. Whitehead, *The Aims of Education*, London: Williams and Northgate, Ltd., 1929, pp. 62–63. Quoted by permission of The Macmillan Company.

[24] John P. Anton remarks that the Greeks saw clearly that in a well-ordered society "moral excellence calls for exalted art; and artistic activity when wisely conducted terminates in consummate social vision. For the art that succeeded in doing exactly this they had a special name; they called it *psychagogia*." "Art and Society: Homer and the Drama of Predicaments," *The Western Humanities Review*, 14:1, 3–12, Winter, 1960.

lessness. It is a sign of moral insensitivity because the means for cultivating an aesthetic life have to be furnished by someone, and we are not absolved from the duty to contribute to those means. I can devote myself to the contemplation of beauty only if someone else raises the food, builds the shelter, and manufactures the other necessities of life for me. It is intellectually careless not to understand this interdependence among the values.

It is quite another matter to *live* aesthetically, to pursue all values so that their aesthetic quality is enhanced. It is one thing to give up civic responsibilities in favor of visiting art galleries; it is another to infuse civic activities with aesthetic quality. Life should be beautiful, but it is a beautiful life rather than beauty as such that is the essence of the good life, and, therefore, of general education.

The good life can have design and express significant feeling. This, in turn, means giving to life a pattern that communicates itself to the beholder. It means being a distinctive personality with high potentialities of pleasure for others.

The aesthetic principles may serve as a guide to self-determination, self-realization, and self-integration. If we ask *why* we want to determine ourselves, *why* we want the maximum of freedom, it makes sense to answer that, like a work of art, life can be a creative expression of distinctive feeling, and there is no creativity without freedom. It also makes sense to think of self-realization as the shaping of our activities in the real world so that they combine into a distinctive whole. And if we accomplish the first two, are we not also to that extent achieving self-integration also?

We do not in our time and in our schools so conceive of life or education. The aesthetic is split off and reserved for ceremonies, room decorations, art training. The notion that a pupil's life can be judged as a more or less adequate work of art has a strange sound. Yet when we speak of a maladjusted person, do we mean anything more than that he is in the grip of unresolved conflicts, that his various doings seem to have no clear relation to each other, and that there is a grating and grinding that give to his whole life an unpleasant aesthetic quality? Our elaborate psychological testing devices help us locate the areas of conflict, the jarring elements, but as a rule the total aesthetic quality of a person's behavior is what "tips" us off as to whether he is or is not maladjusted.

Unfortunately, the very word "aesthetic" connotes an atmosphere in which effeminate men, bohemianism, "overeducated" women, and visionaries all mingle in an amorphous and faintly unpleasant haze. The aesthetic becomes the antithesis of the useful, the rugged, the manly, the efficient, the courageous, the important.

We have tried to show that the aesthetic becomes a genuine social force by the "valence" it stamps on the world around us. It is a universal trait of man to react aesthetically—from tender maid to the toughest gunman. There is, however, a deeper insight which, if we could grasp, might make the aesthetic a more convincing criterion for education than it now is.

This insight Plato enunciated in the unity of the true, good, and beautiful. What is true (in that it apprehends reality) is aesthetically appealing (beautiful) and adapted to its purpose (good). The more efficient a machine becomes, the more aesthetically satisfying its form is likely to become, and the truer it is to the scientific principles it exemplifies. Modern architecture, airplane and furniture design all confirm this principle. Nonfunctional ornamentation, excess weight, redundant parts, and poor articulation all reduce the efficiency of an object—and its aesthetic quality as well. On the other hand, abstract art and music may be new paths to the apprehension of reality.

On this principle it makes sense to think of the good life as one that realizes the whole gamut of values, according to the best knowledge we have. And when so functioning, it becomes aesthetically significant and for the most part aesthetically satisfying. So viewed, the aesthetic need not and should not connote the effeminate, the useless, the sentimental, the weak, and the unreal, but rather their very opposites.[25]

Competence in aesthetic experience, if it transfers at all, probably does so by making the pupil more demanding of form in all experience. The meaningless act, the incongruous act, the awkward act are displeasing to the aesthetically sensitive person. On the contrary, for experience to become "an experience," in Dewey's phrase, it has to have a beginning, a development, and a climax; it has to have a dramatic quality that makes it vivid and significant.

The opposite of the vivid, the significant, and the dramatic is the drab, the dull, the uninteresting. The flight from boredom is also a search for the aesthetically satisfying experience. It is no accident

[25] For a detailed study of this topic cf. Donald G. Arnstine, *The Aesthetic Dimension of Value Education*. Unpublished doctoral dissertation, University of Illinois, 1960.

that the word "interesting" is so much used and abused in education. The dull task is the routine, the prosaic, the loosely organized task and much the same can be said about the dull teacher, the dull worker, and the dull citizen. We have, unfortunately, taken "interesting" to be a quality of objects or people who are or may be useful to our interests. This is unfortunate for two reasons. One is that pupils do not always have "interests" that we can exploit for instruction; another is that it obscures the pedagogical potential of an absorption in what by its very appearance is attention compelling.

Routine cannot be eliminated from life. Indeed, life would be chaotic if it were eliminated and so would school. But it is made bearable and important if it is regarded as a means to the structure of the total drama, just as routine is needed in sports to furnish the means and background of the game's climax. It is the meaningless routine, the practice for a game that never is played, for a concert that never comes off—that is the curse of school and of life itself.

Summary

Within the aesthetic experience we distinguished the aesthetic subject, the aesthetic object, and the aesthetic act.

In aesthetic education we found that we had to distinguish the production of aesthetic objects from the appreciation of them. Further, there was the matter of considering the intrinsic phase of aesthetic experience; of learning to get the maximum enjoyment from the sheer sensuous appearance of things and the instrumental phase of aesthetic values. With respect to the latter, it was shown how by giving psychological valence (attractiveness) to objects, the aesthetic values are used to enhance all other values and as a means of controlling our choices.

We then had to distinguish the various levels of art appreciation and consider the crucial question of standards. The conclusion was that good art is what the connoisseur—the cultivated man—finds to be aesthetically satisfying. The important thing, however, is that each pupil form his own standard on the basis of the kind of training and knowledge that makes for connoisseurship.

In trying to find a perspective from which to view the aesthetic values, we tried to see what it would mean to live aesthetically. We found that there is a figurative sense in which the good life can be understood as a work of art. The good life has the same qualities as does a good work of art, and it was suggested that the educative task could be conceived that way—especially if in reality there was a genuine relation among the true, the good, and the beautiful.

PROBLEMS FOR DISCUSSION AND RESEARCH

1. Read Stephen Pepper's *The Basis of Criticism in the Arts* for a useful classification of approaches to the problems of aesthetics.

2. See if you can classify the view stressed in this chapter in Pepper's scheme.

3. Make an inventory of your own connoisseurship in the arts. How much of the art, music, drama, dance, and literary sections of *The New York Sunday Times* or a similar newspaper do you read regularly? How much of it can you understand?

4. To what extent does your life have design? Unity in variety? Style? Can you detect it in the lives of your friends?

5. Try to analyze a "problem" pupil or personality in aesthetic terms. Does it make sense to try to do so? In what sense is the good life a beautiful one? In what sense would a beautiful life be good?

SUGGESTIONS FOR FURTHER READING

For fuller bibliographical data on the items listed below, consult the General Bibliography.

As an introduction to this topic, the following four items should be helpful:

Pepper, *The Basis of Criticism in the Arts*, entire.
Plato, The *Symposium*, and *Republic*, Book X, 595A–608B.
Rader, *A Modern Book of Esthetics*. (This anthology has an excellent
    bibliography.)
Vivas and Krieger, *The Problems of Aesthetics*. (A book of readings.)

For systematic study of aesthetics as such: (None of it easy.)

Aristotle, *Poetics*, 1448–1454.
Bosanquet, *Three Lectures on Aesthetic*. (Objective Idealism.)
Dewey, *Art as Experience*. (Gives a view of Dewey not sufficiently
    emphasized.)
Ducasse, *The Philosophy of Art*. (Lucid and readable.)
Gilbert and Kuhn, *A History of Aesthetics*. (Revised edition.)
Gotshalk, *Art and the Social Order*, especially for instrumental role of
    aesthetic values.
Langer, ed., *Reflections on Art*.

232

Maritain, *Creative Intuition in Art and Poetry*. (For the advanced student.)
Meyer, *Emotion and Meaning in Music*.
Parker, *The Principles of Aesthetics*. (Widely used as a text.)
Santayana, *The Sense of Beauty*. (For the advanced student.)

More directly related to education:

Commission on Secondary School Curriculum of the Progressive Education Association, *The Visual Arts in General Education*.
Copland, *What to Listen for in Music*.
Fleming and Veinus, *Understanding Music*.
Leonhard and House, *Foundations and Principles of Music Education*.
Lowenfeld, *Creative and Mental Growth*.
Myers, *Understanding the Arts*.
National Committee on Art Education, *The Art in Art Education*.
N.S.S.E., Fortieth Yearbook, *Art in American Life*. (Treats all phases of the subject.)
———, Fifty-seventh Yearbook, *Basic Concepts in Music Education*. (Especially Part I.)
Pearson, *The New Art Education*, especially Chaps. 6–9.
Read, *Education Through Art*.
Seashore, *Why We Love Music*.
Seiberling, *Looking into Art*, especially pp. 15–47 on the nature of form and content.

On mass culture and mass media:

Lerner, *America as a Civilization*.
Lowenthal, Leo, "Historical Perspectives of Popular Culture," *The American Journal of Sociology*, 55, pp. 323ff. 1950.
N.S.S.E., Fifty-third Yearbook, Part II, *Mass Media and Education*. 1954.
Rosenberg and White, *Mass Culture: The Popular Arts in America*.

10

The Moral Values

Moral values arise in the course of moral experience. Moral experience is what we have whenever we deliberate as to what we *ought* to do in a situation that permits us to choose.

Moral Experience

1. The word "ought" is the clue to what is distinctive about moral experience. In the first place, it implies a freedom to choose, for it would make no sense to say that I ought to obey the law of the land if there were no possibility of disobeying it. So, in the second place, the moral experience demands alternatives among which I can choose. These alternatives must have different consequences, and it must not be a matter of indifference as to which I choose. For example, the need to choose between haddock and halibut in a restaurant hardly qualifies as a moral situation.

2. That every moral experience has an "ought" element in it means that we acknowledge principles by which we judge a choice or an

act to be wrong or right, good or bad. If there were no differences between right and wrong acts, it would make no sense to say that one "ought" to do or choose X rather than Y.

3. The rationally moral experience, therefore, is characterized by a feeling of obligation to choose freely *what* I judge to be right and to choose it *because* I judge it to be right. If I choose haddock rather than halibut *because* I like it better than halibut, I have not chosen morally. If, however, I believe that it is right for a man always to choose what he thinks will give him pleasure, and if in this case I judge haddock will do so, then I ought to choose it. It becomes a moral situation, albeit not a very momentous one. It would become a bit more momentous if haddock were more expensive than halibut because then I would have to weigh the pleasure of eating haddock against the pain of paying for it. If I judged that the pain would overbalance the pleasure, my principle would command me to choose the halibut because I ought to make my choice conform to the principle.

One of the important meanings of moral education, accordingly, is the formation of the tendency or disposition in the individual to guide his choices by a desire to do what is right, and to choose what he does choose because he judges it to be right.

Obligation, right and good

If the "ought" is what is distinctive about moral experience, then it becomes important to ask whence this feeling of obligation comes.

We shall say that the force of the "ought" comes from any demand that I acknowledge as a valid claim. Demands are made upon us by situations, men, God, ideas, things, or even by ourselves. The hungry kitten claims our attention by its squeaks, so does a balky automobile. Men clamor for money they claim we owe them; the community claims part of our income; our employer demands our time and effort. I demand attention from my pupils; they demand allowances from their parents; custom demands conformity. Conscience makes demands, and so do ideals.

Not all claims, however, are moral claims. They are moral when they make their demand in the name of the right. A man lends me $100. I promise to pay him and give him my promissory note. If I refuse to pay him, he can take me to court because he has a legal claim on my property. He also has a moral claim, for he might argue: "It is not just that I should lose my money when you have benefited from it. It is not right for you to break your promise because it is not right for anyone to break a promise in these circumstances." On the other hand, when I acknowledge his claim as just and right, then I am obliged to do something about it. If he feels he has a moral claim and I disagree, then we have a moral issue as to whether or not I ought to acknowledge his claim as a moral claim.

What makes an act morally right? What makes it morally good?[1]

An act becomes morally right (1) when it is done because we intend to fulfil a claim upon us that we acknowledge as valid, (2) when the means we choose are adapted to carrying out this intention, and (3) when the action actually does carry out the intention. For example, if I acknowledge that my students have a claim upon me to give them the most up-to-date instruction in my subject, I act rightly if I intend to give them such instruction, keep up with the literature in my field, and convey it to my classes.

Clearly, I could go wrong on one or all three counts. I could, for example, do what my students demanded, not because I thought it was the right thing to do, but because I wanted to be popular with them. Or I could choose the wrong means; or I could fail to convey the information to them. If I went wrong in my intention, I could not be morally right. If I were sincere in my intention, I could not morally be *wholly* wrong, even if I miscalculated on (2) and (3).

Suppose, however, I felt that my class were a frivolous lot, and that it would serve them right to get an examination they could not pass. If I carried this through successfully, I would be morally right. But this sounds all wrong somehow. Can an act that does harm and does no one any good be morally right? Can the intention to do an injury ever make an act right?[2]

This shows us that the rightness of an act involves not only a special *form* or way of choosing, but also a special kind of claim. In other words, a moral claim has to be in behalf of someone's happiness or welfare. The fundamental claim of mankind is to the pursuit

---

[1] For a fuller treatment of this point, cf. C. D. Broad, "Some of the Main Problems of Ethics," in Feigl and Sellars, *Readings in Philosophical Analysis*, pp. 547–563. For a quite different treatment, cf. Kierkegaard, *Concluding Unscientific Postscript*, pp. 116–167.

[2] Remarks Socrates to Polemarchus: "Can it really be a just man's business to harm any human being?" From *The Republic of Plato*, translated by F. M. Cornford, Clarendon Press, 1945, p. 13.

of happiness, and we can no more help asserting this claim than we can help being men.

An act is "good" insofar as it contributes to some rationally chosen goal or end, some hope of welfare, satisfaction, or happiness. It is evil if it frustrates such a hope. To be morally right, therefore, an act must be intended to fill not any claim, but a claim to some good in life.

An act may be right and yet not bring about the intended good. I may do everything needed to give my students the most up-to-date instruction, but if they pay no attention, the intended good will not result. Or I may be planning their downfall, only to have their failure in my examination lead to my dismissal and to my replacement by a more benign and effective instructor.

Inner and outer

This distinction between the good and the right has been important both in the history of ethics and in moral education. The argument reduced to its simplest form is this:

If we concentrate on the rightness of acts, then we emphasize what goes on inside the moral agent: his intent, feeling of obligation, and his deliberations.[3] Unfortunately, he can make mistakes all along the line, so that his action may or may not bring about a result that is for the good of the claimant or for anyone else. With the best of intentions he may lack the skill to insure the goodness of his acts. Hence there develops a tendency to be satisfied with being morally right and leaving the consequences in the lap of the gods. It may discourage action altogether since the moral quality of the act lies so much in the intent of the actor.

On the opposite side, it is argued that the consequences of an act are what make it morally good or not. We should aim at the good of the claimant or of society or of the greatest number. Usually this good has been identified with some kind of pleasantness or happiness, and such a theory has been called Utilitarianism.[4] Here the emphasis is not so much on intent or on feelings of obligation as on the calculation of means that will really bring about desired or desirable consequences.

---

[3] Cf. Wheelwright, *A Critical Introduction to Ethics*, revised edition, pp. 156–158.

[4] *Ibid.*, pp. 257–265.

What everyone wants is a union of the inner and outer such that men choose in the right way, but with an eye to the good of their fellow men.[5] The difficulty resides in the fact that any action puts trains of results into motion that have almost unpredictable effects, especially when they collide with the multitude of other actions that are set in motion at the same time.

Nor are moral situations so simple that any set of principles can tell us baldly the right thing to do. If a man brandishing a gun inquires whether his "good-for-nothing" son is hiding in my house, the principle of "never tell a lie" seems inadequate. To the starving man in the wilderness who comes upon a cache of food, the principle of "Do not take what does not belong to you" seems irrelevant. Only the broadest of principles, such as "Do good" or "Do unto others as you would have them do unto you," cover the assortment of situations that confront us every day. But their very breadth reduces their usefulness as guides in particular instances.

Moral action, therefore, is always a compromise among conflicting goods and evils. This is another way of saying that moral action always involves a gamble so far as results are concerned. We try to reduce the risks by increasing our knowledge, on one hand, and by becoming more and more sensitive to the call of duty, on the other. This automatically outlines the problems and scope of moral education.

Moral Education

Ask a representative body of citizens what they want in the way of moral education, and the answer will be somewhat as follows:

We want our children to develop reliable tendencies to tell the truth, to respect the community's codes of right and wrong, to be

[5] For an Instrumentalist solution to this problem cf. Dewey, *Democracy and Education*, Chap. 26. But note what Dewey says elsewhere: "In principle, their [consequences] role in morals is the same as in scientific inquiry. They are important not as such or by themselves, but in their function as *tests* of ideas, principles, theories. It is possible that at times, in opposition to *ipse dixit* 'intuitions' and dogmatic assertions of absolute standards, I have emphasized the importance of consequences so as to make them supreme in and of themselves. If so, I have departed from my proper view, that of their use as tests of proposed ends and ideals." *The Philosophy of John Dewey*, The Library of Living Philosophers, Vol. I, edited by Paul Arthur Schilpp, Evanston, Ill.: Northwestern University, 1939, p. 591 note.

courageous, to be persevering in the face of obstacles, to withstand the temptations of disapproved pleasures, to be able to sacrifice present pleasures in favor of more remote ones, to have a sense of justice and fair play.

Parents do not expect a guarantee that their child will do this or that at any given time in the future. They are after character traits or reliable tendencies or dispositions to react in certain ways in the presence of difficulties, duties, and conflicts.

The citizens would agree that there is no fixed set of rules to guide their children, but they would insist that in the long run, the principles of truth telling, promise keeping, honesty, courage, perseverance, and strong will are reliable formulas for right action. These principles are part of the culture, reinforced by religion, and consonant with tradition. Parents do not challenge them or spend too much time on the "special" cases where the principles apply neither neatly nor happily.

The school and character training

To sum up the previous paragraphs: parents want children to have a strong sense of duty and a strong tendency to do that duty. There is less concern about reflecting on what duty is and what really would discharge it. In one important sense the parents are on sound premises. They know, as Aristotle pointed out long ago, that the study of ethics does not form the emotional disposition to do the right thing. Only people who already have a strong sense of duty, courage, perseverance, and honesty can profitably study what makes acts right and wrong, good and bad.

What can the school do about such training? We call it training because that is what it is. By living with others and feeling their pleasure and displeasure, we introject their moral attitudes so that we expect from ourselves what others expect from us. It is a familiar story by now that these basic attitudes are formed before the child comes to school. What can the school add?

The answer is clear but disappointing. The school can and does reinforce these attitudes. Teachers praise the virtues and condemn the vices. Some schools use religious teachings to aid in the reinforcement; some do not, but it would be hard to find schools in which the moral principles of the culture are not accepted and practiced. A school which did not would not last a year. Why then the perpetual clamor that the school ought to do more in forming character?

There are at least two reasons for this complaint. Alarmed by the delinquency of juveniles and adults, it is natural for the public to point an accusing finger at the school as well as at the home. To remedy matters, it suggests stricter discipline in both places with more severe punishments for infractions. It also demands more deliberate exhortation of pupils to be good.

The school could punish more and exhort more. Given the children for 24 hours of the day for a number of years, the school could condition them, as apparently the home sometimes fails to do. As matters now stand, more severe discipline by the school would merely drive the recalcitrant ones out of school sooner. It would mean little, if not matched by equal severity in the home and in the community. Actually the school is probably more severe in these matters than is the general community. As for preaching moral character, this is notoriously innocuous so far as forming attitudes is concerned. If you spare the rod, the preaching is useless; if you use the rod, the preaching is unnecessary.

Another complaint comes from educators themselves. Progressive school theorists complain that the traditional school did not make character formation sufficiently central in its program. But what they suggest is not what the public has in mind.

We are told by Dewey, for example, that such traits as honesty, perseverance, and sensitiveness to the demands and claims of others are built into the individual as a direct result of solving problems intelligently. To follow out the ramifications of any social problem automatically leads to enlargement of interest. This is so because social problems are not isolated. The problem of maintaining good health, for example, leads me to discover that my health depends on community health. Interest in my health has to grow to cover the health of others. The requirements of the problem force me to look at it objectively. I cannot abandon the search for data and hypotheses, and, finally, I cannot stop until I have acted to verify the generalizations that I chose to guide my conduct. The scientific method has a morality of its own.[6]

Quite rightly, Dewey regards the search for the solutions to prob-

[6] *Democracy and Education,* pp. 407–414. Cf. also William Gruen, "The Moral Dimension of Science," *Notes and Essays,* No. 23, The Center for the Study of Liberal Arts in Education.

lems a moral as well as an intellectual enterprise. If we meet the intellectual requirements, we are meeting the moral ones at the same time. Perseverance, courage, and open-mindedness all are involved in inquiry. And as the pupil solves more and more problems and finds his life more efficient and more satisfactory, these traits get built into his character as habits. Such discipline is genuine self-discipline.

For this pattern of character training to be effective, the pupils must maintain their interest in the problem. If the group begins with the problem of maintaining its own health and *keeps* that interest, the intellectual work needed to explore and solve the problem will call forth perseverance, open-mindedness, courage, and resistance to distractions. Or if the group or an individual has a strong desire to solve the problem, we will get the same result, even if the interest in health wanes during the inquiry.

Intellectual curiosity or personal involvement or both are needed to make this method produce character training. The former is unevenly distributed and sporadic, and interest fluctuates widely in children and even in adults. We may start with a strong interest in the problem of health, but if the data are too difficult to secure or the hypotheses too complex, the interest may evaporate. As a reliable method for building character traits the claim of this approach loses much of its plausibility.

The other point to be noticed in this approach is that no specific set of fixed moral principles is used as a guide to moral education. The group is honest because the intellectual requirements of inquiry demand honesty about the data as well as a steady eye on the goal and resistance to distractions. Honesty, perseverance, and open-mindedness gain their value from being useful in solving problems and are not practiced on their own account. These principles may, of course, emerge from many problem-solving experiences. When they do they will be held more genuinely and firmly because they have been tested in the direct experience of the pupil. On this view scientists and other professional problem-solvers ought to have the most stable and admirable characters.

It is difficult to appraise this part of the theory because no pupil and no teacher in our culture is completely free from the kind of conditioning that makes him feel that honesty is good on its own account and that lying is intrinsically bad. Whether the problem-solving reinforces, uses, or creates these conditionings cannot, therefore, be decisively ascertained. One can argue about as plausibly that the conditionings help solve the problems, as that the problem-solvings form the dispositions.

We conclude that the Progressive formula probably does not achieve moral training or character formation unless there is a strong intellectual curiosity to begin with, unless interest can be maintained at a fairly high pitch for large numbers of pupils over long periods of time, and unless there has already been formed a conditioned bias in favor of certain moral values.

The school and moral education

The school can do little about character training. Can it do anything about moral education? The answer, of course, is that the whole curriculum is a kind of moral education, and in no merely figurative sense.

1. If morality has to do with the claims made upon us, then moral education means not only to learn *what* these claims are, but also how they arose and how *justified they are in the light of the good life.*

2. Where do we get this kind of knowledge? Clearly, in the sciences of society and of the Self: in history, sociology, anthropology, economics, psychology, philosophy, literature, religion, and the arts.

3. Where do we get the skill to evaluate the diverse claims made upon us? In the problem-solving experiences dealing with genuine social and moral issues. (See Chapter 13.)

What we *can* do we learn from the social sciences and natural sciences. What we *ought* to do is harder to learn. We can in our problem-solving try to clarify the meaning of our duty, and in the guidance program individuals can clear the way for making more intelligent moral decisions in their own lives, but there is no course and no man to tell us what we ought to do. This learning we can produce only within ourselves by reflecting on the moral predicaments of others and of ourselves. (For the role of problem-solving and guidance in the curriculum, see Chapter 13.)

4. What has this kind of education to do with a sense of duty? The good life is the ultimate aim of education, and for each pupil this means to determine himself, realize himself, and integrate himself through the habits of acquiring, using, and enjoying the truth. The good life makes a claim upon the individual. Everything de-

pends on whether the school can persuade him to acknowledge this as a moral claim, as a demand that he judges he *ought* to satisfy.

In one sense, such a commitment has already been made for us because it is human nature to strive to determine itself, realize itself, and integrate itself. In another sense, however, it is not automatic because we need not determine ourselves, realize ourselves, or integrate ourselves *through knowledge.* Only as the pupil through perfecting his habits of knowing realizes that this is the chief instrument for the good life will he become committed to it as a duty.

5. Moral education, as we have conceived it, may strike neither the general public nor parents as satisfactory. In the first place, it is not the equivalent of moral training, which is really what both are after. In the second place, moral reflection in examining the claims upon our sense of duty may prove embarrassing. Such reflection is always a potential danger to conventional morality.

As a notorious example, consider the matter of sexual morality. Every adolescent is concerned with the claims made upon him or her in this area of life by the customs and *mores* of the culture on one hand, and those of the peer group, on the other. Here is a type of behavior in which the glands, a sexually-saturated environment, and opportunity for gratification all combine to test the moral fiber of any girl or boy.

This is a long-standing conflict in civilized societies. The delay between pubescence and marriage has real value for society as a whole but the price for it is exacted from the adolescent. The adults who have solved the sex problem by marriage find it hard to remember their own storms and stresses of earlier days. The adolescents, on the other hand, seeing sex allure rewarded by fame and fortune and celebrated in virtually every advertisement cannot understand the personal and social value of restrictions on sexual behavior. That they will feel about these matters 15 years hence as do their parents *now* is to them almost unbelievable.

Parents want their children to refrain from illicit sex behavior. If this cannot be managed, the next best thing is to keep such behavior from the knowledge of the community. Why such behavior is wrong is hardly a matter for discussion for well-brought-up parents. And if forced into such discussion, they can only answer that the social consequences are such that one had better avoid them. If the adolescent presses the issue and wants to know why the social consequences should be so drastic, the parents become angry, hurt, or both.

Yet in reflective morality these are precisely the sort of questions that will be raised, and they may not be answered at all, or not in the way the parents might like. The role of chastity in the good life is not a simple matter. It is only on a high plane of thought and feeling that a case can be made out for it that will stand up against the objections of the sceptical adolescent.

One would like to hope that as the adolescent goes further and further into the sciences of the Self, he will discover the moral, aesthetic, and religious significance of the sexual act for the personality. Until this discovery is made, the sexual impulse will have to be disciplined by fear or by ingenious chaperones. After the discovery, the discipline will come from a concept of the personality that the adolescent has acknowledged as valid for himself and all others, including members of the opposite sex. Knowledge forms character to the extent that it contributes to such a concept of the Self.

Nevertheless, there is always risk in inquiry, in reflection, and in knowledge. They would be powerless if they were innocuous. But there is no way of avoiding that risk if we intend to be men rather than trained animals. Reflecting on sex morality or other questions is not the same as "bull sessions" or noisy rebellions against the *mores* of the community. Whatever merit these activities may have, they are not characteristic of reflection and study. The study of the principles and problems of morals is ethics and the ideal time to begin this study is adolescence, that is, in high school and college.

Criteria of Moral Education and Development

If self-determination, self-realization, and self-integration are genuine criteria of the good life, then they are criteria for moral action.

Self-determination

Moral education aims at the development of freedom because without freedom of choice no act is moral in quality. How do we educate pupils to be free?

We might urge pupils to want to be free. Ours was a birth in freedom; freedom is celebrated in song and story as well as in history. Do we have to *urge* human beings to want to be free? Do we have to urge people to want to be free from constraint? From fear? From want? From political despotism? No one, I suggest, needs to be told to want this kind of freedom. We usually want more of it than we can possibly have.

There is, however, a freedom which not all of us want. Indeed we sometimes dread it. It is the freedom that carries the price tag of responsibility. A vigorous critic of an organization is at least momentarily disconcerted to find himself its president. Before, he could suggest the wildest schemes, the boldest measures; others would share the responsibility if they were adopted; and there would be no responsibility if they were rejected. Now matters are really up to him.

With the awareness of freedom comes the frightening realization that we have become subject to a claim that we cannot ignore. It is easier, in the short run, to have one's life shaped by others and by circumstances over which one has no control.

We are indebted to the Existentialist writers and especially to Kierkegaard[7] for a recognition of this aspect of freedom and of the existential anxiety that is a part of human nature. We are all anxious, whether we know it or not, because we have an inkling of what human freedom means.[8]

Moral education has to discourage flight from this kind of freedom. To make the individual pupil sensitive to the possibility that at every moment of his life there may be something that *he* can do to shape the next moment is an education for freedom. Self-determination means that one has accepted the responsibility for the making of his future and perhaps of the future of all other men.

The school, you will say, is not the place where pupils make momentous choices. How then can the school educate for freedom? It does so by way of knowledge. As we learn more about our world, our social order, and about ourselves, do we not become more and more sensitive to the claims made upon us? And with this knowledge can we ignore the question as to what our responsibility is to the community, country, family, school, and to our own selves?

Further, the use of knowledge to shape our commitments is what makes them rational rather than capricious. I cannot ever foresee all

[7] Especially in *The Concept of Dread* and *The Sickness Unto Death*. See also H. S. Broudy, "Kierkegaard's Levels of Existence," *Philosophy and Phenomenological Research,* 1:3, pp. 294–312, March, 1941.

[8] For the relation of Kierkegaard's concept of anxiety to that of Freud, cf. Mowrer, *Learning Theory and Personality Dynamics,* pp. 540–546.

the consequences of my commitment, but if I make it on the best knowledge I can summon, my gamble with life has its supreme justification. No man can do more.

The first moral law for every man is to be as rational and as knowing in his choices as circumstances will permit. This law implies another: it is every man's duty to learn as much about the world, the society, and himself as he can.

A reliable symptom as to whether a school or a school system is working at moral education is its respect for knowledge. It matters little whether a school has one or a dozen courses marked "character education." If its attitude toward human knowing is derogatory, if it is anti-intellectualistic in its philosophy, if it gears its curriculum to the minimum needs of getting along on the job or in the group, then that school system has no genuine respect for persons as potential moral legislators in their own right. That system is not aiming at self-determination, but rather at the determination of the pupil by the group, by the economic order, by anything and everything except himself.

However, let us repeat that knowledge as such is no guarantee that every pupil will commit himself to a life according to knowledge. The temptation of pleasure and the urge of lust, fear, and anger can blot out—for a while, at least—the knowledge we do have. The knowledge that guarantees virtue is not simply understanding. It is rather what Plato was speaking about when he said:

> In the world of knowledge, the last thing to be perceived and only with great difficulty is the essential Form of Goodness. Once it is perceived, the conclusion must follow that, for all things, this is the cause of whatever is right and good; in the visible world it gives birth to light and to the lord of light, while it is itself sovereign in the intelligible world and the parent of intelligence and truth. Without having had a vision of this Form no one can act with wisdom, either in his own life or in matters of state.[9]

It is a conversion of the spirit—an emotional commitment to what is revealed about the good life. It is a kind of mystical state, and blessed are those who have experienced it. In a school system it is not easy to arrange for mystical experience. About all one can do is to present knowledge to the student and hope that as he learns to use it, he will feel the force of its claim upon him.

[9] From *The Republic of Plato*, translated by F. M. Cornford, Clarendon Press, 1945, p. 231.

Much of the discussion about freedom in education and education for freedom is concerned with the possibility and desirability of the pupil "making up his own mind." It is important to note the relation between this concept of freedom and the one involved in self-determination.

What does it mean to "make up one's own mind"? Presumably, it is the opposite of taking one's opinions, beliefs, values, and attitudes ready-made, e.g., from textbooks, customs, conventions, traditions, and authorities (experts supposedly excepted). It is argued that the student should accept nothing without making an effort to evaluate and criticize what he is accepting. Conceivably, two individuals could have the same stock of beliefs and values, yet one would have made up his own mind while the other had not.

Freedom of thought means, therefore, the possibility of rejecting a belief even when it is presented with a considerable amount of pressure or persuasion. It means also the right to examine beliefs with the option of rejection. Why do we put so much stress upon this right? Why *ought* we to encourage and even to insist that our pupils form the tendency to examine beliefs?

Because the truth for me is what the *evidence* compels me to believe. Therefore, if it is my duty to seek the truth, it is likewise my duty to examine the evidence for my beliefs. Intellectual competence is thus the first moral duty of the school and the keystone of the formal school's program of moral education. Examining beliefs is admittedly dangerous to the belief; not examining them is disastrous to the soul.

Once more let it be noted that examining a belief is not the same as talking heatedly about it or making rude noises about those who entertain it. For the school and for life this is a fundamental distinction.

Self-realization

We ought to choose freely, but *what* ought we to choose? So far as education is concerned, choice should be to achieve self-realization.

From where the pupil stands, self-realization lies in his own future. For the educator, the goal is the self-realization of all his pupils. Morally speaking, each pupil *ought* to realize his potentialities, and the school *ought* to cultivate the potentialities of every pupil. This seems so obvious as to be trivial, for does not human nature force us to strive for self-realization? Is there any choice, any *ought* in the matter?

The answer lies in the many levels of striving that are possible so that although striving is a universal feature of human nature, its precise character is not. Man can live after a fashion without pushing himself to the limit of his capacity. He can be ignorant of his potentialities, or he can ignore them. There is a choice here, and there can be an *ought*—if we can establish a claim upon him and get him to acknowledge the claim.

As an educator, there is an argument to which one can resort: if I, as a teacher, know the value of a sunset, a friend, a generous act, or an insight into the truth, and if I know you, as a pupil, have the capacity to realize these values, then I ought to disclose these possibilities to you and teach you how to cultivate them. If these values cannot thereafter speak for themselves, there is no more that I can say for them.

Suppose the pupil argues: Does it make any difference to anyone but myself whether I cultivate my capacities or not? Suppose I could become a first-rate poet, musician, scientist, doctor, or carpenter. Suppose I am content to remain second- or even third-rate. Can you tell me that I *ought* to become first-rate?[10]

We can answer in the affirmative, but only if we are prepared to argue that mankind has a claim upon the full self-realization of every man. What could be the basis for such a claim?

We cannot, as a matter of justice, demand that anyone realize his powers beyond what is needed to recompense his fellow men for the values they enable him to realize. If, however, the individual can be led to experience a value of a higher order than he hitherto has achieved, and if he acknowledges it as higher, then he does have a duty to contribute the greatest values of which he is capable. Once he acknowledges that first-rate science is better than second-rate, he is obligated to become the best kind of scientist of which he is capable. He is heeding the claim of value itself. This claim is

[10] A culture by fixing the style of life that is generally regarded as desirable fixes at the same time the amount of self-realization its members, on the average, will regard as desirable. In our own culture, a high degree of self-realization on the part of an intellectual-technological elite has reduced the self-realization needed by the many to earn a decent living, but it has enormously increased the degree of self-realization needed to live really well.

universal, that is, whatever is judged to be good or right is judged to be so for all men in the same circumstances.

That is why in the school we have to take advantage of our position as teachers to set into motion the process of self-realization. Indeed, this becomes our moral obligation. The source of this claim is the nature of man itself, for if we know anything about human nature, it is that the particular direction of human striving is not predetermined by the genes, but by the power of the human mind to envision patterns of possibility. To direct this striving to self-realization through knowledge, therefore, is what the good life demands of the school.

It has been objected that self-realization as an educational goal or as a goal of life smacks too much of individualism, and selfish individualism at that. It seems to connote a narrow devotion to a delightful future for oneself with not much thought for goodness in the lives of others.

However, the situation is not so bad as it sounds. We can only realize ourselves through others. Further, we realize ourselves in the creation of value *for* others. There is no sense in my becoming an engineer if I don't design objects for someone else's use. There is little point in becoming a doctor unless there are people to heal.

Does self-realization mean that I shall realize myself at the expense of the self-realization of others? Ought I to cultivate my own powers if it means that others will have to go without the needs of life, without education, without a place in the sun? If I base my duty to realize myself on the claim that positive value is good in itself, does it follow that only the value I achieve is good?

If, however, there is such a thing as human nature, then a value is what perfects that human nature. If health is good, it is good for all human beings; if education is good, it is good for all. If, in brief, it is my duty to realize my capacities, it is everyone's duty to do likewise. I have to respect this claim wherever it is made. Indeed I have to make that claim for all mankind.

In education, the imperative to self-realization has definite consequences. It means that we have to urge, cajole, and, so far as we are allowed, *insist* that education be not curtailed and truncated for any individual before his capacities for learning have been exploited as far as we have the resources to exploit them. It means that if a boy can learn literature, he will be required to learn it; if he can master trigonometry, he will be required to do so; if he can be artistically competent, he will be required to be competent without worrying too much whether it will get him a job, a house in the suburbs, or membership in the country club.

The vocational usefulness of his school tasks the pupil gauges with uncanny accuracy. It is the usefulness of the school studies to what Aristotle called citizenship and leisure (cultivation of one's rational powers) that the pupil cannot easily discern. Today the intellectual requirements for these are so high that unless the tools for achieving them are perfected in the secondary school, the chances of adequately cultivating one's rational resources in later life are remote.

Self-integration

Self-integration means that we have to put the claims that tug at us from all directions in some intelligible order. Value claims conflict with each other. Until we choose between alternative values, we are torn among them. To decide which values shall dominate and guide our efforts to self-realization is itself a moral decision, perhaps the most serious of all decisions. Moral education in the school, therefore, includes the learning of the means, or at least of some of them, for value integration. How do we go about this?

It is doubtful whether a frontal attack on this problem is possible in the school. The kind of psychological integration the mental hygienist has in mind involves too many non-school factors for the school to control. The guidance program, provided disintegration is not too far advanced, may help the individual alter perspectives so that conflicts can be reduced.

Further, integration is not completed in school because the threats to integration never cease. Vocational failure, the loss of loved ones, disgrace—who knows how well the individual will absorb such calamities?

Finally, it is doubtful whether there is any general integrative formula that will usefully apply to every individual. Some people can integrate their lives through religion; for others, religion is a disruptive force. To some, the aesthetic values are integrative, to some, social service, to some, financial success, and to some, a sense of humor.

Knowledge might be the universal integrator, and in this book it is taken for granted that the school will devote itself to the integrating of life through knowledge. Yet it is silly to urge a boy with modest intellectual endowments to integrate his value system through erudition or to suggest to a musically gifted pupil that he take up farming as a way of simplifying and ordering life. What the school can do is to make an intelligent estimate of the pupil's integrative pattern on the basis of his potentialities. Further, much of the curriculum to be outlined is a study of what men have had to integrate and to what extent they have managed to do so. Because these struggles take place on the stages of history and art, they write our own individual problems in large and luminous letters.

These are admittedly indirect methods. Nevertheless, if the world does not make sense to a man, he is to that degree not integrated. Knowledge tries to find what sense there is in the world and to that extent is integrative for everyone. Studies of mental illness repeatedly disclose an inability or unwillingness to perceive reality. Illusions, delusions, neurotic anxieties are all "bad" because they are self-deceptions. Therapy tries to help the victim recover the sense of reality. The school is not a psychiatric clinic, and knowledge alone may not keep us sound of mind, but in keeping its eye on knowledge, the school is on firm psychological ground.

Therefore, if a general education can give a pupil a confidence in his power to acquire and use knowledge, and if it gives him a realistic sense of his own capacities, his strengths, and his weaknesses, that is, perhaps, a good beginning in integration.

It turns out that criteria of moral education (not moral training) are the criteria of the good life itself, and that moral education is all one with a general education that is aimed at the good life. This means that a school devoted to general education will probably not have a course labeled "moral education" in its course of study. Nor will it devote itself to character training by conditioning, although it will reinforce such training in the ordinary course of school keeping and even design its noninstructional activities with an eye to making such reinforcement systematic rather incidental.[11] It will judge the success of its moral education by the degree to which the pupil becomes sensitive to the demand that he determine, realize, and integrate himself.

---

[11] Due consideration has convinced me that the last phrase in this sentence does not abandon instruction as the primary function of the school.

Democracy as an ethical norm

We have deliberately avoided reference to democracy or to the democratic way of life as a set of moral standards. We have not argued that an act is right if it is in accord with the democratic tradition and wrong if it is not, because this would put the cart before the horse. If democracy is an ultimate good, it cannot be argued about. That is, we could not meaningfully ask whether democracy itself is good. On such a view we would have to say that the challenges to democracy of Hitler and Stalin among others were dangerous but not meaningful. If we wish to defend it against other ways of life, we must do so on the grounds that it meets the claims of human nature and value better than its competitors. I believe that if we examine the value system underlying American democracy, we shall find that it consciously and explicitly acknowledges self-determination, self-realization, and self-integration as the highest goods. The American Creed[12] can legitimately and rationally become a great integrative value system in our own culture and in the American public school.

The study of the Creed, the analysis of its meanings in terms of the good life, and the understanding of how our American practices conform to it or diverge from it constitute moral education in the broadest and most genuine sense. The redefinition of the kind of life style that the Creed calls for in a given epoch is at the heart of moral reflection. If the American Creed turns out *upon rational weighing and analysis* to demand and promote self-realization, self-determination, and self-integration, then we can justify throwing the weight of tradition, authority, and even ritual in its favor. This rational analysis is what the curriculum of general education should promote and does promote if it is knowledge-centered.

Perspective in the Moral Values

In one sense it is pointless to ask what perspective we should take with respect to the moral values because they furnish the perspective of all other perspectives. The moral question is always in order, for it is always relevant to ask: Is this what ought to be done?

[12] Cf. Myrdal, *An American Dilemma*, Chap. 1, and Stanley, *Education and Social Integration*, Chap. 7.

There are, however, certain aberrations of moral activity that the morally educated man tries to avoid.

1. *Moral awkwardness.* When one is learning to ride a bicycle he has to pay close attention to every movement. In time he pays attention only to the larger issues of steering, variations of speed, and other traffic. What practice does for the cyclist the *mores*, custom, and moral principles do for the moral man. When another human being is in danger he does not institute a long process of inquiry as to whether he ought to help him. He does not on every occasion wonder whether he ought to tell the truth, be honest, kind, generous, or loyal. In most situations he reacts spontaneously. It is only when a custom, tradition, or a principle promises to lead to doubtful consequences that he resorts to deliberation. Moral *training* provides moral spontaneity, the raw material for moral education.[13]

2. *Moral rigidity.* Here habituation in the *mores*, customs, traditions, and precepts is so thorough that moral reflection never gets started. "It just isn't done" becomes the sovereign moral maxim. Such people go right most of the time; they are the work horses of the social order, but there could never be any moral growth if it depended upon them.

3. *Overconscientiousness.* Moral questioning always has a place in conduct, but the endless questioning of the propriety of an act can impede action or ruin the very quality for the sake of which it is undertaken. One can, so to speak, become morally muscle-bound. The man who keeps on wondering whether he ought to have paid so much for a theatre ticket or a suit of clothes has neither the money nor the pleasure he hoped to buy with it.

These three aberrations reveal themselves first and most clearly to our aesthetic sensibility. They make a man slightly repulsive, annoying, or irritating to one in the more normal moral state. Like all aspects of life, the moral one, when functioning well, is aesthetically pleasing.

4. *Intellectual smugness.* It is easy, especially in a book that emphasizes the intellectual life, to give the impression that if only we think long and carefully enough, we shall surely guide our lives

---

[13] This is somewhat like the distinction made by Friedrich Schiller in his essay *Anmut und Würde*, in which he differentiates charm, or spontaneous goodness, from dignity, the quality of deservingness that comes from being good from a sense of duty.

in the paths of unbroken properity and happiness. This is a species of intellectual pride that goes before many a fall. The really rational man knows the limits of reason. The truth is that over most factors in our life we have only partial control, and over many others no control whatever. Aside from such natural calamities as floods, tornadoes, earthquakes, and droughts, there are automobiles and other man-made hazards. These, too, can in an instant make a joke out of a lifetime of striving and service.

In trying to predict the future, we dutifully rely on past experience, especially when it has been collected, sifted, and statistically described. If the average life span of the American male is declared to be 65, can we plan our lives accordingly? As a group, yes. On this basis we calculate old-age benefits, the size of the labor market, and the demand for artificial teeth. Can any individual plan his life on this statistical knowledge? Yes, but it is a planned gamble. Will he be in the two-thirds who live to 65? Will he be in the smaller group that dies at 55 or 75? He goes to a doctor who tells him he has a heart condition. "How long shall I live?" he inquires. "Well," replies the doctor, "Our statistics show that 70 per cent of the patients with this condition die in 10 years, 25 per cent in 15 years, and five per cent in 20 years."

The gamble has now been narrowed but not removed. Into which group will he fall? Who knows?

So long as there is no certainty in such matters, the future is not deprived of its dread. The kind of knowledge we have about events lessens the need to make foolish choices, but it does not eliminate the risky ones.

Suppose a man were told by a battery of medical experts that his condition was such that he had two alternatives: one was to do nothing and die within a few years; the other was to undergo surgery which, according to the records, had been 95 per cent successful and would let him live for many years. Suppose that he was a rational man. Here was a risk, but a calculated one with the vast weight of the evidence in favor of the operation. Suppose that he took the chance and died. The effect on the statistics would be slight; on him, considerable.

Does this mean we are not to trust knowledge, the best knowledge available? Not at all, but whoever believes that knowledge will render moral courage, suffering, anxiety, guilt and repentance unnecessary is misunderstanding the nature of knowledge and the nature of man.

Moral perspective is a balanced awareness of the precariousness of our choices and their tremendous import. One can be drowned as effectively in six feet of water as in 6000. It is part of moral perspective not to be overwhelmed by the 6000 and not to despise the six. We do not even know in advance which of our choices will turn out to have been the big ones.

The serious moral attitude is something like our demeanor as a strange dog approaches. We maintain outward calm, tremble a little inside, look the beast firmly in the eye, and hope for the best.

Summary

The distinctive note in moral experience is the presence of "ought-ness." It arises when we acknowledge some claim upon us as a valid claim. To act with the intent to fill this claim is a necessary condition for moral justification, but not a sufficient one. To make an act fully moral requires correctness in assaying the claims upon us and in carrying out the means to fulfilling it. The form of our act, however correct, does not prevent an act from intending and achieving evil. Hence the completely moral act always aims at some good and chooses it in a certain way.

This outlines the requirements of moral education in the school: the production of moral attitudes and goals that will bear moral scrutiny. The program thus falls into two parts: (1) moral training, which the school can only reinforce if already begun outside the school, and (2) moral education, which is the use of knowledge to guide moral choices and judgment.

We found the criteria of moral education to be self-determination, self-realization, and self-integration inasmuch as these are the criteria of the good life itself. Insofar as the American Creed also assumes these criteria, our schools can pursue moral education within a democratic framework, confident that it will withstand the closest scrutiny of moral reflection.

Although the moral values furnish the perspective of all other perspectives, even they are not free from possible aberrations, such as moral awkwardness, moral rigidity, overconscientiousness, and intellectual smugness.

PROBLEMS FOR DISCUSSION AND RESEARCH

1. Study and outline C. D. Broad's article (see reference below) to give you a good notion of the problems found in the study of ethics and for a working terminology.

2. Read the first chapter in Gunnar Myrdal's *An American Dilemma* for an understanding of the American Creed.

3. Study the American Creed to see whether or not it points to self-determination, self-realization, and self-integration as primary values.

4. Organize a panel or round table to discuss the difference between moral training and moral education. Can this distinction be defended theoretically? Can it be maintained in school practice?

5. Read as much as you can of Aristotle's *Nicomachean Ethics* and Walter Lippmann's *A Preface to Morals*. To what extent do you feel that Aristotle's ethical views are outmoded?

6. Can you find an instance where a culture has come to regard as right what it previously regarded as wrong? How would you explain the change?

SUGGESTIONS FOR FURTHER READING

For fuller bibliographical data on the items listed below, consult the General Bibliography.
I would begin by studying quite thoroughly and outlining:

Broad, C. D., "Some of the Main Problems of Ethics," in Feigl and Sellars, *Readings in Philosophical Analysis,* pp. 547–563.

With this as a guide I would read:

Aristotle, *Nicomachean Ethics.* (All of it, if possible.)
Lippmann, *A Preface to Morals.* (A modern and relatively nontechnical book.)
Plato, *Charmides, Lysis, Laches, Protagoras.*

Next might come some study of various ethical theories in such works as:

Edwards and Pap, *A Modern Introduction to Philosophy,* pp. 310–442.
Hill, *Contemporary Ethical Theories.*
Hospers, *An Introduction to Philosophical Analysis,* Chap. 7.
Wheelwright, *A Critical Introduction to Ethics.*

For a critical survey of this field, especially for the advanced student:

W. K. Frankena, "Moral Philosophy at Mid-Century," *Philosophical Review,* 1951.

For samples of the empirical approach to problems of morality:

Hartshorne and May, *Studies in the Nature of Deceit* and *Studies in the Nature of Character.*

Jones, "Character Development in Children: An Objective Approach," *Manual of Child Psychology.*

More directly related to philosophy of education:

Brubacher, *Eclectic Philosophy of Education,* pp. 199–207, 460–475.

———, *Modern Philosophies of Education,* Chap. 13.

Childs, *Education and Morals,* Part II.

Hutchins, *Morals, Religion, and Higher Education.*

Mason, *Moral Values and Secular Education.*

Redden and Ryan, *A Catholic Philosophy of Education,* Chap. 6.

CHAPTER | 11

The Religious Values

Previous chapters tried to isolate the peculiar characteristic that made an experience economic, social, aesthetic, or moral. Can we do the same for the religious experience? Or is it a combination of other value experiences?

When people pray or worship, we say they are having a religious experience. Some report seeing visions of God and angels, and some report other forms of communion with the Divine. William James in his *Varieties of Religious Experience* brings together a collection of reports that reveal the intensity and power of such experiences. What makes an experience religious?

Religious Experience

In religious experience there is a feeling of being in the presence of or in communication with something holy or sacred, of something worthy of veneration and worship.

Many a ragged hermit has given the impression to his followers that he was holy because they felt that way in his presence. Clergy-

257

men are holy in that they are formally related to God and have received authority to speak and act for God. Of course, they may be holy in the hermit's sense also. A church, an altar, or a burying ground becomes a holy object when consecrated; so do clerical vestments, vessels, shrines, relics, and many other objects.

The response to the holy object may be an emotion of fear, of awe, reverence, love, or any combination of them. A painting of a Madonna in an art gallery gives rise to one kind of feeling usually an aesthetic one. The same painting in a church makes us feel differently toward it. To steal the painting from the gallery is theft and puts the police to work; to steal the same painting from a church is sacrilege.

Frequently, in the Old Testament a person had the feeling that he was in a holy place, e.g., Jacob and Moses, presumably because the feeling aroused was similar to that aroused by objects already known to be holy. The holy object is seen as a power that is beyond and different from power as manifested in natural objects, yet so akin to natural objects that it can in some way influence them. Often, but not always, this power is thought of as personal in nature, i.e., as having mind, will, and emotion.

> The religious phenomenon . . . has shown itself to consist everywhere, and at all its stages, in the consciousness which individuals have of an intercourse between themselves and higher powers with which they feel themselves related.[1]

Such an experience, it would seem, is "perfectly *sui generis* and irreducible to any other; . . ."[2]

Pervasiveness of religious values

If the holy object somehow acts upon the world of nature, it can pervade all realms of value experience. God could make or break the economic life of the group by sending or withholding rain or by suspending or promoting the fertility processes. God also could make demands about the relations of men to each other (the moral values). He could also affect what we could know, and He could make the world beautiful or otherwise. And an evil spirit, Satan, could also intervene to influence every realm of value experience.

[1] William James, *Varieties of Religious Experience*, New York: Longmans, Green and Company, Inc., 1902, 1929, p. 465.
[2] Rudolph Otto, *Idea of the Holy*, translated by J. W. Harvey, New York: Oxford University Press, 1943, p. 7.

Some intensely religious people see God's hand in their business, family life, social tasks, their moral struggles, in the scientist's discoveries, and in the artist's inspiration. They see Him in war and in peace, in the thunderstorm and the rainbow. Others see God only in church once a week and on certain holidays, and still others report—usually with vehemence—that they never see Him. Thus, although the religious experience can pervade life, it need not do so, just as it is not inevitable that aesthetic or social values will be equally pervasive for all individuals.

There is the simplest of untutored peasants to whom every twist of the day's work is the work of God; who tempers his rejoicing and sorrow by the belief that such matters are managed by a much wiser mind and hand than his own. We can find men like the philosopher Benedict Spinoza, who, although branded as a heretic during his lifetime, was also called the "God-intoxicated man," filled with *amor intellectualis Dei*, the intellectual love of God. Sainthood varies from the passionate quality of St. Theresa to the intellectual steadiness of St. Thomas.[3] The largest group are the men and women to whom the religious values are real but in whose lives they play a limited role. Some save their religious feelings for the crucial situations of birth, marriage, and death, good fortune or disaster, but rarely let them permeate their daily work. Some exhibit their religious proclivities by speech and behavior; others conceal them behind a matter-of-fact simplicity. Indeed, the Danish theologian and philosopher, Sören Kierkegaard, points out that to find the proper expression of religiosity is itself no easy matter.[4]

If the religious experience cannot be mistaken for any other, is it possible for some people not to have it at all, or not to know that they have it? Probably not. It certainly is true that many men and women deny that they now have such an experience. Fewer deny *ever* having had one. For example, they often say that they had religious experience in childhood, but not in their recent adult life. Others, when asked whether they have religious experience, reply with opinions or even arguments about some particular religion or about religion in general. The chances are pretty fair, therefore, that this mode of experience is about as universal as any other. Whether

[3] Cf. James, *op. cit.*, and Dante's description of the highest circle in heaven in the *Divine Comedy*.

[4] Cf. H. S. Broudy, "Kierkegaard's Levels of Existence," *Philosophy and Phenomenological Research*, 1:3, March 1941, pp. 309 ff.

we are trained to it or born with it is less important than that we have the capacity for it.

Suppose we do have this capacity, and suppose mankind develops it, of what use is it? After all, the argument runs, is not religion made up of childish superstitions that have no place in a scientific mind and age? Have not countless crimes been committed in the name of religion? Wouldn't there be less conflict in the world without it?

The role of religious values in life

We have talked a great deal in this book about the striving for perfection, and we have also noted that in men this striving takes the form of trying to realize the maximum of positive values in every area of life. But we have seen also that this striving is not automatic and its success no foregone conclusion. Men do their striving at different levels of subtlety and intensity. Striving can be inverted so that it results in self-degradation rather than perfection. The good life is not easy; it is easier to lead a pretty good one instead. The early stages of self-perfection are likely to be painful. The good does not seem to be distributed justly among the strivers and the loafers, the good and the wicked.

There comes a time in every thoughtful person's life when he asks whether the battle is worth the effort; whether his value schema is not a will o' the wisp devised by the strong to exploit the weak (Marx), or by the weak to chain the strong (Nietzsche).

Or one can ask whether the universe underwrites these values or is indifferent to them. This is a metaphysical question. It makes no difference to the physicist as a physicist whether the universe is for kindliness, against it, or indifferent to it, just as the universe's attitude toward differential equations makes no difference to the mathematician as a mathematician. Since the physicist and mathematician can solve their special problems regardless of the answer, there is no point in their asking this sort of question.

Of course, when the physicist constructs atomic bombs, he may lose sleep wondering whether such bombs *ought* to be used, but he suffers these qualms and insomnia as a man, not as a scientist. Suppose his bomb does kill several million people. Millions die every year anyhow; heart disease has no concern for man, why should he? Yet he does ask the question, as sooner or later every man must, and insofar as men seek a rational answer to this question they are metaphysicians. For metaphysics is simply the rational attempt to find clues in nature and human experience as to what the value commitment of the universe might be—if any. Theories are not the same as the religious experience itself.

One philosopher defines religion as follows: *"The essence or core of religion is the personal belief that one's most important values are sponsored by, or in harmony with, the enduring structure of the universe, whether they are sponsored by society or not."*[5]

Here the belief in a metaphysical theory is made the core of religion, but the accent is on the belief. In the religious experience we do not argue ourselves into believing that our value commitments have the support of the cosmos. On the contrary, in the moment of religious experience it is immediately felt that a power greater than our own is on the scene and is playing a role—the leading role in the drama of values. Without this feeling, prayer, communion, or worship of any sort are empty rituals.

Leaving aside for the moment the features that distinguish one religion from another, it would seem as if one common characteristic of religious experience is to see and feel ourselves, others, nature, and indeed the cosmos in dramatic terms. There is a plot and there are characters; there is conflict between the good and evil forces; the ultimate outcome is never in doubt; the immediate one always in doubt. The world is understood historically and morally, as a story with a particular plot, conflict, and outcome.

We can see, therefore, how close the religious experience is to the aesthetic. It is aesthetic, for in one unified feeling we grasp a certain kind of significance—a dramatic moral significance. And yet it is not identical with the aesthetic because we do not necessarily apprehend this significance in a perceptible form. The religious experience is also social because it regards the powers of the universe as fellow actors in the drama; it is moral because the drama is a conflict of choice between good and evil. It is intellectual because the plot and characters of this drama have to be understood.

Like the intrinsic phases of all other value experience, this one has an immediately felt unique quality of its own. If a man feels an overwhelming sense of sin, then he feels it. We may argue that there is or there is not a justifiable basis for such a feeling, but there is no denying the feeling itself. The religious experience in its

[5] Peter A. Bertocci, *Introduction to the Philosophy of Religion,* Englewood Cliffs, N.J.: Prentice-Hall, Inc., 1951, p. 9.

intrinsic phase is felt as it is had—satisfactory or otherwise, and with its own peculiar flavor. Whenever we grasp the significance of our own experience in the total drama of being, we are feeling religiously. Like the aesthetic and moral, the religious mode of feeling is a dimension of experience and as real as the sensing of color or sound.

So much for the intrinsic phase of the religious experience. Does it help us in the other areas of life? Some report that it does. It may strengthen the efforts of the person to achieve his value schema, or it may help him to endure deserved or undeserved adversity, or to meet with more than usual serenity the obduracies of ordinary life. Religious activity can give the individual a sense of peace, fellowship, and in some instances, of ecstasy. Some expect God to perform miracles on their behalf—minor miracles for the most part— as when the student who knows that he messed up seven out of 10 questions on an examination hopes for a miracle that will either soften the heart of the instructor or his head, or both. One should expect no fewer gradations in the subtlety of the religious experience than were found in other types of experience. It varies from unbelievable crudity to sublimity no less unbelievable. Finally, some hold that people would not behave themselves if they were not afraid of divine punishment, or that they would tear each other to pieces if they were not enjoined by their religious teachings to love their fellow men. We shall not try to decide these issues at this point. We may get a perspective from which to view them by remembering that once an experience produces consequences there is no telling whether the business will end, if indeed it ever does end. If because of a religious experience I give 10 dollars to a church building fund, then, among other effects, I may help to employ some carpenter, who may use the money to buy a lucky lottery ticket and become so engrossed in the pleasure of the world that he never again enters a church.

Religion has had all sorts of consequences. Religion made the Muslims and Crusaders militant, but it has made the Quakers extraordinarily peaceable. It led to the Inquisition, but also to countless acts of human charity. It has hindered knowledge, but has also preserved it. To have everyone read the Bible, it was necessary sooner or later to found the common school. How, then, are we to answer the question without knowing whose religious experience we are talking about and without knowing what whole train of consequences it engendered?

About the intrinsic phase. however, we can be more sure. Each man knows whether it satisfies him or not and whether one form of it is more satisfactory to him than another. There are connoisseurs and experts in this realm, as in others. For the greatest worth, this, like other modes of experience, has to be cultivated. Those who have done so are the standard rather than those who have not bothered to do so.

Religion and rationality

Is the religious experience anything more than a product of our imagination mixed up with myths told to us in our unsuspecting childhood? Is it merely a grand hoax to frighten us into behaving ourselves? Is it a device of crafty priests to secure domination over us?

Some thinkers believe that the religious experience does not have a unique object, but is rather another name for the loyalty men have to their ideals. On this view, that men seek value is a natural phenomenon, and we do not need to imagine a cosmic drama in which supernatural powers are in the cast of characters. There would be value experience and even religious experience without a supernatural God as object of such experience.[6] In other words, a supernatural God is regarded as a superfluous postulate at best and a downright deception at the worst. On the other hand, there is the more standard view that the religious experience is a special feeling caused by an object that really is holy and supernatural or God.

The debate would have been over long ago if God were an object whose existence one could prove as we prove the existence of the moon, the sun, or electrons. Put more precisely, if God had factual existence or was supposed to have it, to decide whether He existed or not would be a scientific matter.

But how do men conceive God, let us say, in the Judaic-Christian tradition? He is not perceived by the senses; He is not a creature;

[6] Cf. for example, John Dewey: "About all I need to say accordingly about the later writings . . . is that they are devoted to making explicit the religious values implicit in the spirit of science as undogmatic reverence for truth in whatever form it presents itself, and the religious values implicit in our common life, especially in the moral significance of democracy as a way of living together." *The Philosophy of John Dewey*, The Library of Living Philosophers, Paul A. Schilpp, ed., Chicago: Northwestern University, 1939, p. 597.

He is not like men, yet He understands men; He is everywhere, and yet in no particular place; He is eternal, and yet in the Christian tradition manifested Himself on a particular historical occasion on this earth. Theology sets forth in detail the concept of God in a particular religion, but no theology has solved the theoretical problem of demonstrating the existence of such a God to anyone who will take nothing less than an empirical proof. That the world may have a First Cause we may be compelled to believe—if we believe that everything has a cause, but to prove that this cause is God as conceived by any particular religious teaching is a different and much more difficult matter.

There have been innumerable attempts to do this, some more ingenious and convincing than others.[7] Suppose, for example, a crime has been committed which baffles the police. Suppose with the help of science, a number of clues, and cogent reasoning, a master detective deduces that the crime must have been committed by a man five feet ten inches tall, wearing a derby hat, who is a devoted prize fight fan, with a wife who is blonde and overweight. But suppose the most diligent search fails to turn up such a man. The detective may spend his whole life proving to the sceptic that such-and-such a man *must* have existed and committed the crime, but the sceptic will simply retort that he will believe it when he sees the man.

But suppose the detective predicts that such-and-such crimes will be committed by this unfound man, and suppose the predictions are borne out. In that case, the sceptic would waver, for how could the predictions be so accurate unless there were such a man—or unless the detective were himself the criminal? Now, in the case of God, we can infer that such-and-such a Being would be *needed* to produce the kind of world and experience we do have. But we cannot produce God to confront and confound the sceptic. If we begin to predict what He will do, either our predictions may not be verified, or if they are, the sceptic will insist that the events we have predicted can be satisfactorily explained by the laws of science.

The best that men can do with their natural reason is to examine human experience and nature for evidence that will allow them to accept or reject the hypothesis that a power with certain attributes exists.

Since this is not a book on theology, we have argued merely that

[7] Cf. Bertocci, *op. cit.*, pp. 271–304.

human striving guided by human knowledge results in value experiences rewarding in themselves and which promote further value experiences that are also rewarding.

Yet if one could believe with *certainty* that the cosmos was supporting human striving, the significance of life might well be different. This feeling of certainty religious experience can give, but it is a certainty that comes through faith and not through human knowledge alone.

Faith is not merely a willingness to gamble on what we cannot be sure of, as, for example, we gamble with the life insurance company that we will not live so long as it hopes we will. Religious faith is not simply the willingness to take a chance on the existence of God, even though we cannot prove that existence. On the contrary, it is the certainty that comes from a vivid awareness of the presence of or communion with the holy object. This faith may be supported by rational arguments, but there can be faith without such arguments, and there can be arguments without faith. So long as the vivid experience occurs or recurs it cannot be argued with.

Whether such experiences are good or bad for human life individually or collectively depends, as has already been pointed out, on who has the experience, what his concept of the holy object is, and how thoroughly this pervades his whole value schema.

Religious experience and religion

Does one need to belong to a particular church or sect to have religious experience?

Since there are few things in the world or out of it that someone has not worshipped as a holy object at one time or another, it would seem that the religious experience is not tied to any one particular God or to the concept of any God at all.[8] To see the world dramatically is, on the whole, a rather primitive accomplishment if we are to judge by the religions of primitive peoples. A religion when practiced by a group merely clarifies and formalizes the drama into permanent form and prescribes the procedures by which transactions with the Divine are to be conducted. These procedures are the rituals of the religion, just as the drama is contained in its god-story.

[8] Bertocci, *op. cit.*, p. 10 note, quotes from John R. Everett's *Religion in Human Experience*, p. 20, to show that ghosts and spirits in some of the more primitive religions are not the same as the true gods.

Civilized religions have the same structure, but the drama has a more carefully worked out plot; the characters are more subtly drawn, and the ritual tends to become more symbolic than imitative. The more complicated life becomes, the finer our moral distinctions, the more delicate our sensibilities, the more subtle becomes our concept of God. If it does not, there is the danger of continuing to conceive God as a stern, awesome Being who, however, is not up on electronics and nuclear fission.

The purpose of all organized religion is to stimulate the religious experience in the community of worshippers. The use of the same drama, characters, and ritual promotes a unity of religious feeling and the consequent sense of fellowship. Thus it is more likely that a congregation of orthodox Jews will have a common religious experience than a group drawn from various faiths. The values of the group are solidified by their incorporation into the cosmic drama and thus become not only socially desirable, but also divinely sanctioned and demanded. Organized religion is the prime emotional support of a society's value scheme.

Because a religious institution may or may not accommodate itself to social changes, it can happen that the church stands for values the group has abandoned and opposes new ones it has adopted. When this occurs, both society and the church suffer, for the former loses the stabilizing support of the latter, and the church loses its adherents.

Role of ritual

Whatever else ritual is supposed to accomplish, it has the effect of putting the inner religious experience into connection with external physical acts, such as kneeling, bowing, dancing, gesturing, pouring, slaughtering, and chanting. After conditioning is completed the physical act can induce the inner experience. Careful attention to keeping the place of the ritual, certain sounds, odors, and costumes unchanged also aids the conditioning process. The ritual, therefore, is the key to religious *training*, for it is the standard method of inducing the religious experience. The *content* of the experience is furnished by dogma and the creed of the particular church. Both the ritual and the dogma of a religion are in the care of its priesthood or clergy, who have authority in the administration and interpretation of them.

We often hear the complaint that this or that religion is full of "meaningless" ritual. This betrays a misunderstanding. In the first place, it is not meaningless. The religious dance of a primitive tribe re-enacts dramatic events important in the life of the tribe. It may be the historic battle that established the tribe in which certain gods participated, or it may be the ceremony of bread and wine that symbolizes the drama of the transformation of these mundane articles into the body and blood of Christ. In the celebration of the Passover, horseradish or other bitter herbs are eaten as a reminder of the hard lot of the Israelites in Egypt, and cups of wine are consumed at certain points in the service to symbolize certain events and meanings. Insofar as rituals are symbols, they stand for something other than themselves and are not meaningless. They become meaningless only when practiced without reference to what they stand for, in which event they stand for nothing and therefore mean nothing.

Even when these meanings are not fully understood by the participant, the ritual can still induce the feelings intended; this is the main function of ritual. The ritual may be aesthetically beautiful with music and costume, or it may be revolting (to us), as in blood sacrifice, or (to us) obscene, as in some of the ancient fertility rites.

It is somewhat the same with the story or the dogma of the religion. It may be a highly sophisticated system of concepts such as we find in some of the religions of both the West and East, or it may be a rather simple or highly fantastic legend. But to judge it merely as a description of empirical reality is to miss its point, for it is primarily a stimulus to the religious experience.

Religion and education

If the religious experience is the valuable part of religion, and if all men are capable of it in some degree, then why must we have so many separate and warring religions? Can we not in a democracy strip away the peculiarities that divide us and bring forth the new religion: a devotion, let us say, to one God, the freedom of man, peace on earth, and the good life?

Generalized religion. Such a notion deserves attention as does the argument that we can be individually religious and do not need any special institution to administer religion to us.

It is not theoretically impossible to make democracy, communism, or auto racing the focus of a religion. The crucial test would be whether these objects or systems of ideas would arouse a feeling of being in the presence of a holy object that vividly dramatizes the struggle to realize value. If a system of ideas can be fitted into a story that is repeated over and over again while accompanied by a ritual, there is no psychological reason why a generation cannot be brought up to regard it as their religion.

The important point is that without a content and ritual the religious experience remains inchoate, vague, and difficult to elicit or to induce at will. We just have to wait until it happens upon us as it did to the pioneers of every religion, until the spirit of God descended upon them. It might be today, a year from now, or every 10 minutes. There might still be religious experience, but it would be sporadic and highly individualized. It would be difficult to communicate; it could not become socialized. If religion has a social function in a rational society, it must be formalized, symbolized, and institutionalized.

The school has not had much luck in its flirtations with generalized religion, and we can now understand why. Ideals as such do not dramatize themselves. They are too abstract. They may elicit strong loyalties in adults, but rarely in children or childlike adults. The concept of one God, for example, will not arouse the religious experience unless God is felt and recognized as the God who did thus-and-so at such a time to a certain group of people and is still actively concerned with their strivings.

As children mature their concept of God changes also. From a powerful, awesome but benign older man, He is transformed into something more tenuous and spiritual, but by that time if religious conditioning has taken place the religious feeling can be aroused by the ritual and the dogma, even though the precise content of that experience may now be quite different from what it was in childhood.

If a god-story and a ritual are necessary for religious education, which story and which ritual shall the school use? In a public school system this phase of religious education is practically impossible except in those isolated cases where the whole community happens to be of one religious persuasion.[9] The home and the church must take care of religious training if it is to be taken care of.

One cannot understand a social order without understanding the

[9] And legally this might be impossible even in such homogeneous situations.

role of the religious life in it. Promoting this understanding is not religious education[10] because its purpose is not to arouse or to strengthen religious experience, although for those pupils already religiously conditioned it could not fail to have emotional reverberations.

A more direct kind of religious thinking would ask the question: What must my concept of God be to account for the facts of human experience? This is a kind of theology, to be sure, but it is the philosophical part of theology, or, more accurately, it is thinking about God philosophically. Even this is not, strictly speaking, religious training. If the pupil has *already been trained* in religious experience, such thinking will refine it, make it more subtle, and possibly even more intense.

It will do so by the same process that was described in the development of the aesthetic and moral experience; the method of connoisseurship, and connoisseurship means the refinement of immediate felt experience through knowledge. Does this mean that philosophy of religion—for that is what it amounts to—ought to be part of the public school curriculum?

During the latter years of the secondary school the adolescent is desperately seeking precisely this kind of thinking, just as he is eager to talk about moral and aesthetic standards. It is the time when religious doubts arise and when a division of loyalty may also arise. A religiously-trained youngster does not easily lose faith in a particular religion. Nevertheless, he is making new friends who may not share his faith. Loyalty to these friends is also important to him.

The simple concepts of God learned in childhood now seem inadequate. The adolescent wants to know about God's relation to his own predicaments. The stock questions occur to him almost spontaneously: If God is omnipotent, why does He permit evil? And if He permits it, can He be perfectly good? An adolescent is no more prone to make allowances for God than for his parents. Although the shock of science is probably no longer so great as it once was, it still comes as a jolt to the religiously-trained adolescent to find that the story of his religion is not regarded as literally true by some of his most respected textbooks and teachers.

The need for orientation in the value schema of his culture is more acute than it ever has been. Time and experience have not yet

[10] Cf. Oliver Martin, "The Problem of Religious Courses in a State University," *Educational Theory*, 3:1, 76–80.

encased him in the rigid but not uncomfortable stereotypes of adulthood. What about the sex and economic *mores* of the culture? Does the sex act have the religious overtones that his faith declares? Are the glandular imperatives that torment him really illicit, or is this another adult device to frustrate him? Can there be charity and compassion in business?

These are questions that find their way into every adolescent "bull" session. To think these questions through with the help of philosophy would be no small service to any generation. The materials for such instruction are available either in books especially designed for philosophy of religion courses[11] or in more general philosophical and religious literature.

The real obstacle is that people who set great store by religion are not always eager to have it studied philosophically. Why should this be so?

1. To take a philosophical, cognitive attitude toward the religious experience is, in an important sense, to get out of the religious mood. When one feels in communion with God one does not need proof of God's existence. When one feels a genuine sense of sin it means religiously that one has offended God. However, when we raise the question as to what it *means* to commune with God or to offend Him, we are neither in communion nor sensing sin; we are investigators of a conception and its meaning. It is conceivable, although perhaps not likely, that a very competent theologian should not have much or very intense religious experience, just as it is possible to be an expert on philanthropic institutions without feeling particularly charitable. We can understand, therefore, the lack of enthusiasm for a study of religious experience by the young unless it is developed so as to encourage and strengthen it. But this, we have seen, presents insuperable difficulties in the public school.

2. Some feel that to study religion critically will destroy religious faith. The realization that religions have taken so many different forms may shake the student's belief that his religion is the only true one. Also, without the appropriate scholarship, the inconsistencies within sacred books or in dogmas may raise doubts. Finally, it is just possible that such a study would make another religion more attractive than one's own.

The risks are very real, hence the reluctance to incur them. This,

[11] E.g., Bertocci, *op. cit.;* Wright, *A Student's Philosophy of Religion;* and Brightman, *A Philosophy of Religion.*

in turn, makes the logical suggestion that the philosophy of religion be a part of the curriculum of the public school so unrealistic that we shall not even make it in the chapter on curriculum.

Yet for the educated man, such study is a necessity. Our hope is that a good general education will so have equipped him with the habits and skills of acquiring and using knowledge that he will be able to go to the sources of this knowledge on his own.

What the public school cannot do, the church, of course, can do eminently well. Assuming that the home and the church have succeeded in the early conditioning of the child, the task of relating this experience to the questions of the adolescent still remains. More Bible stories and more practice of the ritual will not suffice for this. Something like a philosophy of religion is indicated, and unless the church offers it with a fair amount of scholarship and objectivity the real need will not be met. Youngsters intelligent enough to ask questions will be sharp enough to detect special pleading and this will hardly bolster their religious convictions. It is not, however, the function of a philosophy of education to tell the church its business, although it may not be out of place to point out the problem.

Perspective in the Religious Values

Granting all that has been said about the religious experience, the question still remains whether the good man, that is, the happy man, the intelligent man, the democratic man, needs this religious experience any more than he needs his appendix. Is the value to be derived from it worth the strife, the divisiveness that religion has so often caused?

In many quarters organized religion is openly branded as an enemy of free inquiry, democracy, and the rational life in general. The hope of the world, the argument runs, is science and scientific method by which the evils of the world can be attacked with some hope of success.

This is a brave, optimistic, intelligent, humane point of view and yet, as we review the progress of science and technology, the promised victories bring in their train defeats no less resounding. Ruthlessness has been compatible with scientific competence. Brutal disregard for the human personality was not deterred by the scientific success of the Germans, nor has the ruthlessness of Russia been mitigated by its animosity to religion.

The answer to this argument lies not so much in recrimination between science and religion as in distinguishing more clearly the role we can expect each to play in the good life.

The role of science

What can we expect of science? Science gives us knowledge about matters of fact, and when fortunate and wise, we use this knowledge to control our environment. From science we can expect the means to reduce disease, hunger, poverty, and even insanity. Let us suppose that science is successful beyond our dreams, then what? Then we can say that there remains very little excuse for men not to realize the highest values of which they are capable. Science, therefore, paves the way for value realization by giving man a surplus of power over and above what he needs to supply his physical wants.

By inquiry we discover what is truly enjoyable in life. Empirical investigation can certify with a specified degree of probability that some act or object will in certain circumstances continue to give enjoyment. This is no small matter in the good life for to know what is truly enjoyable is valuable knowledge indeed.

But on what empirical knowledge can we base the moral conviction that man ought to be treated as an end and not as a means merely? Certainly man has not always treated other men in this fashion; he has frequently found it satisfactory to regard him merely as a means or tool for his own purposes. Certainly the world of subhuman nature gives no evidence for the notion that animals or plants regard each other as ends in themselves. Are there not times and occasions when to respect certain individuals as persons requires great moral effort on our part?

On what empirical grounds, on what scientific studies, do we base our conviction that continued effort in behalf of a better world has the sympathy of the cosmos? On the contrary, by a shrewd use of the scientific method we might very well carve out for ourselves a quite satisfactory life in a hostile world. On what empirical grounds should I feel obligated to be intelligent in my behavior? Why should I solve my problems intelligently with an eye to the evidence and to knowledge? Is it not conceivable that by a set of stereotyped responses I may get greater satisfaction than by taking thought in the matter? Why should I realize my own capacities beyond a comfortable degree of adjustment that makes my life tolerably happy? Why should we be "conquered, vanquished, in our active nature by an ideal end"?[12]

If these convictions are based on knowledge it is not the empirical knowledge with which science is concerned. It is rather the philosophical knowledge about the nature of man and the interpretation of his destiny on the basis of that nature. It is an inference about what *man is by nature tending to become* and a study of the forces and factors that promote or hinder that becoming. From the very nature of man's rationality, if we are clear about its meaning, there flows a vision of the everlasting obligation to seek the best that his reason discloses.

It is for such reasons that a life committed to the highest values of which man is capable requires something in addition to scientific activity. It requires a view of reality that does not make such a quest nonsensical. This view a rational metaphysics can construct, and for some men such a highly abstract system of thought is enough to engage their emotions. But for most men this is not the case. Conceptual systems, however consistent and penetrating they may be, are still products of a mind at ease, a mind that has disengaged itself from the drama of human action and emotion. To a mother notified that her son is missing in action or to a man with the choice of betraying his friends or having his life ruined, a conceptual system is cold comfort.

The role of religion

The religious experience, however, does precisely what a conceptual experience cannot do. It gives an intense certainty and vivid awareness of a power that is on the side of righteousness and goodness. It can thus give hope, courage, and comfort, just as it can engender fear, anxiety, guilt, and despair. If a well-acted drama can engage our emotions to the point where we forget that we are in a theater, how much more can the faith that we are actually part of a cosmic moral drama where the stakes are life and value themselves command our emotions? Religion, whether institutionalized or not, heightens the intensity of our awareness of what it is to be a man in a world he did not make; of his peculiar grandeur and insignificance, of his frailty and power.

[12] John Dewey, *A Common Faith*, New Haven: Yale University Press, 1934, p. 20.

That some can, or think they can do without this sort of experience is no more argument against it than the fact that some people do not use banks or doctors. The real question is whether the religious experience does what is claimed for it or not. The evidence must come from those who have had it themselves. The evidence from those who have not is worthless.

Having said this much about the reality and role of the religious experience, we must be sure that we do not claim for it what it cannot deliver. In the first place, the religious experience can make us feel as if we know something—and know it with certainty. Although it feels like knowledge, it cannot qualify as such on any criterion by which we ordinarily test knowledge. That it is really God that I am communing with or praying to I can never prove either by argument or by demonstration. And since I cannot produce for public observation the object to which my experience points, I can never really refute the possibility that I have somehow generated this feeling from within myself as I do my dreams and hallucinations.

If by knowing we mean certifying the existence or the characteristics of an object in any publicly verifiable way either through perceiving the object or coming to the same inference concerning it, the religious experience is not knowledge, although it is the example *par excellence* of faith.[13] And yet before dismissing the cognitive claims of the religious experience, it must be asked: "*What* does the act of faith say about human life?" May it not utter what might turn out to be scientifically true? To say that faith is not knowledge is to emphasize that it does not furnish a proof of *what* it says. Faith asserts; science proves its assertions, and one of the most important assertions of faith is that some assertions can be proved scientifically.

In the second place, it is easy to confuse the teachings of an organized religion, especially as found in its sacred writings, with history or scientific description. As has been argued in Chapter 4, any proposition that purports to be a description of fact has to be

[13] "The realm of faith is thus not a class for numskulls in the sphere of the intellectual, or an asylum for the feeble-minded. Faith constitutes a sphere all by itself, and every misunderstanding of Christianity, transferring it to the sphere of the intellectual may at once be recognized by its transforming it into a doctrine." Sören Kierkegaard, *Concluding Unscientific Postscript,* translated by David F. Swenson, Princeton: The American-Scandinavian Foundation and Princeton University Press, 1941, p. 291. Cf. also Aquinas, *Summa Contra Gentiles,* Book I, Chaps. 3–13, and Part I, Question 2 of the *Summa Theologica.*

certified by the methods of science, whether this proposition appears in a history textbook or in a sacred writing.

This does not mean that factual descriptions in a sacred writing may not be historically and even scientifically true, but if they are, it is not because they are in the sacred book.

However, if the dogma of a religion is regarded as the dramatic symbolization of nature and life, whether it is *literally* true or not becomes more or less irrelevant. For its function is not so much to teach us history as to intensify emotionally the meaning of our participation in the drama of life. Is this then any more than going to the theater and watching a very grand play? In both we identify ourselves with the action. In both the story and characters arouse in us certain emotional complexes. But in the theater we have to maintain psychical distance; we cannot identify ourselves so completely as to forget that this is a play. In church, on the other hand, the point is to abolish the psychic distance altogether. The religious drama is nothing more than an interesting play *unless* there is the faith that it is not a play, the belief that this is the way it must have happened and that we are participants and not merely spectators.

Because of this relation among knowledge, religion, and the religious experience, the school is in an awkward position with respect to it. To assert that it is not "knowledge" is to offend those who are convinced that their religion has not only a symbolic and spiritual meaning, but a literal factual meaning as well. If we accept this claim an irreconcilable conflict between religion and science is inevitable, and there is no honest way for the school or the pupil to avoid it.

On the other hand, to grant that the religious experience is genuine and has powerful effects on human feeling and conduct is to arouse the ire of those who are convinced that it affects human life too much, and that it does so in an irrational, emotional, mystical way that is beyond testing and criticism. They argue that organized religion translates its spiritual mission into social and political tyranny and should be resisted at all costs. They regard any religious note in the classroom as the nose of the camel which inevitably will bring the whole church into the tent.

It is this situation that makes it impossible for us to treat the religious values as we did the others. We are willing to tolerate divergence in aesthetic tastes because, on the whole, these differences do not bring us into violent social conflict. As for moral values, there is really little fundamental difference among our commitments to them, however we may differ in justifying this commitment. But religious differences can be more than religious. They make a difference in the way men vote, and organized religion can be a powerful social force. Diversity in this area is not only a matter of taste, but can become, as it often has become, the occasion for bitter and violent social strife.

It is not difference in belief and ritual that makes one sect so fearful of another. As a matter of fact, we are often "interested" in strange religions—provided they are 3000 miles away and not practiced by our competitors for economic and political power. It is only when religious differences make for conflicting social and political action, that they occasion communal strife.

Yet the remedy for this situation is not the abolition of the religious experience, even if that could be accomplished. The remedy lies in the same medicine cabinet to which we have had recourse so often—knowledge itself.

In each of the value areas—aesthetic, moral, social, economic—we found gradations of complexity and competence. The value experience in both its intrinsic and instrumental phases changes as more reflection is bent upon it. Nor is the intensity of the experience thereby necessarily weakened. Was the religious experience of St. Thomas or St. Francis or Albert Schweitzer less real and less vivid than that of an unlettered peasant because these men reflected endlessly on the meaning of God in human life?

Even if it is true that the core content of the religious experience is a product of conditioning, does the content have to remain in that simple form? Does the conditioned origin of our moral experience prevent it from becoming more and more rational as we reflect on the good life and the choices it necessitates?

Some men wonder that famous scientists are deeply religious and very often in what seem to be rather conventional ways. Is this anything to wonder at, if, as clearheaded men should, they do not react to a symphony and to human tragedy as they do to reactions in a test tube? It is when men begin mixing things up—fighting disease with incantations and testing a religious experience with a slide rule—that we have our best examples of both religious and scientific ignorance. The real scientist does not despise candidates for knowledge because of their origin, and there is a sense in which much of the work of science is to validate and correct the insights of our nonscientific activity. Religion, art, suffering are the seedbeds of our insights into value.

As far as the theoretical task of the school is concerned, it is the same for the religious values as for the others. It is to perfect the habits of acquiring knowledge—knowledge *about* religion and about everything else on which knowledge is available, the habits of using knowledge in reflecting upon the religious experience as on all other kinds, and finally, the habits of enjoying knowledge as it intensifies, subtilizes, and enriches our immediate experience in every value realm.

What the school cannot do is to afford practice in the religious experience, nor can it examine the religious professions of its pupils, but in the concept of the school we have been trying to develop, it is precisely this element of conditioning that we have found difficult to justify in any of the value areas.

Summary

In this chapter we tried:

1. To analyze and describe the mode of experience properly called religious and to distinguish it from other modes of experience.

2. To analyze the components of an organized religion into a dogma, ritual, and clergy and to show how each of these is used to elicit and unify the religious experience in the group.

3. To show the part the school—the public school in particular— can or cannot play in religious education.

4. To show the relation between the religious experience and the quest for values.

5. To show the relation of the religious experience and religion to knowledge, faith, and science.

The religious values, we concluded, stand on the same footing as all the other values. They are real, relevant, and socially important. They do, however, present a problem to the school that at the present time seems unsolvable. About all we can be sure of is that knowledge can produce development in this area of life as in all others, and that this knowledge and not the practice or profession of religion is properly the school's business.

PROBLEMS FOR DISCUSSION AND RESEARCH

1. The reading of *Varieties of Religious Experience* is strongly recommended to give content to some of the points raised in this chapter.

2. How much do you know *about* you own religion? About other religions? Do you find reading *about* religion interesting or boring? Does it affect your faith?

3. How often in your "bull" sessions does the question of religion arise? What forms does it take?

4. Does your church teach what we have called the "philosophy of religion"? Would you be interested in it? How does your clergyman feel about it?

5. To what extent do the religious values pervade the other areas of your value experience? How typical are you of your classmates in this respect?

SUGGESTIONS FOR FURTHER READING

For fuller bibliographical data on the items listed below, consult the General Bibliography.

On the nature of religious experience:

Allport, *The Individual and His Religion.* (A psychological study.)
Bergson, *The Two Sources of Morality and Religion.* (A modern version of mysticism by a sophisticated intuitionist.)
Bertocci, *An Introduction to the Philosophy of Religion,* Chap. 1.
Brightman, *A Philosophy of Religion,* Chaps. 2, 3.
Everett, *Religion in Human Experience.*
Hocking, *Human Nature and Its Remaking,* Chap. 39.
James, *Varieties of Religious Experience.* (Excellent description of religious experience and very readable.)
Wright, *A Student's Philosophy of Religion.* (Good orientation for the beginner.)

On the nature of God and on the relation of science and religion:

Aquinas, *Summa Contra Gentiles,* Book I, Chaps. 3–13.
———, *Summa Theologica,* Part I, Qu. 2.
Bertocci, *Introduction to the Philosophy of Religion,* Chap. 11.
Edwards and Pap, *A Modern Introduction to Philosophy,* pp. 406–544. (Good selections from some standard authors.)
Gilson, *God and Philosophy.*
Martin, *The Order and Integration of Knowledge,* Chap. 10. (On conflicting truth claims.)

Royce, *The Spirit of Modern Philosophy*, Lecture 11.
Wieman, *The Wrestle of Religion with Truth*.
Wild, *Introduction to Realistic Philosophy*, Chap. 16.

Also:

The volumes put out by the Conference on Science, Philosophy, and Religion.

On the more directly educational side:

See references given at the end of Chapter 4, and
American Council on Education, *The Function of the Public Schools in Dealing with Religion*.
Brubacher, *Eclectic Philosophy of Education*, Topics 16, 30.
———, *Modern Philosophies of Education*, Chap. 13.
Butler, *Four Philosophies*. (Chapters dealing with the religious implications of four different philosophies.)
Harner, *Religion's Place in General Education*.
McGucken, "The Philosophy of Catholic Education," N.S.S.E. Forty-First Yearbook, Part I.

PART | III

THE GOOD LIFE

AND THE SCHOOL

12

The Curriculum I

Having described the nature of the good life as the broadest aim of education and having outlined the structure of the personality and of society as the matrix within which diverse types of value can be achieved, we come now to the means of achieving the good life through formal education.

About means we can ask two questions: What is to be learned and how is this learning to be promoted? The latter question can be further subdivided into two other topics: the organization of the school system (Chapter 15), and the methodology to be used in teaching (Chapter 14). This chapter will concern itself with the form of the curriculum, viz., habits and skills, and Chapter 13 with the content of these habits and skills.

The Curriculum Problem

It may be profitable at this point to make several distinctions:
1. There is a difference between an experience that the school

provides for the pupil and the outcome of having this experience. The first we may refer to as an input, just as with a computing machine we first feed in certain data in order to get certain outcomes. For the outcomes to accrue the machine has to perform a number of operations.

2. We may call the operations that go on inside of the pupil "intervening processes." These are of many kinds. Perceiving, remembering, imagining, feeling, analyzing, sorting, combining, judging, choosing, and many others operate on the inputs. To simplify our discussion, however, there are two major kinds of operations in which the teacher and school are primarily interested. They are selective storage and selective recall. Selective storage is important because the human organism would fly to pieces if it were unable to pick and choose from among all the stimuli that are forever bombarding it and vying for its attention.[1]

Learning goes wrong if the pupil cannot or will not select what the teacher intends for him to select. On the other hand, the learning is tested by having the pupil choose from his experience something relevant to a situation, whether it be a fact, a name, a relation, or an image.

3. It has already been pointed out that outcomes of schooling can be distinguished into school outcomes and life outcomes. Among the school outcomes a school may often wish to include the efficiency of the intervening processes. Thus a school may be interested in perfecting a pupil's efficiency in critical thinking or mathematical reasoning or devotion to scientific method. These are also life outcomes in that these traits can come to characterize many aspects of a person's behavior in nonschool life. In school they are tested by school tasks and not life tasks. Consequently, whether they will transfer to later life tasks is something we may reasonably expect but cannot guarantee.

A curriculum pattern or design is distinguished by the way it combines inputs that are intended to secure the different outcomes discussed above. We shall now examine two types of curriculum as to their claims and their shortcomings and subsequently suggest a third type of curriculum as an alternative design.

---

[1] In an illuminating article, "Knowledge: A Growth Process," Paul Weiss indicates that as in organic growth so in knowledge some of the intake is destined for obsolescence and discard. *Science*, 131:3415, June 10, 1960, 1716–1719.

Subject matter curriculum

Controversies over the curriculum are arguments about the *kinds* of experience the pupil shall have in the classroom during his school life. The traditional pattern of the curriculum in the western world has been a set of subjects. Each subject—Latin, English, mathematics, or geography—was a sampling of a whole body of knowledge. It was simplified, of course, both in amount and in complexity to approximate the maturity of the pupil. Within this pattern Latin and Greek have lost their eminence. Typewriting, bookkeeping, safety, and automobile driving have achieved a place in it. But the central pattern is still that of distinct subjects. For the most part this sort of curriculum seemed sensible if the purpose of the school was to provide the pupil with information that the school authorities thought he should have.

It was also hoped that certain habits and skills (intervening processes) would develop as the pupil mastered the information contained in the subject matter: the habits of observing accurately, thinking clearly and logically, sticking to unpleasant tasks unflinchingly, and being prompt, neat, and industrious.

In the last half century criticism of this curriculum has been unremitting, and its has come from both its friends and enemies. We may summarize the main difficulties as follows:

1. *Poor motivation.* The most obvious drawback was that so many children came to regard school as one of the standard miseries of childhood. School interfered with what one really wanted to do. This or that piece of reading might be interesting to the curious, and a few children rejoiced in the favor of the teacher or the respect that high marks brought them. But, by and large, the pupil could not see the connection between accurate reading, precise arithmetical computation, fussy spelling, and the history of the Greeks, on one hand, and the really important affairs of eating, playing, fighting (if he were a boy), fooling, and in the latter days, movies, radio, television, and sports, on the other hand.

Now and then an enterprising school teacher made the subjects "interesting" by turning them into games, by appealing to rivalry or by ingenious story telling. This inventiveness no doubt gave the teacher a reputation of sorts, but it never did meet the underlying difficulty. Systematic geography, history, mathematics, penmanship, and spelling just do not have a high interest appeal to the young.

2. *Low retention.* The schools never had much luck in transferring information from books and teachers to the pupil so that it would stick, because information that finds no home in the clusters of our experience has no place to hang its hat, and like the discouraged guest leaves early. Certain items do stick. Any fact will stick if repeated a thousand times.[2] But the amount of factual information children forget even during one summer vacation is appalling.[3]

This should not surprise anybody, although it invariably does. It incites letters to the editor and resolutions to the school board. If we were to test the letter writers and resolution makers, we would find that they remembered precious little of the *information they* learned in school, *unless* vocation or other circumstances forced them to relearn the information over and over again.

A physician has had sound training in mathematics and chemistry, but what score would doctors make on a high school algebra test? Unless the physician has been using his mathematics for other purposes than to calculate his income tax, the score will probably be modest.[4]

3. *Thinking not developed.* Nor was the avowed hope that the skills of thought would somehow be formed into habits realized. For example, there is a low correlation between ability to do arithmetical computation and arithmetical reasoning.[5] If the emphasis is on skill in computation, there is no automatic increase in ability to reason in mathematical problems. Similarly, rote learning of facts in history, geography, and in other disciplines does not guarantee ability to think *with* these facts.

College teachers often find that the thinking parts of a textbook or lecture are regularly ignored by the student. Twelve years of memorizing items of information has made pupils almost blind to anything else on a printed page. "Thought" questions on an examination are more likely than not to be answered by whatever facts the

[2] This is known as "overlearning" or the practicing of a task beyond the time needed to perform it at a certain standard of quality. For example, if the goal is to repeat a poem by heart with no errors, any practice beyond that point would be "overlearning."

[3] S. J. Bassett, "Retention of History in the Sixth, Seventh, and Eighth Grades with Special Reference to the Factors that Influence Retention," *Johns Hopkins University Studies in Education,* No. 12, 1928.

[4] For a somewhat fuller argument on this point, see H. S. Broudy, "History Without Hysteria," *School and Society,* 58:1494, August 14, 1943, pp. 106–107.

[5] Cf. L. J. Brueckner, "New Data on Transfer in Arithmetic," *AERA, Official Report, Reconstructing Education Through Research,* 9:212–218, 1936.

student can remember. The student, moreover, is surprised and hurt that this is "not what the instructor wanted."

4. *Other objections.*[6] The subject matter curriculum also has been charged with being compartmentalized and fragmented. That is to say, each subject loses its relation to any other subject. History classes seem to have no relation to mathematics classes, and neither to the literature classes.

Further, subjects are built up logically—from elements to complexes. Psychologically, however, learning may not follow such a logical pattern at all. We learn to read a whole sentence or phrase although words are logically more simple than sentences. We tend to learn what concerns us regardless of the logic of the subject matter.

Finally, social problems of current interest have a hard time finding their way into the subject matter curriculum because problems of war, poverty, and political struggles involve many subject matters and, therefore, do not fit neatly into any one of them.

To sum up these objections: the traditional subject matter curriculum as traditionally taught did not make connection between the input and the outcomes expected from it. The intervening processes that were to transfer knowledge to life were not developed, nor were the adult behavior patterns significantly affected by the input.

Problem-centered curricula

Smith, Stanley, and Shores[7] discuss two major types of curriculum organization in addition to the subject matter type: the activity and the core. The activity curriculum grew out of John Dewey's Experimentalist philosophy and was developed by J. L. Meriam, Ellsworth Collings, William H. Kilpatrick and others.

Instead of standard subjects, the purposes and interests of pupils furnish the guide to the activity curriculum. The problem of motivation is thus solved because it is not allowed to rise in the first place.

Under the teacher's guidance, pupils deal with a problem pretty much as does a scientist—defining it, seeking data relevant to it, using what he already knows (generalizations and facts) to propose tenta-

[6] Cf. Smith, Stanley, and Shores, *Fundamentals of Curriculum Development*, pp. 392–399.
[7] *Op. cit.*, pp. 292–419.

tive solutions, and finally testing the solution (hypothesis) that promises success.[8] Thus the pupil learns by *thinking*, which, for Dewey, always involves a *doing* or changing the conditions which put us in doubt, befuddlement, or precarious situations in the first place.[9]

Accompanying this theory is the belief that if a child solves his daily problems intelligently in company with the other children who make up the school community, he will as he grows older find himself embroiled more and more in the problems of the adult community. The good student and the good citizen are, therefore, merely the earlier and later phases of one and the same process, namely, growth.

On this scheme the school is a community in the process of growing up. There are no lessons, only real tasks. Play and work weave into each other. There are no subjects, only funded knowledge as resources to be used as needed. Even the skills of reading, writing, spelling, and computation are developed because they are needed and only when needed to attack genuine problems. In other words, the input is a sampling of real life behavior, of the expected output.

This educational paradise has a somewhat sterner aspect in the modern core curriculum.[10] Here the needs of social living common to all citizens are made the guide instead of the felt interests of the pupil. Every man has to be worker, voter, neighbor, leisure time user, and consumer. This type of curriculum deals with problems in which only the stupidest of pupils could fail to be interested. This is especially the case when adolescents are promised that the school will study the problems that *really* concern them, such as getting along with their own and the opposite sex, their parents, earning money, and becoming a member of the community.

Here too there are no distinct subjects or skills to be learned. The problem or some specialized interest dictates what is to be read or practiced. The virtues claimed for this approach are about the same as for the activity program and for about the same reasons.

[8] Cf. Dewey, *How We Think*, and Kilpatrick, *Foundations of Method*.

[9] Whatever may be said about the theory and practice of some of Dewey's followers, for him doing was always to be, if possible, intelligent doing, i.e., thinking.

[10] The earlier version of the core curriculum sought to blend all subjects by using one study, e.g., history, as a core. Cf. Smith, Stanley, and Shores, *op. cit.*, pp. 312–313. See also the common learnings advocated by Harold C. Hand in *Science Education*, 32:5–11, February, 1948.

But there is even more. Twelve years of group activity should form habits of co-operation, initiative, spontaneity, willingness to experiment, open-mindedness, and a high order of social sensitivity. Real life tasks, therefore, are expected to perfect both the cognitive and attitudinal intervening processes and to provide a store of information as well. This does indeed sound like an educational heaven for teacher, pupil, and community. Nevertheless there are some difficulties even here.

Problems need not require knowledge. The needs, purposes, and difficulties of immature pupils are no less immature. Children in the fourth grade have no more genuine need to find out about the people of India than they have for formal geography and no more natural need for having a school store than for formal economics and arithmetic. If the purpose of the problem curriculum is to entangle the pupil in problems that require knowledge and the methods of knowledge, it will have to interfere with nature.

Problems need not require scientific method. Suppose a high school is facing the problem of what to do when most of its members want to hold the big dance of the year at a hotel and their parents and the faculty make objections. I submit that this sort of problem is more typically "genuine" for adolescents than what to do about slums, world peace, and the current state of the theatre. Do they have to think scientifically about such a problem?

Undeniably the group *could* do so, but there are alternatives. They could, for example, defy the authorities, yield to them, give up the dance, or do whatever the previous classes had done in such situations. Any one of these would solve the problem without scientific investigation. This means that if the school wishes to use problems to provoke thought, it has to select not only problems that are real to the pupil, but also problems that cannot be solved without thought.

How necessary is the school? Suppose, however, we do succeed in finding one, let us say the problem of persuading the community to build a new gym for the high school. Let us grant that caprice, impulse, and custom do not provide a solution. The group is forced to think.

One will inevitably learn much about his community and human nature in such an enterprise. He will become acquainted with the political alignments among the citizens, the reality of taxes, and the reluctance of taxpayers to pay for what will not immediately benefit them. Conceivably he could also learn how to organize a group for political action. But thus far has any learning been mentioned that could not take place just as effectively *outside* of school?

"Raiding" subject matter. In the process of scientific thinking there comes a time when information about the problematic situation is needed. We might need to know, for example, what the gym would cost, the financial conditions of the township or city, what other gym facilities are available, and what the school population might be in five years.

Later in the thought process the problem solver on the basis of study makes a prediction or a guess that "if we do this, that will happen." If, for example, we promise the churches, factories, and fraternal organizations that they can use the new gym for their sports program, then they will rally behind the gym. Or if we dig up some "dirt" on the leader of the opposition, he will become fearful and silent.

We frame these hypotheses on the basis of certain other knowledge that we already have or on certain beliefs that we entertain. The hypothesis that the various groups with sports programs will be a source of strength follows from the belief that people will support what promises to promote their interests. That the leader of the opposition will withdraw his opposition is based on the generalization that most people fear scandal more than withdrawing from a political fight.

With regard to both the data and these generalizations there are great differences of accessibility. Look over the ones mentioned. Most, if not all of them, can be secured by asking questions of the right people, by the consulting of some documents, or by observation. On the other hand, the principles involved in the distribution of stresses and strains of the girders in the gym, the composition of the materials used, the principles of economics that affect tax rates, and the principles of social psychology that govern group attitudes are not laid out on the surface of community life for all to see and use. Where is all this to be found?

A trip to the encyclopedia will engulf students in technical terms. If they trace each of these through the encyclopedia, they may or may not be wiser when they are finished, but they will certainly be older. If they have never studied chemistry or physics, the chances that they can "raid" a textbook on these subjects are slim. It is almost impossible to raid the natural sciences without a prior conquest of them; the case is not much better with the social sciences.

If we can read we can find "data" or information by this kind of research, e.g., that coal costs so much a ton and oil so much a gallon and that one has more B.T.U.'s than the other, but the generalizations that would enable us to *understand* the principles and methods of combustion cannot be picked up out of manuals or almanacs. For a discipline, if it is at all developed, has aspects that make sporadic "raiding" difficult:

1. Terminology or concepts that are short-hand names for very complex and abstract thought processes, e.g., oxidation, marginal utility, specific gravity, and the superego.

2. A whole network of data, facts, rules, generalizations, and theories that have been more or less satisfactorily proved in the history of the discipline.

3. A method of investigation in some sense peculiar to itself.

4. Rules for evaluating evidence.

Any doubting reader can verify this by tackling even an introductory textbook in a subject with which he is unfamiliar. A subject is not a collection of facts and rules to be *memorized*. That is why it cannot be raided at will.

The dilemma. The problem approach to the curriculum is therefore faced with a dilemma. If the problems used do not require the knowledge of the organized disciplines, then the school is superfluous. If such knowledge is required, it cannot be secured except by systematically studying the subject. We conclude, therefore, that the study of organized subject matter is indispensable if the school is not to be dispensable.

Our brief critique of these two views of the curriculum may be summed up as follows: the traditional subject matter curriculum listed lofty objectives, most of which were promptly forgotten as instruction got under way. The only objective to which it was faithful was the memorization of the factual content of the subject, and this was forgotten by the pupil as soon as it was safe to do so.

The problem-centered curriculum has equally lofty objectives and realizes a number of them, particularly certain attitudes desirable for group living. Its chief drawback is that unless it can secure systematic mastery of organized subject matter somehow, the problems with which it can deal in the school are not the sort to which schooling is essential.

A Third View of the Curriculum

To meet the difficulties of the subject matter and activity curricula will require a stroke of genius or judicious patching. The genius being, for the moment, lacking, the patching can be made judicious by keeping in mind some of the observations made earlier in this chapter. First, we need to examine more closely what is general about general education.

General education

General education is that education which presumably every man *as man* should have, as distinguished from specialized education which some men need by virtue of some function that they but not all individuals have to perform.

That a man should have both general and special education would seem to be obvious, yet we have apparently reached a state of affairs that seems to deny the obvious. So specialized have our occupational lives become, and so dominant a role has this aspect of life assumed, that even educated men find themselves "highbrow" in their own specialty and "lowbrow" in practically everything else. Since "highbrows" can converse only with other "highbrows," this means that the routes of communication between members of different professions are closed to all save trivial traffic. There is no common literature, science, art, or philosophy that an educated man can assume every educated man would be likely to know.[11]

By general education one can mean (1) a common program of studies, or (2) a program of studies that are widely applicable because of their general or abstract nature, or (3) a program of studies or activities that all the citizens will find useful. The difficulty lies in a choice between meanings 2 and 3 and is caused by confusing two different ways in which school outcomes can be useful to life outcomes.

Science, mathematics, and literature are useful because they apply to a wide variety of life situations; they have high explanatory and transfer potential. Without them our whole technological and intellectual life would collapse. But because they are difficult to master, it is awkward to insist that everyone study them, that is, to make them common in meaning (1) above.

[11] Cf. The Harvard Report: *General Education in a Free Society*, pp. 53–54.

Problems of citizenship, homemaking, family living, the care of children and automobiles are useful topics of study because they are samples of the life outcomes promised by the school. One could argue also that everyone can profit from these studies. Unfortunately, their explanatory theoretical power is low. Hence we have the paradox of general education: the more general a program is on one meaning, the less so it is on another.

That is why our school program tends to crystallize into two types of general education, despite our commitment to a single track school system on the grounds that it alone is consonant with democracy.

Our schools not only confound these meanings of general education, but compound the confusion by mixing it up with liberal education and liberal arts studies. It would help matters if we reserved "liberal" schooling or education to refer to any study undertaken primarily for self-cultivation rather than for practical utility or to discharge the obligations of citizenship, public or domestic. Liberal arts studies, on the other hand, are certain courses, usually classed with the Humanities, taught in colleges and high schools. Some of these courses, literature, mathematics, and history, for example are general (widely applicable), but not studied "liberally" even at liberal arts colleges. Insofar as liberal arts courses are taken as pre-vocational preparation they are not studied liberally, as will be shown in the chapter on school organization (Chapter 15).

Seeking any set of studies that everybody both ought to know and can master has all the earmarks of a hopeless enterprise. A more promising approach is to seek out those forms of intelligent behavior that are found in all men. It is the cultivation of these forms that constitutes general education rather than any particular set of studies. General education has to be translated into the most universal elements of human behavior, but they must also be elements we can recognize in the classroom. If our elements are not universal, the education will not be general; if they do not issue in observable behavior, they are useless for education. The habits of acquiring, using, and enjoying knowledge would seem to qualify on both counts.

Habits as Universal Forms of Behavior

In *Human Nature and Conduct* Dewey points out that habits are functions not only of the individual to whom they are assigned, but also of the group and environment in which they are formed and operate. They are responses to the demands of an environment, but once established they themselves make demands on the environment.[12] We may similarly say that the school is an environment that makes demands which, if successful, issue in habits of the pupil, and conversely, these habits in turn constitute further demands on the school.

Habit has a *dynamic* nature. It is not simply a tool passively waiting to be used, but rather a tendency that seeks occasions for its own employment. If I have the habits of smoking and reading, they drive me to actions that I might in their absence never undertake. We might call them autodynamic tendencies.[13]

Habits vary in their flexibility. The habit of taking off the left shoe before the right, established when there was no premium on doing otherwise, is an example of a habit with low flexibility. The detective's habit of asking certain questions of all criminal suspects is an example of habit that has high flexibility.[14]

Flexible as it may be, habit still has an element of fixity that distinguishes it from rational reflection. The detective varies the questions to fit the case, but the *habitual* part of the performance is likely to be uniform and fixed. The manipulation of symbolic meanings to frame hypotheses and weigh evidence is not habitual in this sense. Here is a creativity that habit lacks. Yet to seek hypotheses can become habitual. Induction, deduction, critical examination of alternatives—all can become habitual in a variety of problem situations.

It should be clear that if we say that the immediate outcomes of schooling are habits or tendencies or dispositions, we do not mean thereby a set of fixed, semi-automatic responses. Tipping one's hat and repeating the multiplication table may be no more than that. There is, however, a hierarchy of habits based on their generality or the range of their applicability and flexibility. At the top of the hierarchy is the habit of reflective thought, which reduces the rigidity of habit to a minimum. At the other end of the scale are the conditionings that are at best only semi-conscious.

A habit is a unity of content and form. Its content is always particular for we can never think in general, write in general, or eat in general. When we think with mathematical symbols we are not

---

[12] Dewey, *Human Nature and Conduct*, pp. 13–17.
[13] *Ibid.*, p. 25.
[14] *Ibid.*, pp. 51–52. Also *Democracy and Education*, pp. 55–56.

thinking with historical data; when we eat beef we are not eating vegetables. Yet if all learning is particular, the task of education is so vast as to be hopeless. If the arithmetic of papering walls does not apply to dairying, we shall have to teach as many arithmetics as there are occupations. We are saved from this hopelessness by the fact that tasks require the same *form* of a habit even when they vary in content. Thus finding the area of a field and a wall requires the same form of habit. The thinking of the detective in solving a crime and the thinking of the industrialist in solving a problem of production can have the same form although the contents differ widely. We can speak of one habit as more general, more widely applicable, or more usable than another.

Three clusters of habits especially concern us: those that have to do with the acquiring of knowledge; the habits of using it to solve problems; and, finally, habits of using knowledge imaginatively for creative and appreciative activity.[15]

Linguistic symbols and skills

If we ask what habits and skills operate in the widest variety of knowledge-seeking and knowledge-using situations, the answer would be the symbolic ones. Traditionally these are the three R's or the symbol systems of writing, reading, and arithmetic. However they are not restricted to these. Musical notes are symbols, and the visual arts also employ symbols to communicate whatever it is that they do communicate.

The centrality of the three R's in the curriculum of the elementary school has often been challenged. As early as 1898, we find John Dewey writing:

> My proposition is, that conditions—social, industrial, and intel-lectual—have undergone such a radical change, that the time has come for a thoroughgoing examination of the emphasis put upon linguistic work in elementary education.[16]

Dewey goes on to argue that this emphasis on reading arose when there was no other avenue to the control of the accumulated cultural

[15] These habit clusters can be regarded as modes of knowing and will be discussed further. Cf. also Virgil C. Aldrich, "Chess Not Without the Queen," *Proceedings and Addresses of the American Philosophical Association,* 1957–1958.

[16] John Dewey, *Education Today,* New York: G. P. Putnam's Sons, 1940, p. 19.

resources, e.g., the scientific method of direct and free investigation. On the other hand, in early America reading was about the only "escape from the poverty of the intellectual environment." "To learn to read and write was an interesting, even exciting thing: it made such a difference in life."[17]

The situation, Dewey continues, has changed. First, there is now no dearth of direct intellectual stimulation from the environment in the form of travel and art galleries. Today we would add radio and television as well as the pictorial mass media magazine. Reading and writing consequently have lost "their motive and motor force." In the second place, knowledge is no longer hidden behind obscure and difficult symbol systems.

> It is possible to initiate the child from the first in a direct, not abstract or symbolical way, into the operations by which society maintains its existence, material and spiritual.[18]

Further, as Dewey saw, the young child is probably not ready physiologically or psychologically to learn the more abstract symbolic phases of human éxperience, nor does he have a natural need for much systematic training in them.

The defense of the three R's is undertaken by a variety of people. College professors are chronically caustic about the linguistic ineptness of high school graduates. This is understandable because professors in their professions have to use symbols with a fairly high degree of precision, and they expect—with or without reason—themes and papers that exhibit a respectable order of precision. The reading of college textbooks is itself no mean feat of symbolic skill. Enough high school graduates are deficient in all or some of these tasks to force colleges to organize remedial classes in reading.

Complaints come from disgruntled taxpayers who feel that a simplified curriculum of the three R's would reduce school costs. Out-and-out social reactionaries fear that a curriculum that includes discussion of social, political, and economic questions may disturb such features of the social scene that they happen to find pleasant; still others are opposed in principle to anything that was not included in their own elementary schooling.

The Deweyan emphasis on direct experience has often been dis-

---

[17] *Ibid.,* p. 20.
[18] *Ibid.,* p. 22. But obviously this is true of only some of our knowledge. The more theoretically developed knowledge becomes the more "hidden" it is likely to become.

torted into frantic and sometimes comical efforts of elementary teachers to avoid book learning. Boys who have been chased out of the precinct firehouse every other day for years are taken to visit the firehouse lest they have only a "verbal" familiarity with it.

The role of symbolic learning has to be revaluated in the light of what has happened since the turn of the century. To begin with, how sound are Dewey's arguments against the centrality of the symbolic skills? They leave us with the vague feeling that something has been left out of consideration. We may call it the *creative* role of literacy. Language is made up of symbols that represent the *universal* aspects of things (chairness, for example), rather than concrete things (chairs) themselves. They alone enable us to deal with the general and thus free us from the restriction of the particular things and events.

So although it is true that for strictly utilitarian purposes of getting along somehow, the symbolic skill needed by an individual pupil may be very small and may yet become smaller, the argument loses its bite when we regard the pupil's potentialities for self-perfection and society's needs for communication. Whereas other media may be more immediate in their impact and less difficult to use, there is nevertheless no substitute for language symbols in a general education, for they are the road *par excellence* to generality.

Despite the dethronement of verbalism reading is still *the* subject of the elementary grades. The most radically Progressive schoolman knows that even the most Progressive parents are jittery about an activity program until the child has safely jumped the reading hurdle. No amount of happy childhood, finger painting, choric speaking, spontaneous musicianship, and social awareness can quite make up for a prolonged inability to read.

The production of reading materials for children is one of our young industrial giants; courses in reading methods have balanced the budgets of many a school of education; the research into reading —materials, conditions, methods, remedial phases, preventive phases, abnormalities—is the best and most consistently plowed pasture on the educational farm. Those who say that reading is ignored in the modern school simply do not know the facts.

What then is wrong with reading instruction? In one sense, nothing. Children do learn to read. Those who do not probably get more efficient remedial work than did their fathers. Children read quite well on a certain level of abstraction, but this level is not always high enough to handle Shakespeare, Milton, and some of the other "classics" included in the traditional high school curriculum. Nor does it reach the interpretive level demanded by high school history and science. On the expressive side, most children learn to speak and write the language well enough for most purposes. The difficulty comes in satisfying the demands for precision and elegance inherent in high school and college English composition courses.[19]

Another difficulty is this. In their eagerness to teach reading, elementary teachers have understandably succumbed to the argument that since the silent reading of flowing prose is the kind of reading most people do most of the time, that alone is the kind that ought to be mastered. Consequently, rapid reading for comprehension of ideas in simple sequence is the type of reading instruction stressed in the elementary grades.

The most familiar type of reading material is the story or the narrative. Children start with that and very often finish with it. To keep materials within the comprehension of children, great care is taken to maintain the vocabulary load within tested limits of tolerance. The grammatical structure is also kept simple. Wherever possible a bright, dramatic, narrative style is used. Even when description or exposition is needed it is dramatized for vividness. Comprehension comes to mean, accordingly, the ability to follow the plot of a story or the reproduction of the elements of simple description and exposition.

So long as this is the fare no one has indigestion. But when textbooks with technical terminology are introduced in the sixth, seventh, and eighth grades, and when cause and effect relations, complex spatial relations, and chronologies are involved, the reading is likely to break down. This breakdown is of two types: one is due to limits of abstraction potential; in cruder language, the pupil cannot think on this level of generality and hence can merely repeat the words and memorize them. Another type of breakdown is even worse. It is that which befalls the intelligent child who reads a paragraph in a geography text as if it were a narrative and finds to his consternation that there is no plot or character to comprehend. Nothing *happens* in this kind of reading. So a familiarity with the sound or appearance of the words has to suffice. Since the emphasis has been on rapid silent reading with a minimum of rereadings and

[19] On this point, cf. John S. Kenyon, "Cultural Levels and Functional Varieties of English," *College English*, 10: 31–36, October 1948.

analysis, it is hard to blame this child for believing that when he has scanned the material twice, he has "studied" it, and that his only remedy for failure is to "study" it some more.

The writer's analysis of the study habits of many an unfortunate college student has convinced him that the equating of rapid narrative reading with study reading in the early and, for all he knows, in later years of reading instruction is often responsible for their plight. Apropos of which, the remedial reading clinics in colleges that emphasize more rapid reading of easy narrative materials may help the student in courses which call for large doses of such reading, but may not help him to understand philosophy, science, or very adult literature.

So much then for reading. The use of language for communication both in its oral and written form need not be treated separately. The same arguments for and against the development of these skills would apply.

Mathematical symbols

If we ask, "How much mathematics will the average American on the average job living an average life use?" the answer is, "Not much." The day when children had to be taught arithmetic so that they could count and check their change is gone. Furthermore, one can hire a bookkeeper; one's taxes will be made out by a representative of the tax division; and adding machines are more accurate than mental computation anyway. But of course very few Americans lead average lives, so that foreseeing just how much arithmetic a given pupil will need is a futile undertaking.

On the other hand, if we remember that the goal of the good life is the self-perfecting of the individual, then the role of mathematics is relatively clear. For mathematics deal with the quantitative aspects of reality, and to understand mathematics is one way of perfecting oneself. The level of abstraction at which we can operate comfortably in this field varies from one individual to another. Some children will be at their peak when they can perform the four fundamental arithmetical operations on relatively simple elements. Others can rise to such a level that: "How many pencils can you buy for 77 cents if they are priced as 3 for 11 cents?" or "How much interest will 850 dollars earn in 18 months in a savings bank if the rate paid is 2½ per cent a year?" hold no terrors for them. Still others can climb another rung in the mathematical ladder to reach algebra. Others may go to analytical geometry and trigonometry, to Riemmanian geometry, or to mathematical logic. But at whatever level the pupil *can* deal with mathematical symbols, to that level instruction within the time available should bring him.[20]

Two kinds of mathematical habits are essential for general education. One is mastery of the fundamental arithmetic computations to the point of automaticity. The pupil should not have to figure out how to add, subtract, divide, and multiply. He should have the multiplication tables memorized.

The other habit is that of solving mathematical problems. Granted that mathematical understanding is not a matter of habit but of insight, nevertheless there is a habit aspect to the procedures of problem solving. Anyone who has worked with arithmetical problems knows that what was a big job of independent ratiocination in the first problem of two railway trains traveling at certain speeds became fairly routine after the tenth problem had been solved. The problem-solving attitude, the search for unknowns and for possible substitutions and equivalents all are generic operations in the deductive mode and are perfected with repetitions of the right sort just as any other habit is. It is these *generalized habits* that will abide long after specific computational procedures are forgotten.[21]

As for the third R, there is a strong temptation to omit it from this discussion altogether. It is entirely a tool, and legibility is its only virtue.

Artistic symbols

Musical notation, images in paint, clay, language, and gesture are artistic symbols. Aesthetic experience operates via both presentational and representational symbols. Presentational ones convey meaning by looking, sounding, or feeling as they do. The tree in the picture *looks* lonely; the poem *sounds* melancholy, but the artist has to contrive to make them look or sound like this. Some skill in making artistic objects, we have argued in Chapter 9, is essential to enable

[20] If recent research into mathematics teaching has shown anything, it is that we have probably underestimated the ability and inclination of children to deal with the more theoretical aspects of mathematical study.

[21] Cf. National Council of Teachers of Mathematics, *Arithmetic in General Education*, Sixteenth Yearbook, pp. 8–44. Cf. also Beberman and Vaughan, *High School Mathematics*.

us to apprehend the "significant feeling" embodied in well-developed art works.

Representational symbols suggest ideas and images not to be found in the work of art itself. The halo around the head of a saint or the allusions to Greek mythology in Milton's *Paradise Lost* evoke meanings in us, but we have to supply these meanings. Or the table in a picture may refer to a real table outside the picture and thus act as a representational symbol.[22]

To apprehend the import of representational symbolism requires knowledge as well as skill. Yet the literary arts and musical ones make some skill in the use of their symbolism virtually indispensable.

Because skill learning emphasizes semi-automatic responses, it is easy to underestimate its intellectual importance. But in learning to use symbols skillfully, the pupil's thinking takes on the structure of language, mathematics, and the arts themselves. They furnish a kind of intellectual discipline.

Habits of study

A common complaint heard in every academic corridor and in countless homes is that pupils do not know how to study, an odd state of affairs considering that pupils spend so much of their lives in study.

What does the complaint mean? It depends on who is complaining. For one teacher it may mean failure to memorize; for another it means lack of system in preparing home lessons; for another it is synonymous with lack of concentration; for another it is failure to outline the lesson. Failure in school work is due to poor teaching, poor study, or poor capacity, and since teachers are reluctant to admit the first and parents the last, poor study is the favorite explanation although it is not always the pupil's own explanation.

Each subject or discipline has its own method of investigation, its distinctive terminology, and its own basic theories. Together they make up the structure of the discipline. This is the structure to be mastered and understood. There will be elements to be memorized, methods of solving problems to be understood and practiced, and theories to be comprehended.

[22] Whether or not value judgments can be given to us presentationally is a problem that has been discussed by Donald G. Arnstine in an unpublished doctoral dissertation for the University of Illinois entitled *The Aesthetic Dimension of Value Education.*

If the pupil relies on one method of study, e.g., memorization, and if the teacher evaluates his work only in terms of memorization, he will not learn *how* to study for understanding. To understand a textbook is to re-enact the thinking of the author. Outlines, explanations, lectures, underlining, and recitations are all devices to facilitate this reconstruction. Study of a logically organized subject matter in a logically made text is a process of active search and re-search, not merely passive reading.

Not all subjects and texts are logically organized. Some texts and subjects consist largely of lists of items to be memorized or directions to be followed. In a logically organized subject or text, the sovereign skill is that of selection and discrimination. Illustrations are to be distinguished from the principles they are intended to illustrate. Evidence is to be separated from the theory for which it is marshalled. Out of all the facts certain ones are selected as *crucial* to the theory; only these are marked for memorization.

To say that habits of study can be formed is to say no more than that study can be a craft and that the good student is a good craftsman. The notion that study is a mysterious osmosis between a book and a head explains why so little of it is *done* and so much of what passes for it is like the incantation which is supposed to pave the way for a miracle. The good student is, if nothing more, an efficient operator—whether the subject fascinates him or not. Like the good carpenter, he goes about his business with order, method, and ease, whether he is building a palace or a henhouse.

Research skills

Library skills. The materials of knowledge are not arranged in counters and store windows for the casual picking. They are stored in libraries, dictionaries, and reference books, and the use of them is as much a matter of skill and habit as are reading and writing themselves. Therefore, every pupil, regardless of later specialization, should acquire a decent mastery of these generalized research habits.

Observation. The skills and habits discussed thus far have concentrated on the art of getting meaning and understanding from symbolic materials of the linguistic and mathematical kind. But if astronomers did not observe the skies, there might be no books on astronomy. It would be sensible, therefore, to list observation as one of the habits or skills of acquiring knowledge. Observation is not staring. It is a search for what is relevant to a problem. Observation is not a faculty but a skill and a very specific one to boot. The detective is a close observer of criminal situations, but he may not notice what he is having for dinner. We can foster the *habit* of observation by making the pupil as knowing as possible about the discriminations that are proper within each of the subjects he studies.

Experimentation. Experimentation is, of course, the method *par excellence* for the discovery of knowledge and for its validation. No self-respecting school these days is without laboratories for its science work and home economics.

It is to be doubted that much new knowledge is unearthed in these laboratories. Their purpose is rather to make more vivid and convincing the verbal statements found in the textbook. They also give the pupil a perceptual familiarity with such substances as sodium and H_2SO_4 in chemistry. But perhaps the most important function of laboratory work is to illustrate the principles of a science. That the formulas of chemistry and physics, the theories of biology and psychology are not mystifications spun out of dreams can be demonstrated convincingly in the laboratory. This will not happen if the laboratory work is an exercise in following directions in a manual.

To discover knowledge by this method requires a high order of interest and competence in a particular field. Only people so qualified can even raise the questions to which experiments might give the answer; only such persons—and not always they—can recognize the answer when they see it. If the school can generate such interest and competence, it may turn out experimental seekers for the truth in special fields. For the general student this method is rarely a means for discovering new knowledge or even old knowledge.[23]

But, it will be objected, is there not a whole philosophy of education which argues that problem-solving or experimental inquiry is the only reliable way of acquiring knowledge? The purpose of such inquiry, however, is to solve *particular* problems rather than to gain systematic knowledge about the world or about anything else. In the course of such experimental attacks on our problems we certainly do

---

[23] Paul Westmeyer, in an unpublished doctoral thesis for the University of Illinois, 1960, *Development and Preliminary Trial of a Method of Teaching Chemistry*, found that high school students can profit from self-directed experimentation in chemistry and can grow in this dimension if encouraged. Nevertheless, not all students respond uniformly and it is not yet clear just what differentiates them in this respect.

acquire knowledge, but it is subordinate to solving the problem. Only the scientist or the man with theoretical goals uses problems or problem-solving as a means of acquiring knowledge.

Habits of Using Knowledge

In his famous little book, *How We Think*, Dewey analyzed the steps involved in the solving of any problem by the scientific method. We can perhaps condense that treatment by indicating the highlights of the thinking process.

1. When confronted by an obstacle to the flow of action, the human being responds in one or more of many possible ways. If an unlocked door sticks, he may kick it. If a kick doesn't do the trick, he can rattle the knob, push, pull, lift, depress, and shake until something happens. If the door opens, that's the end of this particular problem, but if it doesn't, then either the business of going through the door must be abandoned, or the campaign renewed.

2. It is at this point, when previously learned responses have failed, that reflection or thinking may set in. The person halts the pushing, pulling, and rattling and begins to imagine what could make the door stick. Could it be the swelling of the wood on the door or on the jamb? From his experience there may emerge the generalization that when the weather is damp and warm, wood expands. If this is what has happened—and technically we say, if this hypothesis or guess were correct—then what would reduce the swelling of the wood? Chilling and drying the wood. But how is one to do such a thing? Nothing seems to suggest itself. As he looks over the door and its frame, searching for a clue to arouse another process of more promising imagination, his eye falls on the hinges. His experience seems to churn a bit, and it says: "Drive those pins out of the hinges and the door can be loosened." Mentally he checks whether he has a screw driver and hammer. He then goes into action and off comes the door.

3. Whether it is a physicist in a laboratory or a frustrated man before a sticky door, the process of solving the problem has the same features; a situation that was confused and indeterminate becomes clear and definite. For Dewey, this is thinking and this is truth making. This is Instrumentalism. It is also education because the experience used in the solving of problems is reconstructed so

that the resulting success becomes the wherewithal for further trials and possible successes; it is the tissue of growth itself.

The great truth in Dewey's insistence on problem-solving as a mode of instruction lies in the fact that thinking *methodically* is itself a matter of *habit* formation, and the formation of this cluster of habits is more important than the particular content of the problems that have been used in the forming of it. Of course, if problems of concern *to the pupil* are utilized for the training, there is a neat solution of the problem of motivation, of catching and keeping interest, at the same time.

Note that in steps 2 and 3 of the problem-solving procedure knowledge previously acquired determines how we formulate our problem and the tentative guesses we make for its solution. Where does such knowledge come from? It comes from common knowledge, from deliberate study, and from the solution of previous problems. To get rid of the deliberate and systematic study of the organized fields of knowledge means relying for our generalizations on the other two sources plus the information carried by radio, newspapers, and the like. But fewer and fewer of our really serious problems are solvable by "common" knowledge.

Analytical thinking

The description Dewey gives of problem-solving includes a host of sub-skills which make the total process more or less precise and to that extent more or less fruitful.[24] It takes little or no formal schooling to solve some problems, but it does take formal schooling to think as a physicist, biologist, or political scientist does. Generally it takes formal training to think precisely in any field, and if all men ought to think as precisely as they can about the general problems of life, then precise thinking is one of the habits to be included in general education.

We may accordingly include in our list what might be called analytical or critical thinking. Skill in the framing and testing of definitions, detection of fallacies in thinking, familiarity with the formal properties of both deductive and inductive inference, and classification are samples of the skills to be included under this head.

---

[24] It is with these sub-skills that research in learning theory can be profitably concerned, i.e., with the operations involved in various types of concept attainment, categorization, and inference.

They are not opposed to the more inclusive habit of problem-solving but are rather skills to be used at every turn in problem-solving. They furnish the critical tools for the discrimination and refinement of concepts and their status in propositions and arguments. They make our *thinking* precise. Certainly teachers should be thoroughly sophisticated and facile with respect to these analytical skills.

Deliberative skills

Another cluster of skills and habits prerequisite to general education, especially if that education is to function in a democracy, includes the deliberative skills of group discussion, consensus, and decision. We cannot, it would seem, take for granted that children born and reared in a democracy will automatically assume the democratic posture toward group problems. Consequently, there are "democratic" habits and skills to be learned under deliberate guidance of the school. Solving group problems requires not only an understanding of psychology but also self analysis and the ability to project oneself imaginatively into the feelings of others. This is probably as much an art as a science. Nevertheless, it is an art that is rooted in the science of human relations; indeed, only insofar as it is so rooted can we ever hope to rationalize these human relations.[25]

Evaluational habits

When a principle is taught, it is taught as applicable to a wide variety of situations. Thus the principle of oxidation when taught in chemistry is taught as exemplified in rusting, burning, and spontaneous combustion. The principle of economic cycles is similarly taught as explaining many different examples of economic booms and depressions. It is fair to expect that after a while the *habit* or *tendency* will be formed in the student to ask himself in any problem situation: What principle or knowledge does this situation exemplify? How will this principle illuminate the problem? What hypotheses will it suggest?

Perhaps the most important use to which knowledge should be put is in the judgment of what is valuable. So important is this use that we have devoted the entire second part of this book to its con-

[25] Cf. Benne, *et al.*, *Group Dynamics and Social Action*. Also Moreno, *Psychodrama*, and Raup, *et al.*, *The Improvement of Practical Judgment*.

sideration. Is there a special skill or habit of evaluation? When I am confronted with a choice situation, is there a peculiar skill by which I decide which alternative is preferable?

Aristotle referred to the intelligent evaluation of alternatives as practical wisdom. Yet this is not a different *kind* of intelligence from that used in understanding astronomy. It is intelligence directed to a different goal, a much more complex goal. Which vocation to choose or which man to marry is a far more complicated question than the position of a planet in the solar system.

What we have in mind, therefore, is not a distinctive skill of evaluation. It is rather the *habit* of evaluating a situation or a choice by the use of thought and knowledge.

Do we need to develop such a habit? Yes, because we can evaluate in other ways. For example, we can make our choices on the basis of what the Joneses are doing, on the basis of tastes unconsciously formed, on the basis of fear, on the basis of prejudice and ignorance. We do need to cultivate this habit deliberately and so well that it becomes a reliable tendency, a part of our character. How does a school go about such cultivation?

In Chapter 13 it will be proposed that deliberative skills be developed in a problems course designed for this purpose. These problems will be societal problems—problems confronting society as a whole. There is a real difference between a personal and a group problem. I am completely involved in a personal problem; I may or may not be in a group problem. A high school senior is involved in deciding which band should play at the prom, but not in the same way or degree as he is in deciding whether he can afford to go to the prom or which girl to escort. Although they overlap, the personal and collective problems are never exactly reducible to each other.

For this reason a guidance program in which individual problems are handled individually is indispensable to the curriculum. Such guidance is a way of helping the pupil to confront himself with his own problem and helping him to objectify his situation so that *his* intelligence and knowledge can be brought to work upon it.

Habits of Imagination and Appreciation

In addition to using knowledge instrumentally as a means to accomplishing our ends, we can use knowledge imaginatively. The world can be perceived as bearing qualities that reflect human values.

In Chapter 9 on aesthetic experience this aspect of life was taken up in detail, and earlier in this chapter mention was made of the symbolic skills involved in making and appreciating art objects.

Imagination is broader than art. The scientist uses it in devising hypotheses, the good workman imagines what the inside of the balky engine looks like, and all of us imagine ourselves leading worry-free lives on pleasant shores during the dreary days of winter. Much of what is called creative thinking involves imagination.

Important educationally is the formation of the tendency or habit to be imaginative, that is, to free oneself from the literal, the practical, the observational moods for a flight into symbolic freedom, or what was referred to in Chapter 3 as natural freedom. The aesthetic attitude, a readiness to be stimulated to imagination by a work of imagination, also requires freedom.

Hence the school in aesthetic education, in science, and every other department of instruction can and should encourage and reward the imaginative efforts of the pupil. But the most effective kind of encouragement is success and for this, skill is the best insurance. Although it is not yet clear *how* imagination is cultivated, we can be fairly sure that practice in dealing with imaginative materials in the arts and open-ended situations that permit alternative solutions will result every so often in a happy result. And happy results contrasted with unhappy and indifferent ones will help eliminate inept imaginative gambits and reinforce the successful ones. Now that imagination and creativity have "paid off" in space exploration and military power, they have acquired a respectability they never enjoyed when confined to the fine arts.

It is well to acquire knowledge; it is even better to use it as a means to achieve the good life. But the process of learning should also be enjoyable in itself. To know is a natural human power; to use it should give an immediate satisfaction as well as enjoyable results.

The notorious distaste of youngsters for schooling is a sign that intellectual power is not functioning efficiently. It means that pupils are being asked to do what is beyond the readiness of their powers; it does not mean that children do not like to learn, or that they do not want to learn.

Every achievement is immediately felt as enjoyable, as a sense of power, as confidence, and as an urge to take the next step.

As for *what* the task is, is it so obvious that children have a

"natural" set of things they want to do? Rejecting carefully designed toys, the infant will often be delighted with an old dishpan.
Is learning to read, to write, to draw, to "figure," more "unnatural"
than learning to dress, eat with utensils, go to the movies, and the
scores of other tasks that make up their social environment? True,
the child's desires may not coincide with those of the adult at any
given moment, but that is no more true in the school than anywhere else.

Going to school is as much taken for granted by a child in our
culture as going to the movies. He does not expect to do in the
school what he does at home, in the movies, or on the playground.
The school is the place where one does something special and where
rules of the game are a little different. But there is also a special
kind of excitement and triumph.

To enjoy the process of learning itself, therefore, is a genuine
objective of the school. It is not an impossible one nor incompatible
with the habits of acquiring and using knowledge. Indeed, they
reinforce each other at every step.

Summary

In this chapter we examined and rejected the subject-centered
curriculum *as conceived by traditional schools* on the grounds that
it could not solve the problem of motivation, it could not guarantee
retention of information, and it could not develop thinking.

We rejected the problem-centered curriculum because (1) problems need not require any knowledge beyond what ordinary life
experience could furnish, and (2) problems do not always require
scientific method for their solution. When they are so *designed* as to
require these, the value of natural motivation may be lost, and the
knowledge required is not available by "raiding" subjects that have
never been systematically mastered.

The view of the curriculum being proposed in their stead regards
the habits and skills of acquiring, using, and enjoying truth as the
immediate objectives of general education. This is grounded in the
belief that these habits are universal forms of human activity,
flexible enough to meet the widest variety of learning situations by
varying the particular contents through which they are developed.

An analysis was made of the different types of symbolic, research,
study, deliberative, analytical, imaginative, and evaluative skills and

habits required by general education. In anticipation of the following chapter some indication was given as to the types of curriculum content which might be used to perfect these habits.

For the habits of acquiring knowledge we need to use the organized subject matter as a practice ground to develop the symbolic skills of information and imagination and the skills of observation, research, experimentation, and study.

For the habits of *using* knowledge we need genuine problems to develop the skills of critical thinking and problem-solving. For the skills of evaluation we need to work on collective problems that require group deliberation and a guidance program that exercises the skill of using intelligence in the solution of personal problems.

For the habits of using knowledge for imagination and appreciation, experiences with artistic expression and impression remain the primary resources. But all areas of study provide opportunity for encouraging creativity and the imaginative skills.

Finally, it has been suggested that the very act of learning can become enjoyable and that the habit of enjoying knowledge and its use can be cultivated.

PROBLEMS FOR DISCUSSION AND RESEARCH

1. Smith, Stanley, and Shores in *Fundamentals of Curriculum Development* make out a strong case for the problem-centered curriculum. Do you think that it meets the objections raised in this chapter?

2. You have had at least 12 years of schooling. What curriculum pattern did it follow? Which of the habits or skills do you feel have been well developed? Which do you feel have been neglected?

3. Try "raiding" an organized subject matter that you have never studied. What happens?

4. In Sunday editions of *The New York Times* (or other metropolitan newspapers), can you read and understand special sections on art, science, economics, education, and international affairs? If not, why not? What stands in the way of such understanding?

5. Analyze a day's activity (outside of preparing school lessons) to find out how much of the subjects you studied in high school you use.

SUGGESTIONS FOR FURTHER READING

See list of references at the end of Chapter 13.

13

The Curriculum II

The previous chapter argued that the problem of constructing a curriculum for education that would be really general and therefore the same for all pupils could be solved by having the school concentrate on perfecting the habits of acquiring and using knowledge. Habits were held to be forms of activity that could function in classes of tasks. They consequently could transfer to non-school situations. On the other hand, habits are perfected by developing skill or efficiency of performance. This means that each habit has a content of ideas, images, attitudes, and operations which is particular.

The curriculum, therefore, must have materials and activities that are also particular. These can come only from the culture in which the school operates. Part of that culture is knowledge and this is stored in symbols. Hence the need for the symbolic skills discussed in the last chapter. But there still remains the problem of deciding what knowledge we ought to teach in order that the pupil can use intelligence in his life and to perfect his capacity for acquiring and using knowledge.

311

If we ask, "What would it be desirable for every man as a man to know?" the answer might well be, "Everything." For in general, it is better to know than not to know, and Comenius quite logically, if not very practicably, made the goal of his educational system *Pansophy* (universal knowledge).[1]

Areas of Study

According to Tykociner, we can distinguish the following functions of knowledge:[2]

1 and 2. To systematize knowledge of basic facts and their relations. For this purpose we have the symbol systems already discussed in the previous chapter and the physical, biological, and social sciences. He lists more than a score of basic disciplines in these areas.

3. To systematize the knowledge of how our world, its living things, its institutions and, in general, its culture developed from prehistory to the present time. Although a science often includes something about how its subject matter developed, it need not do so. For example, the science of mathematics can be studied as the relations among certain well-defined ideas about quantity without mentioning the growth of these ideas in the history of mankind. For the designer of the curriculum there looms a choice between studying each basic discipline both as a system of ideas and in its historical development together, or separating study of the disciplines as systems from the study of their development.

4. To project future needs and to regulate the activities of men as they try to fulfill them. According to Tykociner, agriculture, medicine, technology, and national defense are samples of the first, while political science, jurisprudence, economics, and management are samples of the latter. Here too might be included the sciences that serve and regulate our coping activity by disseminating knowledge, e.g., education, library science, journalism, and other mass communication media.

5. To synthesize our knowledge both of fact and of value. Philosophy, general systems theory, ideologies, and religions serve this purpose.

[1] Cf. Beisswänger, *Comenius als Pansophist.*
[2] This classification of knowledge is taken with gross adaptations from Joseph T. Tykociner's *Research as a Science—Zetetics,* privately printed and obtainable from the author at the University of Illinois.

6. To sustain human striving for knowledge and value. Here are included all the fine arts.

7. Tykociner also stresses another function: to sustain, study, and develop research. He calls this the science of Zetetics.

For our purpose these functions together with the disciplines serving them can be grouped as shown in Table I in order to indicate six distinctive strands of the curriculum, each organizing knowledge in a different way in order to achieve somewhat different school and life outcomes. Certain disciplines mentioned in Tykociner's classification are omitted; some because they do not fit into a scheme of general education and many more because of lack of curriculum time.

More important, however, is the fact that the curriculum designer has to keep in mind not only the way knowledge grows and is systematized by the culture, but also how it is to be translated into school procedures and outcomes. Thus to qualify for a place in the curriculum in general education an item has to be indispensable for perfecting the habits of acquiring, using, and enjoying knowledge. Usefulness to society or importance to research may make certain studies valuable, but not necessarily for general education.

For general education a selection has to be made from the area in the first column of Table 1 in terms of the school outcomes listed in the last column. These include the skills and habits discussed in the last chapter plus a *minimum* set of key ideas. Given these skills and ideas one should be able to read, discuss, and think with some facility about any of the topics that concern man as man. He should, to put it roughly, feel at home in the pages of the high quality newspapers, books, and magazines written for the *educated* layman. He will not know everything or even remember all he has studied, but he will know what posture to assume, what sources to consult, and what to admit as relevant evidence for the point at issue. He will also know in every value area *why* some levels are higher than others, and possibly, although this is not absolutely necessary, he will live at these levels.

Modes of Organization

The middle column called "modes of instruction" has to do with the way the materials in the first column are to be arranged. These already have been mentioned, but they need elaboration

Table 1

THE CURRICULUM

Areas and functions of knowledge	Modes of organization for instruction	School outcomes
1. The symbolic tools of learning, thinking, and communication:	As conceptual systems or hierarchies of skills	Intelligent and facile use of these languages— arts of acquiring knowledge
—language of ordinary discourse —language of quantity (mathematics) —language of art (drawing, painting, musical performance, etc.)—all as influenced by modern developments in linguistics, logic, and information theory		
2. Systematization of basic areas of knowledge:	As conceptual systems	Attainment of *basic* minimum key concepts, relations, and familiarity with modes of investigation and criteria of adequacy in each (the mode of scientific cognition)
—physics, chemistry, astronomy, geology —biology, physiology, botany —psychology, sociology		
3. Organization of the past:	Developmental:	Perspective, orientation, and knowledge *about* the culture
—evolutionary account of cosmos —evolutionary account of human groupings (family, communities, and types of state) —evolutionary account of institution sciences, technologies, art, and value systems	—evolutionary —historical —biographical	

Table 1 (continued)

Areas and functions of knowledge	Modes of organization for instruction	School outcomes
4. Modes of analyzing and coping with the problems of the future—the role of agriculture, medicine, engineering, and other arts based on knowledge—also the regulative sciences of law, political science, economics, administration and management—also the sciences of information distribution such as education, library science, journalism, and mass communications	Thematic or as molar social problems, e.g., the problems of peace, world food supply, population distribution, world resources; conflict of ideologies, etc.	Facility in analyzing and structuring (not solving) problems in terms of knowledge from a number of disciplines; skills of deliberation using knowledge (the mode of instrumental knowing or cognition)
5. Value systems that synthesize and integrate man's knowledge and strengthen his aspirations—philosophy and fine arts	Exemplars or models of philosophical systems and fine art of acknowledged excellence and typical of significant epochs in Western civilization	Familiarity with outstanding attempts to formulate value schema and appreciation of their celebration in notable works of art—imaginative use of knowledge (the mode of imaginative cognition)
6. Personal problems	Problems of guidance and counseling	Practice in analyzing personal problems in the light of knowledge about self and situation

because "subjects" in school mean anything from penmanship to physics, and organization of subject matter can refer to the structure of the materials or to the sequence of activities carried on by teachers and pupils in the classroom. For example, historical materials are organized chronologically (in time series), but for teaching purposes an American history class might begin with a movie showing New York City in all its powerful confusion as it *now* exists. How to arrange teaching acts is primarily a matter of methodology.

Languages of all kinds are organized as conceptual systems of meaning (systems of ideas and words) with rules for usage. Grammar, mathematics, and logic are examples of such basic systems of ideas. However, these languages can be used only after skills of speaking and thinking are perfected; understanding the system of meanings is not enough. These two phases *can* be learned independently and often are. One becomes skillful in speaking his mother tongue long before one understands about subjects and predicates, nouns, and verbs. And countless generations have understood the grammar of Latin without ever having acquired the skill of speaking it. The same sort of observation could be made about the roles of skill and understanding in mathematics, literature, and the other arts.

Nevertheless, when the two are allowed to interplay, they can affect each other in important ways. As a result of the development of electronic machines that can process enormous amounts of information in unbelievably complex ways, we have had to look more closely at the theory of language usage and how rules are formulated and employed. Linguistics, logic, and information theory have been called in to help disclose the relations between speech, information, attitudes, and choices. In trying to invent machines that will imitate human thought processes, one is forced to examine how these operate in the human being. And if the machine performs better than the human being, it is possible that we can get a clue to improving the human learning by studying the machine.

As one result of these inquiries, the organization of materials for teaching of language and mathematics is undergoing change.[3] Another is that teaching itself can be conceived as a type of linguistic processing of information by teachers and pupils.[4]

There are grounds for suggesting, therefore, that the materials to be used for developing symbolic skills be organized both conceptually (as subjects) for understanding and as procedures (a set of

[3] Of the numerous articles and books in this area, such samples as *Patterns of English* by Paul Roberts, Harcourt, Brace & World, Inc., 1956, and the University of Illinois Committee on School Mathematics Materials need only be mentioned here as illustrative of this trend.

[4] B. O. Smith, "A Concept of Teaching," *Teachers College Record,* 61:229–241, 1960.

skills) for facile use. The skills themselves are arranged in hierarchies, such that each set is a prerequisite for subsequent ones.

In the second area of study the sciences are organized as separate subjects of instruction because each science is a conceptual system and understanding its structure is the primary reason for studying it. Presumably if one were to apprehend the basic ideas of the basic sciences one could understand the way in which human knowledge is organized and communicated. Note that the primary objective is not skillful scientific work nor skillful application of science to technology.

But the sciences that can be studied in general education and studied carefully as conceptual systems represent only a tiny fraction of all the sciences. The vast stores of information and ideas accumulated in our development cannot be studied systematically. Under such circumstances the developmental approach suggested in area 3 in the table becomes useful. The evolutionary, historical, and biographical modes of organizing knowledge are all developmental in that they concentrate on showing how the present emerged out of the past, but they refer to somewhat different ways of doing so. The evolutionary approach seeks laws or theories that explain how a given form of bird, science, or institution turns into a subsequent form. For example, Darwin tried to explain how any species of animal becomes subdivided into new species by natural selection. Or it is sometimes argued that human institutions like the state or the family evolve from simpler to more complex forms.

One virtue of this approach is that in order to trace the evolution of any cultural development it is necessary to draw from many sources of information. Thus, if one were to organize materials about the family on the evolutionary pattern, one would have to bring in information from archaeology, sociology, and anthropology. This is not an adequate substitute for studying these sciences separately, but it does give the student some understanding of the intellectual resources of the culture and how they can be used.

While all evolutionary treatments are historical in that they proceed from past to present, we tend to use "historical" to refer to accounts that follow a strict chronological order. Thus the historical account of the American family would describe the family as it existed in successive periods. It might end up with "laws" about the development of families in general or it might not.

Biographical treatment is also historical, but it refers more speci-

fically to the description of the life of an individual. By extending
the meaning of the word, we can speak of the biography of a nation
or a science, but this may confuse matters more than clarify them.

The outcomes envisioned from the developmental mode of arrangement is familiarity with the major lines of development of the
sciences, institutions, arts, and the value systems of our culture. This
outcome is not knowledge *of* the sciences and the arts, but rather
knowledge *about* their role in the culture and in our life. Knowledge
of a conceptual system is the primary outcome of the subject matter arrangement of materials.

It may be objected that developmental study will produce a
watered-down and diffuse familiarity allegedly characteristic of survey courses. To which it can only be replied that a map which indicates the outlines of the states in a country is no less precise than
one that includes all the rivers and villages as well, and more useful
for general understanding than an almanac that lists all the geo-
graphical details of a country in alphabetical order. If we cannot
study everything intensively, and if it is disastrous to study everything superficially, then the only alternatives are to study a few
things intensively or to study some intensively and some extensively.

Another mode of organization is represented by the fourth area
in the table. It arranges material so as to bear on a topic or theme.
For example, "food and population" as a topic will suck in, so to
speak, data and theory from agriculture, medicine, biology, ethics,
religion, economics, architecture, city planning, economics, law,
education, and journalism. Indeed, every one of the regulative,
coping, and the disseminating sciences in area 4 as well as some in
the other areas will in some sense be relevant.

But the problem sucks in materials selectively and arranges them
in its own way, not as history or as logic might order them. Because
the outcome is neither *knowledge about* a special field of objects nor
knowledge of such a special field, this kind of organization recom-
mends itself when problem-solving ability is the desired outcome.
As a by-product, problem-solving when practiced on important social problems also contributes *knowledge about* the way knowledge
has been mobilized for action in our culture. Much depends, of
course, on which topics are chosen as nuclei.

The mode of organization in area 5 differs from the others discussed in that it concentrates material in a model or an outstanding
example. Here, for example, is the description of a classic.

WHAT MAKES GREAT BOOKS[5]

The first criterion is that a classic must be a masterpiece in the liberal arts. Its author must be a master of the liberal arts of his time, and his work must exemplify the direction of those arts of thought and imagination to their proper ends, the understanding and exposition of the truth as he sees it.

The second criterion follows from the first. A classical book must be a work of fine art. It must have that clarity and beauty on its surface which provides an immediate intelligibility and leads the mind of the reader to its interior depths of illumination and understanding. This is of first importance in teaching, and its principle is almost universally violated in the textbooks that have developed in the ordinary elective system. A great many of the great books were written for the ordinary intelligent public, and they therefore have the seductive charm of works in the fine arts. They are intrinsically interesting and their disciplines are accepted with pleasure.

The third criterion concerns the internal structure of a classic. A great book has many possible interpretations. This does not mean that it is simply ambiguous, and thus leads to confusion. On the contrary it is possible to discover in a great work such as Dante's *Divine Comedy* or Newton's *Principia* several distinct, complete, and independent meanings, each allowing the others to stand by its side and each supporting and complementing the others. It is the business of a liberal artist to construct such works and also to analyze and understand them.

The fourth criterion demands that a great book shall raise the persistent and humanly unanswerable questions about the great themes in human experience. On the one hand this means that a great book shall be honest about the limits of its powers of exposition, admitting the uncertainties and paradoxes that surround the practice of the liberal arts. On the other hand it means that a liberal artist should not allow a false modesty or scepticism to excuse him from pushing reason and imagination to ultimate questions. The entertainment and exploration of ultimate questions concerning number and measurement, form and matter, causality, tragedy, and God, extend, moderate, and balance the use of our intellectual capacities.

As a design for the total curriculum the great books or masterpieces are inadequate because they do not provide the outcomes listed for the other areas of study. They do not assure symbolic skills, an attainment of the key concepts needed to systematize knowledge, a

[5] *Catalogue* of St. John's College, Vol. IV, No. 1, 1952.

320 THE GOOD LIFE AND THE SCHOOL

familiarity with developmental knowledge, nor skill in structuring social problems.

Yet for exhibiting overarching syntheses that unify men's knowledge and aspirations, they have no equal. For these are creative constructions in logical or imaginative form of what life *really is* or what it looks and sounds like to the artist and the philosopher.

The last mode of organizing knowledge is around the personal predicaments of individual students, and the guidance program to be discussed below does organize knowledge in this way.

The Curriculum

A look at Table 1 together with the foregoing discussion reveals six areas of knowledge each organized in its own way. But the six different ways of arranging the materials correspond to the different functions of knowledge and each function of knowledge corresponds to a school outcome for the pupil in general education. Each area is indispensable to general education and therefore some place has to be found for it between the first grade and the end of secondary school. Some areas of learning are better adapted to the earlier grades, e.g., areas 1, 3, and 4. Others must wait for greater maturity, e.g., areas 3 and 5 and more complex forms of 4.

The placing of these materials at various grade levels is a problem for school organization and methodology. Furthermore, the objection that Table 1 lists far more than our present schools can possibly teach is likewise beside the point. It is for the administrator to devise ways and means. For our purpose the primary question is whether this is even an adequate minimum and whether the suggested styles of organization will do justice to the learning outcomes proper to general education.

To this end arguments will be presented for each area of knowledge and for using the modes of organization indicated in the table. As to symbolic skills, the reader is referred to the previous chapter.

Science

The sciences listed constitute a *minimum* sample of the ways in which the basic facts and relations about nature, society, and selves are systematized. And within each science the content, it is to be hoped, can be reduced to the key concepts strategic for its understanding. In chemistry, physics, and mathematics, for example, a beginning has been made to find these big strategic ideas, and school materials based on them are already being tried out and used. In economics an attempt has been made to identify key issues.[6]

Ordinary observation leads to the suspicion that, in the elementary school, women teachers are not enamoured of science. In our culture few inferiority complexes are produced in females by lack of competence in science and mathematics, despite Sputnik and its aftermath. This is probably due to cultural conditioning, and the reconditioning by teacher training institutions is far from complete. The science curriculum in teachers colleges is likely to be a combination of work in conventional science subjects plus courses in the materials and methods of teaching science at various grade levels. The elementary teacher needs, surely, a knowledge of method, but she cannot hope to learn in detail all of the sciences that she and her pupils will touch upon. Studying one or two sciences as commonly taught on the college level will not do the trick. What she does need is the kind of science that is part of general education, that which covers the major fields but which is restricted to the key concepts, laws, and modes of investigation characteristic of each science. As we shall have occasion to remark later, general science education should be completed before entrance into the teachers college so that the college can give full attention to the professional problems of science teaching.

On the secondary level we are more likely to find science teachers who have had intensive training in one of the special sciences. They have the confidence born of mastery, but they are reluctant to leave out the rich details of their discipline. They are likely to be ill at ease in any discipline but their own. As teachers of prospective college students, they do well enough because the college work will be carried on in the same format. But for general education such instruction with such emphasis is precisely what will not function "generally."

One of the psychological hurdles that secondary and college teachers of science face is the notion that respectable scholarship and defensible scholastic standards are synonymous with and measured by the amount of specific information within their field that the student can recall at examination periods. This conviction has much to

---

[6] For typical writings on this topic see Suggested Readings at the end of this chapter.

be said for it. Science is not science if it is not precise, systematic, and complete, and not the least important ingredient in the scientific temper is a horror of the sloppy, the scattered, and the unorganized. Scientists are understandably nauseated by the glib allegiance to scientific method of educators who have never undergone the rigors of actual scientific investigation.

Nevertheless, science teachers should recognize two educational facts of life. One is that unless the pupil makes a specific branch of science his life's work, the details of that science will not long be remembered. I have discussed this problem in connection with history information elsewhere,[7] but it is equally relevant here. What we do not use will be forgotten unless it is heavily "overlearned." The consoling correlative of this fact is that principles stay with us longer than the details they explain.[8] We can, for example, remember and use the principle of atomic weights long after we have forgotten the specific atomic weights of all the elements, save perhaps hydrogen. The principle of valence can function long after we have forgotten how to balance the equations for many specific chemical reactions. The general relation among the temperature, volume, and pressure of a gas remains with us long after the details of the specific problems on which we practiced the formula are gone from recallable memory.

The second educational fact of life is that in general education it is impossible to achieve the completeness so desirable for the specialist.

Now we may ask: Are the objectives of the teaching of science for generality incompatible with thoroughness, completeness, and system? If only the key concepts, facts, and principles of a science are to be mastered, there obviously has to be a sacrifice of completeness, but, properly taught, there need be little sacrifice of thoroughness and system. For the key concepts and laws should be mastered to the point where the student can *use* them to explain to himself and to others the basic phenomena of that science. If anything, it is a greater tribute to sound scholarship to select and to teach scientific concepts and laws in this fashion than to retail parcels of details as arranged in the standard textbooks. Given a

[7] "History Without Hysteria," *School and Society*, 58:1494, August 14, 1943, pp. 106–107.

[8] Cf. Katona, *Organizing and Memorizing: Studies in the Psychology of Learning and Teaching*.

thorough mastery of the key features of a science, it should not be too difficult in college to go forward to the degree of completeness required for advanced and specialized study. It is important to indicate what is involved in the mastery of a scientific discipline because it is difficult to convince some people that "mastery" and memorization of facts are not one and the same thing.[9]

Every science, and indeed every logically organized subject matter, contains the following elements:

1. A set of entities or units that are described or defined. In chemistry, for example, there are atoms, molecules, elements, compounds. In history there are events. In biology, cells, tissues, organs. In geography there are mountains, lakes, rivers, zones. These entities are sometimes called "constructs" because they are logically constructed by the scientist.

2. These entities are related to each other in some fashion. In history events are related by cause and effect or in chronological series. In geography the relations are spatial and causal. In mathematics the relations between the units or structures of units are deductive. In chemistry the units combine, break up, and recombine according to certain laws.

3. There are facts or data. That is to say, there are statements that are taken as proved or proved sufficiently to spare them any further questioning. The atomic weights of the elements, for example, are taken as facts, although conceivably they could be ascertained in the future with even greater precision. So it is with certain "facts" in geography and history.

4. There are hypotheses that purport to account for certain facts, e.g., the migration of birds at various seasons, the origin of galaxies, the causes of some diseases, and the nature of light energy, which have not yet been accepted as being beyond controversy.

5. There are well-established hypotheses that are accepted by the leaders of the discipline as being warranted on evidence already adduced for them.

6. Each discipline has its own method of investigation.

To master a science is to master all of these elements and to master them in such a way that the total structure of the science becomes clear. For general education, such an understanding of the structure

[9] Cf. Frank C. Wegener, "The Logic of Subject Matter," *School and Society,* 77: 2004, May 16, 1953, pp. 305–308.

and key concepts of a few of the most basic sciences is about all that can reasonably be expected.

The social studies

The social environment is constituted by the expectations of other people and the necessity of living with them in some kind of social organization. We do not choose this aspect of existence; we are, some Existentialists insist, thrown into it.[10] Much has been made of the Aristotelian dictum that man is a social animal by nature. Hobbes argued that he is social by necessity, and Rousseau that he is socialized by fraud. Whatever may be the ultimate truth, the educational task is the same: the perfecting of the individual within a social milieu which entails a reliable tendency to use knowledge in social thinking and action.

We have spoken of the natural order in society. Chapter 4 indicated that each social institution—the government, the family, the church, and the school—had a certain primary function as its reason for being. To discover the primary function of each institution and to discern its relations to other institutions constitute political science. To trace the temporal development of these social institutions is the backbone of history. To undertake an evaluation of how well or ill these institutions have done the jobs for which they were designed involves the philosophy of the various social sciences.

The term "social" is drawn lovingly to the bosom of all modern educators. In the reaction against the *laissez-faire* economic individualism that was supposed to have been rampant on the American scene a century ago, there arose in the thirties an acute conscientiousness about the individual's responsibility to his fellows and even more about the group's responsibility for its least successful and least fortunate members.

> Parodying Marx, the radical intellectual of the thirties used to say, "Intellectuals of the world, unite, you have nothing to lose but your brains"—and probably this was the closest conjunction he ever made between *his* ideality and his reality. For this was in the depression, when many intellectuals were just as badly off as the proletariat. Brains weren't buying much. But even in this crisis, the intellectual never dared speak in his own name. The proletarian spoke in *his* own name, but the intellectual spoke in the name only

[10] E.g., Martin Heidegger, *Sein und Zeit.*

of someone wtih whom he might temporarily confuse himself but who was not, could never be, and never would have wished to be— a proletarian.[11]

The Great Depression of the thirties demonstrated that Horatio Alger was naive in his belief that hard work, honesty, industriousness, and thrift would guarantee success. The depression brought the realization that man's economic destiny was largely in the hands of corporations, cartels, price controllers, and manipulators of money and stock over which the individual worker had no control.

With the depression came also an exaggeration of the strains among the various racial and religious groups within the mixed population of the United States.

Finally, with World War II arrived the problem of survival in an atomic world when nations showed no particular disposition to abandon ancient ambitions and hatreds.

All of these conditions made educators acutely aware of the social dimension of life, the need to get along with others, and the need to plan an economy of plenty and stability to take the place of an economy of scarcity and cycles. It seemed of first and most urgent importance that pupils at all levels of the school ladder become acutely conscious of their social obligations and opportunities. So much so that some educators have advocated social reconstruction as the goal and guide of the organization and conduct of the school.[12] It is not surprising, therefore, that the curriculum should reflect this heightened social awareness by an increased attention to the social studies.

But we are faced here with the impossible task of studying all the numerous disciplines that can be included properly under the social studies. Aside from sociology and something like social psychology that could be included with the sciences discussed in the previous section, it is difficult to make any selection that is big enough to be useful yet small enough to be manageable. Furthermore, these fields are not yet developed to the point where clearcut subjects of study can be defined, not to speak of the welter of conflicting theories that excite the scholar but only confuse the beginner.

[11] Diana Trilling, "A Communist and His Ideals," *Partisan Review*, 18:4 July–August 1951, p. 436.
[12] E.g., Brameld, *Patterns of Educational Philosophy*, Part III.

A solution to this difficulty is suggested by dividing the field of the social studies between the developmental studies of area 3 and the studies that purport to cope with the problems of the present and the future in area 4 of Table 1.

The evolutionary study of the past makes systematic and orderly the conglomerate of history and survey of civilization courses that are now vying for place in the curriculum. By dividing developmental knowledge into that of the world at large, including man; of human societies, and of mankind and its culture, we would have three courses or fields within which the key material in the social studies could be organized. By spreading the materials over the entire range of the 12 grades with appropriate adaptations for learning readiness, a respectable proportion of history and the content of the social sciences would be covered. Because the goal of this segment of the curriculum is perspective and the building of an apperceptive mass, it is not to be taught as a set of separate subjects. Further exploration of this field would take place in the problems course.

Problems course

Although a problems course can clarify the nature and importance of the various fields of knowledge, its chief objective is not knowledge as such. It is rather to perfect the skills and habits of using knowledge *instrumentally*, as means to achieving goals.

Why, it may be asked, do these skills have to be developed directly? Will they not be formed as by-products of studying the symbolic skills or the various other subject matters?

1. Experience points to a disturbing independence between knowledge of the facts, rules, and theories of a subject and success in solving unpracticed problems in that subject. Doing "originals" in geometry or other application problems is the supreme school test. He who passes this test needs no other, but no other test can assure success on this one.

As Woodruff has said:

> . . . in the face of what is known about the relative absence of transfer of training in most school subjects, it is the height of folly to expect students to develop problem-solving skill as an incidental learning unless considerable time and attention is devoted to it, in which case it ceases to be incidental. It is far more likely that something about civic affairs will be learned in a unit on problem-

solving, than that problem-solving will be developed in the typical иниil ииi сivlс аffairs.[10]

2. Problem solving brings into play attitudes,[14] skills, knowledge, and creativity. It employs symbols, concepts, images, facts, and generalizations. Accordingly, problem-solving can go wrong for many reasons, whereas to go right calls for a happy congress of circumstances.

3. Problem-solving skill developed within physics or chemistry may not transfer to problems in taxation and the preservation of peace. An engineer, expert in solving problems in his field, when confronted by a taxation issue may automatically adopt the problem-solving posture and get ready to seek and weigh evidence. But where is he to seek evidence? What is relevant? How does one judge its worth? In his own field he can take these questions in stride; that is why he is an expert. In taxation they become problems because he is a novice.

4. Nevertheless, because we can become more and more efficient in solving problems in a given domain of questions, e.g., physics, mathematics, or taxation, one can hope to improve social problem-solving behavior by instruction.

5. Molar problem-solving or the study of complex social issues affords practice in making judgments of what content is relevant in various classes of problems, and in locating the sources of this content in the appropriate departments of organized knowledge. It therefore presupposes that the student is familiar with the map of knowledge and the methods of using it.

Elsewhere the outline of a problems course has been set down in some detail.[15] Here the principle at stake is whether or not such a course can produce measurable, or at least observable, changes to warrant our inferring that our pupils have improved their efficiency. Only further studies and experimentation can give definitive answers, but on the evidence thus far it would seem that a problems course has a fair chance of achieving the results claimed for it and that these results will not accrue without it.

[13] Asahel D. Woodruff, *The Psychology of Learning*. 3rd edition, New York: Longmans, Green & Co., 1951, p. 301. Quoted with permission of the publisher.
[14] Dewey has called them directness, open-mindedness, single-mindedness, and responsibility. *Democracy and Education*, Chap. 13.
[15] *Report of the Committee to Study General Education in Massachusetts State Teachers Colleges*, directed by John F. Bowler. Boston: Commonwealth of Mass. 1959, pp. 122–127.

The classics

Integrative and aesthetic studies, it is suggested in Table 1 should be organized as exemplars. Reasons for this have already been indicated in earlier portions of this chapter. But it may be noted again that value learning is not the same as learning to do something or to know something.[16] It involves among other things being *impressed* by an idea or an image to the point of captivation, or at least to active approval.

But about the only way one can achieve sensitivity to impression is to be exposed to captivating works of the imagination, whether in the forms of great philosophic syntheses or works of art, classic or contemporary. This is not the history of art (which ought to have been encountered in the developmental sciences), nor is it a way of systematizing special domains of fact (the physical, biological, and social sciences), nor is it a way of coping with problems (area 4). The purpose is to inspire, integrate, and sustain values, and for this purpose the exemplar, chosen with an eye to variations in maturity, seems to be the logical answer.

Systematic courses in philosophy, religion, and the appreciation of all the fine arts are out of the question for general education, but samples of great works in each area are not. We already use this approach in literature, but it could be extended to form a classics course in the other integrative and inspirational fields as well. While this is not an argument for the 100 best books, paintings, musical compositions, and dramas, it is a proposal to make every one acquainted with a relatively small number of such works during his elementary and secondary school life.

The selection need not remain fixed nor restricted to the past. Contemporary exemplars may be more instructive than ancient ones. The important point is that whatever is chosen be chosen deliberately as significant in content, aesthetically compelling in form, and both if possible.

Guidance

How do personal individual problems differ from social ones? Why cannot practice in one be relied upon to transfer to the other? Because commitment to a particular outcome is an essential feature of

---

[16] Scheffler, *The Language of Education*, pp. 79–82.

individual problems, but not of group problems. One can sensibly say, "I am studying the tax problem, but I am not really concerned about it." But it would not make sense to say, "I have a problem in paying my taxes, but I am not really concerned about it."

What really differentiates the two types of problem is that intelligent coping with personal predicaments requires knowledge about one's own personality and resources, and this is difficult to secure and assess—especially in youth.

That men in all walks of life, of all degrees of learning and wisdom, from time to time find themselves estranged from themselves, unsure of their powers and their motives indicates that self knowledge is no easy accomplishment. Can it be taught?

In a sense, "Yes." Insofar as it involves skills and attitudes common to all thinking, there is no reason for not being able to teach it. But in a sense the answer is also, "No," because the relevant content, the crucial data are items in a particular individual life history. They are not, as in school subjects, laid out in textbooks. How to get at these private data and how to interpret and weigh them is an art that the guidance counselor can help the pupil to acquire.

Perhaps this can be done in a group or individually or both, but in either context it is an individual, not a group predicament that is in question, and the goal is not merely knowledge, but knowledgeable commitment.

Guidance is to be distinguished from therapy. The guidance program is not a psychiatric clinic where deep-seated maladjustments are analyzed and treated. It is rather where the healthy soul is kept healthy.[17]

Some objections

It will be objected that no specific provision is made in the curriculum for physical education, safety education, and character education, and that no mention is made of clubs, athletics, orchestras, and bands, which are to be found in the curricula or outside the curricula of the modern high school and to some extent of the elementary school as well.

Our answer is that insofar as health, safety, and character are affected by knowledge and the habits of acquiring, using, and en-

[17] Cf. Jaeger, *Paideia: The Ideals of Greek Culture.*

joying it are concerned, they are in the curriculum. So far as they depend on emotional conditioning and daily practice, they are not, for reasons already expounded in the previous chapters.

On the other hand, athletics, games, gymnastics, and band performances for the public are deliberately excluded from the formal curriculum. These activities may well be carried on *at* the school as part of the life of pupils who congregate there, but they are part of informal education and should be conducted informally. The attempt to formalize such activities and the counter attempt to informalize the study of the organized subject matters both lead to confusion.

Foreign language study presents a special problem for general education. It could be included under the symbolic skills, provided it is judged essential to all members of the social order. At present no one foreign language or any two of them are universally essential. But perhaps we can look forward to some sort of international and indeed interplanetary system of communication that will be essential to general education.

Special education

"Special" education is what all members of the community are not expected to have in common. Vocational education, professional education, and education for beyond average competence in any discipline are all varieties of special education.

This kind of specialization has been enthusiastically cultivated in the United States. College catalogues bulge more and more each year as courses multiply by pedagogical mitosis. There is hardly an occupation for which someone has not established a training institution.

There is nothing wrong with such highly specific education, provided it is not regarded as a substitute for general education, and provided it does not become the tail that wags the dog of general education.

The main argument for early specialization is the extraordinary diversity of occupations requiring highly specific training, but in evaluating this argument it ought not to be forgotten that:

1. Many gainful occupations require relatively little specialized training *in school*. Many industrialists would prefer to teach the specific details of their own machinery on the job. Also, the further the splitting up of operations is carried, the less training is needed by

the performer of each bit of the total operation. It takes less training presumably to tighten two nuts than one nut and one screw.

2. On the other hand, with the advent of automation and technological advances there is ground for expecting that a greater proportion of the labor force will be at the technician level, e.g., electronics technician, medical technician, etc. While this argues for more specialized training for more people, the prerequisites for such training are so near to those required for professional training that the secondary school program need not be sharply differentiated for them. In other words, the prospective electronics technician and the prospective electronics engineer will both need essentially the same high school courses in order to carry on post-secondary schooling.[18]

3. Repeatedly, when employers are asked what sort of vocational preparation they would like for the beginners in the field, they tend to wander off into the areas of attitudes (promptness, neatness, responsibility) and of general competence in the basic symbolic skills rather than insisting on competence in the specific techniques. Of course they want stenographic candidates to know how to take dictation and how to type, but deficiencies in these areas seem to bother them less than carelessness and poor attitudes toward the job.

4. General education conceived as the habits of acquiring, using, and enjoying truth—if really formed—constitutes a surprising proportion of what is prescribed for specialized training even on the upper levels of the professional schools.

5. Our industrialized society, paradoxically perhaps, is headed for less time spent on the job rather than more. The more we go in for mass production, the less do the activities on the job satisfy all of the basic needs of men. Education for the job is not education for the leisure that the workingman is gradually achieving, nor is it relevant to his roles as a husband, a father, and a citizen, or more generally —a happy man.

The popularity of early specialization in our country is symptomatic of the central position the economic role of the individual has assumed in our value scheme. Americans may be vocally opposed to Marxism, but their educational habits afford an excellent verification of economic determinism, because, to the extent that we argue that

[18] A possibility mentioned in a personal communication by M. Ray Karnes, erstwhile head of the Division of Industrial Education and now professor of Higher Education at the University of Illinois.

how a man earns a living determines the rest of his experience, to that extent are we subscribing to this Marxian thesis.

But is this a fact? It is a fact whenever the struggle for material subsistence is so severe that man has little time for anything else. When the material means of life are in constant jeopardy, there is no time for other values. The appeal to the starving man to find consolation in resignation is mean-spirited, if sincere, and downright dishonest, if it is not.

The hope of the world, however, is to have America demonstrate that we can so efficiently solve the problems of production and distribution that man need not be economically determined any more than he is determined by anxieties over water and oxygen. The measure of man's progress is economic indifference rather than economic absorption, although it takes all kinds of struggle to make such indifference possible.

Summary

The problem of curriculum content is that of selection from a store of knowledge far too great to be included in the most ambitious program of general education.

The design adopted in this chapter is based on the functions of knowledge in society and in producing certain school and life outcomes. In order to sample the major domains of knowledge, on one hand, and to develop the habits of acquiring, using, and enjoying knowledge, on the other hand, the materials are organized in different ways: as skills, subjects, developmentally, exemplars, molar societal problems, and individual problems.

Spread through the whole period of elementary and secondary schooling, this content studied in these ways should meet the requirements of general education for all pupils. Special education, it is argued, is indispensable in our society, but given the proper general education, it need not be begun so early or emphasized so much in secondary schooling as has been thought necessary.

PROBLEMS FOR DISCUSSION AND RESEARCH

1. Try to verify the analysis given of an organized subject matter by applying it to one of your textbooks. What are the *key* concepts, facts, hypotheses and theories that are indispensable to it?

2. Have a group study a problem such as TVA or socialized medicine to see how it ramifies into various areas of knowledge. How far can you investigate it without getting lost? At what point do you need the teacher? More subject matter?

3. Examine the observations made on specialized and adult education. Are there any facts which these seem to contradict? Ask a few employers what they want as preparation for their employees.

4. On the proposed curriculum design, what subjects now studied in high school would be omitted?

5. Would you agree or disagree that the proposed curriculum would be regarded as adequate preparation for college? Formulate your arguments for the position you choose to defend.

Suggestions for Further Reading

For fuller bibliographical data on the items listed below, consult the General Bibliography.

Perhaps the most economical way of supplementing Chapters 12 and 13 would be to read:

Brubacher, *Eclectic Philosophy of Education*, Topic 26.

Caswell and Campbell, *Readings in Curriculum Development*, especially Chaps. 3, 7, and 10 on the criticism and defense of the subject matter curriculum.

Smith, *et al.*, *Fundamentals of Curriculum Development*, revised edition, especially Part III which gives an excellent analysis of various curriculum patterns.

For the elementary school:

Beck, *et al.*, *Curriculum in the Elementary School*.

Burton, *The Guidance of Learning Activities*.

Collings, *An Experiment with a Project Curriculum*.

Mayhew, *et al.*, *The Dewey School: The Laboratory School of the University of Chicago*. (An account of an historic venture in American education.)

Morrison, *The Curriculum of the Common School*. (Based on the functions of social institutions.)

Stendler, *Teaching in the Elementary School*.

For the secondary school:

Aikin, *The Story of the Eight Year Study*. (A Progressive experiment on the secondary level.)

Alberty, *Reorganizing the High School Curriculum*. (Typical of attempts to overcome certain difficulties of the traditional curriculum.)

General Education in a Free Society. (The Harvard Report.) *General Education in School and College.* (A reappraisal of the traditional high school and college curriculum by a group of faculty members from prominent preparatory schools and colleges.)

Hand, *Principles of American Public Secondary Education.*

On special aspects of the secondary school studies:

Beberman and Vaughan, *High School Mathematics,* and also the work of the School Mathematics Study Group under the leadership of Edward G. Begle at Yale University.

Conant, *On Understanding Science.*

Council for Advancement of Secondary Education, *Key Understandings in Economics.*

Easley, J. A., "Is Teaching of Scientific Method a Significant Educational Objective?" Scheffler, *Philosophy and Education,* pp. 154–179.

Hunt and Metcalf, *Teaching High School Social Studies.*

Little, E. P.; F. L. Friedman; J. R. Zacharias; and G. Finlay, "The Physical Science Study: Building a New Structure," *Science Teacher,* 24: 7, 1957.

National Council of Teachers of Mathematics, *24th Yearbook,* "Growth of Mathematical Ideas, Grades Kindergarten–12." (Tries to develop six major mathematical ideas.)

Reiner, W. B., "Review of Recent Research in Teaching of Science at the Secondary Level," *Science Education,* 40:341–350, 1956.

Raup, *et al., The Improvement of Practical Intelligence,* pp. 102 ff. (On the deliberative skills.)

Simpson, Ray H., *Improving Teaching Learning Procedures,* Chap. 6.

Strong, L. E. and M. K. Wilson, "Chemical Bonds: A Central Theme for High School Chemistry," *Journal of Chem. Education,* 33:56–58, 1958.

On the organization of knowledge:

Martin, *The Order and Integration of Knowledge.*

Tykociner, *The Science of Research—Zetetics.* (This chapter has been heavily influenced by this volume for the classification of the various types of knowledge.)

CHAPTER | # 14

Methodology

No argument in education starts more quickly and continues longer than the one about method. It engages the emotions of schoolmen and laymen alike. One camp is firm in the belief that "know-how" in teachers is a poor substitute for knowledge of subject matter or enthusiasm; the other camp is equally sure that the untrained teacher is successful only in the anecdotes of aging school administrators.

The Rationale of Method

Method connotes order as opposed to the haphazard, as when we say there is method in his madness. Order, however, need not be consciously contrived. An interesting case can be made for a method that issues from blind automatic tendencies on the part of school teachers to express their concern about the right responses in reading, writing, and arithmetic, just as the home without much planning creates an effective instructional method by expressing forcefully the parental concern about such matters as eating and dressing.[1]

Rational method

To justify a method, however, one has to show that a procedure is *designed* to achieve goals efficiently. It is generally admitted that when we understand *why* we proceed as we do, the results will be under better control and amenable to greater improvement than when we are ignorant of the reasons for the steps we take. An automobile mechanic, for example, can adjust a carburetor without knowing the principles of carburetors. So long as the results are ade-

Table 2

TEACHING-LEARNING MODEL

Inputs ⟶ *Intervening Processes* ⟶ *Outputs*

Inputs	Intervening Processes	Outputs
Instructional acts (task types) Noninstructional school influences Non-school influences	called variously: —intervening variables —mediators —methods of processing data —ways of seeing, classifying, and feeling —types of mental operation The above are either: a. conscious (phenomenological) b. nonconscious	Tests to measure the effects of instructional inputs on instructionally-intended outcomes Changes in nonschool behaviors, e.g., —reorganization of cognitive structures (habits of knowing and inquiry) —reorganization of action patterns —reorganization of feeling patterns (personality structures) Life styles, values schema, or behavior syndromes

quate, the method is adequate. Let the results go awry, and the mechanic is helpless until someone who understands the reasons for the method modifies it to meet the new set of circumstances. What the Greeks called *techné*, an art based on knowledge, is the rationalization of method by science.[2]

[1] J. M. Stephens, "Spontaneous Schooling: A Neglected Feature in Theories of Education," *School and Society*, 73: 1902, June 2, 1951, pp. 337–341.
[2] For a detailed discussion of *techné*, cf. John Wild, "Plato's Theory of Techné," *Philosophy and Phenomenological Research*, 1:3, March 1941, pp. 255–293.

Educational psychology as rationale of method

Whether there can be a rational methodology for teaching depends on the existence of a body of science that furnishes a guiding theory for practice. Otherwise method means little more than tricks of the trade. Presumably educational psychology should furnish the science to rationalize the teaching process because it studies the conditions under which learning takes place, and teaching is one such condition. This, then, is the master *science* of educational method. To it we look for a clue to methods and for a criterion of their validity.

Table 2 is a rough diagram of the teaching-learning process. To the extent that psychology can tell us how inputs are related to the intervening processes and outputs, teaching can be a scientific technology. That progress is being made toward this happy day is undeniable. Articles, monographs, and books on the psychology of learning are enjoying a mushroom-like growth.

The difficulty is that the research is at that unavoidable stage when it keeps finding new factors and making new distinctions. Instead of one power called intelligence, there are now about 50 different intelligences. There is a greater variety of inputs, intervening processes, and outputs to account for than ever before. But the greater the variety of data to be explained, the harder it is to come up with a theory that unifies and fits them all together. We have many theories and it is safe to expect them to become more precise and predictive with every decade.[3]

For this reason a curriculum for teacher training without educational psychology is unthinkable, and yet we cannot expect from it the kind of reliable and straightforward direction that the farmer is getting from biology and chemistry or the engineer from physics. For one thing, there is no way of adequately controlling the input. The influence of attractive and repulsive classmates, the personality of the teacher, and the peculiar pictures on the classroom wall inevitably "contaminate" the effect of the lesson.

Moreover, if no two pupils are at any moment receiving precisely the same input, and if a class may have up to 40 pupils for 45 minutes, what are the chances that any two or three pupils will produce the same output—even if we could assume, as we cannot, that the

[3] For a recent analysis of these theories, see Mowrer, *Learning Theory and Behavior*.

intervening processes are the same and will operate in the same way for these pupils?

Consider also that at every waking moment and in not a few of the sleeping ones, data are being fed into the organism; that every feed-in may change the intervening processes, and that any output may feed back to become another input. Compared to this, the most complex "thinking machines" are like an abacus compared to a Univac.

Finally, even if we could overcome the befuddling complexity of it all; even if we could use a Univac to discover what input will produce a given output (and perhaps we shall one day be able to do so), there is still the task of choosing among outputs for a class of pupils and ultimately for each pupil as an individual.

A philosophy of education cannot and should not be a synopsis of educational psychology. Yet what a philosophy of education says about the teaching-learning process should not fly in the face of well-established psychological fact and theory. It is from research in educational psychology that philosophy of education gets a sense of the distinctions that have to be made, the concepts that are most fruitful, and the lines of investigation that are most promising.

For example, J. P. Guilford's structure of the intellect distinguishes six different products (units, classes, relations, systems, transformations, and implications), each one having four possible types of content (figural, symbolic, semantic, and behavioral) and dealt with by five possible operations (cognition, memory, divergent thinking, convergent thinking, and evaluation). This makes theoretically 120 different combinations of learning task types.[4]

With adequate tests one could identify and measure the pupil's learning readiness for each of these task types. Any school task could be regarded as a prescription compounded of various proportions of various task types. From the other side, failures to learn could be diagnosed by locating the task type at which the breakdown occurred.

Teaching method calls for an organization and analysis of pupils and materials, on one hand, and a set of strategies, on the other. The first may be the work of specialists in testing and curriculum research. The latter only the teacher can perform, but clearly the more thoroughly the first is carried out, the more intelligent and

[4] "Three Faces of Intellect," *The American Psychologist*, 14:8, 469–479, August 1959.

efficient the second can become. In this chapter we shall be concerned with the latter phase of method.

Method and the theory of knowing

Methods of teaching and learning are also related to a theory of knowing, for clearly one outcome of learning is cognition. Thus for Dewey methods of teaching, methods of learning, and methods of thinking all follow the same design. The analysis of knowledge in Chapter 5 stressed its beginnings in the perceiving of actual individual things and its development through abstraction into concepts (ideas) and propositions that asserted truly or otherwise that concepts were related to each other in a certain way.

So while an Experimentalist or Instrumentalist theory of knowing accents the learner's efforts to predict what will extricate him from some predicament, a Realist account of the matter will stress the attainment of accurate concepts and precise relationships among them. Clearly, the strategy of teaching, just as the organization of the curriculum, will differ depending on what is stressed.

Similarly, the role of mind in learning will differ in the two types of theory mentioned above. For Pragmatism and Experimentalism, mind is intelligent, purposeful action; it is a quality of behavior, not something inside the head. Just being aware of the nature of something, of its properties and relations is not to be dignified by the name of "knowing."[5] We are not arguing, however, that awareness of a pattern of relations carries its own guarantee of truth. But to deny that such awareness is cognitive runs counter to common sense and, what is more important, would make cognition a combination of noncognitive elements.

A Realistic theory of knowing, on the other hand, takes awareness and consciousness as a basic aspect of mind. In awareness the perceived situation is grasped in both its concrete richness of sound, color, shapes, sizes, and smells and as objects in their relations. Mind is the "form of forms." Realism, therefore, tends to think of the mind as a processor of data—sorting, classifying, and connecting them—but the data are not regarded as "made up" by the learner and not all sortings are equally good, so to speak. To persuade the learner to perceive, classify, and relate as does the expert in a given domain of

[5] See, e.g., Lewis, *Knowledge and Evaluation,* pp. 9 ff. and Dewey, *Logic: The Theory of Inquiry,* pp. 143–144.

knowledge is the unabashed objective of Realistic teaching method.

Once these "intervening processes" have been shaped, the student is expected to use this cognitive equipment for solving problems, and part of the curriculum is designed to provide practice in doing so (Chapter 13).

In summary, Realistic methodology can be expected to be interested in perceptual reorganization, concept attainment, abstraction, and insight as basic to the learning process. Other theories of knowledge can be expected to stress other aspects.

The Teaching-Learning Process

We shall distinguish in the teaching-learning process the following phases: I. Motivation, II. Presentation, III. Trial Response, IV. Insight or achievement of the model response, V. Incorporation into habit or mastery, and VI. Testing.

I. Motivation. It is a truism that the more the learner apprehends a situation as relevant to his concerns, the greater his attention, effort, and learning. An important part of method, therefore, is to know what the concerns (interests) of pupils really are. Educational psychology has helped us map these interests for various age levels.[6] Yet interests are symptoms of deeper and more pervasive urges to self-determination, self-realization, and self-integration. Insofar as knowledge is apprehended as relevant to these motives, the pupil will not be indifferent to it. But so poorly are these three drives defined in the young child that it is difficult for him to comprehend the relevance to them of much that he is asked to learn in school. Self-determination, self-realization, and self-integration manifest themselves differently at the ages of 5, 10, and 15 years. The key to the pupil's interest is, therefore, how he translates the meaning of success. The energies of the learner, one can be sure, will be channeled accordingly, and much of it does not require school learning.

Nevertheless, the desire to know, to understand, and to perceive clearly are no less natural and ubiquitous than to be strong, agile,

---

[6] For example, Lehman and Witty, *The Psychology of Play Activities.* Dale B. Harris found that adolescents ranked manners and courtesy 4th in 1935 and 10th in 1957, getting along with other people 7th in 1935, but 3rd in 1957, sex adjustment 13th in 1935 and 7th in 1957. The daily schedule and civic responsibilities, however, continued to occupy 15th and 14th (the last two) places respectively. "Life Problems and Interests of Adolescents in 1935 and 1957," *School Review,* 23, Autumn, 1959, pp. 33–50.

and popular. Indeed, the intellectual curiosity of young children is as well known for its strength as for its lack of discrimination. That children prior to adolescence are revolted by aggregates of unrelated "facts" such as the population of Tanganyika, the number of telegraph poles to the mile, and the size of steamships is contrary to the experience of every parent who has listened to an interminable series of "Do you know what?" and the answers to them.

Motivation is often distinguished as being intrinsic or extrinsic. A task is intrinsically motivated when it is done for the sake of performing the task; extrinsically when the reward for performing the task lies beyond the task itself. Now there is a sense in which intrinsic motivation cannot be contrived or engineered. For if a pupil is already interested in a task, no extrinsic motivation is needed; if he is not interested, resort must be had to some goal other than the task itself, in which case the motivation is extrinsic. For this reason, activity programs have no problems of motivation, for either the child is already involved in the learning task or the task is changed to one in which he is involved. An interesting point is raised if it is asked whether an activity program really does rely on intrinsic motivation. When, for example, children absorbed in play *learn about* the dances of Indian children, are they interested primarily in playing or the Indians?

With a more conventional program, however, the pupil who is not interested in learning at a level on which he cannot operate successfully may become interested if the level of the task is brought within his capabilities. For example, a pupil who loses interest in a chemistry problem he cannot solve may become interested in one he can. The motivation thus remains intrinsic. If, however, this gambit does not succeed, the subject matter teacher cannot abandon or change the task. He has to resort to extrinsic motivation, either in the form of a more remote goal, e.g., the learner is expected to stick with the chemistry problem because he wants to become an engineer some day, or in the form of loyalty to a moral principle, such as "One ought to persevere in worthwhile tasks even when one gets no pleasure from doing so" or "One ought to carry out one's commitments to the teacher, school, etc." There is also the cruder motive of avoiding punishment.

This moral appeal is out of place if the teacher has the duty of making the task interesting or the pupil interested. The appeal to self-discipline is also out of place under these circumstances because this kind of control is called upon only when one's commitment to a task breaks down. To be loyal to the demands of a task despite boredom and distraction is really loyalty to a concept of self rather than to the task. It is hard to see on what grounds the pupil should be expected to develop such self-discipline or how one is to develop it if it is insisted that all learning activities be intrinsically motivated.

II. Presentation. The strategy of motivation decided upon, the teacher presents the learning task. Pupils are directed or invited to discuss, read, recite, perform an experiment, watch a demonstration, or solve a problem. The teacher may talk, demonstrate, ask questions, give orders, invite questions, etc. At the close of this chapter a number of historically famous teaching styles each with its characteristic form of presenting the lesson are described.

As might be expected, the manner of presentation depends on the sort of outcome expected, and where different types of outcomes are stressed, as in Chapter 13, the teacher is expected to be skillful in instituting problem-solving, concept attainment, improving a skill, and appreciation.

Presentations are more or less abstract. The more verbal, the more technical; the more theoretical they are, the greater their demand on the abstractive potential of the pupil. Visual aids, examples, diagrams, and demonstrations concretize presentation. Invoking the familiar is another way of lowering the cognitive stress or the abstractive demand on the learner. Herbart's steps of instruction stressed the importance of weaving in the new task with the firmly structured idea clusters of the pupil's experience.

Whatever the devices or procedures, the primary objective of the presentation is to make the pupil *ready* to carry out the instructions. That is why every act of presentation is completed by ascertaining whether the learner is clear as to *what* he is being asked to do, and what a satisfactory response would be like. Of course, if a pupil is *completely* clear in these matters, the learning is over. However, this is rarely the case, so the teacher continues with the presentation until there is reason to believe the pupil has understood the requirements of the task.

It is at this point that analysis of task-types helps the teacher to adjust the mode of presentation both to the type of task and to the learning-readiness of the pupil—or, if possible, of the class as a whole.

III. Trial response. Another ingredient in the learning process is a trial of some kind. It can be a motor act, such as writing or riding a bicycle; it can be a verbal one, like reciting; it can be memorizing something, recalling something, rearranging symbols in the form of inference, or building something—the list is practically endless. The important matter is that the learner has to make some kind of trial symbolically, with his muscles, or both.

We should not construe this activity too narrowly. We cannot learn to ride a bicycle without trying to ride it, but neither can we learn to read without reading, or to think without thinking. Even in just noting something the mind is active—reaching out to its object.

Unfortunately some educators have restricted "doing" to the use of the large muscles. Much of what is sound in the activity program is now in danger because, rightly or wrongly, the public is under the impression that in such programs there is no place for the cultivation of the mind. In their fear of merely verbal learning some schools have turned their classrooms into workshops or little communities where children learn to live together. But if these schools are true to Dewey, they will remember that behavior becomes intelligent as we *note the connections* between what we try and undergo. In other words, symbolic trials are the crux of the matter even on an Experimentalist philosophy.

As far as method is concerned, the trial phase cannot be regarded as automatic. The pupil may hesitate to make the trial for any one of a thousand reasons, or he may not make enough trials, or he may make the wrong trials, or in the wrong way. It is at this stage that the teacher is almost indispensable to the pupil.[7]

The trial response may be no more than an imitation of the instructor's presentation or the uttering of words found in a textbook, or it may be an attempt to use what has been presented in an unpracticed situation, or with very few clues, it may be an attempt to solve a problem of some sort.

The teacher at this point, if necessary, corrects the trial performance or he confirms its correctness. Trials and needed corrections ensue until the pupil has within himself a model of the correct response. He not only knows that it is right, but he has the *feeling* of rightness as well, or what may be called insight.[8]

[7] For some experimental light on the effectiveness of such guidance, cf. Craig, *The Transfer Value of Guided Learning*, p. 65 and *passim*.

[8] It may be that psychologically the value of the trial lies in the stimuli that the learner creates when he makes the response. These stimuli can pre-

IV. Insight—the model response. The next step in learning is a judgment by the learner as to whether the response has been adequate. Sometimes this is obvious, as when a failure to learn the swimming stroke results in being ducked under the water, or failure to get the food tells the rat to keep on running the maze. If hunger persists, one has apparently not succeeded in satisfying it; if the teacher does not smile or approve, something has gone awry; if Mother scolds or slaps, the response was not right. But in any event, nothing goes forward unless some evaluation of the trial is made.

This is a really crucial step in learning. When the learner can evaluate the trial in terms of the task, we have one kind of situation, e.g., when a boy examines his answer to a problem in arithmetic and judges it to be right or wrong, or when falling from the bicycle, he is aware that what he is doing is somehow not right.

When the learner cannot make this judgment, then we have the slow staggering progress characteristic of trial-and-error learning. It takes many trials before chance or the mysterious unconscious workings of reward and punishment give the nervous system the sense to distinguish the right from the wrong response.

In trial-and-error learning, the learner may not *see the connection* between the stimulus and the response that actually brought the success. For example, when Thorndike's cat could not get out of the cage except after a long trial-and-error experience, the gestalt psychologists pointed out that the situation was too complex for the cat to apprehend as a pattern within which the relation between depressing a lever and opening the door of the cage could be experienced. The successful sequence should have stood out as figure against ground instead of merging with many other movements that had no relation to success. We can understand how strong motivation, frequent repetition, and punishment and rewards would prod the cat to isolate the one pattern from the matrix of its irrelevant surroundings, and if the cat were bright, the time needed to isolate this pattern from the others would have been shorter; indeed, is not this what we mean by brightness?

Seeing, feeling, or apprehending a new *pattern* of experience is the moment of learning. The gestaltists call it insight or that sudden

---

sumably become cues to the subsequent responses or attitudes toward the task. See Mowrer, *Behavior and Learning Theory,* Chap. 7. The trial also builds up what E. C. Tolman has called "sign-gestalt expectations." "Theories of Learning" in *Comparative Psychology,* F. A. Moss, ed., pp. 367–408.

awareness of completeness, fitness, or suitability with which we are all familiar and which apparently Köhler's apes also could experience.[9] Critics have held that the sudden insight may not have precluded previous trial and error, and in men certainly trial and error very often precedes the insight. These are interesting psychological details, but for education the important contribution of the gestalt theory is that all conscious learning, at least, is characterized by insight.[10]

Pavlov was able to teach dogs to salivate at the sound of a bell, as they did when food was put into their mouths. When did the learning occur? Clearly when the bell sound was taken by the dog as a sign of impending food—when the sound of the bell was incorporated into the food-saliva pattern.

A boy learns to use a typewriter. When does the learning occur? When the movements of the fingers, images of words, and thoughts about whole sentences become a sequential pattern, or a sequence of unified clusters.

A student is asked to explain: If wishes were horses, beggars would ride. When has the learning occurred? When he apprehends the pattern: beggars have wishes but do not have the means to fulfill them, and without means they are not fulfilled.

From all this we conclude: whether the task is to organize muscle sequences, as in swimming, golfing, and penmanship; or whether it is to connect a new stimulus to an old response; or whether it is to recognize that A is the sign of B; or whether a new pattern of meanings is to be carved out of a welter of meanings organized in other ways—regardless of what is to be learned, *the learning moment* is the one in which the organism achieves the organization.

Possibly this unification takes place in the nervous system without our being aware of it,[11] or it can be a conscious process. If the nervous system of the rat does not select the right pattern, the rat has not learned. If the boy learning to swim does not know what a successful swimming movement feels like, he thrashes about fruitlessly.

It is the business of instruction to help the learner become aware

[9] Köhler, *The Mentality of Apes* and *Gestalt Psychology*.

[10] Cf. Ernest E. Bayles, "The Idea of Learning as Development of Insight," *Educational Theory*, 2:2, 1952, pp. 65–71.

[11] Unless the organism is aware of the unification, it would be odd to call this learning "insight." We shall, therefore, reserve the term "insight" for conscious learnings.

of the pattern that constitutes the right response. Not all tasks are as automatically self-evaluating as swimming. One can give the wrong answer to a problem in arithmetic without immediately suffocating. In the place of immediately felt pains or pleasures resulting from success or failure, the teacher supplies clues; often her pleasure or displeasure or her verbal report is the chief clue.

The same sort of correction is needed for the perfection of details after the main pattern is apprehended. Thus the boy who learns to stay afloat and to move forward a bit in the water has learned the main pattern of swimming, but he is not yet aware of the subpatterns in the learning sequence.

We can now see the proper place of repetition in the learning situation. Traditionally, it was called drill or practice, e.g., repeating the lines of a poem to be learned by heart, repeating the multiplication tables, trying repeatedly to play the right notes on a piano, or trying to hit the right letters on a typewriter. Educational psychology has taught us that repetition *as such* does not improve performance. Properly varied repetition is the opportunity to form patterns when previous attempts have failed.

If the moment of conscious learning is an insight into a new pattern or the attainment of a model response, then is learning an all-or-none affair? If the answer is in the affirmative, what meaning shall we attach to the improvement of learning?

Our answer would seem to be that at any given moment we either do have an insight or we do not. The differences among learnings consist in the patterns apprehended. Some are more extensive than others. For example, I may have the insight that $(a + b)^2$ is an instance to which the binomial theorem applies. Yet I may not have the insight that it applies to $[(x + y) + b]^2$. I may have mastered the pattern of typing words but not phrases.

Similarly, how well we know a subject is measured by the extent of the network of patterns we can comprehend. It follows, therefore, that a learning task that is well structured, which can be patterned, is more easily learned than one which is an agglomerate of unrelated items. It follows also that part of what we mean by teaching is the disclosure of complex and hidden patterns that are not easily accessible to the pupil.

A learning may be improved, therefore, in several ways: we may try to get an insight into subpatterns within a larger pattern already apprehended, e.g., perfecting computational patterns after the theory of the equation has been apprehended, or we may seek a larger pattern that will include smaller patterns that have been apprehended separately, e.g., seeing the general causes of war after having studied the causes of a number of different wars. Finally, one can try to improve the efficiency of a learned response, that is, achieve mastery.

V. *Incorporation into habit.* The tendency to seek patterns, more inclusive patterns, and more subtle patterns is the habit of acquiring knowledge. Part of the habit will be formed by the satisfaction the learner gets from knowing; part of it comes from the tendency of an incompleted pattern to prod its owner to complete it.[12] These factors establish the dynamic tendency of a piece of learning to find opportunities for further use, and this further use establishes the habits.[13]

Mastery comes with the incorporation of learnings into habit. The moment of learning is the moment of insight into a pattern; when the learner has within himself the model response and judges that it is correct. But this is still not mastery; one would hardly care to be operated on by a medical student who has just had his first insight into a surgical procedure.

Mastery makes the successful performance efficient and reliable. In brief, it becomes habitual and semi-automatic, leaving the master free to *think* about the variables in the situations that call for judgment. Mastery without insight and practice is virtually impossible, but insight without mastery is not infrequent. Because not everything in the curriculum need be mastered, efforts to teach for mastery are sometimes misguided and frustrating.[14]

VI. *Testing.* The teaching act is completed by a test in which the pupil is asked to perform the "learned" task without the total complement of clues and aids furnished him during the learning.

It has been observed that this "pay-off" trial is far more potent in shaping the pupil's learning than anything else, because one of the things only the unusually dull student fails to grasp is what pays off in rewards. It is by their tests and not by their printed syllabi that the true aims of the schools are known.

Many school tasks are really exercises of the operations of the

[12] B. Zeignarik, "Das Behalten erledigter und unerledigter Handlungen," *Psychologische Forschung*, 9:1–85; translated and condensed in Ellis, *A Source Book of Gestalt Psychology.*

[13] Some men will maneuver a whole evening for a chance to tell a joke or story they particularly fancy.

[14] Cf. Broudy, "Mastery," in Smith and Ennis, *Language and Concepts in Education.*

mind with little direct relation to life outcomes. Naturally one hopes that school outcomes will produce life outcomes; one hopes that reading Shakespeare in school will result in going to Shakespearean plays in life, but this we cannot test.

It would make everyone involved in the educational enterprise happier if schools promised only those outcomes they have a chance to observe and test at least once in school. It is risky to promise that even observed learnings will operate in life; it is sheer recklessness to promise this about learnings that have not been observed at all.

Method: a preparation for insight and mastery

Insight, the moment of learning, and mastery, the perfecting of habit, are therefore the objectives of teaching method. The means for achieving insight can be characterized as matching the learning readiness of the pupil with the cognitive or noetic demand of the task. Roughly this demand corresponds to the level of abstraction at which the learner is asked to operate. The closer a task is to perceptual experience the more concrete it is; the more a task is couched in concepts, theory, and symbols that do not resemble what they represent, the more abstract it is.

When the pupil fails to learn, one can suspect that discrepancy between the abstraction levels of the task and the learner is responsible. To restore congruity of abstractive levels is the strategy of teaching method, and the strategy is applicable to motivation, presentation, trial, insight, and testing, that is, to all phases of teaching method.

This view of method requires instruments for measuring the learning readiness of the pupil and the cognitive demand of learning tasks. Of the two, the latter is by far more in need of attention. Aside from vocabulary level, textbooks pay little attention to factors which make a task hard or easy to learn, even though the textbook is still the most widely used instrument of instruction.

Examples of method

Historically there have been developed a number of teaching methods, and we shall examine a few of these to see how they prepare for insight and mastery.

Socratic method. One of the most famous teaching methods was practiced by Socrates in the talking places of Athens. He called it a kind of midwifery in that he helped the learner to bring forth what had already been conceived within him and then helped him to judge whether it was a sound child or not.[15] He did it by asking questions; questions, however, that deliberately tested the awareness of the learner as to the implications of his answers. In this way Socrates, in the early dialogues of Plato, tested the soundness of the then current definitions of courage, piety, wisdom, and, in the *Republic*, of justice itself. Socrates had the faith that if men use accurately defined terms and systematically explore their implications, then they would penetrate into the inner meaning of the virtues and thus of life itself.

As a method of teaching, the Socratic dialectic was a way of getting the learner to have successive insights into adequacies and inadequacies of meanings, generalizations, and hypotheses. The whole curriculum of the secondary school in Plato's *Republic* had as its avowed purpose the leading of the mind to the abstract, to the ideas themselves, or, in our terms, to insights at higher and higher levels of abstraction.

The disputation. The medieval method of the disputation may have been more formal, but its purpose was likewise the revelation of deductive conceptual insights to the learner. To make it work one had to have memorized the writings of the authorities that furnished the counters in the logical game which was to follow, but at least one purpose of the disputation was to become aware of the logical or deductive relations that obtained among certain propositions in ethics, epistemology, and theology.

Both the Socratic method and the disputation are suited to the apprehension of a particular kind of pattern. We may call it the pattern of meanings or the pattern that concepts and ideas fall into when connected by certain logical relations, e.g., equivalence, contrariety, contradiction, implication, etc. These patterns are most common in logic and mathematics, but they are not confined to them. In every organized discipline there are idea-patterns, e.g., hypotheses, theories, generalizations. Indeed the most important idea-pattern of all is the relation of a theory to a set of seemingly unconnected facts. The dialectical or questioning method is, therefore, relevant and useful whenever the teaching task is to apprehend idea-patterns, relations among meanings, and concepts.

Memorization. True, it is somewhat hard to see how insight func-

[15] *Theaetetus.*

tioned in those centuries when learning and memorization were held to be equivalent. Without meaning to quibble, the point to be assailed here is not the lack of insight but rather the kind of insight aimed at. For as has already been shown, even the mechanical memorizing of a poem involves pattern. A verbal pattern was incorporated into the speech muscles and the nervous system of the learner. The learner drilled and repeated until with a minimum of cues the pattern could be reinstated. The punishments and devices invented to motivate the learner and to keep him at the task had as their goal this kind of "insight" and mastery. Oratory made use of this mastery, so did the learned professions, and so did the cultured men of the time. One can reject or accept the culture that made this kind of verbalizing profitable, but here we are merely trying to show that to promote the appropriation of the pattern is the goal of all methodology.

A proper criticism of this methodology is that it was not particularly efficient even within its own restricted ambitions. It took ages to learn the contents of a relatively small number of texts[16] and we can understand why this was so. The memorizing of 50 lines of poetry perfected a verbal pattern that did not mate very easily with any other patterns.

Memorization through repetition is indispensable if we wish to form semi-automatic fixed patterns. Whether the repetition is by drill or frequent use in life situations, the method is essentially the same. In every subject there is a core of material that has to be mastered in this semi-mechanical way. Multiplication tables, spellings, arithmetical computations, certain facts in history, science, and language are examples of such materials. The school people who hope to avoid these tasks are wishful thinkers. At best, we can reduce the core to be memorized in school to a minimum and use the hints psychology has given us about making drill effective.

Jesuits. The method of the Jesuits with the prelection and repetition, the frequent reviews, rivalry among pupils and classes, and careful testing also had as its aim the promotion of reliable insights and reliable habits.[17]

Few will deny that these methods produced exemplary results, however limited these results were. It was a methodology designed

[16] Cf. Eby and Arrowood, *The History and Philosophy of Education,* pp. 783 ff., or Butts, *A Cultural History of Education,* pp. 183–188.

[17] Fitzpatrick, *St. Ignatius and the Ratio Studiorum.*

to perfect the symbolic skills and to reinforce certain moral and religious attitudes; it was not designed to inculcate habits of independent investigation. It did very well what it set out to do, which was a great deal indeed. Although much of the pupil's work was memorization and mechanical repetition, yet it was a training for free and easy use of the Latin language and for a confident familiarity with the Classical authors. On the part of the teacher it demanded thorough preparation and no mean expository power.

Lecture method. The lecture method presents patterns of meaning in verbal form. A lecture on the history of experimental psychology, for example, might present a chronological pattern to show how laboratories originated and developed and a causal pattern to explain why the laboratory movement spread to the United States, Great Britain, and elsewhere.

On our analysis of learning, the lecture is an exceedingly abstract form of teaching. It is highly symbolic; it does not demand any physical participation by the student (except to stay awake); and its motivating power is low unless the student is already interested in the subject. It is not, therefore, appropriate to immature learners.

The virtue of the lecture is that it can present materials not found elsewhere or in patterns not found elsewhere. The good lecture simplifies, elaborates, or analyzes in a way that fits the purpose of the instructor. The time needed by a class to bring together the materials constituting the history of experimental psychology might very well—in a general psychology course—be devoted to something else. The lecturer brings this research together in a somewhat simplified form. He makes the outline large so that the contours and articulations are clear. In an hour he does what it would take his students scores of hours to do if they could be persuaded to do it.

When the instructor has a point of view different from that of the text, or has material from his own research, or from sources that have not yet reached print, the lecture is a logical and economical form of instruction. When the lecture is simply an oral repetition of the text, there is no justification for it. The lecture can be regarded as an oral textbook, and when texts were scarce the lecturer was very often no more than a reader from the text. The lecture method, therefore, has little to commend it when adequate printed materials are available.

Activity method. Because the activity method has already been discussed in a number of contexts, no special treatment of it is needed here. Its concreteness makes it suitable for the lower reaches of mental age, the beginning phases of all instruction, and particularly for educational patterns in the form of attitudes and modes of feeling, e.g., co-operativeness, initiative, responsibility, cleanliness, neatness, obedience, willingness to take part in group enterprises, social ease, and a facility in the use of experimental methods. These develop best in lifelike informal situations.

The activity program is the most lifelike of the methods we have discussed. The concreteness of this method promotes insight by engaging the attention and effort of the pupil through a genuine interest in the task. Thus even when noetic insights are the objective, the activity method may be the most reliable means of motivation. The same cannot be said for it in the domain of mastery. This does not exhaust the list of methods.[18] It is doubtful that any one method will facilitate all types of teaching and of learning equally well. When repetition is needed for formation of relatively fixed behavior patterns, Socratic discussion, lectures, or activities won't do. When logical patterns are at issue, drill procedures are virtually useless. When attitudes are the objective, lifelike activities offer the greatest promise.

For these reasons methods must remain plural for the time being at least. The teacher should be able to use all of them as the objectives shift from one type of pattern to another. It is a rough but fairly reliable observation that where a school is devoted to one type of method, it is probably neglecting certain types of pattern formation.

Summary

Two disciplines furnish concepts wherewith the teaching-learning process can be analyzed and rationalized. Educational psychology is one such discipline; epistemology or the theory of knowledge is another. Pedagogy combines these with experience in teaching to form the art of teaching.

From psychology pedagogy has learned that learning is even more complex than had been suspected; new factors in intelligence, motivation, and every other phase of the process are being turned

---

[18] E.g., the Herbartian methods so popular in this country at the close of the last century deserve study on their own account, but it can be shown that they, too, are means of promoting insight, cf. Herbart, *Outlines of Educational Doctrine.*

up by research. The *one* theory to unify this variety has still to be found, but already enough is known to enable us, if we will, to analyze our learning tasks, and the learning readiness of pupils far more accurately than we are now doing.

For the present, however, pedagogy has something to learn from the various theories of mind and knowledge offered by philosophy. Different schools of philosophy tend to stress different types of cognition and different roles of mind in learning.

The teaching act can be divided into six stages, but in a sense the *moment* of learning regardless of type is the moment when the organism appropriates some new pattern into its experience. All teaching methods are in their various ways preparation for insight. Mastery represents the incorporation of these new patterns into the habits of the learner. It was noted that method could be regarded as the attempt to match the cognitive demand of a learning task with the learning readiness of the pupil.

Problems for Discussion and Research

1. Pick two or three of the tasks listed below and if you can do so try to teach them to a beginner. Try to detect the *moment* of learning in each. What more would have to be done to insure mastery? A theorem in geometry; how to solve an algebraic equation; how to tie a square knot; the way a steam engine works; the meaning of a cartoon.

2. In one of your lesson plans identify the six stages of the teaching-learning process.

3. Note the distinction between test-outcomes and life-outcomes of schooling. Do you think this is an important distinction? On what grounds would you argue an affirmative or a negative answer?

4. How much of your method courses (if you have taken any) tie in with your courses in educational psychology?

5. As a student, do you work better with teachers who favor a particular teaching method? If so, which method is it? Can you explain why you favor it?

Suggestions for Further Reading

For fuller bibliographical information on the items listed below, consult the General Bibliography.

For readings and discussion of different views:

Bayles, *The Theory and Practice of Teaching*, Chap. 7.

Brubacher, *Eclectic Philosophy of Education*, Topic 22.

———, *Modern Philosophies of Education*, Chap. 12.

Dewey, *Democracy and Education*, Chap. 13. (The whole book, of course, is a commentary on method.)

Fitzpatrick, *Readings in the Philosophy of Education*, Chaps. 24 and 29.

Herbart, *Outlines of Educational Doctrine*. (A very famous methodology that had a wide influence in this country.)

Horne, *The Democratic Philosophy of Education*, Chaps. 12, 13. (Compare with previous two items.)

Kilpatrick, *Foundations of Method*. (This translates Deweyan theory into classroom practice.)

Koffka, *Principles of Gestalt Psychology*.

Pestalozzi, *How Gertrude Teaches Her Children*. (An educational classic.)

See also:

Eby and Arrowood, *The Development of Modern Education*, pp. 181–198. (A good description of Jesuit school methods.)

Moore, *The Story of Instruction: The Church, Renaissances, and the Reformations*. (A very readable book on the period; see descriptions of university life and of the disputation.)

Plato, *Meno*. (A fine example of Socratic method.)

To see the relations among general psychology, educational psychology, and education, examine any recent textbook, e.g.; Cronbach, *Educational Psychology*.

Also:

Bruner, et al., *A Study of Thinking* and *The Process of Education*.

Guilford, J. P., "Three Faces of Intellect," *The American Psychologist*. 14:8, 469–479, 1959.

Lewin, Kurt, "Field Theory and Learning," N.S.S.E. *Forty-first Yearbook*, Part II, pp. 215–242. Also Chap. 5 by George W. Hartmann in the same volume.

Piaget, *The Origins of Intelligence in Children* and other works listed in the general bibliography.

See also some of the items in the bibliography at the end of Chap. 13.

15

Organization of an
Educational System

An educational system, like any other, arranges different elements into some kind of pattern. When that pattern routes the various elements toward a common goal, we say that these elements or processes have been organized or made to act something like an organism. In organic structures each separate element makes its own peculiar contribution to the life of the whole. The heart, for example, is strategic in the circulation of the blood, and therefore of the life of the organism, but the heart itself depends on the same blood stream for its own maintenance as a heart.

It is dangerous to push the analogy between an organism and a school system very far.[1] Nevertheless, among curriculum, personnel, physical plant, administration, and method there are relations which remind us strongly of the type of relative dependence and interdependence found in organic wholes. As the number of pupils and their needs multiply these functions call for more and more specialization, on one hand, and co-ordination on the other.

[1] On this point see Scheffler, *The Language of Education*, pp. 53 ff.

In whatever way we finally decide to divide the task, certain principles will guide the division. First, that each part contribute to the final outcome. Second, that it does not duplicate the contribution of any other part. Third, that the contribution of one element does not frustrate or cancel out the contribution of any other.

Some Problems of Organization

Certain features of the educational enterprise complicate the problem of its organization.

1. Education is a consecutive and cumulative affair because experience is consecutive and cumulative. Pupils change under our very eyes. What can be taught always depends on what has already been learned. This means that all education makes history—as many histories as there are pupils. Education establishes sequences of experiences over a fairly long period of years. Such conditions confront few enterprises in our culture, so that by comparison the task of machine industry, government, or law is simplicity itself.

2. The problem is aggravated because each pupil, in addition to exemplifying a separate route of educational history, insists on traveling that route at his own rate and in his own pattern. Physiologically a boy may be 11 years of age, intellectually 15 years of age, socially eight years of age, whereas his educational achievement age may be 10 years. Inasmuch as each dimension or trait is a continuous one with an infinite number of possible values, the number of possible patterns of values is beyond calculation, even if we could agree on just what traits should be used as a base for the calculation.

3. The organization of a school system is also limited by the economic resources of a community and the willingness of the citizens to use them for education. In a democracy such as ours with a strong tradition of local control, any logically tight system of schools of any considerable scope soon founders on the reef of local idiosyncrasy. The problem is complicated even more when we try to achieve an educational goal that is national in scope by means of autonomous local school districts.

4. The nature of the curriculum and the nature of method are further limiting factors in organization. The following discussion presupposes the kind of curriculum and method already described in Chapters 12, 13, and 14. Thus a theory which argues for the same

program of general education for everyone in the elementary and secondary school calls for an organization that permits great flexibility of grouping pupils for instruction.

5. Of no less importance is the fact that the organization of a school system institutionalizes the class divisions of a society. Thus a society that is splitting up into more and more specialized vocational classes, and yet is denying that its citizens belong to diverse social classes, is bound to have more than its share of trouble in school organization. We want a comprehensive secondary school to prove our democratic impulses but we also want it to give vocational training. Because occupations do not carry equal prestige, schools that offer a variety of occupational curricula are bound to be divisive, however much pupils fraternize at football games, clubs, dances, and assembly programs.

Organization by age

In America the fundamental unit of educational measurement and management is the school year. One year–one grade is an almost universal formula for promotion, change of rooms, change of program, and change of teachers. Because the year is the unit for so many human doings, it is understandable why it should be adopted for schooling as well.

This formula is so much a part of our educational *mores* that it will take a revolution even to question it. And yet the formula shows signs of having outgrown its original usefulness and is now a positive hindrance to the next logical step in the development of education. Let us see why this is so.

The purpose of grading schools is to secure groups for instruction that are relatively homogeneous with respect to interests, ability to learn, and previous learning. It is assumed that children of the same age are more or less similar in these three aspects, and that if they go through the grades together, their experience will develop at approximately the same rate and on about the same pattern.

This assumption is unwarranted. It has been found, for example, that in an average sixth grade, one third of the pupils would be better placed in the seventh grade and another third in the fifth grade. Studies of the distribution of mental ages in such a classroom show a very broad range.[2] In such a grade some of the girls are already

[2] Cf. Garrison, *Variations in Achievement and Ability Within the Grades.*

pubescent; most of the boys are not. The reading interests of the boys differ markedly from those of the girls; the social and play interests vary no less. Retardation of pupils makes the average undoctored grade no less heterogeneous. In other words, if homogeneity is desirable for efficient instruction, then the one year—one grade formula is a sure way of not getting it.

If it should be argued that the best we can do is to adjust our materials and pace to the middle third of the pupil population and let the other two thirds limp or leap as they can, then the system becomes shockingly wasteful of both time and talent. Furthermore, such a procedure runs counter to the growing conviction that individual differences make valid claims upon the school system and should not be ironed out into uniformity.

Our problem, therefore, is to maintain group instruction and yet to have groupings that are as homogeneous as possible. At this point the reader of current educational literature will object that homogeneous groupings are outmoded on psychological grounds.[3] This is not the place to take up the arguments in detail, but several pertinent considerations can be noted.

Homogeneous grouping

It is argued that if children are alike in mental age they may be so unlike in physiological, emotional, and social age that they cannot work together as a genuine social unit. Another argument, less logical but more potent, is that such groupings publicize differences in mentality, thus making the slow pupil feel inferior, the bright ones superior, and their respective mothers unduly dejected or elated. It is held that the dull children miss the spur of the bright ones, and, finally, that because in life there is no homogeneous grouping, such groupings in school hide from the youngsters the bitter realities of competition, failure, respect for their betters, etc.

Of all these arguments only the first has any educational validity, and it therefore represents a problem to be solved by anyone advocating homogeneous grouping. It may be met by making learning readiness the base of our grouping rather than mental age, IQ, or any other single factor. This makes sense because we are teaching arithmetic, not mental age. Furthermore, there is no reason for a pupil to

[3] For a critique of scientific findings on homogeneous grouping, see Kelliher, *A Critical Study of Homogeneous Grouping.*

be in the same group for all subjects or for very long periods of time. Instructional homogeneity does not mean a perpetual lockstep.

The other arguments are based on (1) the natural dislike of parents to have the quality of their children's mental equipment publicly impugned, or (2) the notion that the school's primary objective is social and emotional adjustment rather than intellectual competence. The latter view, however, overlooks (a) the psychological effects of constant frustration on the dull child in unselected groupings, (b) the ease with which the bright child can fool away his time and become conceited in such a grouping, and (c) the pedagogical difficulties that heterogeneous classes present to the teacher. As for parental resistance, logical or not, any practical scheme for homogeneous grouping has to take it into account.

The principle of homogeneity with respect to scholastic ability will have to be limited, however, by the fact that at adolescence the differences between young men and women on one hand, and children on the other, are more important than whatever similarities they may display in scholastic achievement.

Because puberty heralds a qualitative change in the pupil's experience, and since it is a rather easily observable change, it would seem the part of wisdom to make adolescence the dividing line between the elementary and the secondary school. Children reach this point at various ages so it is not feasible to wait until they reach a uniform age to leave the elementary school. Regardless of accomplishment or ability, the child should enter the secondary school at the onset of adolescence and not until then.[4]

The Elementary School

Educational literature is rich in plans for meeting these individual differences through devices of organization, and some have had the benefit of extensive trials. Most of them exemplify variations of two major approaches to the problem.

1. We may call one the method of the socialized classroom. In this form the grade organization is retained. Each grade has a normal complement of pupils with all their variations. But since the work of

---

[4] It is impossible, of course, to legislate for prodigies. Nevertheless, if adolescence is interpreted to mean psychological adolescence as well as physiological adolescence, there should be no great difficulty in applying the criterion.

the classroom is always some collective activity or project to which each pupil contributes according to his ability and from which each takes what he can, individual differences are taken care of automatically. This not only makes homogeneous grouping unnecessary, but also keeps motivation at a high level and helps the school achieve such noncognitive outcomes as cooperation, initiative, and group consciousness.

2. The other method we may call "diagnostic teaching." Here the learning task is tailored to fit the ability of each pupil, especially in the tool subjects where individual mastery is the objective. On this method, extensive use of tests determines the readiness of each individual to go on to the next step, so that assignments and rate of progress escape from a class lockstep. Obviously the social life of the school in the form of collective experiences has to be provided for in some special way.

The first method has so much to recommend it that its ultimate establishment in the elementary schools is fairly certain. There are, however, learnings that are not collective. Organizing an exhibit can be a collective enterprise. Its success is measured by what the group as a whole has done. Success in arithmetic or reading is measured by what the individual has done. If there are learnings that each individual ought to acquire, the socialized class cannot guarantee that this will take place. To hitch systematic drill in these subjects to the collective approach is a remedy, but it is also a compromise with the method.

Diagnostic teaching is highly efficient in meeting individual needs and abilities, but it does tend to become highly complicated for the teacher, and unless extensive collective activities are provided, school takes on the atmosphere of a workshop where pupils do piecework in each other's presence. Teaching machines that automatically adjust the learning task to the readiness of the learner may be the solution to diagnostic teaching.

The solution would seem to lie either in the socialized approach with generous doses of remedial or supplementary work in the skills, or in some kind of homogeneous grouping so that diagnostic teaching can be applied to groups instead of to individuals. The relaxing of the grade system in the elementary school to enable a child to work with a group of his own ability at all times, regardless of the chronological age of his classmates, would accomplish this even in relatively small schools. By shifting the pupil very frequently—in fact whenever he fell out of step with his group—the school could prevent even conscientious parents from comparing their heirs with other children. By this method of organization, the pupil could work in optimum groupings until he reached adolescence.

There would be no retardation, and acceleration would mean the kind of enriched program that schoolmen talk so frequently about but rarely manage to furnish for the bright child. As the work of the school becomes more diversified into subjects, it would not be unusual for a pupil to work with different groups in art, spelling, reading, and arithmetic.

In effect, a child would enter the elementary school (or kindergarten) whenever he was ready to do so and remain until adolescent behavior and interests manifest themselves. He would not have to be in any grade at any particular time, and in time the grades would disappear from sheer uselessness.

Admittedly this scheme presents some difficult administrative problems, such as the method of assigning teachers, devices for shifting individuals from group to group, evaluating progress of the pupil, teacher-load, and many others. Yet where some form of such an approach has been tried, it has shown genuine promise, and the solving of such problems is certainly not beyond the ingenuity of American school administrators.[5]

It would achieve (1) homogeneous groupings for instruction in a relatively flexible way, (2) individual mastery without sacrificing the social values of group work, (3) automatic acceleration and retardation without "skipping" or "staying back," and (4) acceptance by parents of homogeneous groupings.

But whatever scheme of organization is adopted, the outcomes of the elementary school should be a solid beginning in the habits of acquiring, using, and enjoying knowledge. While the elementary school can never abandon its central responsibility for the symbolic skills, modern curricula will look to it increasingly as the place where the cognitive and evaluational styles of life are shaped by *instruction*. The discovery of new factors in learning and thinking will sooner or later result in a deliberate effort to exercise a wide variety of thinking processes in the early grades. A comparable growth in our knowledge of appreciative learnings will move the acts of imagination far closer to the center of the elementary curriculum than they now are.

[5] Cf. Goodlad and Anderson, *The Non-Graded School.*

The Adolescent or Secondary School

Ideally, the secondary school should complete the general education of the pupil, but it is difficult to say just how long this should take. There is a sense in which general education is never finished, and a sense in which it is finished for some individuals long before they take a diploma. General education has to stop when the community can no longer afford to continue it, when the pupil has to begin specialization, and when he can no longer profit from it. The first two conditions may change from time to time. The last can be determined with some degree of confidence, but not in a hurry. Too many high school drop-outs have the ability to profit from instruction. A minimum of three or four years in the secondary school should be a sufficient guarantee against premature discouragement on the part of teachers or pupils, and a maximum of six years should insure adequate background for the post-secondary schools in our educational system. But at best these are arbitrary figures.

The secondary school has the task of completing what the elementary schools have begun. Its general strategy is to perfect the symbolic skills and to introduce the student to the ways in which human achievements in the arts and sciences can be *systematized, integrated, used,* and *enjoyed.*

If this is the function of the secondary school and if general education is for man as man, then it can have only one curriculum for everyone. It has no room for vocational training as such, nor for specialization as such. Different curricula within one school and multiple schools come to much the same thing.

The only principle of variation compatible with a single track school are differences in learning readiness caused by the genes, previous learnings, or the peculiar conditions of upbringing. If grouping pupils for instruction by their learning readiness for a given area of study is sound for the elementary pupil, it is no less so for the secondary school.

Levels of study

Assuming that six years in the secondary school (Grades 7–12) is the target, each area of study (Chapter 13) first has to be organized on six ability levels. Each level should represent not only an advance in content, but should also demand a higher level of think-ing, organization, expression, and appreciation. We would thus have courses called:

Symbolic Skills:	*Language I, II, III, IV, V, VI.
	Mathematics I, II, III, IV, V, VI.
	Arts I, II, III, IV, V, VI.
Science:	Science I, II, III, IV, V, VI.
	To be be distributed among courses in physics, chem-istry, and biological sciences. Other sciences should, if at all possible, be incorporated under development studies.
Developmental Study:	Developmental Study I, II, III, IV, V, VI.
	To be distributed among the topics:
	development of cosmos and man,
	development of societies and institutions,
	development of mankind and culture.
Integrative and Sustaining Studies:	Classics I, II, III, IV, V, VI.
	To be distributed among literature, fine arts, and other value systems in the form of exemplars from each.

Problems: Societal Problems I, II, III, IV, V, VI.

Guidance: Throughout

Everything depends on how well these six levels of the curriculum can be graded, especially because textbooks do a very rough job of adjusting their abstractive demands on the learner. What I have in mind is the difference between American history studied through a number of historical novels, e.g., *Northwest Passage*, a formal high school textbook, and the works of Charles Beard. Difference in the sheer amount of material to be read, problems to be solved, research to be done is also relevant to the level of study, but the more im-portant difference is the theoretical level at which a subject is studied. The bright student not only can read more and faster, but he can read more mature works. It is the maturity of the learning task rather than its size that is the real challenge to the superior intellect.

It then should be possible with the help of modern testing tech-niques for a pupil to find his appropriate achievement rate each year or half year. Conceivably some can finish up on the sixth level in every area in fewer than six years, and some will take longer. In any event, when tests and guidance converge convincingly on the conclusion that a young man or woman can no longer profit from instruction on any level in any area, secondary school should be

---

* Including such foreign language as can be decided on for general education.

terminated in favor of post-secondary schooling or employment.

Note, if you please, that such a scheme presupposes a uniform curriculum and careful gradation of materials on some rational basis. Since neither condition is satisfied in our present high school, applying this design to it is at present out of the question, although the hope that it can eventually be accomplished is not.

Some advantages

Among the advantages of this kind of secondary school would be that:

1. It provides for individual differences in learning ability without sacrificing a common curriculum. Therefore, it should reduce the number of drop-outs from the secondary school.

2. It enables every post-secondary school and every employer to know with a high order of definiteness just what the applicant has achieved in the way of general education and at what level. This would simplify the mechanics of admission and certification no end, and it would reduce the prospects of failure in post-secondary education enormously.

3. The post-secondary school would not have to spend valuable time in filling in gaps of general education as is now often the case. It could begin its specialized work earlier.

4. It would enable some of the brighter students to begin post-secondary schooling at an earlier age or at a higher level.

5. It would enable the secondary school to do a thorough job of educational and vocational counseling, first, because it could begin the job early, and second, because achievement in general education, when differentiated on six levels, is itself a highly diagnostic aid in prediction of probable success in post-secondary education and in vocations.

6. Those who reach their limit of educability before the sixth year could turn to more profitable types of activity with a minimal loss of time.

7. Assuming an average of 6 years in the elementary school and 6 for the secondary school, a total of 12 years of schooling should give the equivalent in general education of what now takes 14 years. I believe this is possible if the school restricts itself to general education. The time and money so saved could be used for more post-secondary schooling.

The adjustatorium

For some time the American secondary school has been wrestling manfully with the problem of finding something for the nonacademically inclined pupil to do that would warrant keeping him in high school for four years. By nonacademic youth is meant the boy or girl who finds such courses as mathematics, history, literature, and science too difficult to master and too remote from his or her daily life to be interesting.

This is not to say that only nonacademic youth dislike school enough to leave it before the 12th year. Some of the students who drop out are brighter than some who are graduated. But certainly youngsters who find the work beyond their capacity will not want to stay in school.[6]

The solution suggested by many schoolmen is that to make a good citizen, father, soldier, and a defender of the democratic way of life, 12 years of schooling are not too many, and that, therefore, the secondary school years be utilized for this sort of citizenship training. Another argument is that adolescents have problems; that if these are used as the point of departure, young people will be eager to learn. There is also the contention that even academically competent young people need deliberate shaping of attitudes, character, and personality development not available in the conventional secondary school. The secondary school could thus be instrumental in reducing neuroses, juvenile delinquency, and the general unhappiness of mankind.

Now no decent taxpayer would refuse to reduce the general unhappiness of the race on account of a few more years of schooling—provided the longer school term could produce the promised results. The question is, can it?

The answer is probably "yes," provided we design an institution to achieve these ends. The conventional high school with its academic (or specifically vocational) curriculum probably cannot. Nor are the teachers in such schools—for the most part subject matter specialists—the sort of people who think of high school as a place where adolescents live, love, and mature in some "wholesome" way.

On the contrary, the kind of faculty needed would have the training and outlook of guidance counselors, social workers, psychiatrists,

[6] Broudy and Seyfert, *Massachusetts Youth Study*, pp. 92 ff.

and should be counted among those gifted adults who like youth and are liked by them. Conceivably, the doctoring of the present school could in time result in the evolution of a new sort of institution that we might dub an *adjustatorium*.

Although, on the view taken in this book, such noncognitive training is not the function of formal education, it might be desirable to develop an adjustatorium. It would, however, have so little resemblance to a school as as we know it that not much would be gained by calling it a "school." Its objective would not be instruction, but rather to establish an adolescent community in which preliminary trials in the race of life could be run. It would differ from adult life only in that counselors, psychologists, social workers, and physicians would be freely available to diagnose and correct those difficulties which reveal themselves in the trial runs. It would also differ from adult life in that it would not be played for "keeps."

Such an institution would certainly do some adolescents a lot of good and all adolescents some good. But it would do the whole educative enterprise even more good because it would leave the secondary school to do its own job of general education. Such a distinct institution is preferable to foisting upon the regular high school duties and activities alien to its purpose, facilities, and competence. Attendance at such an institution might be required of all youth before entering post-secondary education or the labor market—just as military service may have to be required of all youth in the near future.[7]

An adjustatorium could perhaps become the organizing agent of a youth work corps. The collection of funds for the Red Cross, Community Chest, and other civic enterprises could be carried on efficiently by adolescents. These activities, that now depend on the good will and spare time of adults, would convey to the adolescents a sense of civic responsibility and of personal usefulness that are invaluable to good citizenship. Civic work could help to bridge the gap between adolescence and adulthood. Inasmuch as such service would not encroach on the gainful activities of the citizens, it should arouse no economic resistance.

Fantastic as the adjustatorium notion sounds, it may come to sound less so as parental supervision of highly mobile adolescents becomes more and more difficult. We have here another example of how a

---

[7] Of course it is conceivable that military service could itself fill the role of the adjustatorium.

society lags in adapting social controls to social reality. An adolescent under the eye of supervisory adults and one out of their sight are just not the same adolescents.

Post-Secondary Education

If the task of providing general education to everyone is efficiently accomplished by the public secondary school, as we think it should be, then post-secondary education takes the form of specialized schools. Just as uniformity of content characterized the secondary school, so diversity of content will be prominent among the institutions of post-secondary education.

We can distinguish roughly three types of post-secondary educational needs:

1. There will be those who plan to enter one of the learned professions and will also need selected and intensive study in one or more of the general education areas. Premedical, prelaw, preteaching, prejournalism, etc., students are examples.

2. There will be those who wish to begin technical or vocational training without further ado.

3. There will be adults who have one or more of the above needs.

The American college as we now know it could very well devote itself to meeting the needs of the first group, and specialized technical institutes, trade schools, and business schools could meet the needs of the second group. Adult education presents a special organizational problem.

The American college

The American college is a much maligned but fairly well-loved institution. As its enrollments swell, so does the criticism. A victim of history and circumstances, it is understandably enough a nest of contradictions, crosspurposes, successes, failures, fulfillments and frustrations.

Perhaps the root of most of the trouble is that its aims were those of a high grade advanced boarding school for ladies and gentlemen, whereas its faculty was trained to live out its life in a Prussian university.

A good boarding school for late adolescence helps young men and women develop fine friendships, certain traits of character, standards of value and taste, a fine stock of happy memories for old age, and,

incidentally, some general education. Admirable objectives, and
there was a time when the American college achieved them pretty
well. For many it still achieves them. There is evidence that college
education makes a measurable and marked difference in peoples'
lives although perhaps not by its instructional procedures.[8]

Two factors have confused this rather clear notion of a college.
First, the college has increasingly become a gateway to the professional school in the university. The premedical or pre-engineering
student is rarely in the mood to jump the hurdles of general education, especially of the "cultural" sort.

Second, the faculties of even the smaller liberal arts colleges are
recruited from the tribe of doctors trained in the university for
scholarship and research in special fields of study. These men do not
fit neatly into the boarding school concept of a college. To begin
with, they assume that knowledge in their own field is valuable for
its own sake. Relatively few undergraduates share this assumption.
Hence students enter the classroom without that zealous curiosity
that reduces teaching to the funneling of knowledge from a full head
to an empty one. The college teacher not only is called upon to in-
form the student, but to make him want to be informed. This requires teaching skill that research men and scholars often lack and
are not overly anxious to acquire.

Since prestige and promotion often depend on research and publication, the college professor may come to regard teaching as a
necessary chore wherewith to subsidize the body so that his soul can
devote itself to research and writing. As for character training, these
men may inspire their students by the example of their own rather
harmless and necessarily ascetic lives, but if they do so it is not by
design.

That there has been some dissatisfaction with this state of affairs
is witnessed by the resolutions adopted by the Sixth Annual Conference on Higher Education.

> Whereas, at present, objective evidence of professional service
> and growth is available primarily in areas concerned wtih functions

[8] Harry P. Stedman, *An Analysis and Evaluation of Crane Scholarhip Aid.*
Master's Thesis, State Teachers College, North Adams, Mass., 1940. A quite
different attempt to investigate this is found in P. E. Jacobs, "Does Higher
Education Influence Student Values?" *N.E.A. Journal*, January 1958, pp. 35–38,
and criticisms of it by Paul F. Lazarsfield in A. H. Barton, *Studying the Effects
of College Education*, Edward Hazen Foundation, New Haven, 1959, and David
Riesman, "The Jacobs Report," *American Sociological Review*, 23:733 ff., 1958.

such as research and publication, participation in professional and community organization, and contribution to the college department and the institution, and

Whereas, there is dissatisfaction with present criteria of teaching competence such as years of experience, advanced study and degrees, and judgments of administrative officers,

Be It Resolved: That primary consideration be given to the effectiveness of teaching in deciding promotions in rank and responsibility, and increments in salary, and that continued efforts be made to improve such techniques for measuring effectiveness of teaching as observations of classroom teaching, student ratings of instructors, and actual achievement of students in courses.[9]

The growing emphasis on student counseling and guidance as a separate department likewise indicates a turning away from the more intellectualized, more detached, and less personalized university type of training. The latter assumes that the student is already grounded in the elementary phases of a subject and is competent to study the advanced phases more or less independently, provided only that appropriate facilities in the way of libraries, laboratories, and highly competent specialists are available.

Such an assumption is not warranted. College freshmen exemplify diverse patterns of high school preparation at many levels of mastery. Consequently, the first two years of college often contain elementary courses that should have been taken care of in high school. For example, colleges have to offer freshman courses in English composition, first courses in foreign language, and what amounts to a review of high school mathematics. So long as this is the story, the first two years of college will have to be used to fill in the educational gaps of its students.

There will always be enough demand for the boarding school type of college to nourish a number of private institutions of this sort. They should refrain from hiring their teachers on the basis of research attainments or promise. Rather, faculty should be chosen for broad cultural attainments, ability to work with adolescents, and a genuine zeal for fashioning the kind of character that will not disappoint the expectations of the tuition-paying parents.

College as preprofessional school. But by far our most common type of college will be the liberal arts division of some university,

<hr>

[9] National Education Association, Dept. of Higher Education, *Charting the Course for American Higher Education in a Period of Partial Mobilization,* Ralph W. McDonald, ed., 1951, p. 77. Quoted by permission of the N.E.A.

state or private. This type of college should not give general education or practice in the habits of acquiring, using, and enjoying knowledge. That, as we have argued, is the business of the secondary school.

The bill of fare of the preprofessional college would be composed of studies organized as bodies of knowledge and studied as specialties. The teachers accordingly would be subject matter specialists, but also specialists in *teaching* subject matter. Their advancement would be based on teaching power rather than on research and publication. They would be university-trained people whose profession is teaching, and they would be trained professionally, i.e., in the graduate schools of education, but for college teaching.[10]

From this bill of fare each professional school in the university would select the prerequisites for admission to its own program. It is to be hoped that preprofessional curricula will contain elements from areas of knowledge cognate to the practice of the profession, as well as directly related to it. Fortunately the trend to a broader intellectual base for professional training is already established. In a college such as this the degree of Bachelor of Arts or Science would be a preprofessional degree qualifying its possessor to enter a professional school or department.[11]

Post-secondary technical schools

It is not yet clear what the impact of automation on schooling will be. One prediction is that the need for technicians of numerous kinds will increase, and it is the belief of some educators that regional technical institutes will be the answer rather than junior colleges or four year colleges.

Yet the prerequisites for this variety of technical training may converge on more or less uniform high school preparation. Whether young people with enough intellectual ability to become professionals can be persuaded to settle for technician status is another

[10] I realize that this book may be consigned to the flames by many college professors who may have read this far. Yet if they follow the logic of the argument, they may not be so irked by the conclusion. Why a college teacher should be horrified at the kind of professional training a surgeon or engineer is proud to have is hard to understand, and I hasten to add that unless the school of education is ready to give *this kind* of training, the whole argument collapses.

[11] See the pamphlets issued on this topic by the Publications Institute of Higher Education, Teachers College, Columbia University.

matter, but this is not, strictly speaking, an organizational problem. However, a heavy layer of technical schools, business schools, and trade schools of all sorts can be anticipated as elements in the educational system.

The *total* number of our young people in post-secondary education should increase enormously, for there is little doubt that with a philosophy of guidance on the secondary level that sought to push every youngster to the limit of his learning capacity we would find thousands of young people who could profit from some kind of post-secondary schooling other than a preprofessional college.[12] It will be objected that this view of the American college will set up an undemocratic intellectual elite. But if membership in this elite is not limited by birth, class, or economic status, it is hard to see in what sense it could be undemocratic unless we are to subscribe to the notion that any principle of differentiation is undemocratic.

The university

In America the university is an aggregate of graduate schools, e.g., the medical school, the engineering school, the school of education, etc. Usually some years of undergraduate collegiate instruction are prerequisite for entrance. The graduate school of arts and sciences is also included for those who wish to become scholars in the various disciplines that make up the general studies.

These schools are all instances of special rather than general education—even when general education is the material of instruction. Thus a graduate school of English is a school for budding specialists in English.

The function of the American university is twofold. First, it is a center of instruction in the most advanced and specialized phases of knowledge and skill. In the second place, it is an agency for the discovery of knowledge. Graduate school faculties are expected to carry on research—pioneer research, if possible. It is difficult to say at the present moment which of these functions is primary. Since World War II, industry and government have made the universities subcontractors in research, so that in many a university laboratory the professor is working on problems that have nothing directly to do with instruction or even the materials of instruction.

[12] Cf. President's Commission on Higher Education, *Higher Education for American Democracy.*

To the extent that men divide their interests between teaching and research, one or the other may well suffer and often does. Yet the connection of research to instruction is so close at the graduate level that without it there is no real material for graduate as distinguished from undergraduate instruction. Graduate instruction—when really graduated—consists of little more than exhibiting the methods and results of such research.

It might be urged that a more logical division of labor would be effected if research and teaching were more completely separated. But in this case, where would the basic research be done? In industrial laboratories? But could so-called "basic" or "pure" research hold its own with research on problems of more immediate interest to the industry? Even though it is true that much basic research has resulted from utilitarian interest, is this a reliable motive?

Research might be taken over or provided for by the government. But a government has a hierarchy of interests also. The possibility of war is always in the background, and various segments of our economy naturally would prefer to have the brains of the country concentrate on the solution of their problems rather than on someone else's. If only a single obscure bookworm interested in the philosophy of some pre-Socratic eccentric is denied the opportunity to investigate the pre-Socratic eccentric, the function of pure science is thereby endangered just as genuinely as if atomic research were stifled or ignored.

In America today the university is about the only institution that exemplifies the spirit of knowledge for the sake of knowledge. Plato was wary enough to realize that even those paragons—his Guardians—would not serve truth wholly and unreservedly if they had other interests to divide their loyalty. In other words, the ax of general welfare will be ground only by a group that has no private axes to grind. Do university professors have private axes to grind?

Our culture pays the professor the uncomfortable honor of intense suspicion. Each economic, political, and religious group suspects that the professors are not doing all they could and certainly not all they should to promote *its* interests. Objectivity or impartiality is resented as animosity. In a culture rapidly crystallizing out its interest blocs, a group that can rise above such multiplicity is indispensable, but oddly enough, the greater the logical need, the more suspect such a group becomes.

The ivory tower is not the most popular place on the social scene at the moment. Everyone must be engaged, as the Existentialists insist, and the world might be a better place if good people were more engaged than they are, but the service of the truth requires some acolytes who must first disengage themselves from the pressures of everyday life. To frighten them by constant bullying and exhortation may cook the goose that has laid those wonderfully golden eggs for our modern technological civilization.[13]

It would seem, therefore, that the university would include as part of its primary function the search for and dissemination of truth as such, although in the social order its primary function must remain education, the preparation by instruction for the professions and callings that require a high order of specialization in knowledge. Until our society is willing and able to support a special group of its citizens to conduct research in the genuine spirit of research, this compromise remains as the best of a number of imperfect alternatives.

The preparation of teachers

It would be impossible in any book of this kind to discuss in detail the philosophical issues, the curriculum problems, and the methodology of each of the many forms of special education. There is one type of professional preparation, however, that cannot be omitted, namely, the professional preparation of educators themselves.

The battle to elevate teaching—especially the teaching of younger pupils—to the status of a profession has been a long and bitter one in American history. It continues even after all thoughtful citizens have agreed that good teachers are the pivots upon which all our schemes for the good life turn.

Fundamentally, it might be supposed that the good teacher is a high grade human being skilled in the art of teaching. After the Civil War, under the influence of such European educators as Pestalozzi, Froebel, Herbart, and others, we became conscious of

[13] Chester I. Barnard, Chairman of the National Science Foundation, says, "Science is a value to be cultivated for its own sake. . . . The curiosity, the initiative, the imagination, the persistence, the patience, the frustrations, that must be experienced and endured in science cannot be adequately motivated by the current exaggeration of the usefulness of science, but must be founded on the belief that all this toil is justified as an expression of the superior faculties of mankind and as a contribution to the values of man as a whole." Quoted by Gerald Piel, "Human Want is Obsolete," *The Saturday Review*, 36:26, June 27, 1953, p. 10.

the fact that the art of teaching could be cultivated deliberately; *ergo,* any young woman with decent morals could be trained in this art.

But as the science of education developed, and as we came to realize the psychological complexities involved even in the simplest of learning situations, we found ourselves demanding that teachers not only master the art of teaching, but also that they comprehend the science which made teaching a rational rather than a purely empirical art. This meant that the prospective teacher would have to submit herself to a program of studies requiring a rather high order of mental ability and a long period of time.

The situation has been complicated even further in more recent times. The current emphasis on mental health prescribes that the teacher of younger children be herself mentally healthy in a vocation that is not always conducive to such health. The current emphasis on the teacher's role as a community participant, if not a leader, calls for further personality qualifications. These requirements taken together constitute a blueprint of perfection. But since relatively few men and women in any population can meet these standards, and since the number of teachers in a country such as ours must be large, teacher education is put to it to develop this cluster of characteristics in those men and women whom it manages to attract to the field.

We can clarify the educational requirements for the good teacher by noting that high-gradeness, so far as it can be deliberately produced, is a product of (1) general education, (2) the science of teaching as contained in educational theory, and (3) the skillful practice of the art in some kind of apprenticeship in actual teaching. The proponents of each of these three aspects of teacher training vie for more and more time in the preparation of teachers, so that today the two-year normal school is pretty much a matter of history; the four-year teachers college curriculum is standard; and the five-year program is not too far in the future.

Teacher education as professional education

The solution to this problem is not very difficult. It is to regard teacher preparation as specialized education for a profession. So viewed, it would have nothing to do with general education as such, and if the secondary school could complete general education, the teachers college or school of education could organize its work as does the medical school or the engineering school.

It would prescribe selected preprofessional work in the general areas of knowledge as prerequisites to educational theory and practice. This would be furnished either by the college of a university, or by the teachers college itself if no university college were available for its students. In either case, it would not be concerned primarily with general education as we have defined it.

Much of the bitterness marking the criticism of "educationists" in recent years is due to factors that are more emotional than intellectual, but the key issue is whether or not there is a body of knowledge that uniquely defines professional education. The knowledge need not be unique but its selection, organization, and application must be. Physicians, engineers, and architects, for example, may all use the science of anatomy, but not in the same way.

The organization of knowledge in terms of educational problems constitutes educational theory, and educational theory breaks down into the various dimensions in which such problems can be studied. Thus if we divide educational problems into those having to do with aims and policy, curriculum, organization and administration, teaching-learning, we can study them in the following dimensions: psychological, historical, sociological, philosophical, technical, and clinical, as shown in Table 3.

By filling in each box in the grid a design for a complete program of professional education in both its general and specialized phases can be laid out, and there is now a respectable body of content to provide the filling. Professional educational curricula need not be haphazard collections of information, exhortations, and platitudes, and "educationist" need not be a term of opprobrium any more than "engineer" or "physician."

The professionalization of teaching at all levels may be speeded up by the need to separate the custodial and clerical aspects of teaching from the instructional ones. In other words, an array of technical and semiprofessional occupations may crystallize that require different amounts and quality of training. Tenders of teaching machines, school clerks, and test scorers need not be instructors, yet they would do much of what instructors are now expected to do. Professional status is a reasonable hope only for the teacher as a specialist in teaching.

The difference between a craft and a profession is the relative

Table 3[14]

Problems of	DIMENSIONS OF STUDY						
	Historical	Psychological	Sociological	Philosophical	Technical	Clinical	Internship
Aims and policy							
Curriculum							
Organization and administration							
Teaching-learning							
Special field							

emphases given to practice and theory. A craft gives practice priority, e.g., a tailor or cobbler or carpenter. A profession gives theory priority to enlighten practice. A profession, therefore, screens out those who cannot negotiate the theoretical part of the training; they never get a chance at the practice. The lad who cannot learn chemistry, anatomy, and biology cannot be a doctor, however engaging his bedside manner might be.[15]

The prospective teacher thinks he is preparing for a profession. Caps, gowns, hoods, titles, and degrees help the illusion along, but unless the intellectual discipline for which these paraphernalia are the symbols is there, no one will be fooled—student, other professions, or the public. Either there is a body of knowledge essential to teaching, or there is not. If there is, then it takes intelligence and time to master it. If there is not, then teaching is a craft and not a learned profession. Either teaching is a distinctive profession or it is not. If it is, then teaching is not psychiatry, nursemaiding, politics, or social work. If it is not, then it is hopeless to prepare systematically for it and no amount of organizing, lobbying, and demanding can advance its claims one iota.

[14] The reasons for this design or grid have been set forth in H. S. Broudy, "The N.C.A.T.E. Statement on the Teacher Education Curriculum," *The Journal of Teacher Education,* 10:1, 107–112, March, 1959.

[15] Cf. H. S. Broudy, "Teaching: Craft or Profession," *The Educational Forum,* 20:175–184, January 1956, and M. C. Cogan, "Toward a Definition of a Profession," *Harvard Educational Review,* 23:33–50, Winter, 1953.

Professional status in a society is no small matter. Society puts its life in the hands of the professions. Its whole structure—from the building of roads to the building of souls—is rooted in the learned professions; it depends on a relatively small number of men whose grasp on theory keeps chaos and barbarism at a distance which is always too small for comfort.[16]

What does society demand of the professional as a condition for this great trust? First, unquestioned competence. Second, unquestioned loyalty to the client, patient, pupil, or constituent. Third, an unquestioned loyalty to the ethics of his calling and to the canons of its disciplines.

Unless all three conditions are met, and unless the body politic is convinced that they are being met, it will be grudging of both its trust and its cash. Given that trust, it will pay whatever it has to—it never pays any more—to maintain the source of its several kinds of salvation. It will pay in money or prestige or both. Never so much of either, perhaps, as it will pay to its athletic or entertainment idols—but then no member of a learned profession really needs or wants that much.

Adult education

Ideally, adult education should be self-education. If we have formed the habits of acquiring, using, and enjoying knowledge, we have learned to learn. We should be ready to continue our own education from the intellectual resources of our culture.

We are a long way from such a state. Some have had to curtail their formal education. Some have been thrown into vocations for which they were not prepared. Some would like to get training in order to change vocations.

It is difficult to generalize on this matter, but it does seem as if opportunities for adult education of all sorts are plentiful—both formal and informal. If people do not continue their education, it is hard to figure out why they do not. Certainly there is no dearth of libraries, free lectures, forums, book clubs, and extension courses

[16] By a strange quirk of history we have returned to dependence—almost abject at times—on the specialist. The more spectacularly automatic our mechanical servants become, the more we become slaves to the service man. These men together with their superiors in the technical and scientific hierarchy are the modern counterparts of the ancient magicians and medicine men who also served as intercessionary agents between man and the now-hostile, now-friendly world of physical things.

in addition to what is sprinkled in the entertainment media of radio and television.

Aside from making adult education compulsory, I see nothing to be done in this area beyond providing opportunities so that they are really available to all in terms of time, place, and money.

It may be, however, that we are on the verge of an era when a certain group in our population is about ripe for really liberal education. It will not be the young, who must seek practical education. Nor will it be the young adult who must concentrate on establishing his economic position and rearing a family. Nor can it be the aged, who under benign circumstances ought to be enjoying the fruits of self-cultivation rather than undergoing it. This leaves us with a group that is a bit beyond middle age; this group has achieved a decent order of economic and domestic tranquility and still has a future of some magnitude. This group—not the active leaders in their profession nor in their community—can afford to cultivate themselves. They can afford it economically because they have established themselves in their calling; they can afford it psychologically because they are not driven by unusual needs for prestige and accomplishment, and they can manage it pedagogically because they received the elements of general education in their youth. This is the group that may inherit the earth—the best that our civilization can produce for value realization.

Summary

Our consideration of individual differences in pupils has thus led us to the organization of a series of educational institutions designed to meet the legitimate needs of self-perfection in a society fashioned to meet those needs.

Briefly, the organization that seemed indicated in a culture such as ours was something like this:

The elementary school. The child attends until adolescence. Either an activity program or homogeneous grouping based on scholastic achievement is a suitable principle of organization. If the latter is used, regrouping should be very frequent in every area of instruction. The one year-one grade formula could thus wither on the vine. The elementary school's goal on either method of organization is the establishment of the symbolic habits and skills and a beginning on the other cognitive and evaluational skills.

The secondary school. From the onset of adolescence the pupil attends the secondary school. He leaves when he has completed the highest level of work, when he can no longer profit from general education. The work is organized on many levels and a pupil works at all times at that level of a subject for which his achievement to date fits him. The sole concern of the secondary school is general education.

The college. The college is envisioned as a preprofessional school. It provides a selection of subjects to be studied as a prerequisite for specialized and professional study. The emphasis in the college is more on content than on habit formation, on the advanced phases of subject matter rather than on the introductory phases.

The university. The university would be primarily a professional school with both a research and teaching function.

Specialized institutes, technical schools, and adult education.

This is a single ladder system in the sense that no student is forced to make an early decision in one direction or another. All who can and wish may go through the general education-university sequence. Alternative branches are available only after the potentialities for general education have been exploited within reasonable and practicable limits.

PROBLEMS FOR DISCUSSION AND RESEARCH

1. The student should have some familiarity with the types of school organization in this country and in Europe.

2. Research, if needed, might be done on various current proposals to solve the problems of individual differences.

3. The schemes proposed for elementary, secondary, and post-secondary education in this chapter offer problems for panels or debates. This is a good opportunity for systematic critical thinking.

4. Does the material on the status of the teacher as a professional hold up under criticism?

5. Is the proposed organization of the school system democratic?

SUGGESTIONS FOR FURTHER READING

For fuller bibliographical information on the items listed below, consult the General Bibliography.

If the student has done a fair amount of the reading suggested for the last three chapters, he will realize that books on curriculum and method are also bound to talk about organization. It is assumed that the student will refer to some of the previous readings as well as to the following:

Brubacher and Rudy, *Higher Education in Transition*.

Butts, *The American College Charts its Course*.

Conant, *The American High School Today*.

Flexner, *Universities, American, English, and German*.

Foerster, *The American State University*.

Lieberman, *Education as a Profession*.

Newman, *The Idea of a University*.

Pangburn, *The Evolution of the American Teachers College*.

President's Commission on Higher Education, *Higher Education for American Democracy*.

Reavis, *et al., Administering the Elementary School*.

Smith, *et al., Fundamentals of Curriculum Development*, revised ed., Chaps. 10–14. (These sections deal with the personnel, physical features, and administrative arrangements required by the various types of curriculum.)

16

Building Your Own
Philosophy of Education

If you have struggled through the previous chapters, the time has come to ask yourself the following questions:

1. Could I list the major problems that have to be taken up in a philosophy of education?

2. Could I advance some argument to show why these problems are genuine difficulties?

3. Could I show in some detail how each of these problems is logically related to the others?

4. With respect to each problem area, could I outline the major arguments on either side of the controversy?

5. Could I identify these arguments with some specific writer in philosophy or the philosophy of education?

6. Given a concrete problem in curriculum, methodology, or organization, could I restate it so that it becomes a problem in the philosophy of education?

7. Do I have a feeling that all the arguments seem to have merit when I am reading them, and that it is hard to choose among them?

8. Do I have any urge to read further in the field of philosophy, education, the philosophy of education?

9. Do I find that there are questions which this book has not taken up, or has not dealt with adequately?

10. Do I find some of the views in this book irritating, annoying, or disturbing?

These questions in a sense represent the outcomes the author had in mind for you in this book. If you can give affirmative answers to most of these questions, then you are ready to begin to build your own philosophy of education. There is no pressing hurry, however, for it will take most of what is left of your life to complete it. What you have now are some of the conceptual materials and tools with which to do the building.

Whether you come out finally with a view similar to the one presented here is not unimportant—because I would not have presented it if I thought it to be false—but it is far less important than that you build your own in the light of your own experience and your own reflection.

As you do this step by step, your conceptual lenses will also change. You will perceive pupils, teachers, supervisors, administrators, parents, the community, in new forms and patterns—but there will always be a pattern, the pattern of your developing philosophy.

On another plane you will find that your value perspectives will also change. Your own life will take on new patterns of striving and feeling as your conceptual schema becomes more complete and more refined through the heat of argument, reading, inquiry, and the blows of life itself.

As you continue to philosophize, you will discover why the philosophic quest never ends in one great big bright illumination. Each new era presents the same problems in a new setting; the old solutions never quite fit, just as a suit of clothes fits a growing child only for a very little while. The philosophic mind is the growing mind, and it therefore outgrows its own solutions.

If you are or eventually become a professional educator, your philosophizing will in time reveal to you realms of doubt, despair, and reward that you never dreamed of. You will be engaged not only in what Whitehead has called an "Adventure of Ideas," but an adventure with the lives of others—the most dangerous, the most exciting, the most rewarding of all adventures.

General Bibliography

This bibliography does not list periodical literature referred to in the footnotes. Authors of footnote citations and mentioned in chapter bibliographies are listed in the Index. With very few exceptions, all titles mentioned in the General Bibliography have been referred to in footnotes or in the lists of suggested readings.

Aikin, W. M., *The Story of the Eight Year Study*. New York: Harper and Brothers, 1942.

Alberty, Harold, *Reorganizing the High School Curriculum*. New York: The Macmillan Company, 1947.

Allport, Gordon W., *Personality: A Psychological Interpretation*. New York: Holt, Rinehart & Winston, Inc., 1937.

———, *The Individual and His Religion*. New York: The Macmillan Company, 1950.

Aquinas, St. Thomas, *The Summa Contra Gentiles*, 4 volumes. Translated by the English Dominican Fathers. London: Burns, Oates and Washbourne, Ltd., 1923–1929.

———, *Summa Theologica*, 3 volumes. Translated by the Fathers of the English Dominican Province. New York: Benziger Brothers, Inc., 1947.

Aristotle, *The Works of Aristotle*, 11 volumes. Translated into English under the editorship of W. D. Ross. Oxford: Clarendon Press, 1908–1931.

———, *Selections*, edited by W. D. Ross. New York: The Modern Student's Library, Charles Scribner's Sons, 1927, 1938.

———, *Introduction to Aristotle*, edited by Richard McKeon, New York: The Modern Library, Random House, 1947.

Ausubel, David P., *Ego Development and the Personality Disorders*. New York: Grune and Stratton, 1952.

Bagley, W. C., *Educational Values*. New York: The Macmillan Company, 1911.

———, *Education, Crime, and Social Progress*. New York: The Macmillan Company, 1931.

Baker, Melvin C., *Foundations of John Dewey's Educational Theory*. New York: King's Crown Press, 1955.

Bantock, G. H., *Freedom and Authority in Education*. Chicago: Henry Regnery and Company, 1953.

Bayles, E. E., *The Theory and Practice of Teaching*. New York: Harper & Brothers, 1950.

———, *Democratic Educational Theory*. New York: Harper & Brothers, 1960.

Beberman, Max, and Herbert E. Vaughan, *High School Mathematics*. Urbana: University of Illinois Press, 1959.

Beck, R. H., W. W. Cook, and N. C. Kearney, *Curriculum in the Modern Elementary School*. Englewood Cliffs, N.J.: Prentice-Hall, Inc., 1953.

Beisswänger, Gustav, *Amos Comenius als Pansophist*. Stuttgart: W. Kohlhammer, 1904.

Benne, Kenneth D., *A Conception of Authority*. New York: Bureau of Publications, Teachers College, Columbia University, 1943.

———, Leland P. Bradford, and Ronald Lippitt, *Group Dynamics and Social Action*. New York: Anti-Defamation League of B'nai B'rith, 1950.

Bergson, Henri, *Creative Evolution*. Translated by Arthur Mitchell. London: Macmillan and Company, Ltd., 1912.

———, *The Two Sources of Morality and Religion*. Translated by H. A. Audra and C. Bereton. New York: Holt, Rinehart & Winston, Inc., 1935.

Berkeley, George, *The Works of George Berkeley*, 3 volumes. Edited by George Sampson. London: George Bell and Sons, 1897–1898.

Bertocci, Peter A., *An Introduction to the Philosophy of Religion*. Englewood Cliffs, N.J.: Prentice-Hall, Inc., 1951.

Black, Max, *Critical Thinking: An Introduction to Logic and Scientific Method*. Englewood Cliffs, N.J.: Prentice-Hall, Inc., 1952.

Bobbitt, Franklin, *Curriculum Construction in Los Angeles*. Chicago: University of Chicago Press, 1922.

Bosanquet, Bernard, *Three Lectures on Aesthetic*. New York: The Macmillan Company, 1915.

Boswell, Peyton, Jr., *Modern American Painting*. New York: Dodd, Mead and Company, 1940.

Bowler, John F., ed., *Report of Committee to Study General Education in Mass. State Teachers Colleges.* Boston: Commonwealth of Mass., 1959.

Brameld, Theodore, *Patterns of Educational Philosophy.* Yonkers-on-Hudson, N.Y.: World Book Company, 1950.

Brightman, Edgar S., *Introduction to Philosophy.* New York: Holt, Rinehart & Winston, Inc., 1925.

———, *A Philosophy of Religion.* Englewood Cliffs, N.J.: Prentice-Hall, Inc., 1940.

Broudy, H. S., and W. C. Seyfert, *Massachusetts Youth Study.* The Commonwealth of Massachusetts, 1940.

———, and Eugene L. Freel, *Psychology for General Education.* New York: Longmans, Green and Company, 1956.

Brubacher, John S., *A History of the Problems of Education.* New York: McGraw Hill Book Company, Inc., 1947.

———, *Modern Philosophies of Education.* New York: McGraw-Hill Book Company, Inc., 1950.

———, *Eclectic Philosophy of Education.* Englewood Cliffs, N.J.: Prentice-Hall, Inc., 1951.

———, and Willis Rudy, *Higher Education in Transition.* New York: Harper & Brothers, 1958.

Bruner, Jerome S., *The Process of Education.* Cambridge, Mass.: Harvard University Press, 1960.

———, J. J. Goodnow, and G. A. Austin, *A Study of Thinking.* New York: John Wiley and Sons, Inc., 1950.

Bryson, Lyman, Louis Finkelstein, R. M. MacIver, and Richard McKeon, eds., *Freedom and Authority in Our Time.* New York: Harper & Brothers, 1953.

Burgess, E. W. and Harvey J. Locke, *The Family: From Institution to Companionship.* Cincinnati: American Book Company, 1953.

Burton, William H., *The Guidance of Learning Activities.* New York: Appleton-Century-Crofts, Inc., 1944.

Butler, J. Donald, *Four Philosophies and Their Practice in Education and Religion,* rev. ed. New York: Harper & Brothers, 1957.

Butts, R. Freeman, *The College Charts Its Course.* New York: McGraw-Hill Book Company, Inc., 1939.

———, *A Cultural History of Education.* New York: McGraw-Hill Book Company, Inc., 1947.

———, *The American Tradition in Religion and Education.* Boston: Beacon Press, 1950.

Butts, R. Freeman, and Lawrence A. Cremin, *A History of Education in American Culture.* New York: Holt, Rinehart and Winston, Inc., 1953.

Cannon, Walter B., *The Wisdom of the Body.* New York: W. W. Norton and Company, Inc., 1932.

Carmichael, Leonard, ed., *Manual of Child Psychology.* New York: John Wiley and Sons, Inc., 1946.

Caswell, Hollis L., and Doak S. Campbell, *Readings in Curriculum Development*. New York: American Book Company, 1937.

Childs, J. L., *Education and Morals*. New York: Appleton-Century-Crofts, Inc., 1950.

Collings, Ellsworth, *An Experiment with a Project Curriculum*. New York: The Macmillan Company, 1923.

Comenius, Johann Amos, *The Great Didactic*. Translated and edited by M. W. Keatinge. London: A. and C. Black, Ltd., 1921–1923.

Commission on Secondary School Curriculum of the Progressive Education Association, *The Visual Arts in General Education*. New York: Appleton-Century-Crofts, Inc., 1941.

Committee on Religion and Education, *The Function of the Public Schools in Dealing with Religion*. Washington, D.C.: American Council on Education, 1953.

Conant, James B., *On Understanding Science*. New Haven: Yale University Press, 1947.

———, *The American High School Today*. New York: McGraw-Hill Book Company, Inc., 1959.

Conference on General Education, *General Education at Mid-Century; A Critical Analysis*. Tallahassee, Fla.: Florida State University, 1950.

Copland, Aaron, *What to Listen For in Music*. New York: McGraw-Hill Book Company, Inc., 1939.

Craig, Robert C., *The Transfer Value of Guided Learning*. New York: Bureau of Publications, Teachers College, Columbia University, 1953.

Cronbach, Lee J., *Educational Psychology*. New York: Harcourt, Brace and World, Inc., 1954.

Cunningham, W. F., *Pivotal Problems of Education*. New York: The Macmillan Company, 1940.

Descartes, René, *The Philosophical Works of Descartes*. Translated by E. S. Haldane and G. R. T. Ross. New York: The Macmillan Company, 1912.

Dewey, John, *How We Think*. Boston: D. C. Heath and Company, 1910, 1933.

———, *Democracy and Education*. New York: The Macmillan Company, 1916, 1936.

———, *Human Nature and Conduct*. New York: Holt, Rinehart & Winston, Inc., 1922.

———, *Experience and Nature*. New York: W. W. Norton and Company, 1929.

———, *The Quest for Certainty*. New York: Minton, Balch and Company, 1929.

———, *A Common Faith*. New Haven: Yale University Press, 1934.

———, *Art as Experience*. New York: Minton, Balch and Company, 1935.

———, *Logic: The Theory of Inquiry*. New York: Holt, Rinehart & Winston, Inc., 1938.

——, *Education Today*. New York: G. P. Putnam's Sons, 1940.

Drake, William E., *The American School in Transition*. Englewood Cliffs, N.J.: Prentice-Hall, Inc., 1955.

Ducasse, C. J., *The Philosophy of Art*. New York: The Dial Press, Inc., 1931.

Eby, Frederick, and C. F. Arrowood, *The History and Philosophy of Education Ancient and Medieval*. Englewood Cliffs, N.J.: Prentice-Hall, Inc., 1940.

——, *The Development of Modern Education*. Englewood Cliffs, N.J.: Prentice-Hall, Inc., 1940.

Education in the U.S.S.R., U.S. Office of Education. Bulletin No. 14, 1957. Washington, D.C.: Government Printing Office.

Edwards, Paul, and Arthur Pap, *A Modern Introduction to Philosophy*. Glencoe, Ill.: The Free Press, 1957.

Ellis, W. D., *A Source Book of Gestalt Psychology*. New York: Harcourt, Brace and World, Inc., 1938.

Everett, John R., *Religion in Human Experience*. New York: Holt, Rinehart & Winston, Inc., 1950.

Everett, W. G., *Moral Values*. New York: Holt, Rinehart & Winston, Inc., 1918.

Fairchild, Hoxie N., et al., *Religious Perspectives in College Teaching*. New York: The Ronald Press Company, 1952.

Feigl, Herbert, and Wilfrid Sellars, *Readings in Philosophical Analysis*. New York: Appleton-Century-Crofts, Inc., 1949.

Ferm, Virgilius, ed., *A History of Philosophical Systems*. New York: The Philosophical Library, 1950.

Finney, Ross, *Sociological Philosophy of Education*. New York: The Macmillan Company, 1928.

Fitzpatrick, E. A., *Readings in the Philosophy of Education*. New York: Appleton-Century-Crofts, Inc., 1936.

——, *St. Ignatius and the Ratio Studiorum*. New York: McGraw-Hill Book Company, Inc., 1933.

Fleming, William, and Abram Veinus, *Understanding Music*. New York: Holt, Rinehart & Winston, Inc., 1958.

Flexner, Abraham, *Universities, American, English, and German*. New York: Oxford University Press, 1930.

Foerster, Norman, *The American State University*. Chapel Hill: University of North Carolina Press, 1937.

Frank, Lawrence K., *Nature and Human Nature*. New Brunswick, N.J.: Rutgers University Press, 1951.

Freud, Sigmund, *Civilization and its Discontents*. New York: W. W. Norton and Company, Inc., 1930.

Fromm, Erich, *Escape From Freedom*. New York: Farrar and Rinehart, 1941.

Garrison, S. C., *Variations in Achievement and Ability Within the Grades*. Nashville, Tenn.: George Peabody College for Teachers, 1922.

General Education in School and College; A Committee Report by Members of the Faculties of Andover, Exeter, Lawrenceville,

Harvard, Princeton, and Yale. Cambridge, Mass.: Harvard University Press, 1952.

Gentile, G., *The Reform of Education*. Translated by Dino Bigongiari. New York: Harcourt, Brace and World, Inc., 1922.

Gilbert, Katharine E., and Helmut Kuhn, *A History of Aesthetics*, rev. ed. Bloomington: University of Indiana Press, 1953.

Gilson, Etienne, *God and Philosophy*. New Haven: Yale University Press, 1941.

Goodlad, J. I., and R. H. Anderson, *The Non-Graded School*. New York: Harcourt, Brace and World, Inc., 1959.

Gotshalk, Dilman W., *Art and the Social Order*. Chicago: University of Chicago Press, 1947.

Groos, Karl, *The Play of Men*. Translated by Elizabeth L. Baldwin. New York: Appleton-Century-Crofts, Inc., 1901.

Hand, Harold C., *Principles of American Public Secondary Education*. New York: Harcourt, Brace and World, Inc., 1957.

Handbook of Experimental Psychology. Edited by S. S. Stevens. New York: John Wiley and Sons, Inc., 1951.

Harner, N. C., *Religion's Place in General Education*. Richmond, Va.: John Knox Press, 1949.

Harris, H. S., *The Social Philosophy of Giovanni Gentile*. Urbana: University of Illinois Press, 1960.

Hartshorne, Hugh, and Mark May, *Studies in the Nature of Deceit* and *Studies in the Nature of Character*. New York: The Macmillan Company, 1928.

Harvard Committee on the Objectives of Education in a Free Society, *General Education in a Free Society*. Cambridge, Mass.: Harvard University Press, 1945.

Hayek, Friedrich A. von, *The Road to Serfdom*. Chicago: The University of Chicago Press, 1944.

Heidegger, Martin, *Sein und Zeit*. Halle: Max Niemeyer Verlag, 1927.

Herbart, Johann Friedrich, *Outlines of Educational Doctrine*. Translated by A. F. Lange. New York: The Macmillan Company, 1901.

Hill, T. E., *Contemporary Ethical Theories*. New York: The Macmillan Company, 1952.

Hocking, W. E., *Human Nature and Its Remaking*. New Haven: Yale University Press, 1923.

———, *Types of Philosophy*. New York: Charles Scribner's Sons, 1929.

Horne, Herman Harrell, *The Democratic Philosophy of Education*. New York: The Macmillan Company, 1935.

Horney, Karen, *The Neurotic Personality of Our Time*. New York: W. W. Norton and Company, Inc., 1937.

Hospers, John, *An Introduction to the Philosophy of Analysis*. Englewood Cliffs, N.J.: Prentice-Hall, Inc., 1953.

Huizinga, Johan, *Homo Ludens: A Study of the Play Element in Culture*. Translated by R. F. C. Hull. New York: Roy Publishers, 1950.

Hullfish, H. G., ed., *Educational Freedom in an Age of Anxiety.* New York: Harper & Brothers, 1953. Twelfth Yearbook of the John Dewey Society.

Hume, David, *A Treatise of Human Nature.* 2 volumes. Everyman's Library, New York: E. P. Dutton and Company, Inc., 1911.

Hunt, M. P., and L. E. Metcalf, *Teaching High School Social Studies.* New York: Harper & Brothers, 1955.

Hutchins, R. M., *The Higher Learning in America.* New Haven: Yale University Press, 1936.

———, *Morals, Religion, and Higher Education.* Chicago: The University of Chicago Press, 1950.

———, *The Conflict in Education in a Democratic Society.* New York: Harper & Brothers, 1953.

Inhelder, Bärbel, and Jean Piaget, *The Growth of Logical Thinking from Childhood to Adolescence.* Translated by Anne Parsons and Stanley Milgram. New York: Basic Books, 1958.

Jaeger, Werner W., *Paideia: The Ideals of Greek Culture.* Translated by Gilbert Highet. 2 volumes. New York: Oxford University Press, 1939–1943.

James, William, *A Pluralistic Universe.* New York: Longmans, Green and Company, 1943.

———, *Varieties of Religious Experience.* New York: Longmans, Green and Company, 1902.

Johnson, A. V., and F. N. Yost, *Separation of Church and State in the United States.* Minneapolis: University of Minnesota Press, 1948.

Kant, Immanuel, *Fundamental Principles of the Metaphysics of Ethics.* Translated by Thomas K. Abbott, 8th edition. New York: Longmans, Green and Company, 1947.

———, *The Critique of Pure Reason.* Translated by J. M. D. Meiklejohn, rev. ed. New York: The Colonial Press, 1900.

Kardiner, Abram, *et al., The Psychological Frontiers of Society.* New York: Columbia University Press, 1945.

Katona, G., *Organizing and Memorizing: Studies in the Psychology of Learning and Teaching.* New York: Columbia University Press, 1940.

Kelley, Earl C., and Marie I. Rasey, *Education and the Nature of Man.* New York: Harper & Brothers, 1952.

Kelliher, A. V., *A Critical Study of Homogeneous Grouping.* New York: Teachers College, Columbia University, 1931.

Key Understandings in Economics. Washington, D.C.: Council for Advancement of Secondary Education, 1956.

Kierkegaard, Sören, *Concluding Unscientific Postscript.* Translated by David F. Swenson and Walter Lowrie. Princeton: Princeton University Press, 1941.

———, *The Sickness Unto Death.* Translated by Walter Lowrie. Princeton: Princeton University Press, 1941.

———, *The Concept of Dread.* Translated by Walter Lowrie. Princeton: Princeton University Press, 1946.

Kilpatrick, William H., *Foundations of Method*. New York: The Macmillan Company, 1925.

Kirkpatrick, Clifford, *The Family as Process and Institution*. New York: The Ronald Press Company, 1955.

Klubertanz, George P., *The Philosophy of Human Nature*. New York: Appleton-Century-Crofts, Inc., 1953.

Kluckhohn, Clyde, and Henry A. Murray, *Personality in Nature, Society, and Culture*. New York: Alfred A. Knopf, Inc., 1949.

Kneller, G. F., *The Educational Philosophy of National Socialism*. New Haven: Yale University Press, 1941.

———, *Existentialism and Education*. New York: Philosophical Library, 1958.

Koffka, Kurt, *Principles of Gestalt Psychology*. New York: Harcourt, Brace and World, Inc., 1935.

Köhler, Wolfgang, *The Mentality of Apes*. New York: Harcourt, Brace and World, Inc., 1925.

———, *Gestalt Psychology*. New York: Harcourt, Brace and World, Inc., 1935.

Krikorian, Y. H., ed., *Naturalism and the Human Spirit*. New York: Columbia University Press, 1944.

Kuhlen, Raymond G., *The Psychology of Adolescent Development*. New York: Harper & Brothers, 1952.

Langer, Susanne K., *Philosophy in a New Key*. Cambridge, Mass.: Harvard University Press, 1942.

———, *Feeling and Form; A Theory of Art*. New York: Charles Scribner's Sons, 1953.

———, ed., *Reflections on Art*. Baltimore: Johns Hopkins Press, 1958.

Lee, Vernon, *The Beautiful*. Cambridge, England: University Press, 1913.

———, *Music and Its Lovers*. New York: E. P. Dutton & Company, Inc., 1933.

Lehman, H. C., and P. A. Witty, *Psychology of Play Activities*. New York: A. S. Barnes and Company, 1927.

Leonard, Henry S., *Principles of Right Reason*. New York: Holt, Rinehart & Winston, Inc., 1957.

Leonhard, Charles, and R. W. House, *Foundations and Principles of Music Education*. New York: McGraw-Hill Book Company, 1959.

Lepley, Ray, ed., *Value: A Cooperative Inquiry*. New York: Columbia University Press, 1949.

Lerner, Max, *America as a Civilization*. New York: Simon and Schuster, 1957.

Lewis, C. I., *An Analysis of Knowledge and Evaluation*. LaSalle, Ill.: The Open Court Publishing Company, 1946.

Lieberman, Myron, *Education as a Profession*. Englewood Cliffs, N.J.: Prentice-Hall, Inc., 1956.

———, *The Future of Public Education*. Chicago: The University of Chicago Press, 1960.

Lilge, Frederic, *The Abuse of Learning; The Failure of the German University*. New York: The Macmillan Company, 1948.

————, *Anton Semyonovitch Makarenko*. Berkeley: University of California Press, 1958.
Lippmann, Walter, *A Preface to Morals*. New York: The Macmillan Company, 1931.
Lipps, Theodor, *Zur Einfühlung*. Leipzig: Verlag von Wilhelm Engelmann, 1913.
Locke, John, *Essay Concerning Human Understanding*. 2nd edition. Chicago: The Open Court Publishing Company, 1912.
Lodge, R. C., *Philosophy of Education*. New York: Harper & Brothers, 1947.
Lowenfeld, V., *Creative and Mental Growth*. 3rd edition. New York: The Macmillan Company, 1957.
Madden, Ward, *Religious Values in Education*. New York: Harper & Brothers, 1951.
Mannheim, Karl, *Man and Society in an Age of Reconstruction*. New York: Harcourt, Brace and World, Inc., 1940.
————, *Diagnosis of Our Time*. London: Kegan Paul, Trench, Trubner and Company, 1943.
Maritain, Jacques, *Education at the Crossroads*. New Haven: Yale University Press, 1943.
————, *Creative Intuition in Art and Poetry*. Bollingen Series XXXV. New York: Pantheon Books, Inc., 1953.
Martin, Wm. Oliver, *The Order and Integration of Knowledge*. Ann Arbor, Mich.: The University of Michigan Press, 1957.
Marx, Karl, *Capital and Other Writings by Karl Marx*, Max Eastman, ed. New York: The Modern Library, 1932.
Maslow, A. H., *Motivation and Personality*. New York: Harper & Brothers, 1954.
————, ed., *New Knowledge in Human Values*. New York: Harper & Brothers, 1959.
Mason, R. E., *Moral Values and Secular Education*. New York: Columbia University Press, 1950.
————, *Educational Ideals in American Society*. Boston: Allyn and Bacon, 1960.
Mayhew, Katherine Camp, and Anna Camp Edwards, *The Dewey School: The Laboratory School of the University of Chicago, 1896–1903*. New York: Appleton-Century-Crofts, Inc., 1936.
McCall, Raymond J., *Basic Logic*. 3rd ed. New York: Barnes and Noble, Inc., 1952.
Mead, Margaret, *The School in American Culture*. Cambridge: Harvard University Press, 1951.
Meyer, Leonard B., *Emotion and Meaning in Music*. Chicago: University of Chicago Press, 1956.
Meyers, Bernard S., *Understanding the Arts*. New York: Holt, Rinehart & Winston, Inc., 1958.
Mill, John S., *Utilitarianism*. Everyman's Library. New York: E. P. Dutton and Company, 1910.

392 GENERAL BIBLIOGRAPHY

Mitchell, E. D., and B. S. Mason, *The Theory of Play.* New York: A. S. Barnes, 1948.
Montagu, M. F. Ashley, *The Direction of Human Development: Biological and Social Bases.* New York: Harper & Brothers, 1955.
Montaigne, *The Essays of Montaigne.* Translated by E. J. Trechman. New York: Oxford University Press, 1927.
Moore, Ernest Carroll, *The Story of Instruction: The Church, The Renaissances, and The Reformations.* New York: The Macmillan Company, 1938.
Moore, G. E., *Principia Ethica.* New York: The Macmillan Company, 1903.
Moreno, J. L., *Psychodrama.* New York: Beacon House, 1946.
Morrison, Henry C., *The Curriculum of the Common School.* Chicago: The University of Chicago Press, 1940.
Mosier, Richard D., *The American Temper: Patterns of Our Intellectual Heritage.* Berkeley: University of California Press, 1952.
Moss, F. A., ed., *Comparative Psychology.* Englewood Cliffs, N.J.: Prentice-Hall, Inc., 1934.
Mowrer, O. Hobart, *Learning Theory and Personality.* New York: The Ronald Press Company, 1950.
———, *Learning Theory and Behavior.* New York: John Wiley and Sons, Inc., 1960.
———, *Learning Theory and the Symbolic Processes.* New York: John Wiley and Sons, Inc., 1960.
Mumford, Lewis, *The Transformations of Man.* New York: Harper & Brothers, 1956.
Murphy, Gardner, *Human Potentialities.* New York: Basic Books, 1958.
Murray, H. A., *Explorations in Personality.* New York: Oxford University Press, 1938.
Myrdal, Gunnar, *An American Dilemma.* New York: Harper & Brothers, 1944.
National Committee on Art Education, *The Art in Art Education.* New York: The Committee, 1958.
National Council of Teachers of Mathematics, Sixteenth Yearbook, *Arithmetic in General Education.* New York: Teachers College, Columbia University, 1941.
National Council of Teachers of Mathematics, Twenty-fourth Yearbook, *The Growth of Mathematical Ideas, Grades K–12.* Washington, D.C.: 1959.
National Education Association, Educational Policies Commission, *The Purposes of Education in American Democracy,* 1938.
———, *Moral and Spiritual Values,* 1951.
National Society for the Study of Education, Twenty-fourth Yearbook, Part II, *Adapting the Schools to Individual Differences,* 1925.
———, Fortieth Yearbook, *Art in American Life and Education,* 1941.
———, Forty-first Yearbook, Part I, *Philosophies of Education,* 1942.
———, Forty-first Yearbook, Part II, *The Psychology of Learning,* 1942.
———, Forty-third Yearbook, Part I, *Adolescence,* 1944.

——, Fifty-third Yearbook, Part II, *Mass Media and Education*, 1954.
——, Fifty-fourth Yearbook, Part I, *Modern Philosophies and Education*, 1955.
——, Fifty-seventh Yearbook, Part I, *Basic Concepts in Music Education*, 1958.
——, Fifty-ninth Yearbook, Part I, *Rethinking Science Education*, 1960.
Newman, J. H., *The Idea of a University*. London: Longmans, Green and Company, 1919.
Niebuhr, Rheinhold, *The Nature and Destiny of Man*. 2 volumes. New York: Charles Scribner's Sons, 1941.
Nottingham, Elizabeth D., *Religion and Society: Studies in Sociology*. New York: Random House, 1954.
O'Connor, D. J., *The Philosophy of Education*. New York: Philosophical Library, 1957.
Ogburn, William F., *Social Change*. New York: The Viking Press, 1927.
O'Neill, James N., *Religion and Education Under the Constitution*. New York: Harper & Brothers, 1949.
Otto, Rudolph, *Idea of the Holy*. Translated by J. W. Harvey. New York: Oxford University Press, 1943.
Packard, Vance O., *The Status Seekers*. New York: D. McKay Co., 1959.
Pangburn, Jessie M., *The Evolution of the American Teachers College*. New York: Teachers College, Columbia University, 1932.
Parker, DeWitt H., *The Principles of Aesthetics*. 2nd edition. New York: F. S. Crofts and Company, 1946.
Parker, Francis H., and Henry B. Veatch, *Logic as a Human Instrument*. New York: Harper & Brothers, 1959.
Patrick, G. T. W., *The Psychology of Relaxation*. Boston: Houghton Mifflin Company, 1916.
Pearson, Ralph M., *The New Art Education*, rev. ed. New York: Harper & Brothers, 1953.
Pepper, S. C., *The Basis of Criticism in the Arts*. Cambridge, Mass.: The Harvard University Press, 1945.
——, *Sources of Value*. Berkeley: University of California Press, 1958.
Perry, Ralph B., *General Theory of Value*. New York: Longmans, Green and Company, 1926.
——, *The Realms of Value*. Cambridge, Mass.: Harvard University Press, 1954.
Pestalozzi, J. H., *How Gertrude Teaches Her Children*. Translated by Lucy E. Holland and Frances C. Turner. Syracuse: C. W. Bardeen, 1894.
Phenix, Philip H., *Philosophy of Education*. New York: Holt, Rinehart & Winston, Inc., 1958.
Piaget, Jean, *The Origins of Intelligence in Children*. New York: International Universities Press, 1952.
——, *The Language and Thought of the Child*. Translated by Marjorie Gabain. 3rd edition. New York: Humanities Press, 1953.
Plant, J. S., *Personality and the Culture Pattern*. New York: Commonwealth Fund, 1937.

Plato, *The Dialogues.* 4 volumes. Translated by Benjamin Jowett. New York: Charles Scribner's Sons, 1872.

————, *The Republic of Plato.* Translated by Francis M. Cornford. New York: Oxford University Press, 1945.

President's Commission on Higher Education, *Higher Education for American Democracy.* New York: Harper & Brothers, 1948.

Rader, M. M., *A Modern Book of Esthetics.* New York: Holt, Rinehart & Winston, Inc., 1947, 1952, 1960.

Raup, R. Bruce, Kenneth D. Benne, George Axtelle, and B. Othanel Smith, *The Improvement of Practical Intelligence.* New York: Harper & Brothers, 1950.

Read, Herbert, *Education Through Art,* rev. ed. London: Faber and Faber, 1958.

Reavis, William C., Paul R. Pierce, Edward H. Stulken, and Bertrand L. Smith, *Administering the Elementary School.* Englewood Cliffs, N.J.: Prentice-Hall, Inc., 1953.

Redden, J. D., and F. A. Ryan, *A Catholic Philosophy of Education.* Milwaukee: The Bruce Publishing Company, 1942.

Reik, Theodore, *Masochism in Modern Man.* Translated by Margaret H. Beigel and Gertrude M. Kurth. New York: Farrar, Straus and Company, 1941.

Rosenberg, B., and D. M. White, *Mass Culture: The Popular Arts in America.* Glencoe, Ill.: The Free Press, 1957.

Royce, Josiah, *The Spirit of Modern Philosophy.* Boston: Houghton Mifflin Company, 1892.

Russell, Bertrand, *Education and the Modern World.* New York: W. W. Norton and Company, 1932.

Santayana, George, *The Sense of Beauty.* New York: Charles Scribner's Sons, 1896.

Sartre, Jean Paul, *Existentialism.* Translated by Bernard Frechtman. New York: The Philosophical Library, 1947.

Scheffler, Israel, *Philosophy and Education.* Boston: Allyn and Bacon, Inc., 1958.

————, *The Language of Education.* Springfield, Ill.: C. C. Thomas, 1960.

Schilpp, Paul A., ed., *The Philosophy of John Dewey.* The Library of Living Philosophers, Vol. I. Evanston and Chicago: Northwestern University, 1939.

Seashore, Carl N., *Why We Love Music.* Philadelphia: Oliver Ditson Company, 1941.

Seiberling, Frank, *Looking into Art.* New York: Holt, Rinehart & Winston, Inc., 1959.

Sellars, W., and J. Hospers, *Readings in Ethical Theory.* New York: Appleton-Century-Crofts, Inc., 1953.

Simpson, R. H., *Improving Teaching Learning Procedures.* New York: Longmans, Green and Company, 1953.

Slesinger, Z., *Education and the Class Struggle.* New York: Covici Friede, Inc., 1937.

Smith, B. Othanel, W. O. Stanley, and J. Harlan Shores, *Fundamentals of Curriculum Development*. Yonkers-on-Hudson, N.Y.: World Book Company, 1950, rev. ed., 1957.

Smith, B. Othanel, and Robert Ennis, eds., *Language and Concepts in Education*. Chicago: Rand McNally & Company, 1961.

Smith, T. V., and Marjorie Grene, eds., *From Descartes to Kant*. Chicago: The University of Chicago Press, 1940.

Social Reformers. Donald O. Wagner, ed. New York: The Macmillan Company, 1937.

Spinoza, Benedict, *The Chief Works of Spinoza*. Translated by R. H. M. Elwes. London: G. Bell and Sons, 1883–1884.

Stanley, William O., *Education and Social Integration*. New York: Teachers College, Columbia University, 1953.

Stendler, Celia, *Teaching in the Elementary School*. New York: Harcourt, Brace and World, Inc., 1958.

Stevenson, C. L., *Ethics and Language*. New Haven: Yale University Press, 1944.

Sumner, William Graham, *Folkways*. Boston: Ginn and Company, 1906, 1934, 1940.

Thut, I. N., *The Story of Education: Philosophical and Historical Foundations*. New York: McGraw-Hill Book Company, Inc., 1957.

Tykociner, Joseph T., *Research as a Science—Zetetics*. Urbana, Ill., 1959.

Ulich, Robert, *Fundamentals of Democratic Education*. New York: American Book Company, 1940.

Veblen, Thorsten, *Theory of the Leisure Class*. New York: B. W. Huebsch Company, 1922.

Vischer, Robert, *Das optische Formgefühl*. Tübingen, 1873.

Vivas, Eliseo, and Murray Krieger, *The Problems of Aesthetics*. New York: Holt, Rinehart & Winston, Inc., 1953.

Waller, W., and Reuben Hill, *The Family: A Dynamic Interpretation*, rev. ed. New York: Dryden Press, 1951.

Ware, Caroline F., and Gardiner C. Means, *The Modern Economy in Action*. New York: Harcourt, Brace and World, Inc., 1936.

Wegener, Frank, *An Organic Philosophy of Education*. Dubuque, Iowa: W. C. Brown, 1957.

Welsh, M. G., *The Social Philosophy of Christian Education*. Washington, D.C.: The Catholic University of America Press, 1936.

Wheelwright, Philip, *A Critical Introduction to Ethics*, rev. ed. New York: The Odyssey Press, 1949.

———, *The Way of Philosophy*. New York: The Odyssey Press, 1954.

Whitehead, Alfred N., *The Aims of Education*. London: Williams and Northgate, Ltd., 1929.

Whyte, William H., Jr., *The Organization Man*. New York: Doubleday and Company, 1957.

Wieman, Henry N., *The Wrestle of Religion with Truth*. New York: The Macmillan Company, 1927.

Wild, John, *Introduction to Realistic Philosophy*. New York: Harper & Brothers, 1948.

———, *Plato's Modern Enemies and the Theory of Natural Law.* Chicago: University of Chicago Press, 1953.

———, ed., *The Return to Reason.* Chicago: Henry Regnery Company, 1953.

Woodruff, A. D., *The Psychology of Teaching.* 3rd edition. New York: Longmans, Green and Company, 1951.

Wright, William K., *A Student's Philosophy of Religion.* New York: The Macmillan Company, 1943.

Wynne, John P., *Philosophies of Education from the Standpoint of Experimentalism.* Englewood Cliffs, N.J.: Prentice-Hall, Inc., 1947.

Index

Index

410   INDEX

Trechman, E. J., 174n
Trial-and-error learning, 344–345
Trial response, teaching-learning proc-
    ess, 342–343
Trilling, Diana, 360
Tykociner, Joseph T., 312–313, 334

Ulich, Robert, 41, 104
Ultimate ends, 126, 136 and n, 192,
    251
Universals, see Concepts
Universities, 379
    function of, 371
    organization of, 371–373
    and research, 371–373
Utilitarianism, 26n, 236

Values:
    areas, 140–141
    cultural demands and, 128
    economic, 140
    education and, 125–148
    emotive theories of, 136–138
    experimentalist theory of, 132–136
    general theory of, 132–145
    higher and lower, 143–145
    intrinsic and instrumental aspects
        of, 141
    moral, 126
    norms, 127–132
    as objective, 138–140
    positive and negative, 142–143
    relativity and objectivity of, 129–131
    school's situation with respect to,
        131–132
Vaughan, Herbert E., 300n, 334
Veatch, Henry B., 56n
Veblen, Thorsten, 171

Veinus, Abram, 232
Vischer, Robert, 205n
Vivas, Eliseo, 202n, 231
Vocational education, 153–155, 330
Voltaire, 89

Wagner, D. O., 185n
Waller, W., 104
Ware, Caroline F., 201
Wegener, Frank C., 323
Weiss, Paul, 284
Welsh, M. G., 201
Westmeyer, Paul, 303n
Wheelwright, Philip, 20, 236n, 255
White, D. M., 232
White, R. K., 82n
Whitehead, Alfred N., 112, 226–227,
    382
Whyte, William H., 201
Widen, Irwin, 91n
Wieman, Henry N., 279
Wild, John, 41, 52n, 56n, 59n, 73,
    76n, 103, 107n, 110n, 122,
    137n, 279, 336n
Will, freedom of, 54–57
Wilson, M. K., 334
Witty, P. A., 165n, 171, 340n
Wood, Grant, 215–217
Woodruff, A. D., 179n, 201, 326–327
World War II, 325
Wright, William K., 270n, 278
Wynne, John P., 41

Yost, F. N., 104

Zacharias, J. R., 334
Zeignarik, B., 347
Zetetics, 312–313